THE LIBRARY

COLBY JUNIOR COLLEGE

COLBY JUNIOR COLLEGE FOR WOMEN
PARATI · SERVIRE
MENS · ANIMUS · CORPUS
1837

S0-ACJ-931

NATIONALISM IN JAPAN

NATIONALISM
IN JAPAN

DELMER M. BROWN

an introductory historical analysis

UNIVERSITY OF CALIFORNIA PRESS

BERKELEY AND LOS ANGELES · 1955

DS
·843
B76

4/3/60 Jecerged 3.73

UNIVERSITY OF CALIFORNIA, BERKELEY AND LOS ANGELES, CALIFORNIA

CAMBRIDGE UNIVERSITY PRESS, LONDON, ENGLAND

COPYRIGHT, 1955, BY THE REGENTS OF THE UNIVERSITY OF CALIFORNIA

DESIGNED BY MARION JACKSON

PRINTED IN THE UNITED STATES OF AMERICA
BY THE UNIVERSITY OF CALIFORNIA PRINTING DEPARTMENT

35801

Preface

The retreat of the West from Asia is frequently explained in terms of "the rising tide of Asian nationalism." The cliché suggests, but leaves unanswered, a host of problems concerning the nature of Asian nationalism and its effect upon relations between Asiatic and Euro-American peoples. That these problems have not been solved is apparent not only from the continuous failure of the West to accommodate itself to Asian nationalism but also from the courses of action recommended by both our liberal and conservative "experts" on Asia. Since the people of America do not clearly realize the implications of the sociopsychological fact of nationalism, much of our "conservative" attitude is based on the "old China hand" assumption that the only effective way to convince an Oriental, if words fail, is to use force. The "liberal" attitude also reflects slight appreciation of nationalist sympathies, for it is centered too narrowly upon the conviction that the only way to check nationalist opposition and to kill the Communist virus is to raise the standard of living of the Oriental people. In both points of view little consideration is given to the nationalist aims and attitudes of the people concerned. In order to rectify this situation it is clear that we must gain a better insight into the wellsprings, the drives, and the particular character of nationalism in each Asiatic nation.

In Japan, nationalism has had, and still has, dynamic qualities which not only have deeply affected the country's internal and external affairs but have greatly stimulated the rise of nationalist movements in other parts of Asia. Being geographically isolated off the northeast coast of Asia and having developed, at an early date, a homogeneous people speaking a common language and worshipping indigenous gods, the Japanese soon developed a sense of group unity and, under strong external pressure, became the most nationalistic people in Asia. During most of the nineteenth century, the Japanese, like other Asian peoples, were faced with Western expansionism; unlike other Asians, however, they did not merely resist Western domination but adopted far-reaching reforms that enabled them to utilize techniques developed in the Occident. In the last half of the nineteenth century the reforms led to the emergence of Asia's first industrial revolution, to the establishment of universal education, and to the building of a national army. On these foundations a modern military machine was built, which, in 1895 and 1905, won two successful foreign wars: one against China, that great cultural center of the Far East, and the other against Russia, a Western power. The victories not only aroused the Japanese to a new sense of national pride but quickened nationalist feelings all over the Orient. "Asia for the Asiatics" became a powerful slogan, and various Oriental people became more restive under the strong hand of Western powers.

Japan became the self-appointed and recognized leader of the Pan-Asian movement. Even after 1931, when she embarked upon an ambitious continental program under expansionist-minded military leaders, and when her nationalism reached a fanatical level, Japan insisted that these moves were an integral part of the old effort to rid Asia of domination by the white man. The people of Asia, though suspicious of Japan's role in the program, were greatly influenced by the ideas. Today Japan is no longer the recognized leader of the "Asia for the Asiatics" movement, nor would other Orientals be inclined to give her credit for having had any part in stirring up their feelings of nationalism, but students of Oriental history are quick to see the impact of the Japanese movement.

The influence of nationalism upon Japan's relations with the outside world becomes a subject of vital importance as Japan moves into the center of the Far Eastern sector of the two-world struggle. The fact that she is the only industrialized area in the Far East makes her one of the primary targets of the Communist advance and also the keystone of any effort of the free nations to create economic stability in the non-Communist areas of the Far East. In such a key position it is logical to find a sharp Communist–free world struggle for the support of Japanese nationalist sympathies. In all areas of Asia the Communists have proved themselves to be quite energetic and astute in harnessing nationalist power, and they have already made significant advances in Japan. In this ideological conflict the United States and the free world have definite advantages; but in the absence of enlightened, positive moves that are closely geared to nationalist forces, we may very well meet with still another disastrous failure in the Orient.

During my residence in Japan between 1932 and 1938 I gained an abiding interest in the subject of nationalism. This was the period in which militarists were rising to power through terroristic acts performed in the name of nationalist aims and nationalist symbols, and in the latter part of my stay all information media came to be utilized, as a matter of public policy, to stir the Japanese people to an even deeper sense of loyalty to the nation in preparation for an all-out war against the "aggressive" Western powers. Then, during the Pacific War, I could not but be impressed by the fanaticism which drove thousands of Japanese to participate in such suicidal operations as the "Banzai raids" and the "Kamikaze attacks." Finally, when Japan surrendered, I was amazed to note how the tremendous national solidarity of the country enabled her leaders, through the Emperor institution, to gain a remarkably complete acceptance not only of defeat but even of the Occupation's revolutionary reform program. Long contact with such startling manifestations of national loyalty has given me a curiosity and anxiety about the bearing this social force has had and will continue to have upon Japanese life and upon Japan's relations with the outside world.

In daring to attempt a study of the rise of nationalism in Japan I realize that I am moving in a very rough sea. Social scientists have not come to a definite agreement about what nationalism is, why and when it should emerge, and what effect its rise has upon the life of social groups. Furthermore, the phenomenon in Japan has roots that run very deep into her past and has branches which, in recent years, have penetrated into every area of Japanese life. Nevertheless, the importance of the problem has driven me to do some research in the field and to submit to the student of Asian problems this tentative analysis of the development of nationalism in Japan.

At every stage of this study I have been helped by numerous scholars, students, and friends. Whenever possible this assistance has been acknowledged; but throughout the book there are ideas and interpretations that emerged, often unconsciously, from studies by various Far Eastern scholars, from seminars and classes where alert students were constantly raising new questions, and from profitable hours, in the summers of 1948 and 1952, with Japanese scholars, nationalist leaders, and librarians, who gave me additional information and new slants on different aspects of the problem. It is therefore impossible to name each person who has been of assistance, but I owe a special debt of gratitude to three men who aided me as research assistants: Dr. Royal Wald, Mr. Charles Sheldon, and Mr. Imai Kichinosuke; and to the Rockefeller Foundation for generous financial support during the academic year 1950–1951. For reading part, or all, of the manuscript and for offering helpful criticisms and suggestions I am grateful to the following specialists in Far Eastern studies: Dr. Nobutaka Ike, Dr. Hilary Conroy, Dr. Robert Scalapino, Mr. William Holland, and Mr. Howard Boorman. Finally, I wish to thank Miss Dorothy H. Huggins of the University of California Press for putting the manuscript in final shape at a time when I was out of the country. Although many persons deserve credit for any quality which this study may have, I bear sole responsibility for any remaining errors and for all interpretations and conclusions.

DELMER M. BROWN

Contents

| INTRODUCTION

"Nationalism" is one of the most loosely used words in the English language, and yet it refers to one of the most potent forces at work in the modern world. During the nineteenth century, national movements were a dominant fact in the history of Western Europe, and since the beginning of the twentieth century they have erupted in many areas of the world and have appeared in some truly frightening forms. Nationalism is therefore easily detected, and its importance is generally appreciated; but since it manifests itself in diverse forms, there is very little agreement as to what it is and how it affects human societies. The word thus carries different meanings for different people and has had different meanings at different stages in history. Consequently, in embarking upon this study, it is necessary for me to set forth as clearly as possible what I consider nationalism to be.[1]

The Nature of Nationalism

In terms sufficiently broad to encompass the phenomenon in all its forms and at its various stages of development, nationalism is basically a type of group loyalty. Its most distinctive features, when compared to other types of group loyalty, arise from the fact that the nation is a larger group. Consequently, no high degree of intellectual and emotional unity arises until the nation has been welded together by such modern developments as industrial revolution, popular education, popular press, conscript armies, national radio hookups, and international wars.

Like other types of group loyalty, nationalism has its roots in the conditions and circumstances that lead individuals to feel that they have ties in common with certain others and that, conversely, individuals outside this group are different. Of course these conditions vary widely in their nature, but in general they are the possessions, experiences, ideas, beliefs, hopes, and fears that the members of the group have in common. Obviously, a large group of people have more in common and are more likely to develop a national consciousness—and later nationalism—if they live in a distinct geographical area, believe in a common racial descent, speak the same language, have the same religion, and live under the same government. But few nations are favored with all these relatively constant conditions (called "elements"), and in most nations one or more are not present. Furthermore, not a single one of these elements seems to be essential for the rise of national consciousness, since not one has been present in the growth of every one of the modern nations. However, it seems safe to conclude that, *other factors being present and equal,* the more elements there are present and the stronger they are, the earlier national consciousness is likely to develop and the more intense that group feeling is likely to become.

But the appearance and growth of nationalism cannot be understood in terms of elements alone, for history suggests that nationalism does not become a significant sociopsychological force until the elements have been activated by social and intellectual developments which place the members of the nation into a close, interdependent relationship. Within the nation, developments of this kind are associated with economic expansion and with political and religious centralization. But advances in the field of communications are even more directly related to the activation of the elements of nationalism, for nationalism is basically an intellectual and emotional phenomenon. The changes that are most significant here, whether they be in art, literature, or communications in a general sense, are those that result in a more widespread exchange of ideas and feelings, causing each individual in the group to become familiar with the events, the ideas, the aspirations, and the fears which affect the lives of others, and therefore making it more likely that a greater unity of thought and emotion, as well as a greater sense of group loyalty, will emerge.

Even though all or part of these internal historical developments and some or all of the so-called elements of nationalism are operative within a certain nation, nationalism still may not be a significant social force unless the nation faces competition, rivalry, or danger from other nations. The importance of external pressure is particularly obvious in the rise of nationalism in Asia, for throughout the area there is a close correlation between the emergence of national feelings and the intensity of foreign danger. The danger may appear in different forms; it may be real or imagined; it may even be artificially generated by propaganda; but in any case it is obviously a vital factor in the rise of modern nationalism.

But national attitudes are not merely the product of geographical and social conditions and pressures, for ideas and attitudes carry within themselves power for change. In order properly to understand the developmental process of nationalism, we must not only take into consideration the number and strength of the elements of nationalism and the nature of the internal and external social conditions that weld the group into a more cohesive unit, but we must have a clear understanding of the power and focus of past ideas and feelings about the nation. The thoughts and feelings, national or otherwise, of a given nation are influenced by the ideas and attitudes of previous generations as well as by the peculiar social conditions of the day.

Thus, by considering the presence of certain conditions and the emergence of certain historical developments (social and intellectual), it seems possible to gain some clue to the place and time at which nationalism would logically appear. It also becomes fairly clear that in the development of this sociopsychological phenomenon an increasingly large proportion of the nation—the rulers first and the ruled last—would come to feel a sense of loyalty to the nation, and that the sense of loyalty would gradually prevail over other group loyalties and become an increasingly dominant factor in the history of the nation. But there still remains the question: how does nationalism affect the attitudes and actions of the nation?

Just as egocentric individuals move along different paths and act in different ways, so nations driven by the force of nationalism move toward different goals and act in accordance with different sets of principles. Since the spirit of nationalism forces the nation to give more attention to matters that are peculiar to the nation, a great accent therefore is placed upon its particular way of doing things and upon its special mission. But regardless of this emphasis on a unique way of life and on truly national symbols, the nationalist force tends to make peoples of all nations basically interested in, and even willing to make sacrifices to achieve, greater national strength. Strength may be thought of in cultural, economic, military, or ideological terms—or in a peculiar combination of all these terms—and the determination to achieve or preserve strength will vary widely; but strength remains the major aim of the nationalist drive.

In moving toward the achievement of greater strength, nations adopt policies and take actions that arise out of an extremely complex interplay of conditions and developments peculiar to each nation. But it seems possible to posit still another generalization which may help to assess the independent influence exerted by nationalism upon a given society. It appears that in the nations in which nationalism developed under conditions of relative freedom from foreign danger, and under conditions of unusual economic growth over a long period of time, nationalism does not seem to manifest itself in so virulent a form as in those in which the rise of nationalism is more closely associated with foreign danger and is not accompanied by long periods of unusual economic growth. In the former case, the national attitude tends to be associated with feelings of confidence and pride; in the latter, with feelings of fear and hate. Of course, no nationalist movement ever stands at an absolute position with reference to these two types of nationalism; and no nationalist movement remains at every stage in its history at the same position. But, generally speaking, when national confidence is overshadowed by fear and by feelings characterized as a "national inferiority complex," nationalism—especially in times of crisis and when it is aroused artificially by modern mass propaganda techniques—becomes irrational and fanatical. Under its influence the nation group is tempted to assign mystic qualities to its origins, principles, and goals, and it tends to turn to scapegoats for rationalizing national weaknesses and disasters. The less virulent type tends to be more rational, permitting the nation to be more realistic in its appraisal of the strength and weakness of itself and of other nations.

The two types of nationalism appear to be associated not merely with entirely different manifestations of thought and action but also with the development and preservation of different social structures. In a society in which nationalism emerges as a by-product of a long period of unusual economic growth, with relative freedom from foreign danger, nationalism tends to be "directed inward" and to be led by a segment of the nation which has gained new strength and which, in the name of national ideals and national symbols, works to broaden the base of the political structure and to force greater political and social mobility. Under such circumstances, we have the birth of what has been termed an "open" society.[2] But in Asia and other areas where there has not been this background of prolonged economic prosperity, and where the various nations have been subjected to long periods of foreign pressure, there has been no such impetus for greater social mobility. Instead, the established ruling groups remain in power, and they attempt to make adjustments to the new situations without making any basic alterations in the traditional social relationships. In such areas a "closed" society prevails. Between the "open" and "closed" societies ranges a whole spectrum of social systems. And again, no nation falls completely at one extreme or the other—or remains at the same distance from one extreme. It appears, however, that the major wars of the last fifty years have been fought between nations that have fallen quite far apart on the open-closed society scale, and that the incompatibility of the two types of societies lies at the base of the present two-world struggle. Thus, the character and power of nationalism have a direct bearing on fundamental problems of our age.

"Elements" of Nationalism in Japan

Of the relatively constant conditions ("elements") that tend, other factors being present and equal, to awaken a sense of group consciousness, geographical separateness appears to be the most vital. All the other elements, being far more social in character, are more subject to change. Whether national consciousness arises early or becomes strong depends, in large measure, upon the degree of geographical separateness that the nation enjoys. Japan, with her insular position, is more widely separated from her neighbors than most nations. Until the advent of modern communications the islands were quite isolated even with respect to the continent of Asia. At one point they are separated from the Korean peninsula by a distance of little more than one hundred miles, but that stretch of water (the Tsushima Strait) has served as an extremely effective check on contacts with the outside world—probably a more effective check than the Strait of Dover has been in restricting English contacts with the European continent. The cultural significance of this isolated position has attracted the attention of the eminent anthropologist A. L. Kroeber. On making a survey of certain cultural importations into Japan, Dr. Kroeber found that in many cases there was a cultural lag of several centuries.[3] The Japanese themselves were apparently aware of their geographical separateness in prehistoric times, for the earliest histories contain myths about the divine origin of the Japanese islands—myths which, under the impetus of modern nationalist propaganda, became the basis of a fanatical belief in the divine origin and the divine protection of the Japanese islands. But the special geographical position has been accented not merely by myths but by concrete historical evidence, such as the failure of the powerful Mongols to conquer Japan in the thirteenth century, although the Mongols sent two different expeditions across the Tsushima Strait. In modern times as well, with revolutionary developments in navigation, aviation, and military weapons, the country has not been invaded, and the Japanese still gain some satisfaction from the fact that at the end of the recent war, when Japan was defeated and occupied, she was not, strictly speaking, invaded. Geographical isolation, therefore, has not only made the Japanese feel that they inhabit a separate area, but it has kept them apart from the life of their nearest neighbors, leaving them free from invasion and giving them a historical continuity and cultural unity that have been very significant in the rise of national consciousness.

Geography has done more than place the Japanese in an isolated position. It has given them what the geographers call a "natural region"[4]—a region in which geographical conditions permit or force a certain uniformity of occupation and way of life. In spite of the fact that the islands stretch from north to south for a distance roughly equivalent to that from Montreal to northern Florida, heavy summer rainfall, easily irrigated alluvial lowlands, and the tropical currents make most of the area suitable for the cultivation of rice.[5] Since prehistoric times this cereal has been the prevailing crop, and in modern times more than one-half of the entire cultivated area of Japan is still in rice. It is not strange, therefore, that one of the most popular Shinto cults, even now, is the rice cult.[6] But the geography of Japan also accounts for another occupation, fishing, which prevails throughout the islands and operates to make the country a "natural region." Because of a tremendous length of coastline, the concentration of the population in coastal plains, and the existence of excellent fishing grounds in the waters off Japan, fishing has been engaged in by a very large proportion of the Japanese population for centuries. Today, fishing is the occupation of roughly 20 per cent of the Japanese—a larger percentage than in any other country of the world.[7] This comparative uniformity of economic activity, throughout historic times, has created a vast complex of common social and cultural patterns that helps to account for the early rise of national consciousness.

Probably the second most important element of nationalism in Japan is the belief in a common racial descent. Ethnologists are agreed that the Japanese people have a rather complex racial make-up, predominantly Mongol but mixed with Malay and Ainu strains. And yet, since all the important migrations of people into Japan came from the continent of Asia in early historic or prehistoric ages, there has been a long period of racial fusion, and the Japanese have become one of the most racially homogeneous people in the world.[8] The homogeneity has provided a plausible basis for early myths about a divine origin and has led most Japanese nationalists to place considerable emphasis upon the divine, unique qualities of their race. There is little doubt that relative racial purity has been a truly powerful element in the growth of Japanese national consciousness, causing one nationalist, more than one hundred years ago, to write: "We [Japanese] who have been brought into existence through the creative spirit of the sacred ancestral [gods] are, each and every one, in spontaneous possession of the Way of the Gods."[9]

Since the intercommunication of ideas and feelings is essential in the awakening of national consciousness, the existence of a common language, though not essential, is extremely important.[10] The Japanese have a common language. There are several dialects, but these do not constitute a serious barrier to communication. Since the language is not spoken in other parts of the world, except in the areas affected recently by Japanese expansion, it has done more than facilitate the interchange of ideas and attitudes: it has provided the Japanese with still another unique, exclusive possession to excite the thoughts and sentiments of ardent nationalists. It is true that some Japanese are disturbed because their written language is defiled by Chinese characters and their spoken language contains a large number of foreign words and phrases, but it cannot be denied that Japanese is truly a separate language.[11] Over the centuries it has been enriched by a great body of poetic, prose, historical, and dramatic literature, which has kept the Japanese people closer to their past and has made them more familiar with the thoughts, deeds, and sentiments of Japanese heroes of all ages.

Particularly significant in the development of Japanese nationalism is the existence of common and unique religious beliefs. Religion has played an important role in the rise of many nationalities,[12] especially in periods in which most human activities were still closely related to other-worldly considerations. And this has been true in Japan, not merely in ages past but down to the present time. The symbolic head of the Japanese nation has continued to be the chief priest of a religious cult (the Sun Cult or, in modern times, State Shinto), and this cult is common to the Japanese people and peculiar to Japan. Recent studies show that the Sun Cult has much in common with religious rites in other parts of Asia, especially in Korea and Siberia, and indicate that the cult had continental origins. Nevertheless, after its introduction to Japan it became subjected to so different a set of influences that in time it developed certain unique features. Buddhism, which has left deep imprints upon the culture of the Far East, was introduced into Japan relatively late, after the hereditary head of the Sun Cult—who was also hereditary chieftain of the leading clan—had gained a dominant position among the cults and clans of the land. Consequently, by the time the first written history was compiled, in A.D. 712, the Sun Cult had already taken on a distinctly Japanese coloring and had become closely associated with the emerging Japanese state. Later historical developments further strengthened the position of the chief priest of the cult as the symbolic head of the nation to such a degree that all major political changes were made in the name of the Emperor, the hereditary head of the state. Even in recent years each important political shift has been called a "Restoration"—the name signifying that the Emperor had been restored to his rightful position as the ruler of the state. Furthermore, the early myths were subsequently expanded, rationalized, and fortified until the Emperor became the center of a national entity (kokutai) in which all Japanese were considered to be his children and to have certain divine qualities. The religious element, in other words, has been so powerful in the emergence of Japanese national unity that our great American scholar of Shinto, Dr. D. C. Holtom, is clearly justified in referring to Japanese nationalism as "Shinto nationalism."

The establishment in Japan of a state claiming the right to rule all "eight kingdoms" dates from the eighth century, when the first histories were written. For many centuries the control of the state was not very firm, and at times was almost nonexistent; but from the eighth century until the present the Japanese have always been able to say that under the leadership of the Emperor—the direct descendant of the Sun Goddess herself—there was a government that had an almost unquestioned, divine right to rule over the whole of Japan. This element of a common government has not been a relatively constant factor in the growth of national unity in Japan, for the power and effectiveness of the central government have varied greatly at different periods of history (the government reached its peak of centralization in the 1930's); but it cannot be denied that this common political form has been extremely important in the birth and growth of Japanese national unity.

Although few nations are influenced by all the recognized elements of nationalism, in Japan each of the elements not only is present but exists in an unusually strong form. With respect to the geographical, racial, linguistic, and religious elements, it is difficult to find nations where the elements are stronger. And it will be readily seen that each element takes on more dynamic qualities because of its association with other elements, since, as is true of all social phenomena, no element operates in a vacuum.

All the elements were present in Japan, however, before nationalism was a discernible fact—actually before the appearance of anything that could be properly identified as a nation—for technological progress, economic expansion, political centralization, cultural unification, and foreign pressure were not yet strong enough to generate a strong sense of group loyalty among the people living on the Japanese islands. Since these developments gained momentum only with the passage of time, they can be best dealt with in the following historical analysis of the rise of Japanese nationalism.

2 NATIONAL CONSCIOUSNESS

The nation concept was first expressed in Japan by the word *kokka* (literally "kingdom-house" but generally translated as "state" or "nation")—a word that appeared in histories compiled at the beginning of the eighth century. It was used in reference to the religious-political structure that emerged when the Yamato kingdom, sometime before the fifth century A.D., attained a dominant position among the various kingdoms of the Japanese islands. Under Yamato supremacy the kingdoms were all brought together into a single "house," with Yamato in the dominant position. But only after centuries of increasing social integration, closer contacts with the continent of Asia, and more sophisticated cultural and intellectual achievements, did any significant number of people become conscious of, or identify themselves with, what might be properly called the Japanese nation.

The Yamato State

Just how and when the Yamato kingdom succeeded in establishing its superiority over other kingdoms, and in setting up what is known as the

Yamato state, cannot be definitely established, primarily because the development preceded the first written historical accounts by at least one hundred years, and because Japanese scholars, under the influence of nationalist sentiments, have not until the last few years been free to treat this "prehistoric" period objectively. Modern scholars present various theories about the origin of the Yamato state,[1] but in general they agree that at least by the fifth century A.D. there was a kingdom or state called Yamato (with its base in what is now known as the Nara plain), which was extending its power over neighboring kingdoms and sending military expeditions throughout most of the inhabited areas of the main islands.[2] As the new Yamato kingdom expanded it came into conflict with tribes called the Emishi (probably ancestors of the present-day Ainu of northern Japan). The Emishi were apparently not so well armed as the Yamato, who were mounted soldiers using iron swords and spears,[3] but they were spirited fighters, and their periodic uprisings caused the newcomers considerable trouble. The Yamato people not only met with resistance from the Emishi but were also opposed by the Kumaso, a people of an entirely different stock—they probably were of Malay origin—who dwelt in southern Kyushu. The exact nature and extent of the resistance offered by the Emishi and the Kumaso is not known, but successful campaigns by the Yamato against these people indicate not only that the new state had achieved considerable power and cohesion, but that threats of incursions—from the south as well as the north, and by people who were definitely of different racial origins—may have aroused among the Yamato people feelings of group consciousness. But it is doubtful whether these feelings of identification were as yet beyond the clan or kingdom level. Even the leaders of the Yamato people, throughout the two centuries of military conquest from their base in the Nara plain, probably continued to identify themselves primarily with their own kingdom. *Kokka*, in spite of its use in the eighth-century chronicle descriptions of these events, probably did not yet denote anything approximating the Japanese nation concept.

But with the rise of a reunited China under the Sui and T'ang dynasties (A.D. 589–906) the relations of the expanded Yamato state with the outside world were placed on an entirely different basis. The state was no longer dealing merely with a group of small kingdoms struggling among themselves for power, nor with strange frontier tribes, but with a vast empire that by the middle of the seventh century was reaching out into the Korean peninsula, defeating Yamato armies there and conquering the Korean states that dared to resist. The great T'ang dynasty (618–906) was for the Chinese a period of unprecedented splendor and power and of great cultural achievements. The extension of its military and cultural influence so close to the shores of Japan was therefore a development of extreme importance in the political, social, and cultural history of the Yamato people. It was with this contact that the leaders of the expanded Yamato state seem to have first become clearly aware that the people on the Japanese island chain constituted a distinct social group.

In the early years of the seventh century, only a few years after China had been reunited under the Sui dynasty, the Yamato court began to adopt Chinese court ranks and to use Chinese ethical principles and religious doctrines in order to enhance its prestige and power. In a remarkable document, frequently referred to as the "Seventeen-Article Constitution," and said in Japan's early histories to have been compiled by Prince Shotoku in the year 604, we have clear evidence of efforts to create greater social stability and unity among the people of all kingdoms in the islands (the structure was referred to as *kokka*) and to raise the position of the Yamato ruler to something comparable to that of the emperors of China. All heads of kingdoms and clans were enjoined not to levy taxes, since that was a right to be exercised only by the king (*kimi*)—the title now applied to the ruler of the Yamato structure. In other matters as well, the people of all groups were to be loyal subjects: "When the ruler speaks, the vassal listens; when the superior acts, the inferior yields compliance. Consequently, when you receive the commands (*mikotonori*) of the king, fail not to carry them out scrupulously...."[4]

The Seventeen-Article Constitution, however, was not limited to statements concerning the rights of the king and the responsibilities of subjects in the enlarged kingdom or state. Confucian ethical principles and Buddhist doctrines—both of which had been recently imported from China—were also injected into the constitution to make it more effective in creating the desired unity. In the very first of the seventeen articles the Confucian principle of harmony (*wa*) was upheld, because, as the constitution states, there were "some who disobey their lords and fathers, or who maintain feuds with the neighboring villages." In a later article the principle of decorous behavior (*rei*) was emphasized as an important means of preventing disorder and disobedience and of enabling the state (*kokka*) to manage its political affairs better.[5] Obviously, Prince Shotoku, like many other Orientals before and after him, realized the value of Confucianism as social cement.[6] But apparently he was convinced, too, that Buddhism could serve a useful political function, for in the second article of the constitution he advocated that all people revere the three Buddhist Treasures, stating that these "comprise the destiny of all living things" and that they should receive "the supreme worship of all regions of the world." It has been customary to attribute this support of Buddhism primarily to Prince Shotoku's personal devotion to the Buddhist faith, but modern historians see this also as another effort to increase the political power of the Yamato state. They point out that Buddhism had already shown itself to be an effective means of extending political control. The Soga family, which rose to a dominant position within the Yamato state in 587, seems to have owed much of its success to the support that it gave to the new faith. Temples, built like those in China, and Buddhist priests and paraphernalia imported from Korea not only were impressive manifestations of the superior Chinese culture but were also particularly effective agents for warding off evil spirits. Therefore, the temples, which were further strengthened by the large number of Koreans and Chinese who were migrating to Japan in these years, soon attained positions of considerable influence. And the priests, since they had been supported by the Soga family, and since the Soga family was apparently in control of the major channels of contact with the continent, were undoubtedly inclined to give loyal service to their patrons. In a real sense, then, the Buddhist priests were Japan's first local officials, appointed by, and responsible to, the central government. It is thus understandable that Prince Shotoku, in a document obviously designed to provide greater political power for the state, should have been impelled by political as well as private considerations to urge the acceptance of Buddhism.[7]

Prince Shotoku's use of Chinese ethical principles and religious doctrines to strengthen the moral foundations of the Yamato state suggests that at least some members of the ruling class had been influenced by contacts with China to try to create in the Japanese island chain something approximating the great China. Although Shotoku's constitution was not followed immediately by any extensive implementing measures, there is evidence that the rulers were being driven, in the face of the Chinese example, to look at their state in a different light. In A.D. 607, for example, an official mission was sent to China and, according to Chinese records, the introductory phrase in the note sent by the Japanese began as follows: "The Son of Heaven (*tenshi*) in the land where the sun rises addresses a letter to the Son of Heaven (*tenshi*) in the land where the sun sets."[8] Modern Japanese historians have seized upon this as early proof of Japanese insistence upon national equality with China.[9] It is likely that the choice of words may have been due, in part at least, to a lack of familiarity with Chinese diplomatic usage; but clearly, the Yamato court was now thinking in terms of sovereignty over the entire area "where the sun rises," and it had ambitions that were stirred by what has been called the Chinese Imperial idea.[10] Thus, in the early years of the seventh century there may have been very weak stirrings of national consciousness among some of the leaders of the new political structure. Individuals, in referring to their state, may have even begun to refer to it as "Nippon" (Rising Sun)—a word that was later corrupted to "Japan."

But still Yamato (or Japan) remained very weak, while China under the great T'ang dynasty was becoming increasingly powerful. In 637 the Yamato court was faced by an uprising of the Emishi on the northeastern frontier, and this was followed by internal dissensions which in 645 culminated in a palace revolution. On the continent, T'ang China was extending its influence into the Korean peninsula. In 644—the year before the palace revolution in Japan—the Chinese sent an expedition into Korea to help one of the kingdoms against its neighbors. This development must have been a matter of real concern to the Yamato rulers, for in previous centuries it had been Yamato forces that had been invited in to settle disputes between Korean kingdoms. Thus in 645 there was little evidence that Japan would ever become a strong nation.

But the palace revolution of 645 brought to power men who were apparently challenged by the critical situation and who proceeded to put into effect a reform program that was to bring about fundamental changes in the Japanese political, economic, and social order. Like Prince Shotoku, these new leaders were desirous of welding the various groups into an integrated whole, with the descendants of the old Yamato chieftains at its apex. But, unlike Prince Shotoku, they had the advice of men who had lived long in China and were familiar with the political institutions and techniques developed there. Consequently, after the year 645, a series of reform measures was adopted—measures that were so drastic and that have had so profound an influence upon subsequent Japanese history that the date is well known as the first year of the Era of Great Reforms.

After putting a new Emperor on the throne, the new leaders started a weapons-collection program in order to prevent the outbreak of more internal disturbances. And then, apparently realizing the necessity of a larger and more regular income for the central government, they ordered a land survey and a census—in preparation for a program of equal land distribution and regular tax assessments. Again word was sent out that the Emperor was going to support Buddhism; but at the same time it was made clear that the survey and census were to apply to the Buddhist institutions as well. At the beginning of the following year there was a great clearing away of old titles, and measures were adopted for obtaining efficient, loyal service from local representatives of the central government. New local districts were established; only officials were to be appointed who had a knowledge of writing and arithmetic; the types of tax and the tax rates were clearly defined; and roads, ferries, and post stations were built to simplify the collection of taxes and the supervision of local affairs. In the military field the reformers instituted measures that would result in the establishment of a conscript army which would be responsible to the central government rather than to individual clans or kingdoms. Greater emphasis was placed upon proper training, adequate equipment, and regular inspections. The organization of the central government itself was drastically altered along Chinese lines, but room was left for a peculiarly Japanese bureau (jingikan) that would foster the native traditions of the divine descent of the rulers.[11]

The reform movement was far more than a temporary flurry of political activity. For almost a century after the initial efforts of 645, the rulers, always with advice from those who had studied Chinese institutions and practices, continued to revise and strengthen the new structure. T'ang China was becoming stronger and more prosperous, and the Japanese reformers were therefore constantly reminded that much more had to be done. As early as 651, Korean envoys to Japan were appearing at court in T'ang robes; and in 660 the Chinese sent some 200,000 troops across the Yellow Sea to help the Korean kingdom of Silla against Paekche, a kingdom that had long worked closely with the Japanese. Paekche immediately sent pleas to Japan for help, and in 663 the Japanese did send a force of some 27,000 men; but it was badly defeated by the Chinese, both on land and at sea. This caused the Japanese to withdraw from the Korean peninsula and to give up, for more than a thousand years, any idea of sending another military expedition across the Tsushima Strait. The disastrous defeat of Japanese troops was convincing proof of military inferiority, and it led the rulers, in anticipation of a possible invasion of Japan proper, to concentrate upon the building up of coastal defenses.[12] The reform program, too, was pressed more vigorously, and it resulted in such measures as the promulgation of legal codes, the taking of a census, and the minting of standardized coins.

Nara Japan

The flowering of the reforms came with the establishment of the capital at Nara in the year 710. Until that year each new emperor had moved his capital to a different place because of the old superstition that the site of a capital was defiled by the death of an emperor. But by the beginning of the eighth century the political power had become so centralized that it was no longer practicable to move the capital every few years. Furthermore, the growth of Buddhism and the current interest in Chinese learning had undoubtedly weakened some of the old superstitions. Consequently, it was decided to build a permanent capital and to lay it out on a pattern similar to that of Ch'angan, the fabulous capital of T'ang China. For seventy-four years Nara remained the seat of the central government, and this period, known as the Nara era (710–784), is recognized as one of the most glorious ages in the whole span of Japanese history.

Of the various developments which account for, and which are also manifestations of, the new social unity of the Nara era, the compilation of the first "national" histories is especially noteworthy. Traditionally, the *Kojiki* (Chronicle of Ancient Matters) is the oldest of the extant histories, having been completed, it is asserted, in 712.[13] A reference in the preface to the *Kojiki* shows that in 681 Emperor Temmu ordered the compilation of a historical account in order "to preserve the true traditions from oblivion."[14] It would seem that he wished to strengthen the foundation of the state by showing that the various myths and traditions of the land were in reality centered in and based on the myths of the Sun Cult. The myths recorded in the *Kojiki* made the Emperors divine descendants of the Sun Goddess, who, after certain significant struggles with the gods in heaven, sent messengers down to earth to prepare the way for the descent of her August Grandson. These messengers had many difficulties in dealing with the various earthly deities; but finally an agreement was reached with the strongest, and the August Grandson thrust apart "the many-piled clouds of Heaven" and came down to Kyushu. With him he brought the jewel, the sword, and the mirror—the Three Treasures—which to this day are regarded as the Sacred Regalia, the possession of which still establishes the legitimacy of an emperor's rule. Finally, it is reported, a descendant of the August Grandchild announced his intention of moving eastward to a "fair land." This was Emperor Jimmu, traditionally the first Emperor of Japan, who began his rule in 660 B.C. From that point on, the chronicle covers events in the lives of each succeeding Emperor, the emphasis being not upon an accurate historical record but upon the establishment of a definite genealogical descent of the Emperors from the Sun Goddess. In other words, the account relates the various myths of the land, giving due attention to the many nature deities that were worshiped, but always underlining the supremacy of the Sun Cult and the divine descent of the Emperors. This detailed and carefully worked out account must have been quite as effective as the Chinese court ranks, or the centralized bureaucratic system, in convincing the leaders of the various clans that the Imperial clan had a paramount right to be the religious and political head of the state. It is no wonder that the *Kojiki* received much attention from later nationalists, and that it has even been called the "bible of Japanese nationalism."

During the Great Reform and Nara periods more attention than ever was given to the propagation of Buddhism, in spite of the fact that the Imperial institution itself was firmly based in Shinto mythology. The reformers, like Prince Shotoku, not only ardently believed in the new faith—which was undoubtedly associated in their minds with Chinese greatness—but they appreciated its unifying potential. They saw that it provided additional channels of political control, and that its concept of the oneness of the world could weaken the localizing tendencies of the indigenous cults. And as the two faiths became merged—the Buddhist temples also becoming places for the worship of native gods—the apparent contradictions between the two were submerged and Buddhism became not merely a centralizing force but a further support for the divinity of the Emperor. In order to strengthen Buddhism—and to check the operation of evil forces—the Imperial Court continued to make gifts and issue orders that accelerated its spread. Frequently an Emperor would order a hundred men to enter the priesthood; or he would make gifts of land to certain temples, send out missionaries to outlying provinces, or order provincial authorities to hold lectures on certain sutra. In 685 he ordered every Japanese household to install a Buddhist shrine, place a Buddhist statue in it, and offer up prayers to the statue. It is not surprising, then, that Buddhism, by the beginning of the Nara period—less than 160 years after it had first been introduced into Japan—had come to exert a tremendous influence upon the economic and political, as well as the religious, life of the Japanese people.

But under the reign of Emperor Shomu, who ruled from 724 to 748 and then dominated political affairs from his retirement until his death in 756, Buddhism made its most remarkable advances. The great Buddhist missionary Gyogi was given a free hand, and, traditionally at least, a doctrinal adjustment was made whereby the Sun Goddess (enshrined at the famous Ise Shrine) revealed herself as an incarnation of Buddha. But of still greater significance, from the point of view of the growth of national solidarity, was the Imperial decree of 741, which required that each province build a provincial temple (*kokubunji*). This decree was followed, about two years later, by a plan to build a large temple at Nara to serve as the headquarters of all the provincial temples. The central temple is generally known as *Tōdaiji* (Great Eastern Temple), but its full name is more significant: *Yamato-no-kuni-no-Konkōmyō-Shitennō-gokoku-no-tera,* or "temple for the protection of the Yamato state with the *Konkōmyō* sutra."[15] At the temple there was built a huge statue of Buddha (53½ feet high), which was regarded as the center of the Buddhist faith in Japan. Emperor Shomu himself attended the dedication ceremonies and, standing before the statue, prayed for the welfare and prosperity of the people of Japan. It was not long afterward that an abbot of Tōdaiji, by the name of Dōkyō, gained so much political power that he sought to make himself Emperor. But this was flying in the face of the Shinto myth, to the support of which even the Buddhist institutions owed much of their success. Buddhism had become truly powerful, but the old Sun Cult myth was so strongly rooted in Japanese life that Dōkyō was thwarted. A messenger of the Empress brought back a revealed message, from one of the main Shinto shrines of the day, which stated that from the beginning of the state no subject had ever become a sovereign, and that the successor to the throne must be a member of the Imperial family.[16] Buddhism had served as a cohesive force, but it was not to be placed at the center of the Japanese state.

The national solidarity of the Nara era was more than a political and religious phenomenon. It also had important economic ramifications. Ever since the introduction of Buddhism, if not before, there had been constant economic growth which culminated, in the Nara era, in a spurt of exchange activity that makes the period one of the most remarkable in the economic history of Japan. The rapid spread of Buddhism, entailing the erection of large temples in all parts of the country, created so great a demand for all types of new products that vast numbers of Korean and Chinese artisans, who were acquainted with the various techniques developed on the continent, migrated to Japan. The expansion of industrial activity was associated with greater specialization of economic activity and a more active trade, which, in turn, was both a cause and an effect of improvements in transportation, mining, and coinage. The towns were larger, the markets more numerous, the transportation of goods by land and sea more extensive, and the merchants wealthier and more independent—as a result, the people throughout the nation were bound together in a far more interdependent relationship than before.[17] But this economic growth, of course, was related not only to the spread of Buddhism but also to the rise of a more stable and powerful central government.

It seems safe to conclude, therefore, that in the Nara era the national foundations were greatly strengthened. By this time, governmental control had been extended over most of the area; the position of the Emperor as symbolic head of the state had been firmly fixed; and the rulers, in the face of the T'ang example—and possible T'ang danger—had adopted reforms and pressed policies which resulted in the achievement of a more closely knit social order. The Nara era, however, is even more famous for its literary and artistic activity. Although the literary pieces include the Kojiki—the so-called "bible of Japanese nationalism"—and Japan's first great anthology, the Manyōshū, the literature and art of the period reflect sentiments and attitudes that are only remotely akin to modern nationalism. In most of the literary and art forms the Chinese patterns were followed closely, and even in the Manyōshū, in which many of the poems are written in pure Japanese, there are only a few, such as the following, which express what might be called patriotism:

The spacious Land of Yamato
 Is a land guarded by the gods;
You go upon the water
As upon the land;
You sit in the ship
As on the floor at home. . . .[18]

Group consciousness was still on a low level, being reflected primarily in the activities and policies of the rulers, and was not yet sufficiently strong to color the literature and art of the nation or to influence the thought and actions of the great mass of the Japanese people.

Heian Japanization

Toward the end of the eighth century, about the time the capital was moved to Heian (now called Kyoto), the officials and scholars at the Imperial Court were beginning to lose their feelings of inferiority about the culture and civilization of Japan. Not only had marvelous advances been made since Buddhism was first introduced, in the middle of the sixth century, but T'ang China was no longer so impressive or fearsome. Japanese officials were even becoming less enthusiastic about being sent to China as envoys, and toward the end of the ninth century the practice of dispatching official missions to China was discontinued. Along with the decline of T'ang China, Japan, too, began to lose much of the political unity and economic prosperity that had been characteristic of the fabulous Nara period. A localism began to set in, which is one of the most intriguing developments in Japanese history. There were many contributing factors, including a tremendous increase in the number of people connected with government, religion, and the arts—people not engaged in the production of food. It became more and more difficult for the central government to find resources for supporting these people, particularly after it undertook to build two new capitals—one at Nagaoka and another at Heian—between 784 and 794, and after it was forced to spend huge sums of money in prolonged campaigns on the Ainu frontier. The Buddhist temples, too, had absorbed so large a percentage of the national wealth that their further growth took the form of a centrifugal, rather than a centripetal, force in Japanese society. Gradually, local officials and local temples tended to take over an increasing number of public functions; and finally, by the eleventh century, the central government was unable to prevent robbery, piracy, and civil war. There were no regular exchanges of official missions with China; trading was carried on with rice and silk serving as media of exchange; and the Japanese society, in general, was becoming more and more fragmented.

But throughout this period of localism, in which much of the newly found political and social unity was lost, the court nobility and the Buddhist priesthood continued to give much attention to literary, artistic, and religious matters. Indeed, the Heian period is frequently termed the classical period of Japanese literature,[19] and in that period we find the emergence of a more definitely independent, national culture. The members of the court society still devoted most of their energies to the importation and study of Chinese civilization, especially during the first hundred years of the Heian era; but they were more sophisticated than the nobles of Nara times. They had a better knowledge of things Chinese and, with greater confidence in their understanding and appreciation of Chinese culture, they gradually became more critical. In the latter part of the Heian era there was far more selection and adaptation, and as a result, religious systems and literary and art forms were created which had qualities that were definite variations from the Chinese norm. For this reason, later nationalist historians point to the cultural developments of the Heian era with great pride. They become almost ecstatic, and with much justification, about the vernacular prose literature of the eleventh century, especially the *Genji Monogatari* (Tales of Genji), which is certainly one of the world's earliest and greatest novels. Most modern Japanese are also proud of the colored picture scrolls (*e-makimono*), which did not originate in Japan but, in the latter part of the Heian period, took on a distinctively Japanese character. These developments were extremely important in the history of Japanese nationalism in that they constituted vital steps in the emergence of a truly national culture and therefore contributed, in later centuries, toward the growth of stronger and more widespread feelings of national pride. But it should be remembered that the cultural activities were limited, for the most part, to a small circle of nobles at the Imperial Court, and that there was far less social unity at this time than in preceding or following centuries. There was a luxurious life at the court, but the country was breaking up into small units. The seeds of feudalism were being sown. Furthermore, the Japanese were not in close contact with a strong neighbor. Localism and internal strife, then, rather than national unity and greater national consciousness, were the characteristic features of the Heian era.

Kamakura Unity

In the chaotic Heian times the clan appeared again as the dominant social group. But toward the end of the period, certain clans, by the use of military power, began to rise above the others and to reverse the trend toward social disintegration. Eventually the process resolved itself into a conflict between two great military clans, the Taira and the Minamoto; the history of the twelfth century is for the most part centered around their struggles for supremacy. But in 1185, the Minamoto, after a short period of Taira dominance, emerged victorious under the leadership of the famous hero, Minamoto Yoritomo (1147–1199). The subsequent period, known as the Kamakura era (since the Minamoto headquarters were in the city of Kamakura) was an era of unusual social effervescence, an era in which Japan attained new heights of political centralization, economic growth, and intellectual fluidity, and therefore one in which the people arrived at a new level of national unity.

The wellsprings of the Kamakura unity are not easily identified or evaluated. It would appear, however, that, unlike the situation in Nara times, internal developments may well have been more significant than foreign influences, although again the two operated in an interdependent relationship. In explaining the Kamakura centralization, historians underscore the leadership of Yoritomo, who is considered to have been both a military and a political genius. With the base of his power in eastern Japan, out on the Ainu frontier, he set up his headquarters in Kamakura. But in spite of the disintegrating tendencies of the previous centuries, Yoritomo, even though he was the most powerful figure in the land, did not consider himself an independent ruler but rather the Emperor's agent in charge of military affairs. Yoritomo constructed a highly centralized administrative and judicial system, which was designed as a means of administering the military affairs of the Shogun (the hereditary office which Yoritomo held after 1192). However, the effectiveness of Yoritomo's system and the extent of his clan's military power were such that the local representatives of the Shogun began to encroach upon the prerogatives of the local officials appointed directly by the Imperial Court, and consequently an increasing number of officials and noblemen of Kyoto became desirous of trimming the powers of this military regime and of regaining for the Imperial Court more direct and complete control over the affairs of the country.

The tension between the Court and the Bakufu (military regime) finally broke into open warfare in 1221. Many discontented military groups, various Buddhist organizations, and most of the court nobility sided with the Emperor, who ordered the subjugation of the military organization at Kamakura. But the Bakufu forces, after a decisive victory, marched into Kyoto and placed a more coöperative member of the Imperial family on the throne. Thereafter, remarkable political unity was achieved under the leadership of the Bakufu, but the fiction was still retained that all authority was being exercised in the name of the Emperor. In fact, after defeating the Imperial forces in 1221, the leader of the Kamakura forces felt impelled to explain, before one of the Shinto shrines, that he did not resist the Emperor's mandate for selfish reasons but wished merely to punish the evil councilors who had misled the Emperor.[20]

The greater political unity and stability of the Kamakura era were accompanied by a spurt of economic growth.[21] The elimination of robbery, piracy, and civil war; the rise of new demands for various types of military gear; and the erection of the military center at the relatively distant Kamakura—all were factors that served to stimulate greater production and to create a more active exchange of goods and services. However, there was another development, one that was not so closely related to the trend toward political centralization: the discovery of rich deposits of gold in the province of Mutsu. The Bakufu soon gained control of the new mines, and the gold that was obtained not only accrued to the advantage of the Bakufu but served to increase the flow of foreign and domestic trade.

Large amounts of gold, in addition to wood and miscellaneous items, were exported to China in a trade that had became quite active even before the beginning of the Kamakura era in 1192. China under the Sung dynasty (960–1279) did not reach the cultural heights she had attained under the T'ang dynasty, and yet there was a remarkable expansion in overseas trade that was due, in part at least, to technological developments in shipbuilding and navigation. By the twelfth century, Chinese merchants, especially at Canton, were carrying on a lively trade throughout the Far East. In Japan great profit was obtained from buying up gold and other articles with Chinese copper coins. The demand for these coins in Japan was based on the need for a better medium of exchange. The Bakufu apparently felt that the government's disastrous experiences with devalued coins in the ninth century still made it unlikely that Japanese-minted coins would be accepted; consequently it became convenient and profitable to obtain Chinese copper coins, which, as they circulated throughout Japan, served as a further stimulant to exchange activities.

The phenomenal expansion of trade within Japan during the thirteenth century is reflected in a number of developments, but particularly in the growth of pawnshops (dosō) and in the more extensive use of bills of exchange (kaesen). The pawnshop had come into existence earlier, as an adjunct to religious institutions; but during the thirteenth century it seems to have been associated with purely commercial enterprises—particularly the wineshop—and finally to have emerged as a separate business. By the end of the century, pawnshops had become so numerous and prosperous that the taxes levied on them constituted a very important source of revenue, forcing the military to make an exception for the debts owed to pawnshops when it issued its debt cancellation order (tokusei) of 1297. Bills of exchange too, came to figure prominently in the commercial transactions of the Kamakura era. At first they were used by temples in settling accounts between religious centers, such as Kamakura and Kyoto; but by the end of the century, bills were relied upon in many more types of exchange and were being handled by a greater variety of commercial operators. The level of economic development attained in this period is suggested by the ability of the military government, at the time of the Mongol invasions after 1274, to carry on extensive military operations for a long period of time in the distant island of Kyushu.

But probably the most significant feature of the social cohesion of the Kamakura era was the freer flow of beliefs, ideas, and fears within the nation. In the sphere of religion, for example, there was a movement—frequently termed the Buddhist Reformation—which forced Buddhist beliefs deeper into the Japanese social structure.[22] In that period, three new Buddhist sects became prominent, and the leaders of each showed considerable interest in reaching the new military class. Missionaries were sent out over the country; religious works were written in a language which more people could read; and, still more important, the doctrines made the attainment of salvation easier. Worship in two of the new sects, Shin and Nichiren—both of which were largely indigenous growths—was simplified to the point where the mere repetition of a sacred phrase was almost all that was necessary to obtain Buddha's grace. In the other sect, Zen, enlightenment was to be had not by a long study of religious texts but by intuition. These movements grew rapidly during the thirteenth century, and, since each was aided by a highly organized system of temples and a strong hierarchical priesthood, they affected the life of many more Japanese and established common patterns of worship and belief. Buddhism at this time was not so closely bound up with the trend toward political centralization as in Nara times, but in the realm of beliefs and ideas it laid the foundations for the Buddhism of more recent times, which has been an extremely important agent for establishing the kind of ideological unity that is characteristic of modern nationalism.

The centralization of political control, the spurt of economic growth, and the Buddhist Reformation were internal developments for the most part, and they certainly brought about the greater social cohesion that is essential for any significant growth of national consciousness. But it is doubtful whether the Japanese of this era, if they had not had closer contact with strong outsiders, would have experienced more widespread and more intense feelings of group consciousness than those of the Nara era. But Japan *was* thrown into close contact with a strong, foreign people, and the contact was of a type that struck fear into the hearts of the entire military class. The outsiders were none other than the mighty Mongols, who by 1271 had become the strongest power in all Asia. They had conquered China, had set up their capital at Peking, and had taken over Korea, right at Japan's front door.

Mongol Danger

In 1268 a letter arrived at the Imperial Court from the great Kublai Khan, and it carried very ominous threats:

> The Emperor of the Great Mongols being commissioned by Heaven hereby addresses the King of Japan. . . . It is a teaching of the sages that the entire universe should be one home. Therefore, if Japan should remain aloof and should not establish due relations with us, thus staying outside of the home, it would be contrary to the doctrine of the sages. Neither we nor you would desire to appeal to arms to settle this question. I hereby leave the entire matter to your conscientious consideration.[23]

The Mongol message created a great stir, at both Kyoto and Kamakura. A series of councils was held at Kyoto, and finally a draft reply was drawn up and sent on to Kamakura for the Shogun's approval. But the military men at Kamakura decided to make no reply, and the Mongol ambassador was sent home without even an acknowledgment that the message had been received. Other diplomatic attempts were made by Kublai Khan; but in 1274, after the Japanese had refused to answer a third note, the Mongols decided to use force. An army of some 27,000 men, equipped with superior weapons and trained in the use of advanced military tactics, was dispatched from Korea. Landings were made at Hakata, on the northwest coast of Kyushu. At first the Mongols gained the advantage, but in the midst of the operations a storm arose that destroyed many of the invaders' ships and forced the Mongol troops to withdraw to Korea. To the Japanese this was proof of divine protection. But to the Mongols it was merely an unfortunate accident, and they sent an envoy to see if the Japanese were now ready to change their minds about acceding to Mongol demands. The reply was to seize the envoy and his party and to have them all beheaded. Other envoys were sent by the Mongols, and they received the same treatment. Finally, in 1281, Kublai decided to send against the Japanese a second force, which, according to some, was made up of 140,000 men and more than 4,000 ships. In the meantime, the Japanese had given much attention to strengthening the coastal defenses and, as a result, a stronger resistance was put up. But while the battle was raging and the outcome was still in doubt, another storm arose, and again a huge number of Mongol ships capsized or were wrecked, forcing the remainder of the armada to return to its base in Korea.

For the Japanese this victory was not only undeniable proof of the courage and stamina of their soldiers but also additional evidence that their prayers to the shrines and temples had been answered. They were inclined to give most of the credit to the Sun Goddess who, it was believed, had sent the Divine Wind (*Ise no Kamikaze*) to destroy Kublai Khan's great armada. The failure of the Mongols to carry out their plans for the invasion and conquest of Japan has left a deep imprint upon the intellectual history of the Japanese people. The ability to hold off the powerful Mongols, after so many others had failed, gave the Japanese a confidence and a feeling of national pride that has influenced their thinking from that time to the present. To a person who is aware of the impression that the Mongol invasion made on the Japanese, it is not surprising to find that even in the last World War pilots who "volunteered" for suicide flights were called *Kamikaze* pilots, or "pilots of the Divine Wind." A noted Japanese historian, writing in 1941, has remarked that from the time of the Mongol invasions the word *Kamikaze* "symbolized the faith of the Japanese people in the belief that Providence is constantly with them in times of national adversity."[24]

Besides the success in holding off the Mongols, there were other aspects of the invasions that strengthened feelings of solidarity. Soldiers from all over Japan spent approximately a quarter of a century preparing for an attack by the Mongols. As soon as the first invasion was turned back, the Japanese set to work strengthening coastal defenses in preparation for the second invasion; and for fifteen years after that invasion they fully expected a third. In fact, Kublai Khan until his death, in 1294, continued to push plans for a third attempt. And his son was determined to succeed where his father had failed. The son reëstablished the "Department for the Invasion of Japan" and in 1299 sent a noted Chinese Buddhist by the name of I-shan to Japan to try to gain submission by diplomatic means. I-shan remained in Japan for twenty years, but was unable to carry out his mission, and the plans for further military action were eventually dropped. However, as late as 1419 a force of some 18,000 men, in more than 200 vessels, invaded Tsushima, an island in the strait between Korea and Japan. The Japanese Emperor immediately sent officials to all the leading shrines to pray for protection, and military forces were again mobilized. But Tsushima was able, without assistance, to prevent a landing; and from that time until 1944, Japan was never again seriously threatened by foreign invasion. The fears engendered in the hearts of the Japanese people during much of the thirteenth century were probably more effective than the pride and confidence aroused by the military victories in creating bonds of common feelings and in establishing firm foundations for a more advanced stage of national consciousness.

The evidence of national consciousness among the Japanese people up to the time of the Mongol invasions is found mainly in the actions and policies of the government and, to a minor degree, in the literary and artistic expressions of the nobility. But with the threat of invasion by the Mongols came a deeper sense of national consciousness, as evidenced by the growth of a Buddhist movement which had a definite national focus. The movement was headed by Nichiren (1222–1282), who formulated a "unique truth" which he insisted must be adopted to the exclusion of all the former erroneous religious teachings, and he predicted that the country would suffer from further calamities—even foreign invasion—unless the people abandoned their old religious beliefs and adopted his teachings. At first Nichiren did not gain much of a following, and for his bold accusations and condemnations he was banished to the island of Izu. But when the threatening note of Kublai Khan arrived in 1268, Nichiren rushed back to Kamakura to remind the military officials that he had predicted such a disaster, and to insist that the only way to cope with the situation was for the whole country to turn to his "true" faith. However, too many influential people were angered by his demands, and again he was arrested. This time he seemed destined for execution, when "something bright, like a ball of fire, flew from the southeast to the northwest, and every one's face was clearly visible in its light. The executioner became dizzy, and fell; soldiers were panic stricken" and ran away.[25] Frightened by this apparent display of supernatural power, the officials decided upon exile rather than execution.

While in exile, Nichiren continued to write, and as invasion became more imminent, he became more insistent that national salvation lay in a complete acceptance of his teachings. In a book written in 1272, for example, he wrote: "I will be the Pillar of Japan; I will be the Eyes of Japan; I will be the Great Vessel of Japan."[26] Two years later the relations with the Mongols had become even more strained, and the government rushed preparations to defend the country against invasion. In addition to making military preparations, the government gave much attention to requesting the priests of various temples and shrines to offer up prayers, asking the deities for protection against the foreign enemy. The officials came to fear even that Nichiren had been treated too roughly, and finally an order was issued for his release. Again Nichiren hastened to Kamakura. There he was given a hearing before high-ranking military officials, and again he insisted that the only way to save the country was for the people to turn against the erroneous teachings of the old Buddhist sects and to adopt his teachings. A high ecclesiastical rank and a large gift of money were offered to him, in the hope that he would moderate his condemnations and demands. But Nichiren was not a man to compromise. When the government showed, by calling on the old Buddhist sects for prayers for rain, that it had not undergone a change of heart, he left Kamakura in a huff and went into voluntary exile. As more attention was given to working out the doctrines of his true Buddhism, he became more convinced that a universal church should be established, with its center in Japan, where the prophet of this gospel had appeared: "The Holy See will then be the seat where all men of the three countries (India, China, and Japan) and the whole [world] will be initiated into the mysteries of confession and expiation; and even the great deities, Brahma and Indra, will come down into the sanctuary and participate in the initiation."[27] The final attempt of the Mongols to invade Japan in 1281 seems to have been a source of great satisfaction to Nichiren, although later historians insist that he made a distinction between the actual degeneracy of Japan and her ideal greatness.[28] At any rate, in one of the letters written after the second invasion, he wrote: "An autumn gale destroyed the enemy's ships, and now the people had been captured; while the priests pretend that it was due to the efficacy of their mysteries. Ask them whether they took the head of the Mongol king. . . ."[29] It is clear that Nichiren was not a nationalist of the modern type. He did not describe the glories and unique qualities of the Japanese people; he was not convinced that Japan as a nation had any particular mission, except the one that devolved upon it as a result of his own birth in Japan; and he even expressed some satisfaction at seeing the country invaded. In other words, he was primarily a religious reformer, but he was one that expressed in his actions and words a greater sense of national consciousness. It is no mere accident that the Nichiren sect is still considered the most nationalistic of the various Buddhist sects.

The Mongol invasions did much to create stronger ideological unity, but they also were a powerful disintegrating force—economically, politically, and socially. The trade with China was severed, and the cost of prolonged military preparations—to the military government as well as to the entire military class—was staggering. Because of the absence of so many men from the farms, there was a decline in the production of rice. And since the income of the entire military class was chiefly in terms of fixed incomes in rice, it became increasingly difficult, in those times of economic expansion, rising prices, and increased costs of living, for the soldiers to support their families. In previous campaigns inside Japan the military authorities had been able to distribute among worthy and needy retainers land that had been seized from the defeated enemy, but the resistance to the Mongol invasions did not result in making new lands available. By the end of the thirteenth century the economic distress of the warriors was causing an increasing number of fiefs to fall into the hands of nonmilitary persons, and the military government did not have sufficient economic strength to give its retainers any positive assistance. When sumptuary laws, price fixing, and other legal measures failed to improve conditions among the retainers, the Bakufu, in 1297, was forced to order the cancellation of certain debts owed by the military, and also to order the return of certain fiefs that had fallen into the hands of creditors. But this, too, was somewhat disastrous for all concerned. The measure gave no permanent or substantial assistance to the warriors, and the government found that its own income was endangered by this disregard of creditors' contractural rights. But the measure was symptomatic of the sad state of economic and political affairs facing the military government during and after the attempted Mongol invasions.[30] After the beginning of the fourteenth century the Bakufu became progressively weaker. More local officials began to act independently of the central government, and a series of civil wars broke out. The wars continued on into the sixteenth century and were characteristic of the period of Japan's "Dark Ages" (about 1300–1550). As far as the rise of nationalism is concerned, then, the Mongol invasions had both a positive and a negative effect. They certainly aroused common feelings of fear, pride, and confidence, which made a deep impression upon the thoughts and feelings of Japanese at the time, as well as in later generations; but they also created a strain on the economic and political fabric that resulted in another period of considerable social disintegration.

Japanization in the "Dark Ages"

During the first quarter of the fourteenth century, the military government at Kamakura grew weaker, and finally, in 1320, its armies proved to be ineffective in settling a succession dispute in the Ando family, which held an important post on the Ainu frontier in the north. The poor showing of the Bakufu armies was good news at the Imperial Court, and immediately plots were laid to throw off the shackles of the military regime. Emperor Go-Daigo, advised and encouraged by Kitabatake Chikafusa and other scholars, arranged to gain the military backing of Buddhist monasteries in the Kyoto area and to obtain the support of various military groups that had become dissatisfied with the rule of the Kamakura regime. The situation came to a head in 1331, when the Bakufu decided to check Go-Daigo's maneuvers by placing another emperor, of the alternate line, on the throne. Go-Daigo prepared to resist the order. He left the capital, taking the Imperial seal with him, to assume leadership of the military forces that were drawn up to oppose the Bakufu. But the Kamakura troops were not so weak as had been thought. Go-Daigo's forces were defeated in a series of battles, and Go-Daigo and his two sons were sent into exile. But loyal supporters continued to fight on, in various localities, and finally a number of victories were won that encouraged many others to join the Imperial forces. Then, in 1333, Go-Daigo himself escaped from exile, and whole sections of the country rallied to his support. Kamakura was captured and burned, and thus the military regime came to an end and the Imperial Court at Kyoto once more became the seat of political authority.

For three years, from 1333 to 1336, the Imperial Court was more than the nominal head of the Japanese state. Modern nationalist historians give much attention to this three-year rule by Emperor Go-Daigo, for it was the only successful attempt to restore the Imperial Court to power from Yoritomo's time to the collapse of the Tokugawa Bakufu in 1868. There is a tendency for historians to point to the Go-Daigo restoration as evidence that the Japanese people, more than five hundred years ago, were already so greatly stirred by affections for the Imperial institution that they were determined to restore the Emperor to power. Few will question the conclusion that the Imperial Court had achieved, after centuries of political and religious leadership, tremendous prestige; but it cannot be denied that the fourteenth-century Restoration was for the most part a product of the political chaos of the time. At least one of the modern Japanese historians states that most of the groups that supported the Imperial Court did so not because of loyalty to the Emperor but mainly because of their desire to further their personal interests.[31]

Go-Daigo apparently tried to reëstablish the supremacy of the court nobility without a proper appreciation of the power that had been gained by the military class and by the merchants and financeers of Sakai and other commercial centers. By 1336, discontented, self-seeking elements had banded together, and a new military regime (called the Ashikaga Bakufu) was born. But the rise to power of this regime was not accompanied by the same notable development of social cohesion as was seen at the beginning of the Kamakura era. Ashikaga Takauji (1305–1358), the first of the Ashikaga Shoguns, was unable to marshal sufficient power to bring all the discordant elements under control. Go-Daigo again fled with the Imperial regalia and set up court at Yoshino, while Takauji's candidates for the throne ruled at Kyoto. There was constant fighting between the supporters of the two rival courts during the succeeding fifty years, and only in 1392 was the

Ashikaga Shogun (Yoshimitsu) able to settle the succession dispute. The period (known as Southern-Northern Court era) was a particularly critical one in the history of the Imperial institution. The prestige of the Court was still strong enough to make it imperative that the warring factions support the legitimacy of their cause by fighting, in name at least, for one or other of the claimants to the throne; but it is significant that the Imperial institution itself, the focal point of the development of national unity, was torn by strife and dissension.

Out of this period there did emerge, however, a famous history entitled *Jinnō Shōtōki* (On the Legitimacy of the Imperial Line), which is considered to be one of the key works in Japan's nationalist literature. The author, Kitabatake Chikafusa (1295–1354), was intent upon giving as much support as possible to the claims of the Southern Court. He wanted not merely to show that the Southern Court had legitimate claims to the throne, but also to emphasize the uniqueness, the greatness, and the divinity of the Japanese Imperial line, so that more people might feel impelled to give loyal and unselfish service to the rightful Emperor. He claimed that the uniqueness of the Imperial institution made Japan superior not only to China but also to India.[32] But of greater significance was his emphasis on the idea that a special relationship existed between the Emperor and his people, to which he applied the word *kokutai* (national entity). From that time on, *kokutai* became a favorite subject of discussion for nationalist writers, particularly after the seventeenth century. Its meaning was expanded to include all the unique qualities, possessions, and ideals of the Japanese nation, and it finally took on an extremely mystic character. Thus with Kitabatake's work and his use of the word *kokutai*, national consciousness begins to be identified and stressed in the writings of intellectuals, as well as reflected in the actions of the ruling class. Realizing the significance of Kitabatake in the history of Japanese nationalism, many of the modern writers are inclined to hold him up as the first true nationalist; but it should be remembered that his work was stimulated not so much by a concern for the future of the nation as for the future of the Imperial House. For him, *kokutai* was not endangered by foreign powers but by internal strife.

During the period of conflict between the Northern and Southern courts (1336–1392), there was still another event of some consequence in the rise of national consciousness in Japan. When the Ming dynasty was established in 1368, the Chinese court sent envoys to outlying states asking them to indicate their acceptance of the traditional tributary status. Having removed the foreign (Mongol) dynasty, and being quite disturbed by the activities of Japanese pirates along the coast of China, the Ming court was more determined to force Japan to accept a tributary position. For a time, however, the Japanese refused even to answer the messages. Finally, in 1370, an Imperial Prince replied with a communication that made the Japanese position quite clear:

In the past, the Mongols ranked our country as a barbarian nation and attempted to reduce us to subjects and dependents. We entirely ignored their demands. Later, the Mongol ruler sent his envoy, Chao, to express good will on one hand, although on the other the Mongol armada with a fighting force 100,000 strong suddenly appeared off our coast. This act of the Mongols offended Heaven. Thunder and great winds completely annihilated them. Now, the new emperor in China sent an envoy, also named Chao, with instructions to approach us in similar way. Are not you and also your emperor blood relatives of the Mongols, our national enemies?[33]

Even this emphatic reply did not discourage the Chinese: five more missions were sent to Japan in the following decade. The Japanese note that was sent back with the last of these missions continues to thrill ardent Japanese nationalists:

You, as the sovereign of China, have 10,000 chariots of war at your command. Your cities and fortresses exceed several thousands in number. Your domain extends a million miles. But you are not satisfied with this vast gift of Heaven. You yield to the desire to conquer other nations. . . . We understand that you have a plan for war. We have a plan for defense. We are informed that you have selected trusted generals and instructed them to take the best of your troops to invade our country. Besides our military preparation, we have a geographical advantage; our country has the natural defense of sea and mountains. We shall certainly not kneel down by the roadside and permit your troops to trample over our country. . . . Should we win and you lose, it would bring neither satisfaction nor glory to our country, because we seek reverently to adhere to the instruction of our forefathers; namely, "To maintain peace is the highest aim and to refrain from war is the strongest policy of our nation. To keep people free from the suffering consequent upon war and to rescue them from hardship and misery are the duties of the Ruler." Peace or war is at your command. . . .[34]

This note, together with a plot in China in which certain Japanese were believed to have been implicated, led the Ming emperor to break off all relations with Japan. The failure of the Ming to bring the Japanese into line seems to indicate that even after the lapse of a hundred years, and even in the midst of internal strife, Japanese officials were still influenced by the feelings of pride and confidence that had been aroused by the Mongol invasion.

35801

After the beginning of the fifteenth century, however, Ashikaga Yoshimitsu, the current Shogun, took steps to reopen relations with China. In a note to Cheng-Tsu, the third of the Ming emperors, he not only indicated his acceptance of the tributary status for Japan but called himself the "King of Japan" (*Nihon Kokuo*). This reversal of policy suggests a definite decline in the national feelings that had prevailed in the previous century; but it should be pointed out that Japan under this Shogun was somewhat stronger than before, and that there were now no threats of reprisal from Ming emperors. Furthermore, Yoshimitsu was greatly interested in augmenting his income and obviously recognized the possibility of gaining handsome gifts from the Ming emperor in return for concessions that were dear to the Chinese, namely, acceptance of the tributary status and promises to check Japanese piratical expeditions along the coasts of China. It is probable, then, that Yoshimitsu's actions do not indicate less intense feelings of national consciousness. Yoshimitsu had more reason to be confident about the maintenance of an independent position for Japan; it therefore seems likely that he yielded to the Chinese, with tongue in cheek, in order to improve the financial condition of the Bakufu. The records show that Yoshimitsu did receive large sums of Chinese copper coins, as well as gifts of gold and silver. But on his deathbed he came to regret his Machiavellian moves and asked his son, Yoshimochi, to promise to break off these relations with China. Yoshimochi complied with his father's wishes and refused to obey the numerous instructions and demands of the Ming emperors. In 1419 he made a statement to the Ming envoys explaining the change of policy:

... the gods of supreme power made a revelation through an oracle. They stated that, from the time of the nation's founding, no person had ever degraded himself and his nation so far as to style himself "a subject of a foreign nation." Yoshimitsu ignored traditions and violated the laws of our sacred sovereigns of former days. . . . This [change of policy] is not because we depend upon the geographical advantage of our country's being surrounded by vast waters, but because we desire to obey the instructions of our gods.[35]

But Yoshinori, who became Shogun in 1429, was influenced more by considerations of financial profit than by the sentiments of his older brother. In the notes that he sent to China he signed himself as "Yoshinori, King of Japan and subject of the Ming Emperor."[36] The Chinese were extremely pleased with this development, not only because they had wanted Japan to accept the traditional status of a tributary state but also because they had become greatly disturbed about the devastating raids of Japanese pirates. The arrangements made at this time were so satisfactory to both parties that the Ashikaga Shoguns continued to send tributary missions to China until 1547. Japanese nationalists have been very critical of these Shoguns who degraded Japan and sacrificed national dignity and honor for economic advantage.[37] But political disintegration at home and peaceful relations with foreign nations were not conditions that tended to arouse national feelings of the type that have prevailed in modern times, or that were current at the time of the Mongol invasions.

In the century (1432–1547) in which the Shoguns were sending tributary missions to China in order to increase their supply of Chinese copper coins, the Imperial institution reached a very low level. The Ashikaga shogunate usurped far more of the power of the Imperial Court than did the Kamakura Bakufu, and the gradual loss of Imperial estates placed the Emperor and the court nobility in dire economic straits. Civil wars frequently engulfed the capital itself, and many of the old court functions had to be abandoned. It has been concluded by Western scholars that the Throne had ceased to be of any importance; but recent research by Japanese historians suggests that in spite of the poverty of the Imperial Court there was a definite revival of interest in the Ise Shrine, with which the prestige of the Imperial Household was closely associated. But as much as the nationalists would like to show a continuing growth of national consciousness during the period, it seems that internal strife and relative indifference about relations with the outside world militated against any further strengthening of national ties.

In spite of the prevalence of war, the disgraceful policies of the Shoguns, and the low level of Imperial power, the Ashikaga era is considered one of the most creative periods in the history of Japanese art. It was in these chaotic times that the Noh drama was developed and that pure-ink landscape paintings reached their zenith in the work of Sesshū (1420–1506), the man who was recognized even by contemporary Chinese artists as their superior. Many of Japan's greatest "National Treasures" date from this period, and much of Japan's claim to a unique cultural contribution is based upon Ashikaga art. But it is clear that, as far as nationalism is concerned, the importance of Ashikaga art—like that of Heian literature—lies not in the fact that the art was a manifestation of a new level of national consciousness but in the fact that it aroused, in later centuries, a more profound sense of national pride.   ◇ ◇ ◇

In looking back over this first phase in the growth of national consciousness, one can see that although Japan had already moved quite far toward the achievement of national solidarity, the manifestations of national consciousness were still relatively weak and limited. For the most part, the awareness of national unity was reflected only in the actions of political leaders. With the exception of the establishment of a Buddhist sect with a national focus, and the writing of a history that stressed the *kokutai* concept, there is little evidence that national sentiments had made any noticeable imprint upon the conscious thought of these early centuries. The forces that generate national feelings were operating—there were movements toward internal cohesion, and there were contacts with strong neighbors—but the forces had not yet gathered much momentum. Japan's geographical oneness favored an early rise of internal unity, but her geographical position also isolated her, during most of the period, from foreign dangers. Although the Japanese contact with the culturally superior China, and with the militarily superior Mongols, had probably left most Japanese leaders and intellectuals with a definite sense of inferiority, the rise of greater internal cohesion was the more dominant factor in this early growth of national consciousness.

3 ARTICULATE NATIONAL CONSCIOUSNESS

The arrival of the first Europeans in Japan in 1543 was followed by one of the most dynamic periods in Japanese history and by the rise of intellectual currents which marked the beginning of a new phase in the growth of national consciousness. When the first Portuguese adventurers were blown ashore in southern Japan, the country was torn by civil war. Dozens of feudal lords were fighting among themselves for supremacy. And yet within fifty years the entire country was under the iron hand of Hideyoshi, the great military hero who traditionally started his career as a member of a small robber gang. Hideyoshi gained such tremendous political and military power that in 1592 he undertook to invade Korea, planning to extend his conquests to China and even to India. By the end of the sixteenth century, the Japanese people, having obtained greater political stability and having adopted new techniques of production and distribution, were enjoying unparalleled economic prosperity. Everywhere there was a zest for living that was reflected in gorgeous decorations, imposing castles, richly embroidered costumes, and fabulous tea parties. With the gradual elimination of civil war and the emergence of a period of economic growth, there was more time and opportunity for cultural pursuits. After 1615 the new military regime itself came to advocate that soldiers devote their energies to scholarship, as well as to military exercises. Out of this scholarly activity, intellectual movements emerged which aroused, among a larger segment of the Japanese people, a deeper appreciation of their unique heritage and, in particular, a new sense of the value and significance of the Emperor institution.

Sixteenth-Century Unity

The conventional explanation for the remarkable political centralization and economic prosperity achieved by the Japanese in the last half of the sixteenth century is that Japan was blessed with the leadership of geniuses. And there is no denying that the three men who built the powerful military organization and the strong political structure were exceptional leaders. They knew men; they understood how new weapons could be best utilized; they appreciated the value of a coinage system; and they were masters at perfecting a system of political control. But it must also be recognized that in the last half of the sixteenth century and the first half of the seventeenth there were new techniques, conditions, and opportunities that gave them distinct advantages.

The new unity was certainly related to the great increase in industrial production. In mining, for example, the developments were almost of a revolutionary character. New deposits of gold, silver, and copper were discovered; but of even more importance was the introduction—probably from China—of improved methods of mining and more advanced metallurgical techniques, particularly those that enabled the Japanese to extract silver from their copper ore. Vast new quantities of silver were made available for shipment to China, where the metal was in great demand. When the Portuguese discovered Japan in 1543, Chinese and Japanese merchants were already engaged in the profitable business of trading Japanese silver for Chinese silk. With their bigger and faster ships, the Portuguese lost no time in taking advantage of this trading opportunity. The lively foreign commerce proved to be especially lucrative for those feudal lords who were in possession of territories in which precious metals were mined. It is significant to note that the great sixteenth-century heroes—Nobunaga, Hideyoshi, and Ieyasu—were in control of such territories at an early date.

The possession of precious metals proved to be even more advantageous after Nobunaga (1543–1582), the first of the three heroes, took to using them as money. As indicated above, earlier rulers had preferred the use of Chinese copper coins, even when there was plenty of gold to be had in Japan; but one of the first steps taken by Nobunaga when he seized control of the Imperial Court at Kyoto in 1569 was to issue an order requiring the acceptance of all precious metals and native coins as legal tender. Within a few years the increased circulation of Japanese coins had caused the price of gold to soar, in spite of the fact that vast new quantities of precious metals were being mined in Japan. It even became profitable to import gold from abroad. The widespread use of coins as money after 1569 gave to Nobunaga and his successors—because of their control of rich mines—economic power that obviously facilitated the carrying out of extended military operations and the management of complex political affairs.[1]

Clearly, the new economic power obtained from the greater production and wiser use of precious metals was significant; but it may be that the introduction of long-range military weapons provided the sixteenth-century leaders with an even more crucial advantage. When the Portuguese arrived in 1543, the article in their possession which aroused the most interest and curiosity was the arquebus. Both Japanese and Portuguese accounts reflect the eagerness shown by the local lords in buying guns from the Portuguese merchants and in getting Japanese blacksmiths to learn how to manufacture them. Within just a few years, gunsmiths were turning out firearms even in the most isolated villages of northern Japan; but most of the centers that became particularly famous were in the territories subjugated by Nobunaga. As guns came to be a regular part of the army equipment, generals began to make adjustments which would enable them to obtain greater advantage from the use of the new weapons. And again it was Nobunaga and his generals who took the lead in making those changes.[2]

At the battle of Nagashino in 1575, Nobunaga placed three thousand musketeers behind breastworks and directed them to remain there throughout the engagement. He then divided the musketeers into three sections and issued orders that only one group was to fire at a time, for in those days it took some time to load a gun, and he wanted to make certain that a somewhat continuous fire was maintained throughout the engagement. When contact was made with the enemy, which was far superior in numbers, Nobunaga did not command his men to rush forward in the traditional manner but had his horsemen make feints to convince the enemy that an attack was about to be made. The opposing army was thus aroused to make a frontal attack, and Nobunaga's musketeers, from behind their breastworks, were able to bear down on the onrushing soldiers with a steady fire that settled the issue before the two armies met in the usual hand-to-hand fighting. These tactics were followed consistently by Nobunaga and his generals in subsequent battles. In 1583, after Nobunaga's death, two of his most powerful generals resorted to arms to decide the right of succession. Both had learned well the lessons taught by Nobunaga and were determined to remain on the defensive. Both spent much time in building strong breastworks, and both sent out units to feint attacks. They even exchanged insulting letters, but neither general would budge from his defensive position. After several months of this, the two agreed to become allies. One of the men, Hideyoshi, assumed the dominant political role until his death in 1598; the other, Ieyasu, established the Tokugawa Bakufu, which remained in power from 1603 to 1868.[3]

Still another adjustment to the new type of warfare was the building of castles that would withstand gunfire. Nobunaga and Hideyoshi were also the pioneers in this. Before the introduction of firearms, castles were built of earth and their walls stood only about ten feet high. As early as 1549, however, Ashikaga Yoshiteru, the current Shogun, strengthened his castle walls with stones "as protection against guns." But it was Nobunaga's castle at Azuchi, built in 1576, that set the pattern for subsequent construction. Within the walls of his castle there were four distinct citadels, one within another; and inside the innermost citadel was a central tower, 120 feet long, 102 feet wide, and 96 feet high. All was built of solid rock. Hideyoshi, having learned early and well the military advantages to be derived from the new-type castles, retained the lead in castle construction. In 1586 he built the Osaka castle, which remained the center of his military power and the strongest castle in the land until his death in 1598. This structure went far beyond Nobunaga's stronghold at Azuchi. It was far larger and stronger, having grounds a mile and a half long and a mile wide. The walls were 18 to 21 feet thick and were made of hugh granite stones, some of which were 10 feet wide and 40 feet long. A moat 20 feet deep surrounded each of the citadels, so that an invader would have to cross three moats before reaching the center of the fortress. The building of these huge castles at this early date was not merely a result of greater military and political power; it was also a basic factor in the accumulation of that power, for the protective strength supplied by the new weapons, with which the castles were equipped, was augmented when the castle was strong enough to protect the lord's position from an effective use of those weapons by others. This was particularly true, since, in the days when the political centralization process was under way, cannon were not being used widely and therefore had not yet destroyed the military value of such strongholds.[4]

In a study of the relationship between the introduction of firearms and the political centralization of Japan it should be pointed out, too, that firearms continued to be an important source of power for Nobunaga and Hideyoshi even after other lords took up the use of firearms and had become familiar with the organizational, tactical, and defense techniques best suited to the new long-range weapons. At first, Nobunaga and Hideyoshi had the advantage because they took up the use of the weapons on a large scale earlier, and because they developed the new techniques earlier. They were thus able to outdistance the other lords, even after others had gained the know-how, because of the accumulative propensities of power. Having gained, at an early date, new territories, including those with mines and centers for the production of guns, Nobunaga and Hideyoshi were able to supply larger armies with the more expensive equipment and to build larger castles than the lords who started later, regardless of how clever those lords may have been.

But political centralization was only one of the manifestations of greater social cohesion in the sixteenth century. Probably more basic was the tremendous economic growth, which continued on into the seventeenth century. The increased production of precious metals and their use in the minting of coins have already been mentioned in connection with the accumulation of political and military power by Nobunaga and Hideyoshi; but there were other developments that made the sixteenth and seventeenth centuries one of the most prosperous periods in the history of Japan. The revolution in warfare was of course paralleled by tremendous expansion in military industries, particularly in the manufacture of guns and ammunition and in the construction of stone castles in all parts of Japan. The tendency of the armies to become larger and to remain concentrated at castles, even when not engaged in fighting, created tremendous supply problems which involved far more extensive and complex exchange activities. Then there was the thriving textile industry in which the raw silk from China was made into cloth by the silk weavers in the Nishijin section of Kyoto and other centers. Cotton textile production also soared as a result of the introduction of cottonseed into Japan by the Portuguese. Commercial centers therefore became larger and more numerous, and in them, credit institutions, commercial guilds, and merchant associations grew and prospered. There was such a spurt of economic activity in the last half of the sixteenth century that prices did not rise appreciably, although large quantities of copper, silver, and gold coins were thrown into circulation. The need for money kept pace with the making of coins and the expansion of credit. With all this exchange activity, the Japanese people obviously were experiencing greater unity, economically as well as politically.[5]

Early Seventeenth-Century Rejection of Contacts with the West

Although the new unity was undoubtedly the most significant development of the sixteenth century, as far as the history of nationalism is concerned, it was by no means unrelated to the new contacts with the Western world. The revolution in warfare was of course based upon the introduction of firearms by the Portuguese, and the active foreign trade was closely bound up with the carrying trade of Portuguese merchants. During the last half of the sixteenth century the Japanese had become impressed with the technological superiority of the West, particularly in the fields of gunnery, shipbuilding, and metallurgy. It had even become something of a fad for the Japanese to own some object that had been imported from Europe. But at the beginning of the seventeenth century the leaders began to be increasingly disturbed about the political implications of the spread of Christianity, a foreign religion which had been pressed most energetically by the Portuguese Jesuit missionaries. After the first decade of the century, the Christian movement was considered to be definitely subversive. Although in the latter half of the sixteenth century the relations with the Western world were an important factor in the growth of internal social cohesion, early in the seventeenth century they began to take the form of foreign pressure and to be a more vital factor in arousing among the Japanese a deeper sense of national consciousness.

The danger of the Christian movement was more clearly recognized by Japanese military leaders in the years following the death of Ieyasu in 1616.[6] There were a number of reasons for this concern, but the conservative attitude of the second and third Shoguns and the nature of the new military structure (the Tokugawa Bakufu) which had emerged after 1600 were fundamental. Ieyasu's successors were not as confident as he had been, and because of their fear of political upheavals, they did their best to keep all elements under strict control. But their efforts were not due entirely to their personal proclivities, for the political and military structure did have weaknesses, and might easily have given way had it been subjected to strong subversive forces. The military machine under Hideyoshi had been truly formidable, and with the battles at Sekigahara in 1600 and at Osaka in 1615, Ieyasu had gained the upper hand. And yet the new political framework was more like a loose federation—with the Tokugawas in the strongest position—than a centralized state. There were so-called "outside clans," approximating independent states, which submitted to Tokugawa dominance, but over which the Bakufu was able to exert almost no direct control. Thus, the Bakufu, with its base of power centered in eastern Japan, had to resort to various specially devised techniques to keep the powerful outside clans from increasing their strength and from joining forces against the Bakufu. Under these conditions, Christianity appeared to present a real danger, especially since the Christian movement had been most active in western Japan, the home of many of the powerful outside clans.

From the very first years of the Christian missionary effort—which began with the arrival of Xavier in Japan in 1549—the Jesuits tended to concentrate their appeal on the feudal lords themselves, having discovered that it was much easier to make conversions once the leaders had been won over. In dealing with these lords, the Jesuits became involved in commercial and even political deals which tended to arouse the suspicion that they had goals other than the saving of souls. As early as 1587, Hideyoshi noted this particular aspect of the Christian program, and it was then that Jesuit missionaries were first ordered out of the country. But the decree was not enforced, chiefly because those in power were afraid that the proscription of Christianity would disrupt the profitable Portuguese trade,[7] and Christianity continued to grow.

In the second decade of the seventeenth century, several developments converged to make Christianity seem very dangerous. The Bakufu rulers now were not only quite concerned about preserving the uneasy status quo but they were convinced that Christianity established a very uncomfortable tie between the outside clans (about whom the Bakufu was deeply worried) and the Portuguese and Spaniards (who had extended their empires into all parts of the world). After 1612, plots were uncovered in which Christians were involved. In one case, documents were found which suggested that a Christian official had actually concocted a conspiracy, in conjunction with foreign Christians, to overthrow the Bakufu with the aid of foreign troops. And then, at the battle of Osaka in 1615, when the last remnants of the power of Hideyoshi's son were crushed, many of the leaders of the opposition to the Bakufu turned out to be Christians. One of them, a man by the name of Akashi, had taken his Christianity so seriously that he had permitted the destruction of Buddhist temples. In the engagement some of the troops opposing the Bakufu marched into the fray carrying banners inscribed with Christian symbols. When the castle was finally captured, it was discovered that five foreign missionaries were being harbored in it, although they had all been ordered out of Japan the previous year. By this time, too, the Bakufu officials were becoming convinced that it would be possible to preserve the profitable European trade without having to put up with the missionary activities, since both the Dutch and the English were constantly stating that they, unlike the Portuguese and the Spanish, were interested only in trade. After the death of Ieyasu, the Bakufu therefore began to move against Christianity with far greater vigor and determination.

Not only did it take steps to see that earlier orders were enforced, but it initiated restrictions upon the actions and movements of foreign traders, confining the traders to the ports of Nagasaki and Hirado and allowing them to go to Edo (now Tokyo) just once a year, in very closely guarded groups. In 1617 the first foreign missionaries were executed. In the following year certain high officials created a scandal by accusing each other of harboring foreign missionaries; and thereafter the persecution of Christians became more severe than ever, particularly in the city of Nagasaki, where Christian buildings were torn down and Christian cemeteries were desecrated. The apostates were forced to swear that the Jesuit fathers "by threats of excommunication and hell fire can do what they like with the people, *and all this is their stratagem to take the country of others.*"[8]

The Great Martyrdom was in 1622. In that year, 132 Christians were either killed, tortured to death, or left to die from privations in prison. By this time the Japanese had introduced or devised several types of cruel torture; and torture was used now not only to force Christians to recant but to force people to confess that they were Christians. The misery of the Christian population was further increased by regulations that made it almost impossible for them to earn a living. Consequently, after 1622 there were many more apostasies, and the Christian movement was forced underground. Then, in 1624, the Bakufu, in still another attempt to rid the country of what was considered to be a subversive movement, took its first important step toward isolation by banning all Spaniards from Japan.[9]

In moving beyond persecution to a policy of isolation, the officials of the Bakufu became disturbed not only by the Christian activities of the foreign merchants but by the activities of Japanese merchants. In the first place, most of the Japanese, as well as the foreign, merchant activities were centered in those same outside clans; and in the second place, many of the Japanese merchants came from a class of unattached warriors (called *rōnin*) who served no particular feudal lord and therefore could not be easily controlled. There were tens of thousands of *rōnin* who were constantly on the alert for an opportunity to improve their position. They tended to gravitate toward any group or area that showed promise of achieving greater power. The Bakufu had always kept a careful watch on these *rōnin*, and after 1628 it observed that an unusually large number of them were entering the field of foreign trade. This was not a plot but a development that resulted primarily from a Bakufu embargo on both Dutch and Portuguese trade. The embargo, in 1628, gave Japanese merchants tremendous new opportunities for profit. Trade in Japanese bottoms increased sharply in the following years, and the Bakufu became increasingly anxious about the implications of the trend. Finally, in 1633 it decided that this too should be checked. One of the most telling blows was an order prohibiting the construction of seagoing vessels. Another law forbade Japanese ships to leave any harbor for a foreign port, and finally it was declared that any Japanese going abroad would not be allowed to return to Japan. Thus, by 1636, the only legal foreign trade was that carried on by the Dutch, the Portuguese, and the Chinese. It is to be noted that these particular moves toward isolationism were dictated not merely by the fear of Christianity but by a fear of the political implications of a foreign trade centered in the outside clans and carried on, to a large extent, by the *rōnin*, over whom the government could exercise no direct control.[10]

The final steps toward isolationism followed the Shimabara rebellion of 1638. The rebellion seemed to justify the Bakufu's worst fears: it took place in western Japan; it was led by *rōnin;* and nearly all the rebels were apostatized Christians. There is no evidence to show that the people of the Shimabara peninsula wished to overthrow the Bakufu, or that they rose up merely because of Christian convictions. Rather, it seems that they were aroused to take direct action primarily because of local injustices, especially those connected with a very harsh method of collecting taxes. But as the rebellion gathered momentum, it took on a definitely Christian character. The Shimabara area had been one of the most Christianized areas of Japan, and although by 1637 most of the people had apostatized, they now came forth under Christian banners. Some 37,000 men, women, and children seized whatever weapons they could lay their hands on, and eventually succeeded in taking over a local castle. The Bakufu ordered out approximately 50,000 samurai to quash the uprising, but the people of Shimabara put up such a spirited defense that four months elapsed before the castle could be retaken. Nearly every one of the half-starved defenders were then massacred. The Shimabara rebellion made a deep impression upon Bakufu officials. For some time they had been considering the expulsion of the Portuguese for their part in the spread of Christianity, even though the Portuguese trade was still a source of much profit. The Bakufu was now ready to take action: it banned all Portuguese from the country and permitted no Portuguese ships to enter Japanese harbors. The Portuguese officials at Macao were panic-stricken by this turn of events and after careful deliberation decided to send their most influential leaders to Japan to ask that at least some trade be permitted. They felt that the Japanese should be willing to make some concessions, for many of the Portuguese merchants were still deeply in debt to certain Japanese financeers at Nagasaki. But when the envoys arrived at Nagasaki, they were seized, and sixty-one of them were executed. The few survivors were sent back to Macao with the cryptic message that even if "King Felipe himself, or even the very God of the Christians, or the Great Buddha contravened this prohibition, they shall pay for it with their heads."[11] Thereafter, Japanese contacts with the outside world were limited to the few Dutch and Chinese merchants who were allowed to come to Nagasaki. Even these merchants could not bring in any foreign books that "intended to propagate Christianity."[12] The censorship, instituted in 1630, was enforced so strictly that books carrying even indirect references to Christianity were banned. In effect this amounted to a prohibition against the importation of all Western books. As Sir George Sansom writes: "In the history of relations between Europe and Asia this was the most decided rejection ever given by an Asiatic people to an approach of the Western world."[13]

The Kokutai Movement

With the new social unity of the last half of the sixteenth century and the first half of the seventeenth, and with the fear of contacts with the Western world that led to the adoption of an extremely tight isolation policy, it would appear that Japanese society was subjected to the forces that would tend to produce a more intense and a more wide-spread sentiment of national consciousness. But no notable movement of this type is to be found in the years in which those forces were most active. To be sure, the military heroes of the sixteenth century gave the Imperial Court far more consideration than had been shown by the warring lords in the closing years of the Ashikaga era. But Nobunaga, Hideyoshi, and Ieyasu probably did no more than the earlier lords would have done if they had gained the same political and military power. It is also pointed out that Hideyoshi's campaign into Korea is the first evidence of Japanese national expansion; but a reading of the record shows that Hideyoshi himself did not consider this a national venture but rather a campaign of his own armies. He planned, if he succeeded in conquering China, to set up his capital in Peking. In other words, he seems to have been influenced more by the Chinese univer-salist view of the world than by nationalist drives. Again, when the Japanese officials became disturbed about the danger of Christianity (which had foreign origins, foreign teachers, and foreign leadership), the expressions of fear were primarily those of Bakufu officials. Those officials were not disturbed so much by dangers to Japan as by internal dangers to the political position and stability of the Bakufu. How then do we explain the apparent absence of a higher level of national con-sciousness at a time when forces tending to generate national feelings were apparently so strong?

A closer examination of the history of Japan during the century that followed the arrival of the Portuguese (called the Christian century) suggests, in the first place, that both Western and Japanese histories have tended to overstate the political unity of the Tokugawa era. Since the Bakufu was in the most powerful position and was very jealous of that position, the records of that period are for the most part those kept by the Bakufu or by authors who supported the Bakufu. Also, the modern accounts of that period, being focused chiefly upon the Bakufu, give comparatively little attention to the powerful outside clans that were more like independent states than parts of a united nation. Although Japan had far more political unity than it had in the Ashikaga era, the power of the outside clans was such that they, as well as the Bakufu, worried more about the possibility of an adverse turn of events inside the country than about a foreign enemy which might be a threat to the whole nation.

In the second place, it is clear that, as much as the Japanese officials feared Christianity, the danger did not appear to them in the form of a threat against Japan from foreign enemies. As already pointed out, the focal point of the danger was the possibility that political groups within Japan would be encouraged and supported by outsiders in some effort to overthrow the Bakufu. It is true that many Japanese stood in awe of certain European technological achievements, particularly those in the fields of gunnery and shipbuilding. And some were also disturbed about the rapid expansion of the Portuguese and Spanish empires. The position gained in the Philippines by the Spanish in the sixteenth century, and the conquest of Formosa by the Dutch in 1624, certainly aroused concern; but there is no evidence to show that Hideyoshi, or any of the early Tokugawa Shoguns, felt that the Europeans, without help from elements within Japan, would be able to gain a foothold in the Japanese islands. The fact that in 1591 Hideyoshi sent an emissary to the Philippines demanding the submission of the Spanish colony to Japan suggests that he had no fear of Spanish power. As late as 1637, Tokugawa Iemitsu, the third Tokugawa Shogun, was giving serious consideration to plans for the invasion of the Philippines. His officials estimated that a force of 10,000 samurai would be able to conquer the islands.[14] But the Shimabara rebellion brought an end to these plans, not because there was reason to fear Spanish military power but because the Bakufu had become more anxious about its position at home and less confident in the effectiveness of its samurai forces. In other words, Western nations were not yet viewed as a strong threat to Japan but merely, in combination with political elements inside Japan, as a threat to the position of the Bakufu. This being the case, it becomes understandable that there were no startling new manifestations of national consciousness in the Christian century (1543–1638).

By the middle of the seventeenth century, however, there were intellectual developments which, although they first emerged in the period of new unity, now began to add great strength to the growth of national feelings. But before examining in detail the nature of this intellectual movement, let us give some thought to the more general subject of the communication of ideas. The greater economic growth and political centralization of the Christian century was associated with a freer flow of information and ideas, but the rise of greater cultural unity was not a conspicuous development until after the Shimabara rebellion. Of course, there were improvements in roads, post stations, and so forth, and even movable-type printing was introduced about the year 1590; but until the closing years of the Christian century there was little evidence of any widespread interest in learning or of an appreciable increase in the flow of ideas. Until the battle of Osaka in 1615, warfare seems to have absorbed far too much of the time and energy of the Japanese to permit any widespread interest in intellectual matters. Also, the introduction of movable-type printing was not particularly significant, in this period, for the use of this new technique was not widespread, possibly because it had been too closely associated with Christian missionary work. Therefore, with the rise of Christian persecution after 1612, this type of printing—which would have accelerated the spread of news, propaganda, and literary works—fell into disuse. Still another factor preventing the rise of greater cultural unity within the nation was the policy of the Bakufu to keep the clans over which it did not have absolute control isolated from one another— politically, economically, and culturally. Checking stations along the highways (*sekisho*), spies, and other methods were used to see that the various clans did not become too friendly with each other.

In the closing years of the Christian century, however, several developments operated to bring about a greater exchange of ideas and feelings. One of these was the rise of an intricate, extensive, and regular hostage system (called *sankin kōtai*). The system actually had earlier beginnings. Ieyasu, even before he became Shogun in 1603, had required that Maeda Toshinaga, lord of one of the leading outside clans, come to Edo. But not until after about 1635 did the system reach its final point of development, in which the lord and a very large part of his family and retainers had to stay in Edo, and the lord himself had to stay there one year out of every two. The requirement not only gave the Bakufu better control over the various clans, but it created new demands for an exchange of goods and services and brought about a far wider and deeper interchange of ideas and feelings.

Another development of the first half of the seventeenth century—which did not become extremely important in the formation of greater cultural unity until the middle of the century—was the policy of the Bakufu to encourage both the nobility and the military to become interested in scholarly pursuits. This policy too was associated with the Bakufu's determination to preserve the status quo. The officials were familiar enough with history and with the nature of Japanese society to know that any severe political upheaval probably would be tied in somehow with the Imperial Court. And one of the many efforts made to keep the nobles from meddling in political affairs was the order, issued by Ieyasu in 1613, making it a matter of prime importance that the nobles at the Imperial Court devote themselves to scholarly pursuits.[15] The same device was adopted for keeping military men occupied when they were not needed for fighting, and of course this was a matter of even greater concern to the Bakufu. The introduction and widespread use of handguns had led to the building of huge stone castles, but before there was any extensive use of cannon—which would have destroyed the military value of these castles—peace was established. Consequently, the Bakufu was faced with the problem of keeping a large body of soldiers stationed at the castles, even though there was no fighting to be done. Since the castles, and the forces kept there, had become large, there had grown up around the castles lively commercial centers which not only provided the soldiers with their needs but tempted them with all sorts of luxurious pastimes and diversions. Numerous methods were used to keep the soldiers from indulging in expensive tastes and from becoming involved in political activities. One important policy was to encourage the samurai to devote their time to scholarly pursuits, as the nobles had been encouraged to do. In the Military Code of 1615 the first article stated that "the way of letters and arms, of archery and horsemanship must be cultivated with all the heart and mind. First letters and then arms was the rule ... of old. Neither must be neglected...."[16] Only gradually did the policy of encouraging learning yield results that were significant in the growth of national consciousness. But after the middle of the seventeenth century—particularly after the *rōnin* plot of 1651 led the Bakufu to make even more determined efforts to keep the samurai from meddling in political affairs—there was an upsurge of intellectual activity which was truly significant in the development of nationalist thought. Not only was there a more lively exchange of ideas throughout a larger segment of the population, and throughout a larger part of the country, but there emerged certain intellectual movements that were a direct expression of, and stimulus for, national consciousness. Of particular importance was the new emphasis upon *kokutai*.

Although discussions of *kokutai* were not very prominent in Japanese intellectual life until the last half of the seventeenth century, modern Japanese students detect beginnings of the movement in the writings and teachings of the earliest seventeenth-century Confucian scholars. Fujiwara Seikwa (1561–1619), the first scholar to prove to Tokugawa leaders that the Teishu school of Confucianism (sometimes referred to as "neo-Confucianism") could be a very effective agent for creating greater social stability, was absorbed in the philosophical and ethical principles imported from China. And yet he, as well as his successors, made adaptations that gave to his teachings a definitely Japanese flavor. Not only did he place more emphasis upon loyalty than upon filial piety, but in pointing out, for example, that the Confucian ideal of benevolence (*nin*) was also a feature of Japanese Shinto, he was attempting to show that there was no fundamental conflict between Shinto and Confucianism. And since he did not reject the tradition of the divine descent of the Imperial line and had much to say regarding the special relationship between the Japanese people and the Emperor, he supported the two elements of *kokutai* which remained central to all subsequent discussions of the subject. With justification, then, Seikwa is considered the founding father of the *kokutai* movement in the Tokugawa era.[17]

Seikwa had convinced Ieyasu that Confucianism had political value; but it was his student, Hayashi Razan (1583–1657), who did the most to gain official support for the Teishu school. Hayashi made even more strenuous efforts than Seikwa to associate his teachings with native Shinto beliefs. He wrote a famous book on Shinto, called "A Study of Japanese Shinto Shrines," for the express purpose of "protecting the everlasting and unchangeable dignity of *kokutai*." His basic thesis was that *kokutai* had been defiled by centuries of Buddhist influence and that this harm could best be removed by a complete elimination of Buddhist doctrines and practices from Shintoism. Although Hayashi's interest in *kokutai* was secondary to his interest in Confucianism, he laid important foundations for the later *kokutai* movement.[18] Most of the samurai scholars of the country were steeped in the Teishu school of Confucianism—to excel in that field offered the best promise of advancement in those days—and most of them were undoubtedly influenced by Seikwa's and Hayashi's views on *kokutai*. Furthermore, the Confucian emphasis upon loyalty, although originally thought of as a means of strengthening the Bakufu, served eventually to strengthen the *kokutai* concept, since the idea of loyalty to the Emperor gradually prevailed over the idea of loyalty to the Shogun. Consequently, the contributions of official Confucianism to the *kokutai* movement cannot be overlooked. Even more significant contributions, however, were made by those who turned away from the official brand of Confucianism, especially those who gave more thought to the ideas, principles, and institutions that were really Japanese.

Reactions against Official Confucianism

A number of scholars broke away from the Teishu school of Confucianism in the last half of the seventeenth century. Probably the most important of these was Yamazaki Anzai (1618–1682), who devoted the major part of his adult life to the teaching of Confucian philosophy, but who finally became absorbed in a study of the Sun Cult of Shintoism. He was not willing to break completely with the Confucian teachings, although he did establish a new school of Shinto, called Suiga Shinto, which was an eclectic system that included many Confucian principles. "Man, born with an innate desire after holiness," he wrote, "naturally tended to walk along that Way except when hindered by disturbing influence. The Way has always been known in Japan, where it needed neither foreign nor Japanese books (neither Sutras nor the Kojiki) to illustrate or enforce it; it was suited for high and low alike, and all that walk by its precepts would attain to perfection."[19] Modern Japanese nationalist historians delight in telling this anecdote: Once Yamazaki asked a student what he would do if tens of thousands of men under Confucious as their general should attack Japan. The student felt that he was trapped, but Yamazaki had no doubts and declared that a Japanese should fight back with all his might.[20] In a real sense, Yamazaki Anzai strengthened the principle of loyalty, for he stressed the validity of the principle in terms of native religious beliefs. Because of this service, the Bakufu apparently had no objections to his teachings; but in returning to the Sun Cult, Yamazaki was a forerunner of the Shinto revival, of the next century, which tended to direct loyalties toward the

Imperial Household and away from the Bakufu. In later years, men who favored direct action against the Bakufu, as usurpers of Imperial power, gained inspiration from the works of this seventeenth-century exponent of Shinto-Confucian amalgamation.

Other contemporary scholars reacted, in one way or another, against the wholesale acceptance of Teishu teachings and insisted upon attention to native Shinto beliefs, especially beliefs associated with the unique traditions of the Imperial institution. One of the more notable of these scholars was Kumazawa Banzan (1619–1691), who adopted the teachings of the Oyōmei school of Confucianism, which had long been in conflict with the Teishu school in China. But he seems to have been more of a Shintoist than a Confucianist. In one of his books he pointed out that China was called the land of the star gods, that India was the land of the moon gods, and that Japan was the land of the sun god. Then he added that obviously the moon and the stars were in a less important position than was the sun, and that consequently Japan was on a higher level than either India or China. Elsewhere he explained that Japan's superiority lay in the unique relationship that existed between the Emperor and the people.[21] But Kumazawa does not stand so high, in the estimation of modern nationalists, as some of the other seventeenth-century writers, for he once advanced the theory that the Sun Goddess of Japan was identical with a certain Chinese mythological figure. It cannot be denied, however, that he did his bit to draw intellectuals of the period away from what he considered undue devotion to Chinese philosophy and toward a deeper appreciation of national ideals and institutions.

Still another seventeenth-century Confucianist who turned away from the official Teishu teachings was Yamaga Sokō (1622–1685). Instead of turning directly to native Shinto beliefs, or to the Oyōmei school, he, along with two other leading thinkers,[22] advocated a study of the old Confucian texts; he is therefore considered to be one of the founders of the classical school (*Kogakuha*) of Confucianism. But he also proclaimed the superior qualities of the Japanese people. After commenting upon the well-known theme of the descent of the Emperors in an unbroken line from the Sun Goddess, he wrote:

For seventeen generations after the Divine Age there were none but Sovereigns of great righteousness. With the assistance of wise ministers they established the Way of Heaven and Earth, decided the administration of Court and country and arranged all the affairs of the people, their clothing, food, marriages, and funeral ceremonies and the rest in a most adequate way, in order to set up a standard by which they might live in peace and quietness for countless generations. And here again it was by reason of the virtue of the Sovereign that the way of all, high and low, was made thus clear to them.[23]

But it was his comments on the subject of the superiority of the Japanese warrior that have placed him in an extremely prominent position in the ranks of Japanese nationalists and that have caused him to be considered one of the key personalities in the development of the warrior code of ethics (*Bushidō*).[24] In one book, he outlined the many great military victories of Japan against foreign foes and concluded with the comment that "in strategy and tactics and drill and the equipment of both cavalry and infantry this Empire was the most preëminent of all. How very evident it is then that our valour is greater than that of all other countries."[25]

As important as Kumazawa and Yamaga were, it is clear that the emphasis of Yamazaki was more directly related to the main stream of nationalist thought that prevailed in the next two centuries. It was his attempt to establish a stronger ethical and philosophical support of Shintoism that was most directly related to the subsequent scholastic efforts to learn more about Japan's past, before the introduction of foreign learning, and to revive Shinto beliefs as a vital religious force. Furthermore, it was his teachings, and those of one of his most prominent students,[26] concerning loyalty to the Imperial Household, that gave so powerful an impetus to the subsequent "Revere the Emperor" (*Sonnō*) movement.

Studies of Ancient Japan

The most notable of the seventeenth-century efforts to study things Japanese was centered in the Mito district, where, under the leadership of Tokugawa Mitsukuni (1628–1700) and with the assistance of a number of scholars trained under Yamazaki, one of Japan's most famous histories, the *Dai Nihon Shi*, was compiled. Mitsukuni is said to have spent more than half of his income on the collection and exploitation of historical materials. In a sense, this great project was also a part of the reaction against the inordinate interest shown, particularly in Bakufu circles, in Chinese philosophy and literature. The aim was to obtain a better understanding and appreciation of the literature, religion, and traditions of Japan. Much of the history was focused on the fortunes of the Imperial Court and upon the great exploits of such heroes as Kusu-noki Masashige (1294–1336), who gave his life in loyal service to Emperor Go-Daigo. Modern Japanese have gained considerable satisfaction from the *Dai Nihon Shi* rejection of the theory, advanced in the official Bakufu history, that the Sun Goddess of Japan was identical with Wu T'ai-pe, a mythological figure of China. In fact, throughout the history there is a reflection of the Kitabatake concern with legitimacy of the Imperial line.[27] In addition to the historical work, some scholars of Mito were also encouraged to edit the *Manyōshū,* Japan's eighth-century anthology, and also to write commentaries on the more renowned literary pieces written in the classical period of Japanese literature. In all, the scholarly activities at Mito deepened the interest in Japanese culture and therefore paved the way for the more intense study of antiquarian subjects and for the more outspoken antiforeign sentiments of eighteenth- and nineteenth-century nationalists. Emperor Meiji, who reigned from 1868 to 1912, was not far off when he proclaimed, in a rescript addressed to the departed soul of Mitsukuni: "You proved to be the originator of the movement for reverence and loyalty to the throne, thus making of yourself a wise forerunner of the Imperial Restoration of 1868."[28]

In spite of the relative internal and external calmness that prevailed in the eighteenth century, there were men who continued to build on the foundations that had been laid in the previous century, to probe deeper into Japanese history, and to propagate the principles and ideals of Japanese Shinto. Kamo Mabuchi (1697–1769), for example, was somewhat influenced by the Confucian scholars who were reacting against the formalism of the Teishu school and were returning to a study of the old classics;[29] but he was more deeply stirred by the scholars of the Mito tradition who were intent upon gaining a clearer understanding of Japanese history and culture. Of the many books that he wrote, the one that made the deepest impression upon later Japanese classical scholars (*kokugakusha*) was the *Kokui Kō*. Its central thesis was that the period of Japanese history which preceded the importation of foreign learning was one of "purity" and idealism, a time when the morals of the people were uncontaminated. He wrote: "In ancient time, when men's dispositions were straightforward, a complicated system of morals was unnecessary. It would naturally happen that bad acts might occasionally be committed, but the straightforwardness of men's dispositions would prevent the evil from being concealed and growing in extent. So that in those days it was unnecessary to have a doctrine of right and wrong."[30] In developing his theme he not only attempted to show how righteous and well governed the Japanese were in those early days but also made comparisons with the Chinese, suggesting that they were evil and had degenerate ways: "But the Chinese, being bad at heart, in spite of the teaching which they got, were only good on the outside, and their bad acts became of such magnitude that society was thrown into disorder."[31] As was usual with nationalists then and later, he also made much of the superiority of the Imperial tradition:

While the Chinese for ages past have had a succession of different dynasties to rule over them, Japan has been faithful to one uninterrupted line of Sovereigns. Every Chinese dynasty was founded upon rebellion and patricide. Sometimes a powerful ruler was able to transmit his authority to his son and grandson, but they in their turn were inevitably deposed and murdered, and the country was in perpetual state of civil war. A philosophy which produced such effects must be founded on a false system.[32]

In Mabuchi, therefore, we have a far stronger expression of national sentiment. He not merely delved into Japan's glorious past and placed Japan in a culturally superior position; he also made charges against the Chinese and attributed the misfortunes in Japanese history to the evil influences of Chinese learning—attitudes that more closely resembled the nationalist sentiments of modern times.

A few years before his death, Mabuchi met a promising young classical scholar, Motoori Norinaga (1730–1801), who was to become one of the most outspoken and influential of all the pre-Meiji nationalists. Mabuchi advised the young man to investigate the *Kojiki*, which was considered the oldest extant history of Japan; he thought that this, if properly analyzed, would supply important and valuable information concerning the nature of Japanese life in the glorious days before Japan was subjected to contaminating influences from the continent. Motoori devoted more than thirty years to the work and completed a commentary (*Kojikiden*) of some forty-four volumes (*maki*), which served, probably more than any other single factor, to give the *Kojiki* the reputation of being the "bible of Japanese nationalism." Motoori wrote many other works (58 titles and 182 volumes) on early Japanese history—all reflecting a violent reaction against Chinese principles and institutions, particularly those associated with Confucianism.

The ideas of Mabuchi and Motoori appear to be manifestations of a more modern type of nationalism than they really are. The attitudes of these scholars arose not so much from a feeling of hatred of China as from a rejection of the intellectual leadership of the Teishu Confucianists. The relations with China were then quite calm, and there were no Chinese writings that warranted such an outburst as, for example, this one by Motoori: "As for [the Japanese] paying tribute [to China], the statement is due to the inordinate vanity of the Chinese, who fancy themselves superior to all surrounding nations, whereas they are no better than barbarians themselves and are bound to acknowledge the supremacy of Japan."[33] Those attacks were obviously not a product of anything said or done by the Chinese themselves but of actions and writings of Japanese Confucian scholars of the classical school who had become so enthusiastic about the Chinese sages that they had nothing but scorn for Japanese scholarship. One of the Chinese classical scholars, Ichikawa, had even dared to poke fun at the Japanese Emperor institution:

The name of Amaterasu (the Sun-Goddess) is probably a posthumous title conferred at a later period. If the Sun-Goddess (Amaterasu) is the real Sun in heaven, it must have been quite dark before she was born; and yet it is stated that before she was born there were trees and plants, clothing, weapons, boats, and buildings. If these things existed before her birth, it seems probable that both the Sun and Moon preceded that event. . . . To say that the Sun was born in Japan is a fiction which was probably invented by the earlier Mikados in order to support the assertion that this country is the root, and other countries only branches. The gods in heaven make no difference between different races of mankind who are formed into separate nations as by seas and mountain ranges which divide them off from each other, and the sun shines equal over all.[34]

Motoori's reply to these cogent remarks was not very rational, but it was stated boldly and with energy. Consequently, when read by later nationalists, who were stirred by more serious dangers to the Japanese nation, it was a source of inspiration.

By the middle of the eighteenth century the reaction against Teishu Confucianism had gained momentum. The trend was associated with a tendency on the part of the Bakufu itself to give less support to Confucian scholars. In 1772, for example, Hayashi Nobuyoshi found that the authorities were unwilling to rebuild his Confucian school, which had been burned. The authorities seem to have lost sight of the political function served by the Teishu scholars, and to have become distracted by all sorts of schools of thought, such as the back-to-the-classics teachings of Ogiu Sorai and the Dutch learning of Aoki Bunzo. Many Confucianists were discovering that it was far more advantageous for them to leave Edo and to seek employment in Kyoto, the seat of the Imperial

Court. But at Kyoto the orthodox Teishu school had to compete with several intellectual movements, not the least of which was the classical movement headed by Mabuchi and Motoori. After the middle of the eighteenth century an increasing number of young scholars, from all parts of the country, tended to flock to Kyoto, rather than to Edo. And in Kyoto they naturally fell under the influence of those intellectual schools that laid stress upon the religious and political uniqueness of the Emperor institution.

The "Revere the Emperor" Movement

The prominence of the "Revere the Emperor" (Sonnō) movement was accented by positive evidence of deterioration in the power of the military government. Under the efficient rule of Yoshimune (1716–1744) there were a number of excellent reforms and there was a remarkable increase in the production of rice. But after his death there was a leveling off, if not an actual decline, in rice production. A still more serious matter was the high expenditures, the fraud, and the inefficiency which characterized the Bakufu administration. Furthermore, beginning with a terrific eruption of Mount Asama in 1783, there was a succession of natural calamities that sorely taxed the resources of the government. When more capable leaders rose to power in 1786, they found that military retainers had been plunged into "a bottomless quagmire of indebtedness"[35] and that very drastic steps had to be taken to give them relief. Thus in 1787 a tokusei was issued which cancelled all retainers' (hatamoto) debts that were of more than six years' standing, and decreased the interest payments on other outstanding debts of those retainers.

These signs of economic and political weakness were causing more of the court nobility to think that there might soon be another opportunity, like the one that had arisen in the fourteenth century, for the Imperial Court to throw off the shackles of the military regime. A number of scholars began to speak in more positive terms about the importance of the Imperial institution. Takenouchi Shikibu (1716–1771), in his lectures before court nobles in Kyoto, deplored the conditions of the time and advocated greater respect and reverence for the Emperor. Several times he was hauled before the Bakufu representative in Kyoto and charged with having influenced court nobles to dedicate themselves to restoration of the Imperial rule. Finally, in 1758 he was ordered to leave the city.[36] Eight years later, another lecturer, Yamagata

Daiji (1725–1767), who was a specialist on military tactics and strategy, was convicted of organizing a plot to overthrow the Bakufu. He had just previously written a book, called the *Ryūshi Shinron*, which explained how Japan's dual government had come into existence, and declared that the military had actually usurped the Imperial power. Yamagata believed that it was both human and natural that the country should be under one ruler; he hoped, therefore, that strong leaders would emerge to rectify this situation. Strangely enough, the book itself did not lead to his arrest, and Yamagata became bolder in his lectures, even discussing the military strength of the Bakufu and pointing out means by which the Edo castle could be seized. But in 1766 the military government took action. It arrested Yamagata and almost every person that had been associated with him. The military court, in its recorded verdict, stated that Yamagata had criticized the Shogun's dealings with the Throne, and had attempted to start a civil war. Yamagata was sentenced to death.[37]

But these strong measures did not seem to weaken the *Sonnō* movement. Several famous supporters of the Imperial cause came forth a few years later with programs designed to give additional strength to popular support of the Throne. One of the more prominent of these was Takayama Masayuki (1747–1793), who traveled throughout various provinces of the country and gave public lectures in an attempt to arouse in the people an understanding and appreciation of what he considered the glories of the Imperial institution. Finally, in 1793, he committed suicide, being "afflicted at the state of the country, and offering himself up as a victim to the Imperial cause."[38] Still another of the leading propagandists was Gamō Kumpei (1768–1813). His method of strengthening the prestige of the Emperor was to publicize the sad state of the tombs of the Imperial family. He went about the country investigating the sites of the various tombs, and finally, in 1808, he wrote a book about the Imperial tombs which seems to have had an important bearing on the subsequent growth of the *Sonnō* movement.

From 1786 to 1793 the Bakufu was ruled by the strong hand of the Regent Matsudaira Sadanobu (1758–1829). Two important policies were adopted that were designed to weaken the *Sonnō* movement. In the first place, far more positive efforts were made to keep the Imperial Court in a subordinate position. In 1788 the Regent himself went down to Kyoto to look over the situation, and he returned convinced that the Bakufu had to adopt a very firm attitude toward the Imperial

Court. Therefore, when in 1789 the Court sought the approval of the Bakufu for bestowing a certain title upon the father of the Emperor, Matsudaira—after years of delay—advised that the appointment be disapproved. Furthermore, court nobles who had taken the lead in the affair were punished. This action, however, seems to have aroused members of the Court to further opposition to the Bakufu. When Matsudaira was removed from power in 1793, the Bakufu assumed a far more lenient attitude toward the Imperial Court; more gifts and missions were exchanged, and greater consideration was shown toward the Imperial envoys. The Bakufu was so anxious to conciliate the Imperial Court that relations between the two capitals, during the first quarter of the nineteenth century, were quite cordial.

The other policy adopted by Matsudaira to check the political deterioration was to renew Bakufu support of the Confucian scholars of the Teishu school. During his trip to Kyoto in 1788 he found that something had to be done to gain from the intellectuals stronger support for the Bakufu. He first sought to improve this situation by restoring the old Confucian school, the Seido. Renowned scholars from all parts of the country were invited to Edo to participate in its program. The old system of examinations was revived, and orders and regulations were issued which made official appointments more closely dependent upon the results obtained in the examinations. Finally, in 1795, the Bakufu issued an edict proclaiming that only those who subscribed to the doctrines of the Teishu school of Confucian philosophy would be eligible for positions in the Bakufu. After similar edicts were proclaimed in other districts of Japan, the Confucian scholars of the officially supported Teishu school began to regain much of the prestige that they had enjoyed a century earlier. The policies that were adopted during the regency of Matsudaira, however, seemed only temporarily to weaken the *Sonnō* movement, for a few decades later, under the stimulus of new pressure from the expanding Western powers, it again emerged in so virulent a form that it was a prominent factor in the eventual collapse of the Bakufu.

◇   ◇   ◇

The second phase in the growth of Japanese national consciousness, then, began with a rather startling development of national unity which coincided, quite closely, with Japan's first contacts with the Christian world. There was certainly far greater social cohesion than ever before; but it is doubtful whether Japan's contact with the West was any more significant, as a factor in the rise of more intense and widespread feelings of national sentiment, than her earlier contacts with the Asiatic continent. Western students of Japanese history, realizing the tremendous impact of the West upon Oriental societies in general, have given a great deal of attention to this early period of Japan's relations with the West and consequently have tended to overemphasize the Western influence upon Japan during the so-called Christian century. At least so far as the history of national thought is concerned, these contacts did not arouse any overwhelming sense of danger among the Japanese and were not more important, in the current growth of national consciousness, than the development of greater internal unity. It is significant to note that as national consciousness became stronger during the seventeenth and eighteenth centuries, national uniqueness was generally seen with reference to Chinese, and not Western, ideals and principles. The more advanced stage of national consciousness discussed in this chapter is to be understood, therefore, primarily as a product of internal forces. There were still feelings of inferiority (now in technological as well as cultural terms); but the *kokutai* discussions, the classical studies, and the *Sonnō* movement were primarily by-products of tensions within the Japanese society. The more articulate expressions of national thought were still limited to a part of the samurai intellectuals and were still a far cry from modern expressions of nationalism; but foundations were laid and an intellectual momentum was built up that, as a factor in the subsequent growth of nationalism, cannot be overlooked.

4 EMPERORISM AND ANTIFOREIGNISM

In the last two decades of the eighteenth century, France, Russia, and England each sent exploratory expeditions into the North Pacific. These moves marked the beginning of a new tenseness in Japan's relations with the Western world and the emergence of a more positive form of national consciousness. In succeeding years, these European powers, and the United States as well, continued to be active in Asia, and this activity led Japanese military officials to become increasingly disturbed about the fate of their nation. The fear of domination from the outside gradually made its imprint upon the developmental pattern of Japanese national thought. The old movements, such as those centering on greater respect for the Emperor and those related to the revival of Shintoism, became stronger than ever, and they became tinged with antiforeign, and especially anti-Western, feelings.

Russian Pressure

As early as 1771 the Japanese had heard, through the Dutch at Nagasaki, that the Russians had established a Japanese language school at

Irkutsk. The Dutch passed along their interpretation of the new Russian interest in Japan, suggesting that the Russian empire would profit greatly from trading with, or occupying, Japan.[1] In these years, Russian vessels were sighted frequently in the northern waters of Japan, and this caused more officials and samurai intellectuals to become disturbed about Russian intentions. Then, in 1792, an official expedition (the Laxman expedition) arrived at a port in Yezo. The envoys wanted to negotiate a trade treaty, but the local Japanese officials insisted that all relations with foreigners had to be handled at Nagasaki, in southern Japan. The only concession that Laxman could obtain was a permit to enter Nagasaki for further negotiations. The Russians made no further moves to obtain a trade treaty until 1803, but they had already created a stir within Japan.

Even before the arrival of the Laxman expedition, several samurai scholars had turned to writing memorials and studies which emphasized the urgency of strengthening Japan's defenses against a possible Russian incursion in the north. A notable book[2] of this sort was written in 1785 by Hayashi Shihei (1754–1793), who, in addition to pointing out the weaknesses of Japan's defenses, advocated the seizure of Yezo (now Hokkaido) as a means of heading off the Russian advance. About the same time, another writer, Honda Toshiaki (1744–1821), took an even more advanced stand, insisting that Japan should not only take the island of Yezo but seize Kamchatka and move the Japanese capital to that peninsula. Honda realized that a larger population would be necessary, if such a program was to be carried out; he therefore proposed that the government encourage large families. He was confident that the population could be increased by about twenty times within the next thirty years.[3] Hayashi and Honda, in other words, were not content with a negative policy of defense but favored taking the offense, feeling that expansion would best serve the interests of Japan. For this reason, some have placed these men high among the early nationalists who popularized the idea of a "Greater Japan."[4]

The samurai-scholar declarations in favor of stronger defenses, and expansionist policies, tended to strengthen the Sonnō movement, since the demands for a stronger defense carried the implication that the Bakufu had been remiss in the performance of its military function and that therefore a new realignment of political power under the leadership of the traditional head of the Japanese nation was required. At first the Bakufu officials apparently did not appreciate the significance of these discussions of foreign policy, for they were clearly quite willing to yield to the Russians in order to preserve peace. The Bakufu, in its attempt to freeze the status quo, had become committed to a policy of peace, as well as to a policy of seclusion. But after 1800 the military government at Edo began to wince before the implied charges of the scholars and to be increasingly disturbed by reports of Russian activities. Hence it assumed a more positive attitude toward the foreigners. When the Russians finally decided, in 1803, to make use of their permit to enter Nagasaki for negotiations, the Bakufu was no longer in quite so coöperative a frame of mind.[5] Nikolai Petrovich Rezanov, the leader of the Russian mission, was kept waiting for months and was then told that the Japanese could not alter their traditional policy.

By that time the Russians were more interested than ever in obtaining some trade agreement; Rezanov therefore turned to a consideration of other ways of accomplishing his mission. He decided that a show of force might change the minds of the Japanese, and accordingly devised a plan to drive the Japanese out of Karafuto and to seize Japanese boats engaged in foreign trade in northern waters. However, the direct action actually taken by the Russians was limited to two raids on Japanese communities. The first was made in 1806 at Kushunkotan in Sakhalien and resulted in considerable destruction of property and in the seizure of a few Ainu and one Japanese. The Russians left behind them a message to the effect that more raids could be expected, unless the Japanese changed their minds about signing a trade treaty. The Bakufu immediately dispatched troops to Hakodate and Etorufu and issued orders to attack on sight all Russians, because of their violent behavior toward the Japanese community in Sakhalien. Then, in 1807, came the second raid. This time one settlement on Etorufu was almost completely wiped out. Word of the outrage soon reached the capital, and more troops were dispatched. The local lord was removed—the Bakufu was left in direct charge of all defenses in the area—and northern ports were closed to native junk traffic.[6]

As information and rumors about the Russian activities spread, the samurai scholars became even more energetic in their denunciation of military inefficiency. In the previous decade some had had sufficient confidence in the military strength of the Bakufu to advocate a program of expansion, but none did so now. One famous scholar of Dutch learning, Sugita Gempaku (1733–1817), was convinced that the only wise course for Japan to follow, in view of such military impotence, was to yield to the Russian demand for trade in order to give the Bakufu time to reorganize its army and to strengthen its defenses. He felt that it would be about fourteen years before the Bakufu would be able to cope with the Russians.[7] One other noted writer, Hirayama Kōzō (1758–1828), made proposals that reflected an even deeper pessimism about the ability of the Japanese soldier to protect the country against invasion. He suggested the organization of a huge national army, including even pirates and bandits, to drive back the Russians. The suggestion that robbers and pirates be called in to help the proud samurai was indicative of the current attitude toward the military regime, an attitude which was a vital factor in the growth of the *Sonnō* movement.[8]

In addition to making desperate efforts to improve the defenses, the Bakufu gave serious thought to means of showing greater respect for the Imperial Court and thereby weakening the effect of charges made by the Imperialist writers. Gradually, much of the old distrust and suspicion between the Bakufu and the Imperialist Court—which had been aroused earlier when the Bakufu followed a strong, rather than a conciliatory, policy toward the Imperial Court—disappeared; but the classical scholars continued to gain ground in their efforts to arouse a deeper sense of loyalty to, and appreciation of, Japanese traditions and institutions.

The most notable Japanese classicist of the period was Hirata Atsutane (1776–1843), whose first book appeared in 1805, the year before the Russian raids in the north. Immediately after the raids, he too wrote down his ideas about how the "barbarians" could be restrained,[9] but his greatest contribution to the cause of nationalism was to strengthen Shinto as a religious, political, and intellectual force. He was not content with condemning all that was non-Japanese and non-Shinto, nor was he satisfied merely with making investigations of Japan's "glorious" past. He chose to focus his energies on the formulation of a religious system, headed by the Emperor as the direct descendant of the Sun Goddess. Into this system he incorporated some of the basic principles of Confucianism, laying special emphasis upon filial piety as the basis of all good actions, and upon devotion to the memory of one's ancestors as the mainspring of all virtue. With Hirata, the Japanese classical scholars returned to a kind of Shinto-Confucian amalgamation of the type suggested by Yamazaki Anzai (but rejected by subsequent Japanese classical scholars such as Mabuchi and

Motoori); and with this union, Shintoism (of the Imperial Cult variety) became a more dynamic force for the creation of greater national unity. In his voluminous writings, Hirata reiterated much that had been said by nationalists before him, particularly by his teacher, Motoori; but in addition to formulating a brand of Shintoism that had a far broader ethical and religious base, he placed great emphasis upon the theory that every Japanese was a descendant of the gods. This concept, which became a common ingredient in subsequent nationalist thought, was extremely important in the rise of nationalism, for beliefs in divine ancestry strengthened racialism, a powerful element in the growth of many forms of modern nationalism. Hirata also spoke of national superiority, as did his predecessors, but he broadened the scope of his comparisons to include the Western powers as well as the great cultural centers of Asia. He wrote in 1811: "Between the Japanese people and the Chinese, Hindoos, Russians, Dutch, Siamese, Cambodians, and other nations of the world, there is a difference of kind rather than of degree."[10] And again: "from the divine descent of the Japanese people proceeds their immeasurable superiority to the natives of other countries in courage and intelligence."[11] Hirata's teachings played a truly vital role in the rise of national Shinto, a central theme in Japanese nationalist sentiment; he is therefore an outstanding figure in the early growth of Japanese nationalism. In 1840 the Bakufu finally realized that Hirata's efforts were providing too much support for the Sonnō movement, and consequently ordered him into exile.

British Pressure

The Russians seemed gradually to lose interest in Japan after the raid of 1807. They sent an expedition to survey the northern waters in 1811, but in 1813 word was relayed to Japan that the raids of 1806 and 1807 had not been approved by the Tsar. In the meantime, however, the Japanese had become anxious also about the English, whose expansion into the Far East was gathering great momentum. After the British-Dutch War of 1780–1783, they pushed energetically into areas that previously had been monopolized by the Dutch, and in 1795 the Vancouver expedition was dispatched to the North Pacific—just seven years after the French La Pérouse expedition had explored roughly the same area. The Japanese were aware of these moves, but it was not until 1808 that they began to fear the English as much as the Russians. In that year an English ship, the *Phaeton*, entered the harbor of Nagasaki in its search for Dutch vessels. The captain asked for supplies and threatened to sink the junks in the harbor if the supplies were not forthcoming. The local Japanese officials realized that this was a flagrant violation of the seclusion policy; but the size and fire power of the English ship was so impressive that they had to yield to British demands—at least until more troops had arrived from neighboring provinces. Although the *Phaeton* departed before the Japanese had gathered a force strong enough to venture an attack, the incident created a tremendous stir in Nagasaki, since the impotence of Japanese defenses was made readily apparent to all. The ranking local official expressed his feelings by committing suicide.[12]

The *Phaeton* incident would not have made so deep an impression had it not been preceded by the Russian raids in the North, and had not the Dutch at Nagasaki been giving the Japanese ominous reports about the depredations of the English in other Asian lands. After the incident, it appears, the Dutch also attempted to strengthen their trade monopoly in Japan by further amplifying earlier accusations that England and Russia were working together in their expansion into the Far East. The plan, according to the Dutch, was to divide China and Japan between them.[13]

But the British had no special interest in Japan, as yet, and in the next fifteen years there were no moves that gave the Japanese any particular cause for concern. In 1824, however, another British ship appeared off shore near Kagoshima. On this occasion, the captain, instead of making threats in order to obtain supplies, actually sent men ashore to seize what was wanted. Cattle were slaughtered and food was stolen. Under the circumstances, the local officials had no alternative but to resort to the use of force in an attempt to drive away the intruders. In the fighting that ensued, men were lost by both sides; but the English, having obtained the supplies they needed, withdrew. As a direct result of the affair, the military government issued an order which constitutes the strongest statement of the seclusion policy ever made by the Bakufu. The "Don't Think Twice" decree concluded with the demand that "should any foreigners land anywhere, they must be arrested or killed, and if the ship approaches the shore it must be destroyed."[14]

These incidents, together with Dutch reports of British strength, caused the Japanese samurai intellectuals to revise their views on foreign policy. Instead of pressing merely for stronger defenses and more positive measures to head off advances in the north, the scholars began now to give some thought to checking British advances from the south. Again the importance of stronger defenses was emphasized, and again the expansionist solution was suggested; but the expansionist programs took on an entirely different character. In addition to the men who advocated moves into Hokkaido and Sakhalien, there were those who spoke out in behalf of continental expansion. The man best remembered for his early support of such a program was Satō Nobuhiro (1768–1850), who proposed that Japan first adopt thoroughgoing internal reforms, and that she then accept the "duty" of helping other peoples of the world by conquering China, where there would be plenty of land and resources to strengthen Japan for moving on into Siam and India—to meet the advances of the English.[15] From this positive expansionist program many ardent nationalists of modern times have gained great inspiration.

For fifteen years after the "Don't Think Twice" decree of 1825 there were no particularly disturbing events in Japan's relations with the West. And yet these were years in which the major powers were developing new interests in the Far East, interests which led them eventually to show an even greater determination to bring Japan within the orbit of their growing commercial worlds. This period was also one of economic and political deterioration within Japan, making the military government even less able to resist the pressure of Western expansion, once it should be brought to bear upon the traditional seclusion policy. In the early 1830's a series of poor crops, coupled with a further debasement of the coinage, caused a sharp rise in the price of rice, and further economic distress. The military government, plagued more than ever by inefficiency and reckless spending, did little to improve the situation. As a result, discontented groups, in both rural and urban areas, became extremely restless.

There were many uprisings. The most serious one broke out in Osaka in 1837. A minor scholar official by the name of Ōshio Heihachirō (1792–1837) had become concerned about the misery of the starving people, and, having failed to convince higher officials that something ought to be done to alleviate their suffering, he decided to use his own meager funds to help them. It was his hope, apparently, that the more wealthy citizens would follow his example; but here, too, he was disappointed. Finally, in 1837, he decided that there was nothing left to do but to resort to mob action. A manifesto was circulated which de-

nounced the corrupt, selfish officials. A plan was drawn up to seize
control of Osaka and to "deprive the merchants of their inhuman gains."
But word of the plan leaked out, and Ōshio had to move ahead of
schedule. Fires were started, and men were sent out to urge the people
to seize what they needed. There was an immediate and enthusiastic
response to the call; and in spite of the fact that all the troops of the
area were ordered out and that the people were not well organized,
the rioting continued for days. A large part of the city of Osaka was
reduced to ashes, and many important buildings and bridges were
destroyed. The outbreak in Osaka struck a sympathetic chord among
people in other parts of Japan, and a series of riots broke out in other
cities.[16] But even with these sharp reminders of social discontent, the
government was unwilling, or unable, to make any basic changes in its
policies or methods.

While Japan was still plagued with these serious economic and political problems, information was received about the pressure the English
were exerting against the Chinese. Even before the actual outbreak of
hostilities in China, certain Japanese writers were spreading the alarm.
One scholar of Dutch learning, Takano Nagahide (1804–1850), wrote
in 1838 that the British Navy had 25,860 vessels and 1,000,000 men,
and he recommended that in the face of such danger Japan scrap the
seclusion policy.[17] Of course, after the actual fighting started in 1840,
and after the Japanese learned how easy it had been for the British
fleet to move up the Yangtze River and to dictate terms of peace at the
very gates of Nanking, far more officials and intellectuals gave more
serious consideration to the implications of this startling development.

The officials decided immediately that changes must be made in
both the internal and the foreign policy of the country. Internal reforms
were adopted, and though several of them were quite drastic, they did
not produce the desired results. The most celebrated part of the reform
movement was the abolition of the old guild system; but the Confucian
scholars who had recommended the measure did not understand the
operation of economic forces and were surprised to find that conditions
in Edo, instead of improving, actually became more serious. Finally,
in 1851, two years before the arrival of Perry, the old guild system was
reëstablished. Other measures were equally ineffective. As for the foreign policy, the Bakufu soon came round to the view that the old
"Don't Think Twice" decree of 1825 was too severe and that it might
cause trouble unnecessarily. Therefore, in 1842, it was toned down.

One part of the revised decree reads as follows: "It is not thought fitting to drive away all foreign ships irrespective of their condition, in spite of their lack of supplies, or of their having stranded, or their suffering from stress of weather. In accordance with the ordinance of 1806, after investigating the circumstances of each case, you should, when necessary, supply them with food and fuel and advise them to return, but on no account allow foreigners to land."[18] But in spite of unsettling news from China, the Bakufu could go no further than this in the revision of the established seclusion policy.

The samurai intellectuals had always reacted quite quickly to any foreign developments that seemed to endanger the seclusion policy, and after the disastrous defeat of the Chinese by the British, their reactions were even stronger. Many more were critical of the weakness of Japan's defenses and had more definite ideas about measures that should be adopted for improvement, but few were sufficiently confident of the power of the military class to support expansionist plans. Not only were more writers talking about the changes that should be made in the defense system, but more of them were speaking out in behalf of the importation of certain military techniques developed in the West. The scholars of Dutch learning therefore suddenly found that they were obtaining a more attentive hearing and that even the Bakufu was willing to consider some of the innovations proposed by Takashima Shuhan (1798–1866) and other noted students of Western military science. In 1841, Takashima was permitted to demonstrate gunnery exercises and Western-type infantry drill before Bakufu officials; and in spite of the objections of conservative Confucianist advisers, the government ordered Takashima to teach these foreign military methods and techniques to officials. But eventually the Confucianists got the upper hand, and Takashima was imprisoned—only to be released in 1853 when the arrival of Perry served to remind the officials once more that the traditional military methods were inadequate.[19]

More significant than the advocacy of drastic reforms in military defense was the tendency now for some scholars to propose that Western methods of production, administration, and education, as well as warfare, be introduced. The leading exponent of this more advanced view was Sakuma Shōzan (1811–1864), who, as a scholar of Dutch learning, was well posted on developments abroad and was somewhat of an expert on Western military science. For a time after the Opium

War he seems to have differed little from others who were issuing warnings of danger. For example, in 1840 he wrote:

Once they [the British] have finished off the business in China, they will send warships to Nagasaki, Satsuma, and Yedo. They are a people who are swayed only by a desire for profit, and they are not likely to go to the expense of sending a large expedition against us all the way from England. But they already have a considerable force just across the water from us, and all they have to do is to take advantage of the recent incident in Uraga [referring to the visit of the *Morrison* in 1837] and, making a warlike demonstration, to insist upon opening trade. If this were refused they would pester us until they gained their point at little expense and would stop at nothing. There is therefore no advantage in attempting to deal with them in accordance with the laws of courtesy.[20]

But by 1842, Sakuma had taken a more advanced position. In that year he outlined an eight-point program which he felt ought to be adopted if Japan was to avoid the disasters that had fallen to the lot of China. As yet, Sakuma was not recommending a complete reversal of the seclusion policy; but he did feel that military reforms, in order to be really effective, would have to be supplemented by basic economic, political, and even educational changes. His most remarkable proposal was that schools be established throughout the country and that a modern education system be provided, "so that even the most stupid men and women may understand loyalty, piety, and chastity."[21] In 1842 such a proposal was startling, but before three more decades had passed, a universal education system had been adopted by the Japanese government. Sakuma, stirred by an awareness of national danger, was moving toward the view that his country must achieve a much higher degree of political, economic, and ideological unity in order to be able to defend itself against the Western powers.

After 1843, Sakuma was not in a position to exercise much influence in Bakufu councils, but his study led him to the conviction that Japan was much more retarded than he had at first supposed. He therefore undertook a study of the Dutch language in order that he might be better able to learn the things that would be of the greatest help to his countrymen. By 1849 he had developed so great a respect for Western learning that he attempted to gain the approval of his feudal lord for the printing of a Dutch-Japanese dictionary. Such a dictionary, he pointed out, would make it possible for "many Japanese to learn the long and short points, the abilities and failings, of the Western nations and to understand thoroughly conditions in those countries."[22] By 1853, when his country was faced with Perry's demands, Sakuma had laid important foundations for Japan's unique response to Western expansion—a response that was closely bound up with, if not dependent on, the relatively high level of national consciousness which had been aroused, in large measure, by fears of oppression at the hands of Western peoples.

American Pressure

The Russian and British expansion had alarmed the Japanese first, but it was the Americans who were at the forefront of the Western moves which eventually forced Japan to revise, and later to drop, her seclusion policy. After the Revolutionary War, American vessels began to enter the lucrative Canton trade and were soon calling at ports in the American Northwest to buy up furs for sale in Canton. Since Japan lay so close to the route from the Northwest to Canton, the American merchants gradually became interested in establishing some kind of commercial relationship with the Japanese. As early as 1791, two American vessels tried to sell a cargo of sealskins and sea otter peltries at a port in the province of Kii, but were unsuccessful. Then, between 1797 and 1809, eight different American vessels were chartered by the Dutch to make the annual voyage between Japan and Java. It was not until 1837, however, that American traders became sufficiently interested to take concrete measures to obtain a revision of the Japanese trade policy. The first effort took the form of an unofficial expedition, called the *Morrison* expedition, which was dispatched by an American firm in Canton. But the *Morrison* was driven away, by gunfire, from two different Japanese ports.[28]

The decade 1840 to 1850 was a period of great expansion in American trade on the Pacific. With American settlement of the West Coast, the perfection of the new, fast clipper ship, and the increased production of cheap cotton textiles, there were far more opportunities for gaining profit in Far Eastern trade. After 1850, American merchants gained further advantages from the British navigation laws and from English involvement in the Crimean War. The sharp increase in transpacific trade, together with the active whaling industry, forced a larger number of American vessels to seek shelter and supplies in Japanese ports. In many cases, however, the American sailors were not well treated. Usually they were arrested, and, according to some reports, sometimes they were made to trample on crosses to prove that they were not missionaries. Gradually the American public began to insist that the government take steps to reach a satisfactory agreement with the Japanese government regarding the treatment of shipwrecked American sailors. Also, as companies began to consider the use of steam vessels in the Oriental trade, there were demands for the establishment of a coaling station in the Japanese islands.

Between 1832 and 1844 a few moves were made with a view to initiating negotiations with the Japanese; but nothing very positive was done until Commodore Biddle, with two warships, visited Edo in 1846 to request trading privileges. Biddle was not fired upon, for the Japanese were now following a more liberal policy; but the request was denied.[24] Within the next few years, public demands for an understanding with Japan became even more insistent, since the rapid development of the West Coast had sharpened the interest in Far Eastern trade. Therefore, in 1851, the United States government started another move to open negotiations. This time, however, the request was to be backed up by a larger naval force; and in 1853 Commodore Perry entered Edo Bay with four ships, including two that were propelled by steam. He was instructed not to resort to the use of force, unless in self-defense; but the Japanese did not know about these instructions. To them, the approach of four huge, well-armed ships cleared for action was a frightening spectacle. The first local officials to come near the ships were rebuffed. Commodore Perry announced that he would deal only with a high-ranking official and that a suitable man should be sent to receive a letter from the President of the United States to the Emperor of Japan. To the local officials this was indeed a terrifying attitude, and the situation began to look even worse when the American naval force, while awaiting a reply, began to move up the bay toward Edo. In just a few days the Bakufu took the necessary action to see that officials of daimyo rank were sent to meet Perry. The letter from the President was delivered, and then Perry, after announcing that he would return the next year for a reply, sailed away.[25]

The arrival of the Perry mission sent tremors of anxiety through the ruling class. According to one contemporary account, the samurai "were greatly alarmed at the prospect that war might break out at a moment's notice, and began to run hither and thither in search of arms. . . . The people carried their valuables and furniture in all directions to conceal them in the house of some friend living farther off."[26] The sudden withdrawal of the ships tended to quiet their fears somewhat, but everyone soon fell to fretting about what was to be done when the "black ships" returned. The panic in official circles was reflected in the unprecedented decision to ask for the opinions and advice of all high-ranking samurai—a strong indication that the officials lacked confidence in their ability to cope with the problem.

As the requested memorials were presented, it was seen that the views and recommendations fell into two categories. Either they insisted on a strict enforcement of the old, time-proven policy of seclusion, or they veered toward the views of those scholars of Dutch learning who proposed that the ban on trade be temporarily lifted in order to give the Bakufu time to strengthen its defenses. Those who stuck to the traditional policy tended to be anti-Bakufu men. They may have been honestly convinced that the old policy was best for the country, but it is probable that they were primarily interested in embarrassing the Bakufu. Even those outside clans who had been in closest touch with the outside world, and who were gaining profit from illegal trade with foreign merchants, were quite emphatic that the American requests be denied. The Prince of Mito, a junior member of the Tokugawa family, took the lead among the conservatives, probably because his position with the Tokugawa family gave him new freedom to speak out. His argument ran as follows:

If we are frightened by [these foreigners'] aggressive lying stratagems and give them what they ask for (as they have a cunning and treacherous object) they will go on from bad to worse. At first they will give us philosophical instruments, machinery, and other curiosities, will take ignorant people in, and trade being their chief object, will manage bit by bit to impoverish the country; after which they will treat us just as they like; perhaps behave with the greatest rudeness and insult us, and end by swallowing up Japan. If we don't drive them away now we shall never have another opportunity.[27]

But many men close to the Bakufu (this organization, it will be remembered, was originally responsible for the adoption of the policy, in the seventeenth century) were sufficiently realistic to see that, since their military organization was no match for that of the foreigners, it would be folly to insist on a policy that could not be enforced. For the most part, they feared the effects of free contact, and they were opposed to it, but under the circumstances they felt that a compromise, for the time being, was unavoidable. The arguments of these men, according to a contemporary source, ran like this:

If we once get into a dispute, we shall have an enemy to fight who will not be easily disposed of. He does not care how long a time he will have to spend over it, but he will come with several myriads of men of war and surround our shores completely: he will capture our junks and blockade our ports and deprive us of all hope of protecting our coasts. However large a number of his ships we might destroy, he is so accustomed to that sort of thing, that he would not care in the least. Even supposing that our troops were animated by patriotic zeal in the commencement of the war, after they had been fighting for several years their patriotic zeal would naturally become relaxed; the soldiers would become fatigued, and we should have ourselves to thank for this. Soldiers who have distinguished themselves are rewarded by grants of land, or else you attack and seize the enemy's territory and that becomes your own property; so every man is encouraged to fight his best. But in a war with foreign countries a man may undergo hardships for years, may fight as if his life were worth nothing, and as all the land in this country has already owners, there will be none to be given away as rewards; so we should have to give rewards in words or money. In time the country would be put to an immense expense, and the people be plunged into misery. Rather than allow this, as we are not the equals of foreigners in the mechanical arts, *let us have intercourse with foreign countries, learn their drill and tactics, and when we have made the nations as united as one family, we shall be able to go abroad and give lands in foreign countries to those who have distinguished themselves in battle; the soldiers will vie with one another in displaying their intrepidity, and it will not be too late then to declare war.*[28]

The argument of this group was further strengthened by information that the Russians had just sent another expedition to Japan to request a trade treaty. Since 1847 the famous Nicholas Muraviev (1809–1881) had been serving as governor-general of Siberia, and after the establishment of a Russian settlement at the mouth of the Amur River in 1850 he was determined to open up trade with Japan. The naval expedition under Putiatin, then, to the Japanese officials and intellectuals was an indication that the old Russian danger was reappearing. Yoshida Shōin (1831–1860), one of Japan's most famous nationals of these years and a student of Sakuma Shōzan, wrote a book at this time in which he presented, in a most emphatic manner, an expansionist program of the Honda Toshiaki variety, which called for the colonization of Hokkaido, the taking of the Kuriles and Kamchatka, and the seizure of Korea, Manchuria, Formosa, and the Ryukyus.[29] All this was to check the Russian advance. But fortunately for the Japanese, the Crimean War served to keep both the English and the Russians occupied elsewhere.

When Perry returned in the spring of 1854—this time with seven ships—the Japanese submitted a reply to the President's letter which indicated that all the requests were to be granted. Perry however demanded a formal treaty. A few weeks later, the treaty was signed, and within a few months other European powers rushed to Japan to gain the same rights.

"Revere the Emperor! Expel the Barbarians!"

The reaction to the Bakufu's tradition-shattering steps was immediate and violent. All the political groups that had been gaining power, as the Bakufu was losing it, were merciless in their condemnations of this weak-kneed attitude toward the "barbarians." As one writer put it: "All the patriotic and honest men in the Empire were enraged at the doings of [the] Shogun's officials and did not cease to censure them; all sorts of arguments without end were started about this question; and thus was laid the foundation of trouble at home and difficulties abroad, and of manifold troubles and misfortunes."[30] To make matters worse, a large number of foreign vessels began to enter Japanese waters and ports. None of these ships, however, were sent to make attacks on the Japanese islands. Some were on surveying expeditions, many were engaged in whaling or in trade, and some were British and Russian warships which, since the Crimean War was in progress, were searching out enemy vessels. But an increasing number of Japanese were led to believe that an attack on Japan might be made at any moment.

The Bakufu and all the clans speeded up their defense programs— it was no longer necessary to have the military weaknesses pointed out by the scholars. And attention was no longer restricted to traditional weapons. Between 1853 and 1856, reverberatory furnaces, used for smelting a better grade of steel for guns, were built almost simultaneously by the Bakufu and the leading clans. Large sums of money were spent in importing new-type weapons and ships, and the construction of foundries and shipyards was also started. By 1857, Satsuma and Chōshū, as well as the Bakufu, had shipyards in which ships were being built and equipped with heavy guns. The manufacture of gunpowder and the modernization of coastal batteries[31] were also under way. The concentration upon military reform undoubtedly arose from a clear realization of military inferiority; but the reform programs probably were designed not merely to afford better protection for Japan against foreign domination but to improve the position of each clan in the impending realignment of political power within Japan. Concern for the safety of the country may very well have been secondary to a concern for clan position.

But again, there were a few intellectuals—Sakuma Shozan and his group, for instance—who felt that there was far more to be learned from the Westerners than the techniques of making guns and building ships, and who began to feel that the clans should be worrying more about the Western powers than about each other. In fact, Sakuma was thrown into prison for his part in encouraging his student Yoshida Shōin to stow away on one of Perry's ships in order to learn about the West firsthand. While in jail, Sakuma wrote his most famous book, the *Seiken Roku* (Reflections on My Errors). This is a clear and positive statement of the policy he favored, and it was eventually adopted by the leaders of the Restoration of 1868. In one paragraph of his account, Sakuma wrote: "It is inevitable that 'if we know neither the enemy nor ourselves, we shall be defeated in every battle.' Even if we knew both the enemy and ourselves, at the present time we should still not speak of fighting. Only after we have mastered everything that the enemy can do well, without losing the abilities we already have, can we begin to speak of that."[32] The ruling class was aroused by the 1853–1854 crisis to take more energetic action in modernizing the military system; but only after the incidence of other crises did the more drastic steps, suggested by Sakuma and his students, become acceptable.

Before the frantic efforts to institute military reform had yielded the power necessary to check the Western nations, these foreign powers began to make new demands for additional commercial privileges. The Americans in particular were dissatisfied with the "wood and water treaty" settlement of 1854. And they took the lead in obtaining revisions that would provide better commercial opportunities. No naval force was sent to back up these demands; but the American representative, Townsend Harris, was most adroit in pointing out the dangers of not yielding. There are several facets to his success, but an extremely important factor in the final decision was the receipt of news from the continent regarding the new treaty settlement that had been extracted from China by the Western powers. Harris took full advantage of the news and warned the Japanese that it would not be long before British and French warships would be sailing into Japanese waters to demand the opening up of Japanese ports. He apparently convinced the officials that signing a commercial treaty with the United States would be the best method of preventing excessive demands from other Western powers.[33]

In signing this treaty—and then similar ones with the other Western powers—the Bakufu stirred up violent opposition from conservative groups. Samurai in all parts of Japan were irritated not only by the inability of the Bakufu to keep foreigners out of the country but were particularly agitated by its failure to obtain the sanction of the Imperial Court before agreeing to so important a treaty settlement. Actually, the Bakufu had tried desperately to gain this approval, but the conservative opinion at the Court, expressed in the following terms, was too strong:

... the Shogun's officials, by a wilful error, have given permission for friendly relations and commerce; worse than this they have promised to open ports, acts which must excite the profoundest indignation. If they go on in this slothful and supine way, they will gradually fall into the snares of these people, the fundamental laws of the state will be altogether lost, we shall be insulted, get our Government and laws from jurisdiction of barbarian States. *Then the national glory which has lasted for thousands of years, will be utterly tarnished; then it will be too late to gnaw our entrails with rage, and disgraced as a country we shall become a dependent state.*[34]

When news of the Treaty of Tientsin arrived, Bakufu officials, headed by the famous Ii Naosuke, decided that the treaty must be signed, even though Imperial sanction had not been obtained.

The decision threw the court nobles into a great rage, and lords and samurai who for one reason or another opposed the Bakufu poured into Kyoto to offer their support to the Imperial Court. Even high-ranking members of the Tokugawa clan, notably Tokugawa Nariaki of Mito, wrote memorials to the Shogun, expressing their opposition to this reversal of traditional policies. Finally, when the Bakufu learned that the Emperor was beginning to take independent action, it decided to adopt repressive measures. Several nobles were arrested and placed in prison, and later many of these were excuted. Tokugawa Nariaki himself was placed in retirement, and a few daimyo who had shared in the conspiracy were forced to turn their fiefs over to their sons and enter private life. Finally, the Bakufu was successful in getting the Emperor to agree not to forbid the conclusion of the treaty; but in order to gain this concession it had to promise to expel the foreigners within a short time—reportedly in five years.

The new treaties came into force in July, 1859. Foreign diplomats took up their residence in Edo, and the port of Yokohama soon became a busy center of foreign trade. The country after more than two hundred years of seclusion and exclusion was definitely opened, and leaders and intellectuals throughout the country were aware that great changes were about to take place. Some of the Japanese merchants immediately discovered that profit could be obtained by trading with foreign merchants. They were satisfied with the new turn of events, but many suffered financial loss and others were irritated by the behavior and actions of the foreign businessmen and their governmental representatives.

One of the most annoying developments arose out of the discovery by foreigners that the value of gold was much lower in Japan than elsewhere in the world. A clause in the treaties had provided that the exchange of foreign coins for Japanese coins should be on a weight for weight basis, and this gave all foreigners an easy way of making money. They used what silver coins they could obtain to buy up Japanese gold coins at the rate current in Japan and then took these coins to some foreign market where they could be disposed of at a profit of about 100 per cent. It did not take long for this practice to spread, and soon the Japanese discovered that vast amounts of gold coins were leaving the country. This loss of gold coins was related to the current economic dislocation, and thus it was an additional source of discontent.[35] The situation was blamed on the profit-hungry foreigners and upon the weak-kneed policy of the Bakufu.

Only one month after the treaties were placed in effect, foreigners began to suffer from acts of violence by irate Japanese. In that month two foreign missions were pelted with stones, and Russian sailors, wandering through the streets of Edo, were stoned by a mob. A few days later, a Russian lieutenant and two seamen were murdered in Yokohama. Members of the foreign community, greatly alarmed by these incidents, undertook to arm themselves against attack, and to urge various forms of reprisal. Some even proposed the destruction of the entire city of Yokohama. But the Japanese officials expressed their regrets, and a satisfactory settlement was made.[36]

In the ensuing months several other acts of violence were directed at foreign residents and also at Bakufu officials who had taken the lead in signing agreements with foreign representatives. The most notable and significant attack on officials was the assassination of Ii Naosuke on March 24, 1860. He was the most powerful and influential figure in the Bakufu at the critical time when the treaty settlement of 1858 was being made. He had tried desperately to gain approval of the treaties from the Imperial Court, and when he failed in those efforts, he assumed responsibility for signing the treaties without the approval of the Court. He apparently had the greatest respect for the prestige of the Imperial Court, but when he heard of British and French advances in China he decided that action had to be taken immediately. The

Sonnō movement, as well as the antiforeign feelings, had serious implications for the Bakufu; and Ii was determined that they should be kept under control. It was he who was primarily responsible for the "Great Persecution of Ansei" of 1859 and 1860. Several of Japan's best-known nationalists, including Yoshida Shōin, were eliminated by capital punishment in these turbulent days.

As antiforeign feelings mounted, Ii's part in the treaties, and particularly his failure to gain Imperial sanction for them, made him a logical target for the tirades of those who felt that the national honor was being sacrificed. While Ii was on his way to the Shogun's palace in 1860, his party was attacked by a group of eighteen samurai, and he was killed. The assassins' statement shows how intense their antiforeign sentiment had become.

> While fully aware of the necessity for some change in policy since the coming of the Americans to Uraga, it is entirely against the interest of the country and a shame to the sacred dignity of the land to open commercial relations, to admit foreigners into the castle, to conclude a treaty, to abolish the established custom of trampling on the picture of Christ, to permit foreigners to build places of worship of their evil religion, Christianity, and to allow the three Ministers to reside in the land. Under the excuse of keeping the peace, too much compromise has been made at the sacrifice of national honor. Too much fear has been shown in regard to the foreigners' threatenings. Not only has the national custom been set aside, and national dignity injured, but the policy followed by the Shogunate has no Imperial sanction. For all these acts the Tairo Baron Ii Kamon-no-Kami is responsible. . . . We hope to see our national glory manifested in the expulsion of foreigners from the land. Thus will the whole nation be established on a basis as firm and unmovable as Mount Fuji itself.[37]

After the death of Ii, the Bakufu ceased to resist the onward rush of the Sonnō movement. Compromises replaced repressive measures and, as a result, the momentum of the Sonnō movement was increased and opposition to the Bakufu's revision of the traditional policy of isolation was heightened.[38] The slogan "Revere the Emperor! Expel the barbarians!" became more popular than ever; but after the death of Ii another slogan was adopted that seemed to be an even better expression of non-Bakufu samurai sentiment. It was: "Revere the Emperor! Down with the Bakufu!"

"Revere the Emperor! Down with the Bakufu!"

The less forceful officials who replaced Ii Naosuke tried to appease the Imperialists but soon found themselves on a toboggan, which they seemed powerless to guide or to stop, headed for disaster. First they proposed that the Bakufu allot funds for repairing and redecorating the Imperial Palace, and that a marriage alliance between the Bakufu and the Court be arranged. These and other steps, however, increased the power of the Court at the expense of the Bakufu. One of the more notable developments in this trend was the insistence, in 1862, by the great Chōshū clan of western Japan, that the Bakufu recognize the supremacy of the Emperor:

Since the conclusion of the treaties the people of this empire have done nothing but protest against them. They declare that you have disregarded the Mikado's wish that the country should be closed to foreigners, and that you treat him as if he were not of the slightest importance. I beg most earnestly that the Shogun will recognize the supremacy of the Mikado, so that the harmony existing between the two may be made evident, and the comments of the people be put a stop to.[39]

But for a time, the Satsuma clan was possibly more prominent than Chōshū as a champion of the Imperialist and antiforeign cause. In the year 1862, when Shimazu Izumi, the father of the Prince of Satsuma, arrived at Himeji on his way up to Edo, he was met by several hundred men who complained to him about the Bakufu and asked if he would not be their leader in "doing some great deed [to] restore the old state of things."[40] Shimazu went to Kyoto, not to Edo, and reported the matter to the Court; thereupon the Emperor ordered him to remain at Kyoto for a while "to quiet the excitement among the rōnins . . . and [to] give tranquility to the Empire."[41] Shimazu complied with the order, and, according to the Genji Yume Monogatari, "The officials of the Bakufu were terrified by the decision and energy of the Shimazu family and by the fierceness of the rōnins."[42]

About this time, the Prince of Chōshū left Edo for Kyoto, apparently desiring to take advantage of the growing political influence of the Imperial Court. He, too, received an order from the Emperor—to assist Shimazu in "quieting the excitement of the rōnin." With the military support of these two great clans, the Imperial Court began to act far more independently. It immediately freed the nobles who had been placed in confinement for pressing the Imperial cause when Ii Naosuke was in control at Edo, and it bestowed posthumous titles upon the old Prince of Mito and other noted supporters of the Imperial Court. Furthermore, there was a general house cleaning, which resulted in the removal from office of all those who had coöperated too closely with the Bakufu in the two or three critical years immediately after the treaty settlement of 1858.

The new political independence of the Imperial Court is most closely seen, however, in the Imperial message sent to the Bakufu in the summer of 1862, which condemned the Edo officials and ordered the Shogun to proceed to Kyoto to exert himself in the task of expelling the foreigners and "restoring tranquility to the Empire."[48] Furthermore, the Emperor demanded that certain men be given positions of responsibility. There had been such a shift in political power and policies that now, less than three years after the death of Ii Naosuke, the Shogun meekly complied with all the demands of the Imperial Court. In quick succession other steps were taken which continued to undermine the old autocratic power of the Tokugawa regime. The most drastic of these moves was a revision of the old hostage system whereby daimyo and their families had been required to spend approximately half of their time in Edo. By the revision, the daimyo were required to spend so small a portion of the time in Edo that the system no longer served as an adequate check on their political activities. Thereafter, the daimyo, particularly in the more distant regions, were much less inclined to obey the commands of the Bakufu; therefore, the Tokugawa Shoguns quickly lost much of the prestige and power which they had enjoyed during the previous two centuries.

The rising tide of antiforeignism, together with the increased political power of those who supported antiforeign policies, tended to make for a larger number of more violent actions against foreign residents. Incident after incident broke out, and the representatives of Western powers found it necessary to spend much time in insisting that the Bakufu respect the treaties that had been signed, and in making demands for indemnities and apologies for crimes committed against their nationals. Pressure on the Bakufu by these foreign powers thus was increasing at a time when the Bakufu itself had lost much of its independence of political action. It was being constantly called upon to enforce treaties that were unpopular with the Imperial Court and with the strong clans that had come to the support of the Imperial House. The military regime, therefore, was placed in the anomalous position of agreeing with foreign representatives to abide by the treaties and at the same time agreeing with the Imperial Court to expel all foreigners. To have made a definite stand for free contact with foreign countries would probably have brought immediate civil war, whereas a clear-cut stand for isolation probably would have resulted in war with foreign powers. In the summer of 1863 the balance was in favor of expelling the foreigners; and when steps were taken to enforce exclusion, the reaction of the Western powers was unequivocal.

On June 5, 1863, the Emperor issued an order that all foreigners be expelled, which was to become effective twenty days later. Immediately, the representatives of foreign powers made objections in the most positive of terms. Even Pruyn, the United States minister, who had tended to be quite friendly toward the Japanese, and whose country was then engaged in a bloody civil war, now became convinced that a show of force must be made in order "to preserve to the world what has thus been gained."[44] He recommended to the Secretary of State that the treaty powers combine to keep a fleet in Japanese waters for some time. In a note to the Bakufu, Pruyn wrote: "A solemn treaty has been made by the government of Japan with the United States granting to its citizens the liberty to reside and trade at these ports. The right thus acquired will not be surrendered, and cannot be withdrawn. Even to propose such a measure is an insult to my country, and equivalent to a declaration of war."[45] The French minister declared that the expulsion order was without precedent in the history of civilized nations and might bring some chastisement upon those who were responsible for it. But the British note was even stronger, for the Japanese proposal was considered "unparalleled in the history of all nations, civilized or uncivilized," and constituted "a declaration of war by Japan against the whole of the treaty powers, and the consequences of which if not at once arrested, it will have speedily to expiate by the severest and most merited chastisement."[46]

The Bakufu was apparently convinced that the Western representatives meant what they said, for it tried desperately to convince the Imperial Court that the order should be rescinded. But in this it was unsuccessful. At the Imperial Court, and in many of the clans, news of the order was received with great enthusiasm, and in Chōshū—the clan then most influential at Kyoto—preparations were made for enforcing the order. When the day fixed for the expulsion arrived, the first foreign ship to pass through to Chōshū waters was fired upon. By chance that ship was a small American steamer, the *Pembroke*, which was on its way to Shanghai from Yokohama. Although it was subjected to armed attack by two Chōshū boats, no lives were lost and very little damage was sustained. But a ship flying the American flag had been attacked by Japanese vessels. As soon as word of this reached Yokohama, the captain of the U.S.S. *Wyoming*, which happened to be in the harbor, and Mr. Pruyn, the American representative in Japan, both agreed that the *Wyoming* should proceed immediately to Chōshū to seize the offending vessels. But before it arrived there, a French steamboat and a Dutch steam sloop were also fired upon by Chōshū shore batteries. Thus, on the very day that the *Wyoming* arrived in Chōshū waters and was fired upon, a French admiral was leaving Yokohama to seek reprisals for the unprovoked attack on a French vessel. The *Wyoming* sank two Chōshū vessels a few days later. The French warships, when they arrived, landed a small force, destroyed one of the batteries, and burned a small village. On the day that the French ships were making their strike, a British vessel left from Yokohama for Chōshū, although no British ships had as yet been attacked. The British apparently expected that this ship would also be fired upon, and that all four of the major treaty powers would then be in the same position. But Chōshū sent word to the commander of the British vessel that the vessel would not be attacked unless it fired first.[47]

Although the British had no reason to attack Chōshū, they did have what they considered to be a justifiable cause for attacking Satsuma, the other powerful anti-Bakufu clan of western Japan. In September of the preceding year, in the midst of antiforeign incidents, a British citizen had been murdered by retainers of the father of the Lord of Satsuma. At that time, the British representative, Colonel Neal, had taken a moderate position; but several months later (on March 14, 1863) he received a dispatch from his home government instructing him to demand reparations from both the Bakufu and the Satsuma clan. After Admiral Kuper arrived in Yokohama on March 22 with a squadron of five ships, he sent an ultimatum to the Bakufu demanding a sum of 100,000 pounds and allowing twenty days for a categorical reply. If the answer was not satisfactory, the message stated, Admiral Kuper would within twenty-four hours "proceed to enter upon such measures as may be necessary to secure the reparation demanded."[48] An extension of time for the reply was granted by the British, since the Shogun was absent from Edo; but just before the end of the period and as the Japanese populace was beginning to leave Yokohama in anticipation of hostilities, the British representative suddenly decided to "offer their naval forces" (now a sizable force) to the Bakufu and to grant a further extension of time for an answer to the ultimatum. The British had apparently decided that it was to their advantage to support the Bakufu, the only political force in Japan that seemed to favor continued foreign intercourse. But the Bakufu rejected the offer of assistance, realizing that this would be certain to bring civil war, and offered to pay the full indemnity.[49] At just this time, the Chōshū incidents occurred, and the British negotiations with Satsuma were delayed. But on August 6, 1863, a British squadron of seven ships left Yokohama for Satsuma, and when they reached there the admiral issued an ultimatum.

Since the Satsuma reply was not considered satisfactory, the admiral ordered the seizure of three small steamers in the harbor. Immediately the shore batteries opened up, and the British returned the fire. Fighting continued on into the next day, and when the admiral ordered his ship to return to Yokohama, the entire town of Kagoshima was apparently in ruins.[50]

There has been a tendency among Western writers to conclude that the attack on Kagoshima forced the Satsuma clan to favor the policy of opening relations with foreign countries. Nevertheless, there is evidence which suggests that the clan was inclined to favor a revision of the traditional isolation policy even before the bombardment of Kagoshima. In the preceding year, the leaders apparently had become displeased about developments in Kyoto. Although the displeasure was, in part at least, based on the opinion that Japan should give up the old isolation policy, the change may have been due primarily to the fact that Chōshū, a rival clan, dominated affairs at the Imperial Court.

In the summer of 1864, while Chōshū was attempting to regain its position at the Imperial Court, a joint Western naval force was being organized to punish the clan for its unprovoked attacks on foreign ships the previous summer. The expedition, originally proposed by Sir Rutherford Alcock, was made up of seventeen warships. It arrived in the Shimonoseki Strait on September 5 and fired upon the shore batteries of Chōshū without making any attempt at negotiation. On the first day of the attack, five batteries were put out of commission, and the next morning a landing party took possession of eight of the principal batteries. After spiking the cannon and destroying the ammunition, the men returned to their ships. Hostilities continued for two more days, but in the meantime the Chōshū leaders sought to negotiate. They sent word that they felt no enmity toward foreigners and that their sole desire was to have peace. An agreement was drawn up in which Chōshū agreed to the following: (1) to open up the strait to the ships of all countries: (2) to build no new forts; and (3) to pay the expenses of the expedition and a ransom for the city of Shimonoseki, which "might justly have been burnt."[51]

Again, the decision to agree to foreign demands was not brought about by a display of military power by the Western nations, for a political group (the so-called Vulgar View party) which was not in favor of an uncompromising antiforeign policy had seized power before the expedition arrived. In fact, the expedition, together with a military defeat at the hands of the Bakufu soon afterward, so weakened the influence of the moderates that they were unable to prevent the old antiforeign faction from regaining control. The joint naval expedition thus strengthened rather than weakened the conservative position.[52]

The leader of the conservative group, Takasugi Shinsaku, correctly surmised that as soon as the Bakufu heard of this development within Chōshū, another military expedition would be dispatched against it. In the face of possible opposition from the Bakufu, the Imperial Court, Satsuma, and the foreign powers, the future for the conservative leaders looked very dark. But support suddenly came from an unexpected quarter. Satsuma was now regretting that it had given help to the Bakufu in the preceding year. The reason for this change of heart is not quite clear, but possibly the author of the *Kinsei Shiriaku* is correct in stating that the Satsuma leaders were concerned about national unity.[53] At any rate, Saigo Takamori, the great Satsuma military hero, opened up negotiations with Chōshū which resulted in an understanding between the two western clans. When the Bakufu sent out orders for the mobilizations of troops in preparation for another expedition against Chōshū, Satsuma showed no willingness to coöperate.

The Bakufu's expedition against Chōshū did not materialize until 1866; in the meantime, the Western powers, under the leadership of the energetic and impatient British representative, Sir Harry Parkes, made another display of force, which resulted in new concessions for Western countries and new embarrassments for the Bakufu. When faced with requests for the postponement of indemnity payments, Sir Harry convinced his diplomatic colleagues in Yokohama that a naval expedition, "with no hostile intent," should be sent to Osaka. "And it also occurred to me," he wrote, "that whatever result might attend our negotiations, the appearance of a fleet off Osaco [sic] could not fail to exercise a beneficial effect both on the Daimyos who surround the Court of Kioto, and have had little opportunity of satisfying themselves of our power, and also on the people generally of that vicinity, whom it is well to begin to accustom to the sight of foreign visitors."[54] On November 4, 1865, a group of twelve Western warships—six British, three French, and one Dutch—appeared in Osaka Bay, and finally, on the ninth, a conference with a representative of the Bakufu was held on board ship. As an alternative to prompt payment of the indemnities, the powers proposed that two-thirds of the indemnity stipulated in the Convention of October 22, 1864 (held after the naval expedition against Chōshū) be cancelled in return for the immediate opening of Hyogo and Osaka, the ratification of the treaties by the Emperor, and the "regularization of the tariff" on a 5 per cent basis. The proposals posed serious problems for the Bakufu, and it requested time for consultation. When it began to appear that the reactionaries were carrying the day at Court, the foreign representatives sent identical notes to the Shogun, insisting that unless a categorical reply to the proposals was received in ten days, the representatives of the powers would consider the failure to reply a refusal and would feel free "to act as we may judge convenient." The threat was effective. On the tenth day, word came that the Emperor had ratified the treaties and had agreed to a lowering of the tariff. The ports of Hyogo and Osaka, however, would not be opened, but the full amount of the indemnity would be paid at the stipulated time.[55]

The joint display of naval force before Osaka in 1865 is an important event in the history of Japanese nationalism. It has been long considered a source of national humiliation, for it was then that Japan was forced to agree to the "regularization of tariff"—one of the most disturbing aspects of the "unequal treaties," the revision of which absorbed much of the attention of Japanese diplomats during the remainder of the nineteenth century. And yet it was after this display of Western naval power that antiforeign demonstrations came to an end. With the Emperor's approval of the foreign treaties, contact with the outside world became an accepted fact. From this time on, the old slogan "Revere the Emperor! Expel the barbarians!" was almost completely replaced by "Revere the Emperor! Down with the Bakufu!" Samurai in all parts of Japan were not merely condemning an unpopular policy of the Bakufu; they were condemning the Bakufu itself.

One of the traditional explanations for the Bakufu's relatively weak resistance against the attempts made to undermine its position is that the Shogun in power was willing to make sacrifices for the good of the nation. National safety may very well have been one consideration, but later historians, under the influence of nationalist feelings, have obviously placed far too much emphasis upon this factor. The impending collapse of the military regime in Edo was already apparent to all. Thus, it was probably realized by Bakufu officials that even the most spirited defense would not suffice. There was still another development, however, which had some bearing on the Bakufu's decision to turn over its authority and holdings voluntarily to the Imperial Court: the growing interest in Western systems of representative government. Various political groups—outside the strongest western clans—were influenced sufficiently by this movement to give serious thought to advocating some form of representative government which would preserve a modicum of power for those who were not at the forefront of the "Restoration" movement. The Shogun in the final announcement of his resignation[56] clearly indicated his hope, if not anticipation, that a representative system would be established. Voluntary resignation, in other words, seemed to offer to the Tokugawa family a means of retaining some of its old influence.

The young samurai leaders of the western clans were quite willing to lend their ears to talk of representation, so long as it helped to increase their political and military control. But as soon as the Shogun came to Kyoto and placed himself more or less at the mercy of the Emperor, a coup d'état was arranged which showed that the western clans would not be satisfied with a compromise arrangement. Only then was the Shogun forced to resort to military action. From the first, he seems to have realized that there was no hope for a military victory, and it may be true—at least in part—that he could not put his heart into a struggle against forces that were operating, nominally at least, under the orders of the symbolic head of the Japanese nation. At any rate, the fighting between the "Imperial" forces and the Bakufu troops was extremely desultory. By 1868 the Emperor, with the help of the western clans, was "restored" to power.[57] The Sonnō movement had reached its logical conclusion, for by the Meiji Restoration of 1868 the Emperor was made, nominally at least, the actual ruler of Japan, not merely its symbolic head.

✧   ✧   ✧

The restoration of the Emperor and the stronger antiforeign feelings were obviously manifestations of a more positive form of national consciousness. Earlier evidence of national thought and feelings had been limited, for the most part, to the writings of the samurai-scholar class, but now manifestations of concern for the nation also took the form of direct action by a large number of men who were willing to endanger their lives to do their bit in "restoring" the Emperor to power and in driving the hated foreigners from Japan. Thus the Japanese nationalist historians, in tracing the rise of nationalism in Japan, are inclined to point to these years of foreign pressure as the period in which modern nationalism was born.

But as important as these developments were, it is also clear that subsequent nationalist feelings caused writers to overlook the fact that internal political rivalries were probably as important as the national urge and the foreign pressure in bringing about the Restoration and in attracting attention to antiforeign slogans. Recent studies are beginning to show that the western clans, toward the end of the Tokugawa era, were beginning to gain such economic strength that they would logically have taken up the Imperialist cause, the traditional means of effecting a realignment of political power, even if there had been no danger from Western nations. In such a situation the western clans and the other supporters of the Imperial Court would have seized upon any means that would have embarrassed the Bakufu. The "Revere the Emperor! Expel the barbarians!" slogan, therefore, was a double-edged attack on the established military regime, not merely an expression of deeper nationalist sentiments arising from a sense of foreign danger. The Western powers were clearly interested, at this time, in a continuation of trade relations, not in seizing territory, and some recent Japanese scholars point out that a few officials understood this. In other words, it is quite probable that Western and Japanese scholars alike have overemphasized the sense of danger aroused by the Western naval expeditions and have overstated the depth and intensity of nationalist sentiments.

Some foreign observers in Japan at that time noted that the antiforeign feelings were limited entirely to the samurai class and that the common people seemed to favor free intercourse with other nations. Sir Rutherford Alcock guessed that the samurai were antiforeign because they realized that their social position would be endangered by the rise of a merchant class, but it is more likely that they realized the political advantage to be derived from embarrassing the Bakufu. The Sonnō (Revere the Emperor) element in the Sonnō Jōi slogan must not be forgotten.

Still another significant factor in the antiforeign sentiment was the peculiar nature of the traditional Confucian system of foreign relations.[58] By this system the familial pattern of social relations was extended to dealings between states. One state assumed the position of father; the others took the position of filial sons or younger or older brothers. There were no relations of equality. States were either inside or outside the system. Inside they were tribute-bearing or tribute-receiving states; outside they were "barbarians" who were to be kept at arm's length. With centuries of indoctrination in the Confucian system of international relations, the ruling class of Japan saw no alternative to treating these foreigners, who would not abide by the old rules, as "barbarians." "Expelling the barbarians," therefore, was probably not so much an emotional outburst of hatred against foreigners as it was a long-established attitude toward all outsiders who did not conform to the Confucian theory of what was proper in the relations between states.

There is little doubt that the display of naval power by Westerners, in the years 1863 to 1865, made a deep impression upon the clans. It was a decisive factor in the shift of political power from the hands of the Bakufu to the western clans—clans which did not carry the onus of having participated in the scrapping of the traditional seclusion policy, and which had never relied on military support from foreign nations. Also, the foreign naval expeditions had definitely established the fact of Japan's military inferiority, and as a result, there were more samurai who were coming round to the advanced view of Sakuma and others that only by determined and unified action could disaster be avoided. It is not merely a coincidence, then, that after 1865 the slogan "Revere the Emperor! Expel the barbarians!" was gradually replaced by another one which, in terms of the current situation, was far more meaningful: "Rich country—Strong army!" The leaders were gradually shifting from antiforeignism to reform and, as we shall see in the next chapter, the drive for reform, as far as the history of nationalism is concerned, was an even more significant development. It cannot be denied that the *Sonnō* movement and antiforeignism, even though they were associated with internal political rivalries, were manifestations of a more advanced form of national consciousness. They indicated that additional foundation stones for modern nationalism had been laid, but did not prove that modern nationalism had arrived.

5 NATIONAL REFORMS

The Restoration of 1868 was followed by a sharp decline in the anti-foreign movement. Thereafter the young leaders of the country were busy laying the foundations for a modernization program along Western lines. The shift of emphasis, however, was not as revolutionary as it would at first appear. As has already been pointed out, the antiforeign feelings were not so widespread or so deep as has been supposed. And the modernization program was by no means completley free of anti-foreignism. A great mass of evidence could be marshaled to show that the leaders of the reform program urged closer contact with, and knowledge of, the West, not because of any upsurge of friendship for the West, but because of a firm conviction that Japan's military inferiority could be eradicated only by making use of all Western techniques. This is made clear not only by evidence found in the writings of the new leaders but by an analysis of the nature of the emphasis, and the process, of the reform program. Each modernization effort was clearly related to the central problem of increasing the wealth and power of the nation, and almost every major move was initiated and pushed by the national state in order to serve clearly defined national aims. The period from 1868 to 1887 was therefore not a temporary lull in the growth of nationalism but a distinct period of development in which preoccupation with expansionism was subordinated to the task of creating greater national strength and solidarity. The greater social cohesion and the improved channels for the flow of ideas and feelings added the last, and probably the most important, block to the foundation of modern Japanese nationalism.

"Rich Country—Strong Army!"

The center of political gravity shifted from the Tokugawa Bakufu to the western clans at the time of the Meiji Restoration of 1868; and intellectual movements that had become popular in the western clans— movements which were for the most part anti-Confucian, Royalist, and progressive—were greatly strengthened. Consequently, the Restoration meant a sharp break with traditional Confucian attitudes and the emergence of a progressive outlook that characterized the thinking of many of the leading scholars of western Japan. Sakuma Shōzan and other men of the so-called Dutch learning school had gained a better hearing after the arrival of Perry in 1853; but the man who was most closely associated with the progressive policy adopted by the Meiji government was Yoshida Shōin (1831–1860), a man who to this day is revered as one of the most farseeing and influential of Japan's nationalist heroes.

Yoshida was born the son of a samurai scholar in western Japan. At an early age he inherited the headship of the local Yamaga School of Military Science. In 1849 he went down to Kyushu, apparently to study military science under scholars in that area, and in 1851 he traveled with his lord to Edo. On these trips he became absorbed in other intellectual movements—mostly those that would not have been acceptable to the Teishu Confucianists at Edo—and became more conscious of Japan as a country distinct from the countries across the sea. The travels aroused in him such an urge to visit other parts of Japan that he was glad to give up his fief and his samurai title in order to gain the freedom necessary to see Aizu, Echigo, Sado, and particularly Mito, where the Royalist movement was strong and where, he said, he came to know "the reason for the existence" of his country. But in addition to being inspired by the Royalist movement of the day, Yoshida became a student of Sakuma Shōzan, who, by this time, was insisting that Japan, to gain sufficient strength to avoid foreign domination, must adopt a broad program of reform. Yoshida was so deeply impressed with Sakuma's arguments that when he heard of the Perry expedition he decided immediately to stow away on one of Perry's ships in order to gain firsthand knowledge of Occidental strength. But his plans were so carelessly laid and executed that he was caught and arrested for his trouble.

After his release from jail, Yoshida returned to his native clan, and he became the respected and revered teacher of some of the most influential leaders of the Meiji era. As Coleman says, Yoshida's school "was the altar on which was kindled the fires of the Restoration." Prince Itō, the author of Japan's constitution, and Prince Yamagata, the founder of Japan's modern army, were merely two of the more famous leaders trained in Yoshida's school between 1855 and 1858. Throughout his lectures there was a constant and spirited plea for greater loyalty to the Imperial institution and also a stress upon the necessity of instituting reforms as the best means of assuring the defense and growth of the Japanese nation. Yoshida was not satisfied with discussions alone. He wanted and expected action. He therefore soon turned his thoughts to revolution—to backing any group that seemed to show promise as a means of overthrowing the Bakufu and restoring the Emperor to power. Again his actions were more spirited than wise; consequently he was soon arrested and sent to prison for a crime he did not commit. While in prison he blurted out a confession of his part in a plot to overthrow the Bakufu. He was immediately tried and condemned to death. The judgment of the court, in listing the crimes Yoshida had committed, stated that he had attempted to go to the United States, that he had opposed hereditary accession to office, and that he favored the selection of men of ability by a popular election.

In spite of the Bakufu's strenuous efforts to keep the Royalists and reformists down, their numbers and influence increased in direct proportion to the decline in the power of the Bakufu. By 1868 a large number of men were ready to take positions of responsibility in the new government who thought, as Sakuma and Yoshida did, that Japan must achieve greater unity and must adopt extensive military, economic, and educational reforms in order to assure national independence and national growth. Under their leadership, "Rich country—Strong army" became the popular slogan of the post-Restoration period.

Military and Political Unity

While the Bakufu troops were still offering some resistance, a government was set up under the Emperor which was eventually to develop into one of the world's most highly centralized political structures. But even the most astute observer could not have guessed, in looking at the 1868 government, that it would have so brilliant a future. Its income was meager, it had no army directly under its command, and its political control was very weak. The men responsible for the new order were obviously operating under the assumption that a representative system, along American lines, might cause neutral clans to submit voluntarily to the authority of the government. The interest in Western institutions had caused Bakufu officials to favor a peaceful settlement in 1867, and it was apparently assumed for a time that it would continue to be of service in establishing greater political unity.

Soon after the Restoration of 1868, the new leaders issued a statement that was designed to win over those feudal lords who had not yet given enthusiastic support to the Imperial cause. The statement, which has come to be known in English as the "Imperial Oath," had five articles, but the one that the leaders of the government were obviously most interested in emphasizing was the first one. It declared that an assembly was to be established and all matters were to be decided by public opinion. The other articles outlined the government's policy of reform: political unity was to be achieved; every person was to be permitted to follow the occupation of his choosing; old "absurd" customs and practices were to be discarded; and finally, knowledge was to be sought in all parts of the world "in order to establish the foundations of the Empire."[1]

Whether they were actuated by the promise of representation or by some other factor—such as the overwhelming military power of the western clan combination, or the agreement that the old local lords would be appointed as the governors of the same area, or concern for national security—most of the clans did follow the Satsuma-Chōshū-Tosa-Hizen lead in handing over all the lands and revenues to the Emperor. In setting the example, the four western clans issued an explanatory statement, in 1869, which focused attention on national security. The closing sentences were: "[We] also beg that all laws, decrees, and military regulations, extending even to military dress and accoutrements, may be issued by the Central government, so that all matters of state may be decided by one and the same authority. *In this way both name and reality will be secured, and this country will be placed upon a footing of equality with foreign powers.*[2] The fact that such an argument should be presented is indicative of the rise of a higher order of national consciousness; but it is doubtful whether, in the minds of those samurai leaders who followed the Satsuma-Chōshū-Tosa-Hizen example, interest in building national strength ever overshadowed the desire to protect and, if possible, to strengthen their position within the new political structure.

As soon as the Bakufu forces had been defeated and the support of most of the feudal clans had been gained for the new Imperial government (at least nominally), the leaders instituted a series of administrative changes which were designed to strengthen the control of the government and which were obviously based upon the assumption that any further development of the Western representative institutions would operate to complicate rather than facilitate the work of achieving greater political and military unity. With each reorganization, the pattern of government became less Western and less conducive to the effective operation of the representative legislative bodies.[3]

But real unity was not to be achieved by legal measures alone. Actually, there is some evidence to support the conclusion that between 1869 and the summer of 1871 ground was lost. Even Satsuma and Chōshū, the clans that had taken the lead in setting up the new government, were continuing to exercise almost complete independence within the territories of their own clans. Their subservience to the will of the Imperial Court was more nominal than real. However, certain influential young samurai from these two clans continued to work toward the goal of political centralization. They realized that it was necessary, if the new structure was to be anything more than another Bakufu, for the Imperial government to have its own military force, so that it would have the power to enforce its control over the various local groups. But establishing such a central army, subject only to orders from the central government, was a task of no mean proportions. By the summer of 1871, however, an agreement was reached between Chōshū and Satsuma whereby each clan was to supply troops to the central government for an "Imperial Guard" of 10,000 men. It is significant that soon after this a step was taken which was probably the most important single move made to bring about the destruction of the old, decentralized, feudal regime. By Imperial decree the clans (*han*) were all abolished and prefectures (*ken*) were set up; thus the boards were cleared for the organization of local government that would be truly responsible to the central authority. Again the steps were taken in the name of national unity. An Imperial rescript explained the order in these terms: "We are of the opinion that in a time of radical reform like the present, if We desire by its means to give protection and tranquility to the people at home, *and abroad to maintain equality with foreign nations, words must be made to mean in reality what they claim to signify, and the government of the country must centre in a single authority.*"[4]

After the summer of 1871 the central government was in a position to move forward on all fronts in its reform program. In the economic and educational as well as the military and political fields important changes were soon made. At this more advanced stage of modernization, reforms in one field had to be closely integrated with those in others, but throughout the complex interplay of reform measures there was a consistent concentration upon the goal of achieving greater strength for the national state and there was a continuous development in the direction of greater political centralization. In 1873 there were two measures that were particularly significant politically: the adoption of a modern tax system and the organization of a modern conscript army. Each brought changes that were of almost revolutionary proportions, and that were particularly important in the rise of that high degree of social interdependence which is a *sine qua non* for the emergence of a truly modern variety of nationalism.

Until the new state had established a regular and adequate income, it was impossible for it to organize the intricate bureaucratic system which was required in a highly centralized state. It was necessary, then, to see that a larger percentage of the tax payments reached the central government and that the taxes did not decrease in periods when, for one reason or another, there was a decline in production.[5] To take care of the first problem it was necessary to arrange that all taxes be paid directly to the central government, or its agents, and not to some relatively independent local administrator. The "prefectural" system that was set up in 1871 was an important preparatory step. It eliminated the clans, to whom the taxes had been traditionally paid, and established local districts that were administered by officials responsible to the central government. In December of the same year another order abolished the "samurai land" (*bukeji*) and the "townsman land" (*chōji*), which had always been tax exempt. Then, in 1873, a tax law was passed which required that taxes be paid in money rather than in produce. Obviously this simplified the handling of the tax income. The new system also made the owner of the land, rather than the cultivator, responsible for the payment of the taxes. In order to implement this policy, the principle of private ownership of land had to be established; consequently after January, 1872, the government began issuing deeds (chiken) to those who seemed to have the strongest claims to title. The placing of the tax burden on the owner of the land obviously made the collection of taxes on a large scale far simpler and more dependable. Then, in order to handle the problem of regularizing the income, the tax law stipulated that taxes were to be levied on the assessed value of the land, rather than upon the yield, as had been the custom. This change meant that the government would be assured of the same tax income regardless of the actual yield. The farmers, especially in years of famine, were greatly incensed at the operation of this modern system which paid no heed to the effect of natural disasters over which the farmer had no control; but the government could not be moved to change a policy which served to provide a regular tax income for the state. As the new tax system was implemented and improved, the state was gradually placed in a stronger financial position, which enabled it to provide more positive support for the remainder of the reform program.

The other important step taken in 1873 was the establishment of a national conscript army[6] to replace the old locally controlled feudal armies made up of hereditary samurai. The samurai scholars had long studied Western military science, but their attention was focused chiefly upon weapons, ships, and strategy—not upon army organization. Some had seen the advantage of a centralized army with a broad base, but it was realized that reform along this line had to be preceded by basic political changes. With the establishment of the "Imperial Guard" and the "prefectural system" in 1871, the necessary groundwork was laid; in the following year the government abolished the hereditary samurai system, and in 1873 it passed a conscript law which made all males, at the age of twenty, subject to three years' service in a national army. The adoption of this system was of so revolutionary a nature that the new governmental structure was seriously threatened for several years by opposition from the declassed samurai, who had long been the social elite of the country. The government adopted a number of measures to appease these men, and gradually it succeeded in placing the new military system on a solid foundation. The system was subjected to a severe test in the Satsuma rebellion of 1877. But the army succeeded in that struggle, with extensive technical assistance from abroad, and by 1888 had become a force which, according to its leader (Yamagata), was "ready for any continental operation."[7]

The ease with which the ethical standards of the old samurai class were adjusted to the needs of a strong national army helped to make the military reforms more effective. Of course, many of the intellectual movements of the eighteenth century and first half of the nineteenth had tended to orient samurai loyalties toward the Emperor rather than toward the military superior. But the leaders of the "Restoration" government gave particular attention to accelerating the process. Many new religious, administrative, and educational policies were products of that interest. The military training itself was soon geared to the task of effecting the intellectual and emotional reorientation. In 1882, for example, the Emperor issued the famous Imperial Rescript to Soldiers and Sailors, which started off as follows: "The forces of Our Empire are in all ages under the command of the Emperor." It went on to state that for several centuries leaders of the military class had held sway. This was a most deplorable development, the Emperor said, since they were acting "contrary to the fundamental character of Our Empire and to the law of Our Imperial Ancestors"; but now a new order has been established, and the "supreme command of Our forces is in Our hands." Having established the true source of military authority, the rescript went on to underline the military virtues and to relate the exercise of these virtues to the fulfillment of the soldiers' "duty of grateful service to the country."[8] By continuous effort along these lines, the samurai code of ethics (*Bushidō*) tended to become the code of ethics for all loyal citizens of the Japanese state, but particularly for the soldiers in the new national army. In the past, the military leaders were interested in the development of *Bushidō* as a means of strengthening the Tokugawa military regime; but in the hands of the post-Restoration leaders, *Bushidō* not only became a powerful cohesive force within the army but served gradually as a very effective means of directing the loyalties of all Japanese citizens to the Emperor, the symbolic head of the nation.

By taking these positive steps toward centralization, the leaders of the Meiji government aroused considerable opposition, since many persons suffered from the changes. For a few years, much of the opposition took the form of direct action; but after 1877 it was limited chiefly to political-party movements, criticism from the press, and secret-society activity. At the time of the great crisis in 1881, it looked as though the political parties, with their opposition demands for a constitution and a truly representative form of government, had gained the upper hand; but by 1888, with judicious compromise measures and determined countermoves, coupled with developments which weakened the opposition, the government had established itself in an extremely strong position. A Western pattern of control had emerged; but the oligarchy's position was firm—the Japanese nation had been brought together under a highly unified, modern state.

Economic Reform

An integral part of the reform program was the government's drive to increase production, for the leaders of the new regime were well aware that strength for the new state was mainly dependent upon the possibility of increasing the wealth of the nation. The current slogan *Fukoku Kyōhei* (Rich country—Strong army) was indicative of their concentration upon the problem of economic expansion. The slogan also indicated that economic expansion should be toward the development of military industries. The economic reform, like the political and military reform, was therefore to be molded in a way that would best serve the immediate aims of the state. The leaders, most of whom had come from the old samurai class, were inclined to think, especially in view of their recent experience with the Western powers, that military strength was basic to national strength. Also, they knew enough of military developments abroad, as well as at home, to realize that a modern military machine, to be really powerful, had to have the support of a strong, well-integrated, military industry.

After the arrival of Perry in 1853, the old military regime, as well as the various feudal clans, directed attention and money to the manufacture of modern weapons and modern ships;[9] but after the Restoration, the government embarked upon a much more ambitious program of industrial development. It took over all the factories and workshops that had been built in various local areas and initiated a program of expansion and integration which, in a relatively short time, provided the new army with needed supplies and equipment.

But the Meiji government soon found that military industries of the modern type could not exist apart from other industries, and that specialized equipment and the assistance of foreign technicians could not be obtained without the production of goods for sale abroad. Consequently, in its effort to provide an adequate base for its modern army and navy, the government soon found itself operating model factories, subsidizing small companies, and taking a direct hand in various fields of production and distribution. Not only the munitions industries but mining, transportation, and banking enterprises were controlled and aided by the central government. By 1880 the government was so deeply involved in so wide a range of economic endeavor that an attempt was made to transfer ownership of the more marginal concerns—that is, the nonmilitary ones—to private firms. But a pattern of industrial growth had already been set which gave Japan's economic growth a peculiar character that has persisted down to modern times.

The remarkable economic expansion of the first two decades of the Meiji period accounted for a far greater degree of social cohesion within the Japanese nation. With the introduction of the factory system and with the adoption of many new specialized industrial techniques, there was far more specialization of economic activity and thus a greater degree of economic interdependence. But the special character of the expansion made it even more significant as a cohesive development. Since the program was based, in large measure, upon government initiative, there was far greater integration than there would otherwise have been. Not only was there a military focus but there was a high degree of centralized capital investment, either because the government put up the capital or because private investors did so with government backing. Since the economic development followed this pattern, there was comparatively little economic growth that resulted merely from private investors entering a field for profit. Consequently there was very little fragmentation of industrial effort arising from private enterprise. Likewise, the economic growth was not accompanied by the growth of a large, independent "middle class"—a development which not only would have made it more difficult for the government to achieve the same degree of unity in its economic program but also would have made it far more difficult for the oligarchy to preserve, as well as it did, so high a degree of political control over the new, centralized state structure.[10]

Establishment of State Shinto

As fundamental as the political and economic reforms were, the attempts made to create greater ideological unity were related more closely to the rise of modern nationalism, for nationalism is basically an ideological phenomenon. Since the decline of the feudal regime was paralleled by the growth of the "Revere the Emperor" movement, it was quite natural that the leaders of the new regime should use those ideas and feelings as justification and support for the establishment of a new order. Thus the political change of 1868 came to be known as the "Restoration" (the "Restoration" of the Emperor to his rightful position). There had been restorations before, but in this case the leaders took special precautions to see that the symbolic leadership of the Emperor was given more than ceremonial recognition. Statements of public policy took the form of Imperial rescripts. The Imperial Court was moved to Edo (thereafter to be called Tokyo), and thus the impression was given that the Emperor was going to assume direct control of the affairs of state. But the most effective means of giving real substance to the claims of an "Imperial Restoration" was the raising of the Sun Cult of Shinto (of which the Emperor was the hereditary head priest) to the level of a state religion.

That the Meiji leaders had this goal in mind from the start is indicated by the inclusion of a Shinto Department (*Jingikan*) in the new Western-style government that was set up early in 1868. Soon thereafter a series of orders was issued requiring the complete removal of Buddhist paraphernalia and Buddhist ceremonies from the Shinto shrines. For centuries the Buddhist sects had gained strength from associating themselves with native Shinto cults, but now that the Sun Cult was to serve as the focus of greater ideological unity it had to be "purified." The Buddhists had been so closely bound up with the old Tokugawa Bakufu that the "purification" process, in some areas, amounted to persecution. On the island of Sado, for example, several hundred temples were closed up and hundreds of priests were forced to become farmers.[11]

With the government reorganization of 1869, the Shinto Department was placed in a still higher position (on an equality with the Council of State itself),[12] and two months later a Shinto missionary program was set up to proclaim the State Shinto ideology to the people. The Shinto missionaries were sent to various parts of the country, but particularly to the areas in which Buddhist, and sometimes Christian, influence was strongest. In January, 1870, an Imperial rescript was issued to explain why this program had been adopted:

The Heavenly gods and our Heavenly Ancestor have constituted the highest principle, and upon it they founded the first undertakings of a great achievement. Ever since, the Emperors in line have acknowledged, inherited and proclaimed it. The ideal of "the unity of religion and state" is held by the whole Nation; the right ways in polity and education are clear to those on high, and the customs and manners of those below are in perfect order. . . . At this time the Heavenly Course of the Nation has turned, and thus all things are become new. By all means, polity and education should be made clear to the Nation, and thus the Great Way of *Kannagara* should be promulgated. Therefore preachers shall be ordered to propagate the Way far and wide.[13]

After this rescript was issued, other steps were taken to strengthen the Shinto missionary effort, such as forcing the local han, as well as the central government, to send out missionaries, and requiring all people in the country to register at some Shinto shrine.

By the summer of 1871 the government was still dissatisfied with the results of the Shinto program and consequently decided upon a reorganization of the entire Shinto structure. Twelve grades of shrines, ranging from one that included the small local shrines to one that included the Ise Shrine—where the Sun Goddess herself was enshrined— were established, and government control and regulation thus were made easier. But of greater significance was the order abolishing the hereditary rights of the Shinto priesthood and declaring that all priests, from those at Ise down to those in local shrines, were to be appointed by the government. Immediately after these drastic administrative changes were made, the government attempted to revitalize its missionary program by carefully spelling out its objectives. In no uncertain terms it insisted on greater respect for the Shinto deities and more wholehearted acceptance of "high moral principles" in order that the people might serve the Emperor with deeper feelings of loyalty.[14]

But the Shinto program had proved, after four years, to be very disappointing. It may very well have served to accelerate the substitution of loyalty to the Emperor for loyalty to local clans, but it had not been influential in Buddhist circles. In fact, on a religious level, the Shinto program, down to 1872, may have created greater disunity. In 1872, therefore, still another basic revision in the program was made: the missionary work was to be carried on by Buddhists as well as by Shintoists. The Shinto Department became the Religious Department (*Kyō-busho*), which had jurisdiction over both Buddhism and Shintoism, and the missionaries were to be chosen from Buddhist as well as Shinto priests. However, the goals of the propaganda were to remain basically the same. All missionaries, whether Buddhist or Shinto, were directed to support the principles of reverence for the Shinto deities, reverence for the Emperor, and obedience to the authorities.[15] When it was discovered that the Buddhist priests were not able or willing to serve as propagandists for Shinto-national principles, the government established special training schools. But the attempt to bring the Buddhists into the program was obviously a failure, and on May 3, 1875, the program was reorganized. The Buddhists were removed from active participation in the program, and a policy was adopted whereby the whole Shintoization process would be played down.

The shift in policy was related to a number of circumstances. The continuous opposition of the Buddhists was undoubtedly an important factor, since an increasing number of officials saw that the Shinto propaganda was creating dissension rather than greater ideological unity. But the Japanese, after 1873, had become extremely sensitive to the attitudes of Western powers, because of the impelling desire to gain recognition of equality from Western nations as a means of assuring a revision of the unequal treaties. Since the Western nations placed great store by the principle of religious freedom, and since they were criticizing the Japanese for their persecution of Christians, it seemed advisable to drop, nominally at least, the policy of making Shinto a state religion.[16] But still another contributing factor was the growing realization in official circles that the new universal education system appeared to be a more promising medium for achieving ideological unity.

Educational Reform

From the very beginning of the Restoration period the officials had decided that "Knowledge shall be sought for all over the world, *and thus shall be strengthened the foundations of the Imperial Polity (kokutai)*."[17] For two years after the Restoration the government was too busy with more pressing problems, such as the military campaigns against remnants of Bakufu power, to give much attention to the development of its educational program; but by 1870 a few measures had been taken to implement the stated policy. In that year an order was sent to local officials instructing them to send the most capable students to Tokyo.

From these, the most promising were to be sent abroad for study. Then, in January, 1871, a Department of Education was set up, and educators were sent abroad to study foreign educational systems. Mori Arinori, the chargé d'affaires in the United States after 1871, invited prominent American educators to submit suggestions that might be of help to the Japanese. One of the men approached was Dr. David Murray, a mathematician and astronomer at Rutgers University, who was so coöperative and helpful that he was given a position in Japan as an educational consultant. Finally, in June, 1872, a normal school was set up to train elementary school teachers, and in August of the same year, the "Code of Education" was promulgated.[18]

From the beginning, the new universal education system was thought of primarily as a tool for providing Japanese citizens with technical knowledge that would be of assistance to the state in the implementation of its huge reform program. A large pool of trained personnel was needed for the expanded bureaucracy, for the industrial program, and for the modern national army. The assistance of American advisers and the introduction of certain American educational methods led at least one noted writer to observe that "no less a feat than the reform of the entire educational system was chiefly the work of a handful of Americans."[19] Although certain American forms and methods were adopted, the Japanese officials always considered education primarily as a means of strengthening the state and only secondarily as a means of enriching the lives of individual students. As one Japanese educational leader remarked, "the propagation of education was felt to be *an urgent state necessity.*"[20]

In the 1870's the new educational system was used primarily to introduce Western scientific knowledge into Japan. The agricultural, commercial, and trade schools were given the most support. And Mori, the Education Minister, went so far as to propose that English be substituted for Japanese, since, he said, the Japanese language was not a suitable medium for the expression of modern scientific concepts.[21] But gradually a larger number of officials came round to the view that the educational system could also be used to advantage in creating greater ideological unity. Those who took the lead in advocating such a revision were the Confucianists. Throughout the Tokugawa period (1603–1868) they had enjoyed official support; consequently, for a time after the Meiji Restoration, they were not in good standing with the leaders of the new regime. But it was not long before some of the Confucianists were beginning to write books, make speeches, and organize societies which advocated greater attention to the old Confucian ethical principles, in order to counterbalance the recent stress on the material aspects of life. This appeal became particularly attractive to government leaders, as it was becoming more apparent that the teaching of Western technology was leading to more interest in Western principles of government. And ideas of individual freedom and representative government did not sit well with men who were bent on increasing the power of the state. Also, the officials were beginning to realize that the Confucian emphasis on loyalty and filial piety—particularly when focused upon the Emperor—could be very effective in achieving greater national unity. Thus, in order to head off what was considered to be the subversive influence of Western liberalism, and in order to follow through with the program of creating greater ideological unity, "moral" education gradually became more important than "scientific" education. Both were considered means of increasing the strength of the nation, and both were obviously important in establishing greater social cohesion; but clearly "moral" education was more directly related to the rapid spread of national feelings.

As early as 1875 a noted Confucian scholar, Nishimura Shigeki, became head of the textbook section of the Department of Education. But the most positive move toward greater emphasis upon "moral" education came with the 1880 revision of the Code of Education which placed the "morals" courses in a far more prominent position in the school curriculum and made "moral character" an essential qualification for teachers. Military drill was also introduced into the curriculum, and retired army officers were used to implement this part of the program. The usual explanation for the decision to include military training in the schools was that since all able-bodied men were subject to a period of military service, it was desirable to introduce them earlier to training in the military arts. But it was also pointed out that military exercises would serve to strengthen the moral and intellectual training of the students.[22] Military training undoubtedly did supplement the morals courses in creating a greater sense of national solidarity among the students, particularly after 1882, when the Imperial Exhortation to Military Men was issued and the ideals of Bushidō came to play so vital a role.

In 1880, Motoda Eifu, the most noted Confucian scholar of the period, wrote a book entitled *Yōgaku Kōyō* (An Outline of Learning for the Young), in which he said:

Although at one time we took the best features of the West and succeeded in getting new things, the serious defect was to relegate benevolence, justice, reverence and wisdom to a secondary position. *The thing to fear of blindly seeking after Western customs is that in the end great principles governing the relations between ruler and subject, and father and son will be forgotten.* ... People should cultivate sincerity and moral conduct, and after that they should pursue the various subjects of learning to the best of their ability.[23]

The Emperor himself wrote the foreword, thus ensuring high approval of the book. The *Shibun Gakkai* (Society for the Study of Confucian Culture) also was organized in 1880, and its avowed purpose was to strengthen the foundations of the state by promotion of Confucian principles.

By 1887, the educational system, as a means of serving the state, had been broadened. In addition to training men to be bureaucrats and soldiers, and providing the necessary technical education to equip men for the new industrial enterprises, the schools instilled into the students a deeper sense of loyalty to the nation. Under the leadership of Mori Arinori, who was Minister of Education from 1885 to 1889, education in Japan came to have a nationalistic, as well as a utilitarian, emphasis.

Still another phase of the educational reform was important in strengthening the foundations of nationalism in Japan: the extension of literacy. By 1880, 41 per cent of all the school-age children in Japan were in school, and by 1895 the percentage had risen to 61.[24] Before the Restoration a very large part of the samurai class, as a result of the Bakufu support of Confucian learning, was able to read and write, but now with the adoption of compulsory universal education, an increasingly large segment of the whole Japanese population was being influenced by a mass communication of ideas and feelings.

Popular Literature

As important and basic as education was in deepening and widening the channels for the transmission of ideas, there were other developments which accelerated the process. In the first place, mention should be made of the revolutionary changes in the Japanese written language. For centuries it had been customary to write in a formal language that was weighted heavily with Chinese words and phrases. The more erudite scholars had preferred to write in pure Chinese. But after the Restoration a number of men began to write in the everyday spoken style, so that all could understand. One of the leaders in the movement was Fukuzawa Yukichi, who tells of reading his manuscripts to a servant and then rewriting them if the meaning was not clear. It has been said that in the years following the Restoration the Japanese written language was altered more drastically than any other language at any time in history. As these changes became generally accepted, a student could learn to read in a much shorter time. Thus, in a few years a large reading public was created.

Still another change which served to facilitate the flow of ideas by means of the written word was the development of modern techniques of printing, and the publication of truly popular newspapers, books, and magazines. As was true of so many new developments in the Meiji era, the appearance of modern newspapers was closely associated with, if not dependent upon, governmental efforts. At the very beginning of the Restoration the government issued the *Dajōkan Nisshi* (Journal of the Grand Council), which was more an official gazette than a modern newspaper; but this was followed by the publication of news organs by prefectural authorities and, in a short time, by a few private newspapers. At the end of 1868 there were ten different official gazettes and fifteen private newspapers. This early growth undoubtedly was due primarily to the public interest in the civil war that accompanied the Restoration, for in the next two years there was no comparable expansion. Printing was still limited to the use of hand-engraved wood blocks, and the reading public was still small. But in 1870, a newspaper, the Yokohama *Mainichi Shimbun,* was printed with movable lead type, and in consequence of this, newspaper circulation increased significantly. Soon afterward other techniques were used to make newspapers more interesting and attractive. Phonetic symbols (*kana*) were placed beside the Chinese characters so that even persons who had not learned many Chinese characters could understand what was written. Also, illustrations and human-interest stories were added. Finally, in 1874, the steam press was introduced. By this time not only had the new universal education system increased the number of people who could read papers, but the political crisis of 1873—over whether or not Japan should invade Korea—had aroused a tremendous new popular interest in public affairs. By 1874 the circulation of newspapers had passed the 10,000 mark, and by 1877 one newspaper alone enjoyed a circulation of more than 19,000. In this last year, the year of the Satsuma rebellion, 140 new papers were started and the total circulation was estimated to be more than 100,000. During the next decade the industry continued to expand by leaps and bounds, for more people could read and more of them were becoming interested in the news and in the stories that the papers carried.[25]

Only gradually, however, did the newspapers come to be a strong agent for creating greater ideological unity or for arousing more intense feelings of national sentiment, since in the first decade of their growth they were closely associated with opposition to the government. At the time of the great political crisis of 1873 some of the most influential newspapers came out in opposition to the government position. Many writers were so outspoken that by 1875 the government had to resort to censorship and strict press regulations. Still, criticism of the government could not be stopped, and it is said that by 1876 there was hardly an editor in the country who had not been punished for criticizing the government. In January of that year, for example, one writer wrote that he wished to start a rebellion like the one the thirteen states of North America had raised against England, in order to establish in Japan a republican form of government. The man was sent to jail for three years.[26] Others continued to speak out, and the government was forced to take even more positive action against the papers. It should be pointed out, however, that these outspoken opponents of the government, like the liberal leaders of the day, expressed their views in national terms. In October, 1876, Yokose Fumihiko attacked the government in these words:

If wicked Ministers and vulgar officials take advantage of their power, and abuse the people by making tyrannical rules and collecting too heavy taxes; and if men of high ideals, anxious for *national welfare* and representing the will of the people, frankly discuss the merits and demerits of the government's policies and the official practices, and are restricted from discussion by means of severe punishments; then the *very independence of the nation is at stake!* If such government is not promptly overturned, there will be no other way than to wait for the *decay of the state as a whole. At this time of national crisis,* why should the subjects of such a state remain in subjugation to the tryannical government longer? What should they do then? My reply is "Just test the sharpness or dullness of the people's swords on the necks of those dishonest Ministers and vulgar officials!"[27]

Gradually, however, the press was brought into line, not merely by restrictive methods but by the operation of the historical process in which the reform program as a whole had resulted in a strong, centralized state with a much higher productive power and a greater degree of social cohesion. After the Satsuma rebellion of 1877 there were few direct-action moves against the government, and after the political crisis of 1881 the leaders of the Meiji government moved forward rapidly in the building of a strong and rigid political, economic, and social structure. The opposition movements slowly disintegrated and the newspapers gradually came round to a basic support of government policies. By the end of the national reform period the newspapers had become a powerful and influential agent for the growth of modern nationalism.

The new techniques, conditions, and interests which accounted for the great expansion in the newspaper industry also affected the publication of books and magazines. As more people were able to read, more books were written in everyday Japanese, and these, like the newspapers, reflected the new interest in the Western world and had an increasingly popular appeal. At first a large proportion of the books were translations of American, English, and French works. As early as 1870, Smiles' *Self-Help* was rendered into Japanese and was enthusiastically received by the Japanese public. Biographies of Napoleon, Shakespeare, Voltaire, and Bacon were also translated, and romantic novels were widely read. In selecting Western works to be translated, the Japanese were obviously guided by utilitarian motives, as we can readily see from the following phrase found in the preface to the translation of Robinson Crusoe: "... if men will read [this] carefully they will see that it shows how by stubborn determination an island can be developed."[28]

In the political novels, which became extremely popular in the 1880's, we have even more positive evidence that the Japanese were strongly influenced by utilitarian and national interests, even when translating and reading Western books. After a period during which most of the novels published were translations, the Japanese began to write their own. One of the first, written between 1883 and 1884, was *Keikoku Bidan* (The Saga of a Classical Country), which described the patriotic deeds of ancient Greece. It was read with avid interest by young Japanese who wished to do their part in building a strong Japan. The most famous of the political novels, however, was *Kajin no Kigū* (Chance Meeting with a Beautiful Woman), which was published serially sometime after 1885. It told of the adventures of a young Japanese, Tōkai, who visited Independence Hall in Philadelphia and there met two beautiful young women, an Irish blonde and a Spanish brunette. As he became better acquainted with them, he learned that they understood and appreciated his concern about the future of his country. After he returned home, he became utterly disgusted at the failure of Japanese diplomats to obtain any satisfactory results in their negotiations with Korea. Tōkai traveled again, in Europe and China, but throughout the tale he continued to be concerned about his country and to protest against the arrogance and conceit of foreigners.[29]

In what might well be deemed to be the least significant field of reform, that of manners and customs, we see a reflection of the same national concerns. At first glance one might doubt whether adoption of Western-style clothes would serve national interests, and yet when foreign dress was prescribed for all court and official functions in 1872, it was explained that "the people must not be soft, but must strive to build up a martial state." As Sansom explains, legalizing trousers and abolishing flowing robes symbolized the change from a leisurely life to a "busy practical striding about the market place." Public notices were posted, urging the eating of beef, on the grounds that it would "create energy for the performance of patriotic duties and strengthen the national physique." In many other changes in customs and manners can be seen the desire of the Japanese to appear to be civilized and thus to warrant the revision of the unequal treaties and the removal of the hated extraterritorial privileges. In 1871 the Tokyo *Nichi-nichi* carried an order against nakedness; the headline read: "Do not be laughed at by foreigners." Orders requiring the separation of the sexes at the public bathhouses, prohibiting obscene performances at the theater, and prohibiting the display or sale of pornographic art were all issued to head off criticisms from foreigners. In 1870 a leading newspaper condemned Japanese travelers who did not conduct themselves properly while abroad, pointing out that the "doings of one business man could cast shame upon the Japanese people in the eyes of the whole world."[30]

◇   ◇   ◇

In the two decades of reform, between 1868 and 1888, Western nations did not again subject Japan to military pressure, although both the French and British expressed some willingness to participate in the internal struggles for power that followed the Restoration. But as the Japanese set to work to learn the secrets of Western strength, their new knowledge tended to accent further their feelings of national inferiority. Japanese travelers brought back amazing stories of material wealth and mechanical achievement, and soon books and magazines were disseminating information about the superior material accomplishments of the Western world. So deep an impression was made that the Japanese not only became more determined to modernize their country along Western lines, but they tended to adopt generally the tastes, interests, and trappings of Western culture. For a time they even showed a distaste for their own artistic and literary standards.

The driving force behind the entire Meiji reform program was the urge, on the part of the young leaders of the new government, to achieve greater national strength. The pattern of the reform movement was accordingly dominated by a military theme, and it carried, to an amazing degree, the imprint of government sponsorship. For these reasons, the political, military, economic, social, educational, and religious developments of modern Japan all bear characteristics which vary considerably from the norm established in France, England, and the United States. The concentration on industries that would provide the most vital support for the new army, on the promotion of a foreign trade and commerce that would accrue to the military advantage of the nation, on the establishment of a political organization that would assure the greatest degree of political strength, and on the adoption of educational and religious institutions and philosophies that would foster greater ideological unity and more loyal, efficient service to the nation, obviously gave to the program a consistency and a direction which were indeed remarkable. But under this governmental sponsorship, impelled by the urge for greater national security, the reforms tended to stifle the growth of democratic forces. The industrial spurt was not accompanied by the growth of a great class of small industrialists; the political organs tended to check any dispersal of political power; and the policies in regard to education and religion gave slight attention to human values and individual rights. It is clear, however, that because of an absence of powerful democratic forces, the government was able to achieve, in a shorter time, greater degrees of political centralization, economic expansion, and ideological unity, and by doing so, created national strength and moved the country farther and faster along the road toward modern nationalism.

6 PRESERVATION OF "JAPANESE NATIONAL ESSENCE"

In the summer of 1887 the Japanese became highly indignant at their government for agreeing to a treaty revision which they considered insulting to the nation. The incident itself was not so serious a threat to the nation as, let us say, the joint Western-power naval expedition against Osaka in 1865. And yet the reaction in 1887 was far more intense—it was felt throughout the country and deep down in the social order. Feelings ran so high that the negotiations had to be dropped. The cabinet was ousted, and strong measures were adopted in order to quiet the opposition. This upsurge of feeling marks the beginning of modern nationalism in Japan.

Clearly, a popular reaction of this kind can be understood only in terms of the social and ideological developments which had made the Japanese nation a more cohesive unit. Now that the reform programs and the earlier growth of national thought had welded the people into a tighter whole, any apparent danger to the nation aroused a far more dynamic response. Another pertinent factor, however, was the psychological reaction against Western principles and ideas. Westernization had caused many persons to reject the old religious, ethical, and political principles; but the rejection had left a sort of moral vacuum which could not be filled by Western thought. Consequently the sense of being cast loose from intellectual and moral moorings led eventually to a turning back to traditional patterns. The reaction of 1887 therefore not only took the form of a deep-seated aversion to the government's weak-kneed foreign policy but included anger against Western powers for their unfair and unreasonable attitude toward Japan, and it was associated with a revulsion against Western thoughts and with a new interest in traditional Japanese ideals. Just a few months before the crisis of 1887, Premier Itō had given a grand Western-type costume ball for some four hundred guests. The ball, like so many other social events and activities of the day, seems to have sprung from the conviction that the adoption of Western ways would not only strengthen Japan but would help her to become an acceptable member of the society of nations. After 1887, however, there was an apparent denial of that assumption. We find thereafter a definite rejection of Western manners, an enthusiasm for traditional Japanese standards, and a greater interest in expansionism as a means of further strengthening the Japanese nation.

The "Japanese National Essence" Movement

A number of developments, besides the reaction to the insulting treaty revision, attest to this change of attitude; but the one that has received the most attention was the organization in 1885 of the True Teachings Club (*Seikyō Sha*) by a group of conservative intellectuals. The club undertook to publish a magazine, called *Nihonjin* (The Japanese), which soon became noted for its strenuous opposition to all Western ideas and customs and popularized the demand for the preservation of the "Japanese National Essence." In the early issues there were articles under such titles as "The Future National Policy of Japan Should Be to Decide Matters in Accordance with the Principles of the Preservation of National Characteristics" and "On the Basic Principles of National Essence." But there were other societies and magazines of the same order. For example, there was the Society of the Great Way of Japan (*Nihon*

Kokkyō Daidō Sha), which made a declaration of its principles (in its own journal) in these words:

The national religions are [basic to] the spirit of the country. The spirit of our country is found in the three religions of Shinto, Confucianism, and Buddhism. In the unity of these three we have the Great Way (*Daidō*). In [stimulating] loyalty to the Emperor and love for our country, nothing is superior to Shinto. [In helping us] to deal with the affairs of the world, nothing is superior to Confucianism. And in coping with world passions, nothing is superior to Buddhism. In ancient times these three "Ways" were harmonized, and consequently a state religion was established, and for this reason we have the spirit of the state (*kokka*). It was on this basis that society was organized and the basis of morals established. From this we have the phenomena of loyalty and love. From this there evolved reverence and respect for the *kokutai* . . . but in recent times the work of former Emperors has been destroyed, the spirit of the state is being undermined, the organization of society is being disturbed, and the basis of morals is being weakened.

The religions of foreign countries have eaten into the spirit of our country. . . . If we are to maintain for all ages the Imperial country of Japan without losing any territory, then we must respect the work of previous Emperors and solidify the spirit of the state. We must also keep in order the organization of society, we must strengthen the foundation of our morals, we must claim the spirit of filial piety and love (*chūai*). It is to support these aims that the *Nihon Kokkyō Daidō Sha* was organized. We are to band together into one group, and avoiding private opinions, to give our attention to the work of these previous Emperors. We want to restore the national religion, to proclaim the spirit of love and filial piety, to strengthen the basis of morals, to improve the organization of society, and to unify the spirit of the state.[1]

There were many intellectuals who energetically gave their support to these "Great Way" (*Daidō*) principles; but the movement was merely one of the more prominent aspects of the general interest in purely Japanese ideas and ideals. In almost every area of thought and action we can find evidence of the same emphasis.

"Japanese National Essence" and Shintoism

In Shintoism, for example, there were developments after 1887 which indicate the presence of a more definitely nation-oriented intellectual atmosphere. The Sun Cult of Shintoism, of course, had long been the focus of the growth of early national consciousness. The so-called Shinto revival of Tokugawa times and the establishment of the Sun Cult as the state religion of Japan at the time of the Restoration are merely two of the better-known developments in which Shintoism was at the center of the movement leading to the rise of modern nationalism. For a decade or so before 1887 the government-supported Shinto program had not been pressed openly or energetically, since it was deemed advisable to give the impression that the Western principle of religious freedom was respected in Japan. The Meiji leaders, however, never ceased to consider Shinto—that is, the Sun Cult of Shinto—as essential in creating greater ideological unity;[2] and after 1887 the Shinto program reëmerged as an extremely vital force, not merely in the realm of thought and religion but in politics and education as well.

Probably the most startling evidence of the new stress upon Shinto traditions is to be seen in the Constitution of 1889, which in purpose and in form was a product of Western influence.[3] It was promised by the government only after opposition groups—which advocated Western concepts of representative government—had become sufficiently strong to force the government to yield to their demands. Nevertheless, it is clear that the Shinto traditions served as foundation stones for that historic document. Even in its formulation we see the mark of Shinto traditions: it was drafted within the Imperial Household, not in an assembly elected by the people, and it was considered to be a gift from the Emperor. The whole first chapter of the Constitution was about the Emperor—his status, function, and powers. Article 1 states: "The Empire of Japan shall be reigned over and governed by a line of Emperors unbroken for ages eternal." Another article declares that the Emperor is "sacred and inviolable." Subsequent sections of the Constitution further implement the Shinto concept that the Emperor (the hereditary, divine head of the Sun Cult) "combines in himself the rights of sovereignty." Itō Hirobumi, the man most responsible for drafting the document later wrote:

All the different legislative as well as executive powers of State, by means of which He reigns over the country and governs the people, are united in His Most Exalted Personage, who thus holds in His hands, as it were, all the ramifying threads of the political life of the country, just as the brain in the human body is the primitive source of all mental activity manifested through the four limbs and the different parts of the body.[4]

By the Constitution of 1889, then, the Sun Cult of Shintoism was given higher legal status as the state religion of Japan.

The new emphasis upon Shinto traditions was also reflected in the Imperial Rescript on Education of 1890. As pointed out above, there had been a tendency in the 1880's for the government to use the new educational system as a means of arousing a greater sense of loyalty to the state, as well as a means of providing students with training in the sciences. But after 1887 the Department of Education took even more positive steps to see that "morality based upon the native doctrine of the Empire" should be made an important part of all educational work.[5] The most significant of these steps was the proclamation of the Imperial Rescript on Education in 1890,[6] which, as one of the men associated with its formulation later admitted, was designed primarily to counteract the growing influence of Western thought. The Emperor, in this rescript, set forth principles and concepts that were to be considered the basis of Japan's educational philosophy. It begins: "Our Imperial ancestors have founded Our Empire on a basis broad and everlasting, and have deeply and firmly implanted virtue; Our subjects ever united in loyalty and filial piety have from generation to generation illustrated the beauty thereof. This is the glory of the fundamental character of Our Empire, and herein also lies the source of Our education. . . ." Then, after outlining the Confucian ethical principles that were to be taught and practiced, the rescript concludes in this strain: "The Way here set forth is indeed the teaching bequeathed by Our Imperial Ancestors, to be observed alike by the Descendants and the subjects, infallible in all ages and true in all places. It is our wish to lay it to heart in all reverence, in common with you, our subjects, that we all may attain to the same virtue." When the rescript was first proclaimed, there were some who felt that it was an undesirable, reactionary step; but in later years, as feelings of nationalism became more widespread and intense, the rescript gradually took on the character of a sacred text.

The new interest in Shinto doctrine, however, was by no means limited to government circles, for a number of nonofficial intellectuals wrote books—and associated themselves with societies—that provided a powerful impetus to the new emphasis upon Shinto. One of the more famous Shinto societies that cropped up at this time was the *Ishin Gakkai* (Society for Restoring Learning), which published a magazine called the *Kannagara*, an old word for "Shinto." The prospectus of this society ran as follows:

In 647, Emperor Kōtoku issued an Imperial Edict that said: "The Empire was entrusted [by the Sun Goddess to her descendants, with the words]: 'My children, in their capacity of Deities (*Ishin*) shall rule it.' For this reason, this country since Heaven and Earth began has been a monarchy. From the time that our Imperial ancestor first ruled the land, there has been great concord in the Empire, and there has never been any factiousness."[7] It has been explained that Shinto, as something established by the Imperial Way (*Kōdō*) and [received] from the descendants of the gods, or from the Imperial ancestors, is something that should be respected by our Japanese race. . . . But by the time of the Taika era (645–650) there were many immigrants that had entered the country from the neighboring country of China, disturbing the minds of men and complicating the administration of the country. . . . So by issuing this Imperial Edict the aims of the subjects were made clear. One thousand two hundred and fifty years separate us from the Taika era [and in that period] there have been even closer relations with China and the burden of assimilating foreign peoples has been much greater. Internal and external relations have been complicated, and political parties and religious sects have been thrown into far more disorder than was the case in Taika days. Under such circumstances the Imperial Constitution was promulgated and the concept of obedience pointed out. . . . We have set up a historical association by which we plan to investigate the divine features of [our] divine country and to clarify the Imperial Way. . . . By [the study of] ancient customs we will clarify the basis of politics and religion; by words we will identify the differences in races; by considering the systems of ancient and modern times we will learn the lucky and unlucky ceremonies; by [learning] the proprieties (*rei*) we will bring tranquillity to those above us and [effective] rule to the people. We will go about making speeches, or will publish magazines. . . . We will clarify the divine (*Ishin*) Imperial Way (*Kōdō*).[8]

"Japanese National Essence" and Confucianism

The reactionary trend which emerged after 1887 was also reflected in the field of ethics, where Confucianism emerged once more as a dominant force in the intellectual life of the Japanese people. As pointed out above, Confucian scholars had been discredited, in the years immediately following the Restoration, by their close association with the old feudal regime. But after a decade or two, certain responsible government officials turned their efforts once more to a reawakening of interest in Confucian standards of conduct. It was clear to them, as it was to the Tokugawa rulers before them, that a more widespread acceptance of Confucian principles of loyalty would help to create the kind of ideological unity they desired, and would tend to weaken the liberal Western principles that caused them so much anxiety. Iwakura Tomomi, one of the most influential of the Meiji leaders, and other men in high government circles joined hands in 1880 to set up a Confucian society, the *Shibun Gakkai*. The purpose was to strengthen the basis of the state by fostering Confucian thoughts. Three years later, the society, with the help of a yearly stipend from the Imperial Court, established a school which later played an important role in the Confucian revival.[9]

After 1887 even more positive support was given to the further spread of Confucian ethical principles. The courses on morals were given greater importance in the curriculum of all schools. They were more heavily loaded with nation-oriented Confucian teachings. Again, the clearest and most positive evidence of this emphasis is seen in the Imperial Rescript on Education; in this we find that the educational philosophy of Japan thenceforth was to be based not only upon proper appreciation of Shinto traditions but also upon a wholehearted acceptance of Confucian ethical principles. After setting forth the unique position and qualities of the Emperor (as given above), the rescript states:

Ye, our subjects, be filial to your parents, affectionate to your brothers and sisters; as husbands and wives be harmonious, as friends true, bear yourselves in modesty and moderation; extend your benevolence to all; pursue learning and cultivate arts, and thereby develop intellectual faculties and perfect moral powers ... *should emergency arise, offer yourselves courageously to the State; and thus guard and maintain the prosperity of Our Imperial Throne coeval with heaven and earth....* [10]

As in the new interest in Shintoism, private scholars as well as government officials added their support to the reawakening of interest in Confucian principles. The leading nonofficial Confucian scholar of the day was Nishimura Shigeki, who, as early as 1886, wrote a book entitled *Nihon Dōtoku Ron* (A Discussion of Japanese Morals), which was widely read and is considered a landmark in the new enthusiasm for Confucian teachings. One of the societies in which Nishimura was active, the *Nihon Kōdō Kai,* (Japanese Morals Society) made a declaration of its principles in September, 1887—just two months after the negotiations for a revision of the unequal treaties had broken down. It reads, in part, as follows:

Upon observing the conditions of the moral world of our country since the Meiji Restoration, we find that we must avoid the destruction of our traditional morals by the moral principles of Europe and America, and we must prevent our own Japanese people, who have been clouded by the glitter of foreign culture and by the confusion of the Restoration period, from destroying their own traditional morals. We must come to grips with both of these enemies and fight it out to the finish. If the moral army, before it sees the color of the enemy, destroys the base of those morals and forces them to withdraw and if it destroys their stronghold and forces them to flee, then in the field of present day morals there will be no enemies.... These are the unalterable aims of the *Nihon Kōdō Kai.* [11]

The society also issued a magazine, sponsored public lectures, and in 1890 organized a women's auxiliary. At the ceremonial opening of the auxiliary, Nishimura made a speech in which he spoke out against the Western-type education and stressed the unique virtues of Japanese women.

Influence of "Japanese National Essence" Movement in Other Fields

How much the whole of Japanese life was affected by the new attention to the preservation of Japan's "national essence," can probably be understood more clearly if we note the effect in fields outside Shintoism and Confucianism, the traditional ideologies that were now being revitalized as a matter of public policy. First let us turn to the field of art. In the first two decades of the Meiji era the Japanese artists had become almost completely absorbed by the artistic styles, forms, and techniques of the West, and they seemed to lose all interest in Japan's old art treasures. Mary Fenollosa, in her preface to Ernest Fenollosa's *Epochs of Chinese and Japanese Art,* has written as follows concerning art in early Meiji times: "Collections of painting, porcelains, lacquers, bronzes and prints were scattered, and treasures that are now almost priceless could at that time be bought for a few yen. It is even said that among the extreme foreignists some of the collections were burned as rubbish." But by the 1880's, Ernest Fenollosa, an American student who was then living in Japan, was able to arouse some interest in "saving" Japanese art. In 1885 an art commission decided to approve Fenollosa's suggestion that purely Japanese techniques of painting should be reintroduced into the schools. Finally, in 1887, the year of the diplomatic crisis over the revision of the unequal treaties, the Normal Art School of Tokyo was opened, and Fenollosa was given the task of registering the art treasures of the country.[12] At this time an increasing number of Japanese artists became interested in these moves, and soon there emerged what has been termed a national art movement.

In the field of history, too, scholars began to concern themselves with studies of Japanese institutions and Japanese ideas, and to give less attention to foreign history. Japan's first historical journal, the *Shigaku Zasshi,* appeared in 1889. Dr. Shigeno, one of the historians backing the venture, contributed a short article in which he expressed the hope that the new historical association would benefit the state and that Japanese scholars would turn to an examination of Japanese history.[13] The titles of articles included in the early issues indicate that Dr. Shigeno's hopes were shared by others, for most of the historical studies were now directed toward Japan's own past.

After 1892 the conflict between Shintoists and Christians became increasingly intense, for Christianity was considered a foreign religion which was a threat to the traditional Japanese faith. Inouye Tetsujirō, the leading exponent of anti-Christian thinking in those days, was writing in strains such as this:

Our Imperial Rescript on Education is based entirely upon nationalism (*kokka shugi*), but the Christians in our country have not received this [rescript] well. We have had cases in the schools of [Christian] students refusing to respect the Imperial picture. The logical conclusion of this is that Christianity is absolutely anti-national. . . . Since it places emphasis upon the quality of all before God, it does not accept reverence for the Emperor and consequently places no value upon the idea of loyalty. It cares not the least whether the state deteriorates. . . .[14]

Under the pressure of this national sentiment there were a number of Christians who attempted to show that there was no basic conflict between Christianity and Japanese patriotism. Buddhists, too, entered the fray, and by 1894 the struggle was being fought out in newspapers and magazines, at public debates, and in religious and educational conferences. When the anti-Christians would enumerate the harms Christians had brought to the social and political world of Japan, the Christians would point out all the contributions they had made in the importation of Western culture. But the disputes also reached a much lower level. The Christians resorted to accusing the non-Christians of being bigoted and nonprogressive, and the non-Christians would reply that Christians were obstinate and spiritless. Inouye was called a literary sycophant and a pseudo-philosopher, and the Christians were called "infamous fellows who indulge in liquor, keep women and engage in loaning money at high rates of interest." As one patriotic writer put it, "Christianity places stress on charity (*hakuai*) and love of enemy and therefore leaves no room for the Japanese spirit."[15]

Expansionist Sentiment

The more positive form which nationalist thought took after 1887 affected, and was affected by, developments in the field of foreign relations. During the previous two decades the sense of national inferiority had been so strong that the new policy of increasing the nation's strength primarily through an intensive and extensive reform program seemed to be the wise and logical course for the country. There had been many, particularly among the declassed samurai, who felt that national strength could be most easily and surely acquired by expansion abroad, but they had not been allowed to control the formulation of foreign policy. However, as Japan moved into this new phase in the rise of national thought, those advocating the expansionist course became more influential, and gradually expansionism began to overshadow internal reform as the dominant theme in Japanese nationalist endeavor.

In earlier decades, expansionist sentiments were by no means nonexistent; it is therefore essential, in attempting to evaluate the expansionist sentiment of the post-1887 period, to review briefly the nature and form of earlier movements. Yoshida Shōin, that great intellectual leader of the Meiji adjustment, considered expansion a necessary corollary to internal reform and an important means of achieving greater national power. In one of his works he declared:

The nation is destined to decline unless it advances and flourishes. Therefore, those who know how to look after the welfare of their country should not be satisfied with maintaining and protecting that which their country already has, but at the same time should aim to reform and improve upon that which their country already possesses. They should also strive to gain and add that which their country has not, thereby extending the power and glory of the nation beyond its borders. Present-day Japan should first of all complete her military preparations, by building the necessary battleships and by providing herself with all sorts of military weapons and ammunition. Then she should develop and colonize Yezo and entrust its rule to worthy feudal lords. At her earliest opportunity, Japan should occupy Kamchatka with an army and place the Sea of Okhotsk under her sole control. Liu Chiu (otherwise known as Lu Choo or as Ryu Kyu) should be instructed to make her king come in person to pay homage to Japan so that he and his kingdom may pay reverence to Japan as do all the feudal lords in the homeland. Japan should upbraid Korea for her long negligence in the observation of her duty to Japan, and have her send tribute-bearing envoys, and Japan should also instruct Korea to give hostages to Japan for her good behavior, as she did during the glorious imperial period of ancient Japan. In the north, Manchuria should be sliced off . . .[16]

In the early years of the Meiji period many of the samurai leaders were convinced that the strengthening of Japanese control over Korea was a necessary first step in the expansion of Japan. Soon after the Restoration, the Meiji government itself dispatched envoys to Korea with a view to establishing closer relations, but the Korean government would not receive them. Other missions were sent. The Koreans, however, became more firm in their refusal to resume relations with the Japanese, and the Korean attitude tended to increase the intensity of the expansionist sentiment in Japan, especially in 1873 when wide publicity was given to a Korean note that was couched in most insulting terms.[17] But the rise of an expansionist urge in 1873 was probably more closely related to the implementation of the government's policy to abolish the hereditary privileges of the samurai class than to the Korean rejection of the Japanese overtures. The destruction of the official position of the samurai left a large group of discontented men who took up the cry for a war against Korea in order to create a situation in which they might regain their old social standing in Japan. The demands were such that the government, at one point, actually decided to send an expeditionary force to Korea. But eventually, the so-called "peace party" won the day by hammering away at the thesis that it was to Japan's advantage to follow through with the program of internal reform.[18] The peace party's case, of course, was placed on a foundation of national interest, as is shown by the following statement attributed to Okubo: "Of all the foreign powers Russia is the most to be feared, and her southward movement is well known; so that if Japan and Korea fight with one another, both will fall as easy prey to Russia. England is also a powerful nation, from whom Japan has already borrowed much money, so that if Japan and Korea fight and we can not pay the interest in consequence of the war, she would make it a pretext for interfering in our internal affairs thus making Japan another India."[19] The crisis of 1873 provides clear evidence of early interest in continental expansion; but since the demands for a stronger policy toward Korea were so deeply embedded in the internal political rivalries of the day, one should not accept this expansionist movement merely as a manifestation of national feelings. Even though the proponents for this course of action stated their case in national terms, they were certainly driven by strong, nonnational motives.

When the government decided against sending an expedition to Korea in 1873, a serious political crisis arose, for several influential men withdrew from the government and assumed leadership of opposition movements. Some of these movements took the form of plots leading to direct action; others took the form of political-party activity. But both types of opposition, for a time at least, were tinged with convictions that a stronger foreign policy should be followed. This was especially true of the direct-action movement in western Japan, where Saigo Takamori was active. Even the government was not completely free of the desire to strengthen Japan's position abroad, as we can readily see from its earlier efforts to gain title to outlying islands and from its decision to send an expeditionary force to Formosa in 1874.

Again, however, the Formosan expedition cannot be interpreted simply as a manifestation of nationalist urges, for the decision was bound up with consideration of political expediency. For one thing, it was deemed politic for the government to give some evidence of following a strong foreign policy, in order to weaken the charges of the discontented samurai that it had adopted a negative attitude in its handling of foreign affairs.[20] The government continued also to do what it could to strengthen the Japanese position in Korea by methods short of war. In 1876 it decided to follow the Perry technique in opening up Korea. A naval force of two gunboats and three transports, with about eight hundred men, was dispatched to Korea to present "a request" for the resumption of diplomatic relations. The result was a treaty of commerce between Japan and Korea, signed on February 26, 1876, which served to break the traditional tributary relationship between Korea and China and to give Japan a new basis for a further extension of her interests on the continent.

In spite of these gains the opposition of discontented samurai continued to grow, and in 1877 the government was faced with a serious rebellion in Kyushu, where Saigo Takamori had amassed a large following of men who were not content with the way the central government was conducting foreign affairs. There were objections of various kinds. First of all, the rebels were convinced that the process of westernization would be disastrous for Japan, and they were still positive that a military expedition against Korea would be the best means of strengthening Japan's position. But another reason for their opposition was the hardship which had been caused by the government's decision, in 1876, to force all samurai to accept their pensions in a lump sum. But it is clear that the rebels explained their action most convincingly as an act of loyal service to the Emperor. Even in modern times, the members of the Satsuma clan, and especially Saigo Takamori, have been held in high esteem for their spirited support of the Emperor.

The government's victory against the rebels of Satsuma marked the end of direct-action opposition to the government, but it did not wipe out demands for a more positive policy on the continent. Instead, those demands came to be pressed by the so-called "nationalist" societies. The first of the nationalist societies to gain fame was the *Genyōsha*, which was organized in Kyushu in 1881, four years after the Satsuma rebellion had been suppressed. Its principles were stated in unmistakably nationalistic terms: the Emperor was to be revered; the nation was to be loved and respected; and the people's rights were to be defended. But the name of the society provides a better indication of the area in which it chose to center its activities, for "Genyō" was the name of the sea separating Japan from the continent of Asia. Members of the society were drawn mainly from the discontented samurai who had followed Saigō Takamori, and it soon became apparent that they were determined to follow up Saigō's efforts to strengthen Japan's position on the continent of Asia. Now that the road of direct action against the government was closed, the society directed its efforts toward influencing, rather than overthrowing, the government.

The *Genyōsha*, an elite group of samurai under a strong leader, used propaganda, personal influence, intrigue, and even blackmail and assassination, in order to win the support of key figures in military, government, and business circles. A relatively small part of their work was directed toward winning popular support for their cause, since they understood well that popular opinion as yet had relatively little bearing upon the formulation and implementation of public policy. In its early days the society tended to be somewhat sympathetic to the liberal movement, headed by Itagaki Taisuke, for it, too, was opposed to the government. But by 1888, after the death of the society's first president and the collapse of the government's effort to obtain a satisfactory revision of the unequal treaties, the *Genyōsha* repudiated any connection with, or sympathy for, groups favoring internal reform. Thereafter it devoted its full attention to "guarding the nation's prestige," to insisting upon what it considered proper action in the face of slights and insults by foreign powers, to demanding that more attention be given to building up the army and navy, and to advocating that the government assume a more positive foreign policy—more specifically a foreign policy that would lead to the expansion of Japanese interests abroad.[21]

By about 1885 a quite powerful group within the Japanese government was favoring military action against China. Its attitude was undoubtedly due in part to the influence exerted by the *Genyōsha* and other nationalist societies, but it also was closely related to the success of the reform movement in Japan and to a situation on the continent which seemed to offer unusually promising opportunities for an extension of Japanese authority. The leader of the expansionist group in the government was General Kuroda, who was reported to be alarmed at China's naval expansion after her war with the French in Tongking. He and his group wished to make an attack on China before she became too strong. The leaders of the opposing group were Itō Hirobumi and Inouye Kaoru. They argued that Japan was not yet ready for foreign war, that the navy should be made stronger, and that modernization in various fields should be pushed much further. Also, they felt that China would soon lapse into inactivity and that the conservative Chinese officials would continue to resist reforms. Itō's group, backed by the Emperor, won the day, and the urge toward expansion on the continent was checked once more.[22]

After the upsurge of national feelings in 1887 there was greater sympathy, both inside and outside the government, for the efforts of the *Genyōsha*. Its own accounts and those of the *Kokuryūkai*, a later offshoot, give credit to the society for winning crucial support in high circles for a declaration of war on China in 1894.[23] It would be difficult to prove, or disprove, the validity of the claim; but the society undoubtedly did play a prominent role in arousing a more intense expansionist sentiment. The agitation for more positive action, in fact, had become so great by the summer of 1894 that the government was forced to suspend a number of journals. The trend, however, was not merely a product of nationalist-society activity. For one thing, the general reaction against westernization and the growing resentment against Western powers for refusing to yield on the question of treaty revision were operating to strengthen the urge to show the foreigners that "by the usual tests of power politics which prevailed in the West" Japan was entitled to a position of equality.[24]

Resentment against Western Nations

The growing urge to "show the West" was closely associated with a succession of failures to obtain a satisfactory revision of the unequal treaties, after the failure of 1887. In 1888 the popular liberal leader Ōkuma Shigenobu was invited back into the government as Foreign Minister, and of course his major task was to gain an acceptable revision of the treaties. Ōkuma was a brilliant man; he had some new tactics, and he made tangible gains. But when terms of a draft treaty with England were printed in the London *Times* in 1889, there was another upsurge of popular indignation. A former samurai was so infuriated that he tried to kill Ōkuma, and then committed suicide. Ōkuma was seriously injured by the bomb the samurai had thrown and, feeling that he had to yield to popular disapproval, resigned his government post. By that time the popular insistence on a treaty revision which comported with the national dignity of Japan made it extremely difficult for the government to obtain satisfactory results in its diplomatic negotiations. Toward the end of 1893, opposition groups in the Diet directed attention to the treaty-revision problem by demanding "strict enforcement" as the best means of forcing the Western powers to make the desired changes. They felt that by a strict enforcement of the terms of the treaties the foreigners would be driven to support treaty revision. Eventually, the government, embarrassed by this opposition, had to dissolve the Diet; and in the election of March, 1894, "strict enforcement" was the major issue. Mainly as a result of governmental interference in the election, the opposition groups lost some seats. But when the next session was opened in May, the opposition was even more determined and outspoken on the treaty issue. An address to the Throne complained that the government had neglected both reforms at home and national interests abroad.[25] The Diet was again dissolved, on June 2. Before the opposition could martial its forces again for an attack on the government, a treaty with England had been signed (on July 16) and the war with China had started (on July 23). The declaration of war at a time when the government was having so much difficulty with opposition demands for a stronger foreign policy has led some observers to conclude that war was decided upon in order to silence the political-party opposition, but the demands for a stronger policy were by no means limited to members of the Diet. Such sentiments were sweeping the country.[26]

As early as January, 1894, the *Nippon* had been suspended for its strong statements in behalf of a stronger foreign policy, and even the so-called "progressive" papers, such as the *Mainichi Shimbun*, were declaring: "Strict enforcement of the treaties is now demanded by the public opinion of the country. Apart from a small number of men intoxicated with Western ideas, and also men who observe nothing beyond their own selfish interests, nobody can see the treaty rights of the country trampled on without feeling deep indignation."[27] The *Nippon*, the *Niroku Shimpō*, and the *Chūō Shimbun* were all suspended in January for their support of "strict enforcement."[28] By the following summer the popular indignation against Western nations was more widespread and more deep-seated—a condition which caused the Japanese to be more responsive to the critical relations with China.

On June 7, 1894, the Chinese made a statement which made it clear that they still considered Korea a tributary vassal; and when it was learned that the Chinese had decided to send troops into Korea to help put down the Tong-hak rebellion, the Japanese nation as a whole—not merely the government—took a determined stand. The government took decisive steps; but in view of the prevailing atmosphere of the times, it is doubtful whether a less positive approach would have been acceptable to the nation. As Edwin Dun, the American minister to Japan, wrote on June 14, ". . . the restless and aggressive spirit of her [Japan's] people will not permit the government to draw back, even should it desire to do so. The nation is united to a man in its support of the government's Korean policy. . . . The Japanese government cannot draw back. They have committed themselves to a task that the nation insists shall be accomplished."[29] Two days later, Captain Francis Brinkley, who was then residing in Japan, wrote that it was apparent "that the restless energies of the people yearn for employment in a foreign war. The real difficulty that the Japanese cabinet has now to grapple with is not China's aggressive demands upon the peninsular Kingdom, but the control of the warlike spirit aroused among its own countrymen."[30] A few papers were advising against strong action, but even the "moderates" were now welcoming war. One of the moderate writers, Hoshi Tōru, declared that a war with a foreign country would be more delightful to him than his daily meals.[31] Thus, the demands had shifted. Instead of mere demands for a strong policy, there were now demands for war. And now the demands did not come from nationalist societies and chauvinistic writers only—even the moderate newspapers were taking up the cry. Clearly there was a ground swell of nationalist feeling which gave the government very little freedom for independent action.

The Sino-Japanese War

News of the actual outbreak of war was received enthusiastically throughout the nation. Partisan political-party activities in the Diet ceased, and when the next session was convened, each section of the lower house gave loyal support to the cabinet. The newspapers began to urge that the war be pressed until China was completely crushed, and before a month had elapsed several papers were talking about dictating the terms of the peace in Peking. Although Japan's leading English-language newspaper, the *Japan Mail*, was urging caution, warning against the wasting of Japan's resources, and suggesting that if Japan went too far the Western nations might intervene,[32] few Japanese nationals could look at the situation so calmly. The *Mainichi*, in one of its editorials, stated that Japan "is now determined to obtain for herself a commanding position in the East, and to raise her prestige among the various Powers of the West."[33]

After the Japanese military victory against Chinese forces at Ping-yang in September, 1894, popular enthusiasm for pressing the war into Manchuria and China increased. It was generally felt that peace offers or threats of intervention should be resisted with determination. There was more talk of annexing Chinese provinces and requiring the payment of large indemnities. Within a month after the Ping-yang victory, many of the leading papers agreed that Japan should receive a cession of territory, and groups within the Diet drew up a manifesto stating that "a righteous war can not admit of mediation, and it is therefore certainly the duty of Japan to humiliate her antagonist so far as to be able to dictate terms of peace under the walls of Peking."[34] The *Kokumin* declared that the cession of territory should be "a condition without which the present war should never be brought to a conclusion." The *Hōchi* went further, declaring that it lay "in the path of Japan's mission, as the peace-maintainer of the Orient, to bring China under the flag of the Rising Sun. . . ."[35]

The New Year of 1895 was a season for national self-congratulation. One of the more cautious newspapers, the *Mainichi Shimbun*, even boasted that "at no time have we [Japanese] ever had so much cause to rejoice, and so much reason to congratulate ourselves. Hitherto Europe was blind to Japan's true greatness and apt to slight her. . . . But this war has wrought a sudden change in Europe's attitude toward Japan. This New Year's Day is the beginning not only of a new year, but also of a new era of Japanese greatness."[36] There were those also who suggested that since Japan had proved the strength of her military, it was proper that every effort be made to prove her superiority in other fields, such as scholarship, literature, and education.[37]

Victory and Peace

After the start of peace negotiations, the feelings of national confidence became complicated by a concern that somehow "diplomacy, by a slight blunder, may undo all that the expeditionary forces had hitherto accomplished," and that there might be some "troublesome foreign intervention."[38] But the early attempts at negotiation failed, and few Japanese were disappointed. The armies continued to fight on, winning more victories which stirred the hearts of patriotic subjects; and with the capture of Weihaiwei in February, predictions were made that soon the flag of the Rising Sun would be flying above the walls of Peking.[39]

Toward the end of February, word was received that the Chinese were sending Li Hung Chang, one of their most prominent statesmen, to negotiate for peace. Although many Japanese were skeptical about the possibility of agreement, all felt that China's decision to send one of her great men was an indication that Japan's new status in world affairs had been recognized. Still, the fear prevailed that Western powers might step in to deprive Japan of the territories to which she felt entitled. The *Mainichi* reported receipt of a telegram to the effect that France, Russia, England, and the United States had agreed to prevent Japan from annexing any part of the Chinese continent. The report was labeled "a mere canard, invented by some Englishman for putting Japanese courage to the test";[40] but the fear could not be downed, and there was some indication that, as a result, the demands were being narrowed considerably and were being presented in more definitely moral terms. Writers were beginning to say that "no Japanese demand is proffered for the selfish aggrandizement of the Island Empire," and that the demands "point to the benefit of the whole East."[41]

The announcement on April 16 of the peace terms of the Treaty of Shimonoseki was welcomed with "undisguised joy." On that day and the following day, the government was forced to suspend more than half a dozen newspapers, probably to prevent strong expressions of dissatisfaction with the terms. But most papers considered the treaty a matter for "sincere congratulations,"[42] and at least one wealthy merchant expressed the opinion that it was only the hotheaded politicians who were dissatisfied and that all the people were greatly delighted.[43] Schools declared holidays, and throughout the land there was rejoicing. In part, it was due to a sense of relief that the fighting was over, but also there was a deep feeling of satisfaction that Japan had become a world power.

⋄   ⋄   ⋄

In reviewing the nature and extent of nationalist sentiment between the years 1887 and 1895, we find that group consciousness was for the first time something that could be properly identified as modern nationalism. In previous decades there had been nationalist thought and action, but it was limited principally to one section of the ruling class. The great mass of the people were still illiterate. They had little or no knowledge of national affairs, and their loyalties were, for the most part, local in character. Only by 1887 had sufficient social cohesion been created to permit a truly popular response to national danger. It is significant that the threat to Japan in 1887 was relatively slight when compared with the Western naval expeditions of the 1860's; but a popular press, a national army, a universal education system, and a strong central government, had created a far deeper sense of national unity, and the danger, slight as it was, was sufficient to arouse a tremendous upsurge of national resentment.

In addition, there was a new awareness that traditional values had been destroyed by the importation of Western learning. There was a reaction against Western ways and a reawakening of interest in Japanese patterns of thought and action. This reaction meant, of course, a more definite identification with the nation and a tendency to make sharper distinctions between that which was Japanese and that which was not Japanese.

Furthermore, the reform program of the previous decades, in addition to creating greater solidarity, had resulted in the building of a modern army that gave the Japanese a new sense of confidence. In the face of earlier dangers there had been a helpless feeling that resistance would prove to be disastrous; but now there was not only a greater insistence upon international justice (as the Japanese interpreted it), but a new dynamic urge to prove, by military action, that Japan was entitled to her "proper position" among the nations of the world.

These conditions were conducive to the rise of a more positive form of expansionism, to a more definite insistence upon a higher status in the society of nations, and to a more ready acceptance of any challenge that might be offered by neighboring nations. In a real sense, then, the Sino-Japanese War was a product of the force of modern nationalism in Japan, as well as a powerful stimulus for a further growth of the phenomenon.

7 JAPANISM

Russia, France, and Germany dispatched identical notes to Japan one week after the signing of the Treaty of Shimonoseki, advising her to return the Liaotung Peninsula to China. The presence of thirty Russian warships in Asiatic waters was a grim reminder that the intervening powers were ready to resort to the use of force, if necessary. Japan, therefore, decided to accede to their "advice"; but the decision was a humiliating step for a victorious nation to take. The popular reaction to the intervention was so great that the government was forced to suspend many of the leading newspapers. Enough of the views and feelings was revealed in other papers, however, to indicate that the entire country was enraged, not merely at the intervening powers but at the Japanese officials who dared yield to the humiliating demands.[1] Some emotional patriots protested by committing suicide, but more realistic persons turned to a consideration of ways to increase the nation's strength so that Japan would never again have to suffer insulting treatment by foreign powers.

If the Triple Intervention left doubts about Russian intentions, the doubts were soon dispelled by developments in Korea, where the Japanese had instituted an ambitious modernization program. Many Koreans had come to resent the demands made upon them by the Japanese, and after the Triple Intervention, certain elements in the Korean court began to look to Russia for support. Japan could not allow Korea, as well as Liaotung, to slip from her hands. The responsibility for dealing with Korea was therefore placed in the hands of a man of action, General Miura Gorō. For a time, Miura attempted to carry out his program by controlling the established regime in Korea; but by October, 1895, he apparently had become impatient with the lack of coöperation at the court and therefore connived at a plot in which the Korean queen, who had become quite friendly with the Russian minister to Korea, was murdered. Up to this time, the Japanese had enjoyed some backing within certain segments of the Korean ruling class, but the murder of the queen by Japanese agents aroused deep resentment. There was even some criticism in foreign capitals, and the Japanese government hastily recalled Miura and had him court-martialed. But the damage could not be repaired, and within a short time conditions at the court made it possible for the Korean king to "seek refuge" in the Russian legation. Thereafter the Russians exercised considerable control, through the king, over the affairs of the kingdom.

The part Russia had taken in the Triple Intervention was humiliating enough, but for Russia to seize control of the internal affairs of Korea—where military campaigns had been fought and won by Japan—was almost more than ardent Japanese nationalists could bear. One of the conservative newspapers insisted that troops be dispatched to Korea to protect Japanese lives and property, and to escort the king and crown prince back to their palace.[2] But the Japanese government leaders realized full well that Japan could not afford another war—for the time being at least—and they therefore attempted, by a series of diplomatic steps, to salvage as much of their influence in Korea as possible. In June, 1896, Japan and Russia signed the Yamagata-Lobanov Convention, which seemed to place the two countries on an equal footing in Korea; but it was not long before Russia was sending in military advisers and gaining lucrative concessions, such as the timber concession on the Yalu River and mining rights on the Tumen. It looked to the Japanese as though Russia were aiming at complete control of the peninsula, and that if she accomplished this she would be a truly formidable threat to the security of the Japanese nation.

The "Japanism" Movement

In such an atmosphere of national anxiety, and in a society that was now more closely tied together by economic growth, a higher literacy rate, and greater political centralization, it was only natural that the Japanese people should be more firmly united by these common concerns about their newly won position on the continent. A review of the opinions expressed in the press and in books and magazines shows the presence of a far more positive type of national consciousness. The Japanese intellectuals of that day readily recognized the difference in these feelings and adopted the new term "Japanism" (*Nihon Shugi*) to distinguish them from those that had prevailed in the years before the Sino-Japanese War. The term came into prominence in 1897 as a result of the writings of such leading nationalists as Takayama Rinjirō, Kimura Takatarō, and Inouye Tetsujirō. But even before 1897 there were intellectual activities which were a significant prelude to Japanism.

In November, 1894, there appeared a new journal, the *Kokugakuin Zasshi* (Magazine for the Institute of Japanese Studies), which remained for many years a very important outlet for nationalist writings.[3] Articles therein indicated that national feelings were already moving beyond a level that could be properly ascribed to the "Japanese National Essence" movement. Foreign ideals were not merely rejected, they were berated; and the Japanese people were urged to follow the Japanese way of life (*dō*).[4] Also, new organizations which suggested a more positive identification of the people with the nation were being formed by men in all walks of life. The Greater Japan Education Society (*Dai Nihon Kyōkai*), for example, was organized for the purpose of making the Imperial Rescript on Education something more than a formal statement of educational philosophy.[5] And the Japanese Religions Society (*Nihon Shūkyō Sha*) was set up by Christians who were attempting to integrate Christian principles into the intellectual and social patterns of Japan. Christians apparently realized that the new climate of opinion was such that Christianity, if it were to survive in Japan, had to be Japanized. But their efforts were still in behalf of Christian ideals; consequently not a few non-Christian intellectuals reiterated the thesis that there was only one Japanese religion (Shintoism) and that in Japan no other religion was needed.[6]

The man most responsible for the popularization of Japanism was Takayama Rinjirō. Like the members of the Greater Japan Education

Society, he laid great stress on Shintoism, but he favored a rejection of all religions imported from abroad and insisted that the Japanese, as a single nation-family, accept the "original national aspirations" and worship their national ancestors. This ideology he termed "Japanism." Concerning it he wrote: "Japanism is an expression of the aspirations and the ideals of the Japanese people (*Yamato minzoku*). It defines the Japanese philosophy of calm resignation (*anshin ritsumei*). It is the principle for the national fulfillment of morality."[7] The Greater Japan Education Society became extremely active in supporting the ideals of Japanism. An examination of the society's principles shows that the men associated with it were now moving beyond the fields of education and religion. In addition to advocating the worship of Imperial ancestors and working toward a development of national spirit, they urged that the people give more attention to creating greater national solidarity, to honoring the military, and even to bringing about world peace and promoting ideals of human fellowship. In June, 1897, Takayama Rinjirō and Kimura Takatarō wrote an article entitled "In Support of Japanism," which marked the beginning of an intense propaganda program designed to popularize the movement.[8] And the society's magazine, appropriately entitled *Nihon Shugi* (Japanism), was soon flooded with articles on such topics as "Philosophy and Japanism," "Deploring Public Opinion on Japanism," "The State and Religion," and "A Danger to National Morals."[9]

Expansionism Again

In November, 1897, the *Taiyō* carried an article on "Our National Polity and New Territory" which expressed expansionist sentiment of the type that colored Japanist thought after 1898. In this article, the theory that the one-family structure of Japanese society did not permit the inclusion of other peoples was rejected with the comment: "In regard to the problem of what to do about the rule of these new territories, it is nothing but a matter of power relationship. Having built a firm national polity (*kokutai*) of a single 'Emperor-people' household, there is nothing for us to do but use this power in dealing with these people while treating them with benevolence (*jinkei*)."[10] But the expansionist tinge to Japanism was not really prominent until after 1898, when other developments in the field of foreign relations not only made Japan more incensed at the Russians but also brought England to her support and gave her an opportunity to participate in the competition for rights and privileges in China.

The event that marks the beginning of this new trend was the Convention of March 27, 1898, by which Russia leased from China for twenty-five years the southern tip of the Liaotung Peninsula—the very peninsula which Russia, Germany, and France had forced Japan to give back to China less than three years before. The reaction of the Japanese was immediate and loud. Some newspapers, such as the *Hōchi Shimbun*, advocated war. It insisted that the situation was analogous to that which prevailed before the Sino-Japanese War:

Japan believed [in 1894] that the peace of the East could not be maintained unless the independence of Korea were secured, and she did not shrink from war to attain that end. Russia now occupies the place that China held in 1894, and the China of today is the Korea of that time. . . . Whatever reasons existed to fight China in 1894 exist with incomparably greater force to fight Russia today. There is no excuse, no palliation, for Russia's conduct in Manchuria. To look back upon the events connected with the retrocession of Liaotung and to contrast them with the events that are occurring now must make every Japanese thrill with indignation. If ever there was a time when the country should assert itself, now is the time.[11]

Even the Russians seemed to realize that this was stepping on Japanese toes a little too heavily, for soon afterward they began to show a more conciliatory attitude, indicating a willingness to give Japan a freer hand in Korea. In April, one month after the convention with China was signed, Russia agreed to the Nishi-Rosen Convention with Japan. By it, both countries recognized the sovereignty and independence of Korea; in addition Russia agreed not to impede the development of industrial and commercial enterprises sponsored by the Japanese. The Russians may have been trying to appease the Japanese, but they were now also more intent upon the exploitation and development of Manchuria. It is certain, however, that few Japanese nationalists were mollified by the convention.[12]

With the aggressive moves of Russia in Manchuria, Japan found herself working more closely with the British—a development which greatly enhanced Japan's position in the international rivalries of the Far East and gave Japanese nationalists far greater confidence about the future destiny of their country. When, in April, 1898, England joined with Japan in a display of naval force in order to prevent Russian control of Korean finances, it was beginning to be clear that in opposing Russian advances Japan was to have a powerful and influential ally. It was undoubtedly this new relationship with England that enabled Japan to extract a promise from China that she would not alienate land in Fukien province "to any other power." In the face of the impending break-up of China, and with the new confidence that was aroused by new indications of British support, an increasing number of ardent nationalists became certain that Japan was destined to play an important role in the future of Asia.

In November, 1898, the East Asia Common Culture Society (*Tōa Dōbun Kai*) was founded. The society's purpose was to sponsor study and research of conditions in Korea and China, with a view to bringing about reforms in those countries and to reviving interest in Japan's proper role in Asia. Influential businessmen, politicians, and nationalists participated in the activities of the society. Branch offices were set up in several places in China, and the society accumulated a great mass of information that was designed to aid the Japanese government in assuming a more positive role on the continent. The society felt that it was its mission to save China from the predatory Western powers, but it hoped also that a more profitable trade relationship between Japan and other Oriental nations could be developed. Members of the East Asia Common Culture Society gave much of their attention to arousing patriotic sentiments among the Chinese, feeling that this was necessary if their program of reform was to succeed. The society soon became associated with a number of groups with similar interests, and it broadened the scope of its activities to include research in almost every field of Chinese commercial and industrial activity. It gave particular thought to the study of railroad needs, mineral resources, investment possibilities, and new industrial enterprises.[13]

The depth and breadth of the Japanese interest in "East Asianism" was such that Ōkuma, who was Premier between June and November, 1898, made declarations and adopted policies which were closely akin to the sentiments and aims of the East Asia Common Culture Society. The "Ōkuma doctrine," which was popularized in 1898, was based on the conviction that since Japan was the first Oriental nation to profit from modernization along Western lines, it was her duty to protect China from Western aggression and to aid her in adopting political, social, and economic reforms. It was Ōkuma's belief that a national hero would soon arise in China to awaken the country from slumber, to arouse feelings of patriotism, and to lead China to a place of importance among the world powers. Ōkuma further declared that since

Japan had received so many rich cultural and spiritual gifts from China in past centuries it was only right that Japan should show her appreciation by helping China in these trying times.[14]

Liberation from Extraterritoriality

The summer of 1899 was also a memorable time in the history of Japanese nationalism, for it was then that Japan freed herself from the shackles of extraterritoriality that had been forced on her by Western powers in 1854. It will be recalled that Japan's diplomats had long been concentrating their efforts upon the revision of the unequal treaties, and now that they had succeeded, there were widespread feelings of relief—feelings, however, which were also mixed with a resentment against the powers for waiting so many years to comply with Japan's "just" claims.

Less than one month after the extraterritoriality privileges had been eliminated (on August 3, 1899) the Japanese Department of Education issued its famous "Order No. 12," which prohibited all religious practices in the schools. It was clearly a move against Christianity (since Shinto was legally not a religion and therefore would not be proscribed by the order), and was a logical product of the growing anti-Christian sentiment which was associated with, and greatly stimulated by, the Japanist movement. While the unequal treaties were still in effect, it had been deemed inadvisable for the government to take any steps that might be interpreted as being contrary to the principle of religious freedom. But the removal of the extraterritorial privileges, together with the confidence that arose from the new relationship with England, allowed the government greater freedom of action in the religious and moral field.[15]

Shortly before the "Order No. 12" was issued, Kimura Takatarō had further agitated the religious question by the publication of a book entitled Yaso-kyō Kōnin Kahi Ron (Against the Official Recognition of Christianity). Kimura's answer was that on moral, educational, philosophical, and political grounds Christianity should not be recognized. More specifically he wrote:

In Japan loyalty and filial piety are the focal points of morality. But in Christianity the focus is on God and Jesus, and loyalty and filial piety are denied. . . . Those who slight loyalty and filial piety are unlearned people who have not read the classics and who do not know the beauty of our national family system. They have been swept into the current of individual selfishness. Christianity has rejected the teachings of filial piety, because such teachings are inconsistent with Christian doctrine.[16]

Kimura's views were soon answered by Christian supporters with charges that Japanism was narrow-minded and nonhumanitarian. Consequently, by the summer of 1899, when "Order No. 12" was issued, considerable heat had been generated, and there was strong support for the proposal that concrete steps be taken to check the influence of Christianity.[17] Inouye Tetsujirō, Dean of the College of Literature of the Tokyo Imperial University and the leading exponent of anti-Christian views, was then encouraged to make his most positive declarations about the danger of Christianity to the Japanese nationality. He stated, in December, 1899, that Christianity was inconsistent with the Japanese family system, which was the foundation of the Japanese state; that Christian individualism tended to destroy loyalty and filial piety and thus to imperil the state; and finally, that Christianity was not in accord with *kokutai*.[18]

Anti-Russianism

But it was the growing anti-Russian sentiment, not anti-Christian sentiments, that became the most prominent characteristic of nationalism at the turn of the twentieth century. The feelings and sentiments that were manifested in the program of the East Asia Common Culture Society became more intense and widespread after 1900 as a result of the Boxer rebellion of that year. But with this Chinese revolt, both the Japanese and the British became more suspicious of Russian intentions in the Far East. Russia, in moving her troops into Manchuria and showing a disinclination to withdraw them even after the rebellion had been put down, aroused the enmity of a great number of Japanese nationalists. Furthermore, since the Chinese nationalists, with Japanese assistance, had failed to seize power in 1900, the supporters of the East Asia Common Culture Society and similar organizations became discouraged about the possibility of the rise of a strong China. Consequently, the more expansionist-minded nationalists in Japan began to turn their attention from China toward Russia. Even the members of the East Asia Common Culture Society seemed now to be more interested in opposing Russia than in implementing the society's announced policy of pressing for Chinese reforms under Japanese guidance. Also, new secret societies were organized in September, 1900, when it looked as though the Japanese government was inclined to accept a Russian proposal that Russian and Japanese spheres be delineated at the Tae-dong River. A powerful group of men organized the People's League (*Koku-*

min Dōmei Kai) in order to pool their efforts in working toward the expulsion of the Russians from Manchuria. The league's preliminary statement declared that Japan had to wake up to her responsibility of preserving the peace of East Asia.[19]

The most active and significant of the societies organized at this time, however, was the *Kokuryūkai,* which is commonly known in Western writings as the Black Dragon Society (the term that will be used here) but which would be more accurately translated as the Amur River Society. It was established in January, 1901, and, as the name implies, its purpose was to extend Japan's sphere of influence as far north in Manchuria as the Amur River. The society was primarily concerned with driving Russia from eastern Asia and then welding Manchuria, Mongolia, and Siberia into a solid base for Japanese control of the continent. It published a journal called *Kokuryūkai Kaihō* (Journal of the Black Dragon Society), the second issue of which contained a seventy-page thesis on the subject of "An Estimate of the Power of Russia and Japan to Determine the Advantages and Disadvantages of War and Peace." The article was considered by the government to be inflammatory and to be a deterrent to peaceful relations with foreign nations. The issue was therefore banned. Nevertheless the article had great influence, both on officials and the public at large. According to the official history of the society, the journal thereafter became the guiding star of all persons interested in Russian affairs.[20] But the platform of the Black Dragon Society was written in broader terms:

We shall renovate the present system, foster a foreign policy aiming at expansion overseas, revolutionize domestic politics to increase the happiness of the people, and establish a social policy that will settle problems between labor and capital thus strengthening the foundation of the empire. We shall uphold the spirit of the Imperial Rescript to soldiers, promote a military spirit, and realize the fruits of the universal conscription system—thus perfecting the organs for national defense. We shall bring about a fundamental change in present-day education, which is copied after European and American systems, and build the foundations for a national education based on *kokutai*—thus fostering the virtue and wisdom of the Yamato race.[21]

As it became more obvious, in 1901, that the Russians had no intention of withdrawing from Manchuria, the activities of the Black Dragon Society and similar organizations became more energetic and were received more enthusiastically by the Japanese public. Then, when the signing of the Anglo-Japanese Treaty was announced in February, 1902, the people as a whole showed a new confidence in their ability, with the support of their new ally, to press forward with their demands upon Russia. The treaty recognized Japan's special interest in China as well as her special political, commercial, and industrial position in Korea. It therefore gave to Japan not only the backing of a great Western power but served to lay the foundations for future programs of expansion on the continent of Asia. The enthusiasm for the treaty was so great that some writers felt impelled to warn the public against raising its hopes and expectations too high.[22] Nevertheless, it is clear that the government, as well as the public, was encouraged to take a more positive stand in efforts to protect and to expand Japanese interests abroad.

Up to the time of the Anglo-Japanese Alliance, the Black Dragon Society, in its Russian program, had centered attention on the weakness of Russia and on the ability of Japan to resist Russian aggression. But with the encouragement and confidence which the Anglo-Japanese Alliance gave, the society, in addition to trying to make the people warminded, now turned its attention to espionage for the army and to activities that anticipated Russian defeat and Japanese acquisition of new territories. In this latter connection the society was responsible for the organization of the Japanese-Russian Society (*Nichiro Kyōkai*). The need for such an organization arose from the conviction that in the impending war Japan would win and might well gain possession of Russian territory east of Lake Baikal. Plans therefore had to be formulated and preparations had to be made in order that Japan might maintain a firm grip on the area and avoid interference from the United States and other countries. Furthermore, it was felt that in preparation for the revolution in Russia, which had been predicted, plans should be laid for closer relations with Russian people in order to "help" them and thereby preserve the peace of the Far East. Prince Itō, who had failed to effect a closer tie between Russia and Japan before 1902, was invited by Uchida Ryōhei, the president of the Black Dragon Society, to join the Japanese-Russian Society. In his plea Uchida admitted that up to this time he and Itō had been following different paths—Itō had been working for peace and Uchida for war—but he felt that the aims of both men could be furthered by participation in this society. He hoped therefore that Itō would join it, and finally Itō did.[23]

In the months following the Anglo-Japanese Alliance there was far more than the positive moves of the Black Dragon Society to indicate a stronger national sentiment. When it became increasingly clear that the Russians intended to retain their dominant military and political position in Manchuria, the press became more outspoken in its insistence upon a showdown. The stronger attitude was particularly apparent after the spring of 1903, when the Japanese government succeeded in obtaining a loan from the Rothschilds in London, to cover war costs,[24] and when the Russians failed to keep their promise to carry out the second phase of their withdrawal of troops from Manchuria. It was soon afterward, in August, 1903, that the Anti-Russian Comrades Society (*Tairo Dōshi Kai*) was born. The group immediately made known its intentions by passing this resolution: "It is the mission of the Empire to make Russia carry out the terms of the treaty by which she promised to withdraw her troops [from Manchuria], to see that Manchuria is liberated for China and thus to preserve for all times the peace of East Asia. We hope that our government, if it is not hopelessly negligent, will carry out this [mission] immediately."[25] At a meeting two months later, the society took a more advanced position, as is shown by another resolution: "We recognize, after studying the present situation, that this is the opportunity for immediately taking final steps. There is absolutely no excuse for the slightest hesitation by the authorities."[26] Toward the end of 1903 there was a general insistence upon war. The nationalist journal, *Nippon*, of course complained that the government was delaying a decisive blow.[27] But even the more circumspect *Asahi* reminded the Japanese that they must prepare themselves to give not only their treasures but their lives in this coming struggle.[28] At a banquet in Tokyo on January 15, 1904, Sonoda Kokichi, president of a huge Tokyo bank, made a speech in which he said: "I see no reason why we should not be able to bear a much heavier burden [in this coming war] than we did [in the Sino-Japanese War]. Besides, gentlemen, the temper of the nation has reached its highest pitch, and when a patriotic people are strongly united in one common cause as we are at the present moment, I am sure everyone is prepared to sacrifice even his last penny. We fear not therefore war expenses. We fear not the result of the struggle."[29] By the end of that same month the editor of a Tokyo English newspaper observed a widespread "sentiment of wrath and of an impatient resolve not to be played with any more." The same writer added: "The Japanese people may be said to have set their teeth for a fight. They are wholly and completely weary of shuffling, and it evidently appears to them that of all humanly acts nothing can be more unmanly than to stand vacillating in the presence of an enemy while he gets ready to fight."[30] One Japanese Christian writer declared that, if necessary, he would give up his membership in the church for the national cause.[31]

The Russo-Japanese War

The announcement of war on February 10, 1904, was received with great popular enthusiasm. There was a sharp increase in the number of volunteers for military service, and, as one observer said, the whole literary world had gone crazy. A large number of new magazines appeared, and newspaper circulation mounted.[32] Within the Diet the political parties dropped their opposition tactics and gave full support to the government. The patriotism shown by all was readily recognized not only by Japanese observers but by foreign residents. One of the foreigners, Henry Dyer, wrote a book in 1904 in which he said: "If I were attempting to sum up briefly the qualities of the Japanese which have enabled them to make such wonderful developments in such a short time, I would mention as the important factor the intense loyalty of the people which compels them to make any sacrifice—even life itself—when they consider it necessary for the honour of their country."[33] It is with considerable justification, then, that observers have termed the Russo-Japanese war a "popular war."

As reports began to pour in about the excellent discipline and bravery displayed by the Japanese soldiers, and as the reports gained wide circulation in the press, the unique qualities of *Bushidō* again became an object of discussion in academic, literary, and journalistic circles. In the October issue of *Taiyō* (The Sun) there were two articles which claimed that Japan's remarkable success against the Russians was due primarily to *Bushidō*. Because of this military moral code, one journalist said, Japan has been able "to turn out such fine specimens of fighting humanity as are now upholding the honour of the national flag in Manchuria," a fact that "is worthy of the attention of the whole civilized world."[34] A number of writers soon turned to a treatment of *Bushidō*, and even Christians and foreigners began to express enthusiasm for the ideals of that ancient military "code." In October, 1904, the London *Times* carried an article that praised the patriotic fervor shown by the Japanese nation:

Of all the remarkable circumstances of this Far Eastern war, the fact that dominates everything else is the courage and conduct of the Mikado's armies. *We recognize almost grudgingly and in spite of ourselves,* the existence of a moral force that appears able to govern and sway the whole conduct of a whole people, inspiring not a caste but a nation from highest to lowest, to deeds that are worthy to rank with the most famous of history or of legend. We want to know what this force is, whence it comes, and what it means; the sense of its existence makes us jealous, uncomfortable, almost annoyed.[35]

But the pitch of national fervor rose much higher in 1905, for that was the year of great military and naval victories against a Western power—victories which were truly heady wine for a nation that had developed a gnawing sense of inferiority and that had long complained of unequal and unjust treatment at the hands of the Western nations. The first great victory was the capture of Port Arthur in January. Throughout the country, formal celebrations were held, and the Emperor himself addressed a message of appreciation to General Nogi and Admiral Tōgō. Although there was still some anxiety about the final outcome of the war, there was already evidence of greater confidence about Japan's position in world affairs. Viscount Watanabe wrote an article, in the January issue of *Taiyō* entitled "The Point of Contact between the Oriental and Occidental Civilizations." It carried the thought that, as a result of her victories, Japan was in a position to make a unique contribution to civilization. In fact, the author felt that the Japanese were beginning to realize that they occupied a place of leadership in the "Moral World" and that Japan was going to be "the medium for uniting Eastern and Western ideals."[36] There was more talk of the bravery of Japanese soldiers and more discussion of the peculiar qualities of *Bushidō*. One Christian magazine carried an article which, after outlining the new features of *Bushidō*, presented the view that Christianity not only approved of *Bushidō* principles but embodied them in its teachings.

The expansive feelings of national pride and confidence that were aroused by the decisive military victory at Port Arthur were further compounded by a most impressive defeat of the Russian Baltic fleet in May, 1905. The victory in Tsushima Strait was followed by outbursts of joy which suggested to Westerners that from here on there would be no holding Japan back. Even before the battle of Tsushima, Ōkuma had written an article in *Taiyō* in which he laid great stress on the importance to Japan of following up the victories with the economic exploitation of Korea and Manchuria.[37] But after the historic battle, more grandiose plans were laid. The *Yomiuri Shimbun* had the temerity to state that, as one condition of peace, Russia should surrender to

Japan the whole Siberian coast.[38] One journalist, Ōishi Masami, in an article entitled "Taking of St. Petersburg," contended that Japan could march an army right into the Russian capital and there make terms directly with the Tsar himself. He added, however, that probably a more reasonable objective, since it would not cost so much money, would be the seizure of all Russian territory east of Lake Baikal. At the very least, he argued, Japan should certainly keep the Liaotung Peninsula and hand Manchuria back to China.[39] Such views were by no means limited to journalists. Seven university professors made a joint declaration, demanding vast new territories. They insisted that Japan's terms for peace should include (1) an indemnity of 300,000,000 yen, (2) the cession of Saghalin, Kamchatka, territories along the coast of the Sea of Okhotsk, and the Liaotung Peninsula, (3) the handing over of all Russian rights and possessions in Manchuria, and (4) certain definite limitations on Russian power in the Far East. One of the seven professors, Dr. Tomizu, declared that Japan would no longer be satisfied with the situation that prevailed before the war. "She is impelled," he said, "by an imperialistic spirit and feels the necessity of enlarging her borders . . . We are destined to expand and govern other nations."[40]

Social Solidarity

The tenseness in Japan's relations with the outside world, which culminated in the remarkable military and naval victories against Russia, was undoubtedly a powerful factor—and probably the most immediate factor—in the rise of a more intense form of nationalism. But it must not be forgotten that there were also strong social forces at work within the nation which were basic to the movement. As pointed out earlier, by the 1890's the broad-based reform program of the post-Meiji period had greatly strengthened the foundations for the development of great political centralization, economic growth, and ideological unity. But it was between the Sino-Japanese War and the Russo-Japanese War that this social integration reached truly modern proportions.

The economic growth after the Sino-Japanese War was such as to warrant the use of the term "industrial revolution." In 1895 the export trade of Japan amounted to approximately 137,000,000 yen;[41] but in 1904 it was more than 341,000,000 yen. In 1890, Japan had about 143,000 tons of merchant shipping; but in 1903, the figure had reached about 657,000 tons.[42] In the production of iron and steel, in the mining of coal, in the generation of electricity, in the manufacture of textiles, and in many other fields there were equally startling increases. With this tremendous spurt in productive capacity the country was not only able to support a much larger population—which had grown from 35,000,000 in 1873 to 45,000,000 in 1903—but could afford a more intricate governmental structure and a much larger military organization. Truly remarkable material progress had been made.[43]

In politics, too, a greater degree of social solidarity had been achieved as a result of the successful efforts of the ruling class to extend and strengthen its control over a wide range of social activities. Before the Sino-Japanese War there were strong political movements that were centered on demands for the establishment of a government that would be responsible to the elected representatives of the people. By 1881 this "liberal" movement had become strong enough to force the government to promise a constitution which would provide an elective assembly. But immediately thereafter the ruling oligarchy adopted a series of measures which led to the erection of a political structure that was patterned after representative Western institutions and yet did not materially broaden the base of political power.[44] From the time the Constitution was promulgated in 1889 until the outbreak of war in 1894, the "liberals" put up an energetic and determined fight for reforms which would make the cabinet responsible to the new Diet; but the outbreak of war in 1894 forced them to drop these demands in favor of a policy of coöperation with the government. After the war, the same liberal parties revived, for a time, their old demands for a responsible cabinet; but they found that the war had seriously undermined their support and had greatly strengthened the hand of the ruling oligarchy. The war accelerated the process of integrating the old samurai class into the new centralized structure; and the rural gentry, too, were now convinced that they could gain more from a close liaison with the Meiji leaders than from an association with the liberals. But the prestige of the oligarchy was greatly enhanced by the credit it received for leading the country through a successful war. The new modern army had now become a powerful political force which served to raise General Yamagata to new heights of political influence. For a short time after the Triple Intervention, the government was somewhat unpopular because it had yielded to the demands of the Western powers; but as relations with Russia became more strained, the popular resentment was directed more toward foreign enemies than toward leaders of the government. By the end of the century the old liberal movement was all but extinct. The major political rivalry thereafter was between two members of the oligarchy itself: one under General Yamagata and the other under Itō Hirobumi, the author of the Constitution. In an effort to counter the growing influence of Yamagata, Itō became the leader of a political party, the *Seiyūkai*. But he was not a strong supporter of the principles of representative government, and since he used the party primarily to strengthen his own political position, his association with elected representatives of the people did not serve to weaken oligarchical control. After the signing of the Anglo-Japanese Treaty in 1902, there was little effective opposition to Army dominance in politics, and until the very end of the Russo-Japanese War a general served as Premier. There was no longer any strong demand for a revision of the political structure, and the Diet was giving full support to the program and policies favored by the elite group of "advisers" to the Emperor. This unity in political procedures operated to add further strength and momentum to the growth of national solidarity.

Economic growth and political centralization were also closely associated with an accelerated development of ideological unity. The educational system came to include almost all the youth in the land; newspaper circulation rose to greater heights; and other media for the printed word served to direct the thoughts and feelings of the Japanese into a common mold. It seems safe to conclude, then, that the expressions of national consciousness, between 1895 and 1905, not only were indicative of a more definite identification with the nation but represented the thoughts of a far larger segment of the Japanese nation. It was no mere accident that Western books on Japan of that day seldom refrained from commenting on the breadth and depth of Japanese patriotism.

◇   ◇   ◇

The first phase (1887 to 1895) in the rise of modern nationalism in Japan was associated with a victorious war against China, an Oriental neighbor; but this second phase (1895 to 1905) was contemporaneous with a period of opposition to Russia, a Western power. The two conflicts were on an entirely different level: China had been merely attempting to preserve her traditional position in one of her old tributary states, but Russia was attempting to push her expansion program farther afield and into areas that seemed to endanger Japan's continental interests. But of even greater significance was the fact that Russia was a European nation. China, like Japan, had been subjected to Western pressure; and quite early in the nineteenth century there were stirrings of Pan-Asianism which caused many Chinese and Japanese to feel that their nations must work together in the face of these common enemies. The Pan-Asian sentiment in Japan, therefore, was an element in the intellectual atmosphere which made the people ever more responsive, intellectually and emotionally, to the conflict with Russia. Here Japan was fighting against one of the Western nations that had imposed their wills upon Asian countries, subjecting them to unequal treaty settlements and seizing territories and "spheres of influence" where special commercial privileges were demanded. In fighting the Russians, then, the Japanese felt that they were not merely expanding in the face of opposition from a strong nation, but that they were striking a blow against injustices inflicted upon Asian peoples.

The war against Russia marked a new level of nationalist development also because it gave Japan an opportunity to prove her claim to, and to satisfy her urge for, a position of equality with Western nations by a matching of strength with one of the Western powers. Victory against an Oriental neighbor had not been sufficient to gain the recognition to which Japanese nationalists felt entitled. But victory against the Russians was another matter. People throughout the world, Asians and Europeans, now recognized Japan's military strength and were ready to assign her a prominent position among the world's great powers.

Although this more mature stage of national development in Japan was a product of the interdependent operation of many forces and conditions, it is clear that the dominant factor was the tension in Japan's relations with Russia. Since Russia had been identified, in Japanese minds, with the Western world—comparisons with which had given the Japanese a feeling of inferiority—the Russian challenge met with a response that was far from calm. A review of the nationalist sentiment in the prewar years shows signs of fear and hate. In this intellectual and emotional climate the effect of victory logically was greater, and yet the victory tended to remove the old feelings of inferiority and to mark the beginning of a period of nationalism characterized by confidence rather than fear.

8 NATIONAL CONFIDENCE

The victory against Russia marked the beginning of a period in which Japanese nationalism took on a "confident" rather than a "fearful" character. In addition to the sense of national pride aroused in the Japanese by a decisive victory against a Western power, there was great satisfaction because Japan was now considered a world power and also the most progressive nation in Asia. In the years between the Russo-Japanese War and World War I, Japan felt no fear of aggressive acts by foreign powers, and she experienced one of the most remarkable periods of economic growth in her history.

Nationalist action and thought, therefore, were of a different order. In the place of the old determination to serve the country in an all-out effort to defeat a foreign enemy, and to gain recognition for Japan's "proper position" in the world, there were calmer efforts to expand Japanese interests on the continent by peaceful means. And instead of emotional declamations in behalf of Japanism and against Western ideologies, there was a strong interest in various Western intellectual movements. Many of the old Japanist subjects were discussed, in terms of the same national symbols; but there was not the same frantic searching for sources of nationalist strength. After the Russo-Japanese War, Japanese discussed *kokutai* and *Bushidō* as means of rationalizing Japan's greatness.

During World War I the sense of national confidence was strengthened further by unusual opportunities for the expansion of interests on the continent of Asia. Among many groups there was a tremendous enthusiasm for empire building, and the government was under constant pressure to be more energetic in taking advantage of new opportunities. When Japan emerged victorious from World War I—as an ally of France, England, and the United States—nationalism reached its most confident level. In many circles, nationalist loyalties were overshadowed by internationalist interests.

Victory and Peace

After months of absorption in military and naval victories and in fantastic press comments about what Japan should demand from Russia at the conclusion of the war, the public was not prepared for the reports that their representatives at Portsmouth were yielding to Russian demands and were showing a "compromising" attitude. There was an upsurge of disgust at the spineless behavior of Japanese leaders. Throughout the country, meetings were held, organizations were formed, petitions were signed, and demands were made—all in an attempt to convince the government that a continuation of war was preferable to "concessions that would embolden Russia and encourage a spirit of aggression." Ambassador Komura, the head of the Japanese mission at the Portsmouth Peace Conference, was accused of having lost his nerve, and other responsible leaders were subjected to similar charges.[1]

News of the peace terms was received with even greater indignation, particularly since no indemnity was to be paid.[2] A few newspapers felt that the aims of the war had been achieved, but most were very critical of the government and its envoys for a "craven and discreditable surrender" to Russian demands. Some went so far as to insist that ratification ought to be refused, and at least three papers hinted that the members of the cabinet ought to be assassinated. Finally, the government decided to suppress the more outspoken newspapers; but public resentment continued to mount, and on September 5, four days after the news was first released, a mass meeting was called in Tokyo. When people arrived at the designated place, they found that the meeting had been banned by the police. A riot ensued and the crowd headed for the residence of the Home Minister, whom it blamed for the issuance of the ban, with the intention of burning him out. But facing too much police resistance there, it moved on, destroying police boxes and gathering more supporters. In the following two days the situation became worse, and finally martial law was declared. Eventually, however, order was restored, and the public became somewhat resigned to the treaty settlement when Prince Yamagata, the leading Elder Statesman of the day, made a statement to the effect that "peace was made because in the unanimous opinion of the Genro and Cabinet Ministers such a step was wisest, having regard to the Empire's financial resources, to the sequence of its expansion, to the difficulty of striking a decisive blow at Russia in East Asia, and to the opinion of the world."[3] Within the following month the Emperor ratified the treaty, stating that it was in full accord with his wishes. But feeling was still running so high that when Komura returned to Japan two days after the ratification, government officials arranged for him to land at a secret place. For two months, according to a foreign resident in Japan at the time, there was no more unpopular man in all Japan. The attitude of one writer was expressed as follows:

When on land and on the sea Japan won victory after victory, the nation reached a state of jubilance which had never before been experienced in the same degree. Self-confidence that was quite new was the natural mental product of the unparalleled success. Then we began to say to ourselves, "If we have shown ourselves capable of doing such great things in war, there can be no task in time of peace that is too difficult for us." Our young men saw visions and our old men dreamed dreams concerning the nation's future greatness. One of the new conditions of peace, we thought, would be the payment to us of a huge indemnity that would enable us to occupy an unrivalled financial position in the Far East. In international politics as far as this quarter of the world is concerned we were to take the lead. In civilisation, instead of continuing to borrow from the West, we were to figure as the pioneers of the new type of civilisation we Japanese have evolved, a type which has blended the best elements of the Oriental and Occidental systems. The yellow peril indeed! We felt that we had it in us to show that we could prove a yellow blessing to the world. Prior to the Portsmouth peace as a nation we were up in the seventh heaven of delight. When the terms of peace were made known our spirits dropped to zero. The feeling throughout the country was one and the same. We felt that we went to the Portsmouth Conference as conquerors, that we stated our terms as conquerors, but that when pressure was brought to bear on us we gradually receded from the position we had taken up and accepted the most unfavorable terms. There is no doubt an explanation or there may be several explanations of how this came about. But unfortunately these explanations do not help much to remove existing national dissatisfaction . . . And there are not a few who are beginning to say that the war was a foolish affair and that if patriotism commands only such mean notice as it has received it had better not be encouraged.[4]

The Portsmouth Treaty was really disappointing, but it was realized that Japan had emerged from the war as the dominant power of the Far East. Her navy had won an overwhelming victory in what has been considered one of the greatest naval engagements in history; and although her armies made no such spectacular showing, the fighting spirit of the soldiers was praised in the capitals of Europe and America. The repercussions of these military achievements were felt around the world. The American public, fearing that the Philippines might be in danger, became anxious about what Japan might do next. And England was sufficiently impressed to agree to a revision of the Anglo-Japanese Alliance that would recognize Japan's new position in Asia. But probably the greatest impact was upon Asian peoples, who were stirred by Japan's defeat of a Western power. Those who had been subjected to Western political domination were encouraged to seek independence. Japan was not only respected everywhere for her military strength but was placed in the enviable position of having no neighbors with sufficient power to threaten her or prevent her from strengthening the newly won position. For a nation that had been so helpless in the face of Western advances only forty years earlier, Japan had really accomplished a remarkable feat.

The government soon initiated diplomatic negotiations with the powers in order to gain recognition for the new position, since it was well understood that other powers might singly, or in combination, prevent Japan from making the most of her military victory. Even before the conclusion of the war, the Foreign Office had begun work on the construction of a pattern of foreign treaties and agreements that provided strong international sanction for concessions on the continent. First, a number of agreements with Korea were signed, which made the peninsula a "modified form of protectorate." Then came the treaty with Britain, signed on August 12, 1905, by which that country specifically agreed that Japan possessed "paramount political, military and economic interests" in Korea and that Japan had the right "to take such measures of guidance, control, and protection in Corea as she may deem proper and necessary to safeguard and advance those interests . . ."[5]

While these negotiations were being carried on, Japan was also ex-changing the notes that resulted in the Taft-Katsura understanding. William Howard Taft expressed the opinion, to which he believed President Roosevelt would concur, that "the establishment by Japanese troops of a suzerainty over Korea to the extent of requiring that Korea enter into no foreign treaties without the consent of Japan was the logical result of the present [Russo-Japanese] war and would directly contribute to permanent peace in the East."[6] Finally, in December, 1905, Japan signed a treaty with China which gained Chinese acqui-escence in the terms of the Portsmouth Treaty.[7] With this approval from the nations that might have challenged her, Japan was freer to move forward with a more positive continental program.

The strength of Japan's political and military position was no more remarkable than the industrial, commercial, and financial advances made during and following the Russo-Japanese War. This spurt of economic growth has led scholars to assign the period a special position in the economic history of Japan. In the field of steel and iron produc-tion, the output of Japan before the war amounted to about 55,000 tons a year; but by the beginning of World War I the figure had been almost quadrupled. There were also tremendous increases in textile production. In the cotton-weaving industry, for example, twice as much cotton cloth was produced in 1914 as in 1903.[8] In foreign trade, both imports and exports were nearly doubled in the same period. A number of new financial magnates emerged; the value of stocks rose to unprece-dented heights; and business people throughout the land became able to afford gawdy displays of wealth. Even the women, it is reported, became absorbed in such expensive pastimes as gambling and horse racing, and the young people were tempted to break loose from tradi-tional restraints and to accept what was termed "principles of selfish-ness." By 1908, government leaders deemed it necessary for the Emperor to issue an Imperial rescript warning the people against the "evils of the time."

Kokutai and National Morals

With the prevalence of these feelings of national confidence, national security, and national well-being, the Japanese people assumed a quite different attitude toward other countries and toward themselves. The old fear and resentment against Western nations was gone, and the feeling of inferiority was less noticeable. There was no longer the same violent, emotional drive to fight for a national cause, regardless of cost or sacrifice, but rather a strong feeling of confidence that permitted a more detached interest in the life and thought of foreign peoples. The interest in foreign ideas was not merely based on utilitarian considerations, as that of the 1870's had been, but was sufficiently broad to encompass intellectual, philosophical, and artistic movements that had no direct bearing on the welfare of the Japanese nation. Some of the intellectuals who had previously gained fame as exponents of Japanism even turned to a study of naturalism, a movement which had gained popularity in artistic as well as in philosophical and literary circles. Iwano Hōmei, who had previously supported Japanism, wrote a book in 1906 which rejected all ancient morals and old religions and advocated what he called monistic representation (*ichigen byōsha*).[9] A writer in 1908 said that the naturalist school was dominant among the novelists of the day, and explained the emphasis in these terms: "No question arises as to whether it is a manifestation that is common or whether it is eternal, or beautiful, or ugly. The main problem is whether or not it is as is."[10]

But an even clearer indication of the effect of national confidence upon the climate of opinion in Japan in the postwar years was the popularity of socialism, a movement that carried internationalist overtones. The socialist movement had emerged in Japan long before the war, and by 1903 a socialist newspaper (the *Heimin Shimbun*), which supported pacifist principles, was being published. In the early part of the war, the socialists continued to display remarkable energy in behalf of pacifism, but finally their newspaper was suppressed. The movement also suffered from the upsurge of aggressive nationalist sentiments. But after the war, in an atmosphere characterized by economic prosperity and national confidence, there was a new interest in socialist thought. In the closing months of 1905 two different socialist organs were launched: the *Shin Kigen* and the *Hikari*. Abe Isō and Katayama Sen became particularly active in writing socialistic articles and books, and in 1906 the Japanese Socialist party (the *Nihon Shakai Tō*) was organized. Unfortunately for the movement, however, an anarchist plot was discovered by the authorities in 1907; and since the leader, Kōtoku Denjirō, had been in communication with socialists, repressive measures were adopted which seriously retarded the growth of socialism in Japan.[11]

The popularity of internationalist movements did not mean, however, that nationalist thought was no longer present. The pre-1905 flow of books and articles on Japanism, the continuous reference in newspapers to events and developments that were considered to have a direct bearing on the future of the nation, and the constant emphasis in education upon the proper training of students for loyal service to the nation—all had made a deep imprint upon the minds of the Japanese people. And although the conditions after 1905 did not make loyalty to the nation so compelling, a habit of mind and a philosophy of education had been established which continued to exert a strong influence upon the thoughts and actions of the people.

For some time after the war, the deeds of war heroes and the victories of the Japanese army and navy in the war were prominent themes in contemporary literature, and there was still considerable preoccupation, among the intellectuals, with the nature and development of *Bushidō*, for the remarkable accomplishments of Japan since the arrival of Perry had to a large extent been attributed to the peculiar character of this traditional ethical code.

The subject that received the most attention among conservative intellectuals, however, was the old subject of national entity (*kokutai*). This was clearly a less aggressive type of nationalist thought than that associated with prewar Japanism, for the reflection upon *kokutai*, instead of emerging from a general feeling of national danger, was based on a desire to rationalize the new status achieved by the nation. Even before the end of the war, in December, 1904, the Confucian philosopher Inouye Tetsujirō contributed an article on *kokutai* to the *Nihonjin* in which he said that *kokutai* was "the mighty wellspring of Japanism" (*Nihon no kyodai naru genin*). Here he reiterated the qualities of Japanese national entity, giving the greatest importance to a peculiar unity of the Japanese people around the Imperial Household. Later, another famous intellectual of the day, Katō Hiroyuki, gave a lecture on "Our Political System of Constitutional Family-Father Control," in which he pointed out the uniqueness of the Japanese sociopolitical system. In 1907, Katō took a more advanced stand on *kokutai* by discussing it in relationship to Christianity, thus harking back to a conflict that had arisen as early as 1887. In reviving the old issue, Katō emphasized the point that since Christianity and Buddhism were internationalist in character and were not national religions, they were subversive to Japan's *kokutai*. People who believed in these world religions, Katō argued, automatically subjected themselves to controls that lay outside the state, and therefore they could never become true servants of the state. Thereafter several books on *kokutai* appeared, and finally Inouye organized a society of scholars engaged in studying the subject.[12]

After a few years in which national thought was directed chiefly toward considerations of *kokutai*, a new conservative movement arose, which was known as the *Kokumin Dōtoku Undō* (National Morals Movement). Participants in this movement, like those who discussed *kokutai*, were stimulated by feelings of anxiety about the spread of naturalism, individualism, socialism, and other ideologies which were believed to be destroying the moral fiber of the nation. The term "national morals" had been used back in 1886, when Nishimura Shigeki, a famous Confucian scholar, wrote a book on the subject; but he thought of Japanese morals primarily in terms of Confucian standards. The writers who returned to the subject after 1910 had a broader approach—one that was geared rather closely to principles set forth in the Imperial Rescript on Education. The man who did most to popularize the National Morals movement was Inouye Tetsujirō. In 1910, his society, the *Tōa Kyōkai*, which had been set up for those engaged in the study of *kokutai*, held a three-week conference on "National Morals." Soon after that, the Department of Education itself became interested in the movement, and Inouye and two other speakers were invited to give lectures at a meeting of teacher-training school officials, held in December, 1910. These lectures were later published. Thenceforth much was written and said about national morals, but probably the most significant book was the one written by Inouye Tetsujirō in 1912 called *Kokumin Dōtoku Gairon* (An Outline of National Morals). In discussing the basic elements of Japan's unique moral structure, Inouye placed *kokutai* in a position of primary importance and then moved on to Shintoism, assigning, of course, far more value to State Shinto than to sectarian Shinto. In addition, *Bushidō* and Japan's unique family system—as well as the Confucian principles of loyalty—were stressed. Most of the writers on national morals based their discussion on these same elements, emphasizing their value for Japan and the Japanese people.[13]

Still another indication of the nature of national thought after the Russo-Japanese War was the change that took place in the editorial policy of the leading national journal. Until early in 1907 this journal had been called *Nihonjin* (The Japanese), and in the years preceding and during the war it had been the major outlet for Japanist thought, just as, before the Sino-Japanese War, it had been the major outlet for writings on the preservation of "Japanese National Essence." But in February, 1907, the journal was renamed *Nihon oyobi Nihonjin* (Japan and the Japanese), and the editor, in outlining the new editorial policy, said that hereafter Japan should

strive to show her gratitude for the benefits received from foreign countries by benefiting them in return. If concerning things material she has had much to learn from them, in things mental and moral there is much that she can teach them. They have hitherto assumed, unwarrantably, that the white races have a monopoly of all that is best connected with humanity and human institutions. In religion, and ethics, as well as in the knowledge of physical laws and their application for mechanical purposes, Europeans have considered themselves superior to all Asiatics and Africans. Japan has begun to explode that theory. She must keep on doing it.[14]

At a time of economic prosperity and of relatively calm foreign relations, even the most nationalistic writers had thus adopted a more tolerant attitude toward foreign ideas and institutions. While still proclaiming the "spiritual" superiority of Japan, they were willing to admit that there was still "much to learn" from foreign countries.

Activity of Nationalist Societies

The Black Dragon Society, which had taken so prominent a part in the nationalist activity before 1905, continued to be prominent after the war. Its program, however, was drastically revised, for there were now new and different ways to serve the nation. Throughout the period 1905 to 1918 the society was primarily concerned with the extension of Japanese influence and with the development of Japanese commercial and industrial enterprises on the continent of Asia. Its activities were first directed primarily toward Korea, then toward Manchuria, and finally toward China, as Japanese expansionism gathered momentum. Since two wars had been fought to establish Japan's position in Korea, the Black Dragon Society's policy of encouraging the development of the Korean peninsula was acceptable to most Japanese; the society's agents consequently found themselves working closely with the government in their attempts to integrate Korea—economically, politically, and culturally—into the Japanese Empire.

But there was little that could be done in Korea beyond what the government was doing; the society therefore soon transferred its major advance base of operations to Manchuria. At first the government did not appear enthusiastic about the encouragement and support of Japanese commercial and industrial enterprise there, but ardent nationalists had long seen the advantages to be derived from the development of the area and soon gained government backing for their program. By 1906 the government was giving wholehearted support to the development of Manchuria. As early as March, 1906, American diplomatic agents reported to the State Department that American businessmen were complaining about Japanese official support of Japanese commercial interests in the principal towns of Manchuria. It was felt that there was little or no opening for other foreign trade.[15] In June, 1906, the South Manchuria Railway Company was organized to manage all Japanese railroads in the area. The government owned one-half of the capital stock and controlled the appointment of the principal officers. The company, in addition to managing railroads, was permitted to engage in mining, transportation, electric-power, real estate, and warehousing enterprises within the railway zone, and even to collect taxes and handle the zone's administrative affairs. In August, 1906, the Government General of Kwangtung (*Kwantō sōtoku fu*) was also established to administer the Kwangtung leasehold. After these two organs had been set up, tremendous energy was applied to railroad development. So much capital and effort was poured into Manchuria that nationals of other countries, particularly of Britain and the United States, began to fear that the "open door" was being effectively closed. This concern was closely associated with an intensification of international rivalry, and with a growing fear of Japanese expansion, which in turn led to talk of war.

But the Japanese government, being determined to accomplish its ends in Manchuria without war, turned to a series of diplomatic moves designed to gain recognition for its special position in that area. In June, 1907, an excellent start was made with the signing of the Franco-Japanese Treaty, by which France and Japan each agreed to the spheres of interest of the other—and Japan's sphere of influence was understood to include Manchuria. Then Japan turned to her former enemy, Russia, and within a few months several conventions were signed that clearly delimited the parts of Manchuria in which each would have prior rights and privileges. Finally, in October, 1907, Japan assured the United States that she wanted to avoid war and that she wished to reach an understanding with regard to the special interests of the two nations. Eventually there emerged, in November, 1908, an exchange of notes, known as the Root-Takahira notes, which were somewhat ambiguous but which, according to Griswold, suggested that "the United States had given Japan a free hand in Manchuria" in return for Japan's renewal of the pledge to respect the United States' position in the Philippines.[16] With this pattern of diplomatic agreements and understandings, Japan gained additional freedom for an even more energetic program in Manchuria. And although the United States attempted for a time to extend her financial and commercial interests into the area, by 1914 Japan had made great progress toward building the foundations which were to make Manchuria an important block in Japan's "Greater East Asia" structure of later years.

While the government was concentrating upon the development of Manchuria, the Black Dragon Society and its associates turned more of their attention to new frontiers, especially to China, where the internal political struggles seemed to offer bright prospects for a further extension of Japanese interests. As has already been noted, certain nationalist societies were active in China even before the Sino-Japanese War. They had been working with the Chinese nationalist movement, hoping to aid in the overthrow of the old Manchu regime and in the establishment of a government which would adopt a progressive reform program of the type followed in Japan. The Japanese nationalists were tireless in their support of this movement because they felt that a program of modernization in China would offer new opportunities for an expansion of Japanese interests on the continent, and that a strong China would enable Japan to put up a stiffer resistance to Western advances, particularly those of Russia. The desirability of aiding the Chinese nationalists seems to have been generally accepted, for Black Dragon Society activities received backing from high-level government officials.

After the Russo-Japanese War, however, the desirability of helping the Chinese nationalist movement was not so obvious, and government officials tended to withdraw their support from Black Dragon Society activities in China. The change was due, in large measure, to the fact that Japan had become more sure of her position in the Far East, and to the apparent conviction that she would stand to gain more from a weak China. Furthermore, government support of Japanese secret-society activities in China was likely to arouse the suspicions of Western nations, and at this time Japan was determined to follow a peaceful penetration policy, to act in accordance with the standards of Western international law, and to avoid any impression that Japan was fishing in muddy waters. Finally, there was the fear that the Chinese nationalist movement was too radical and that its success might lead to subversive developments even in Japan. Consequently, many of the more influential members of the Japanese oligarchy were consistent in their refusal to back the Chinese revolutionary movement.

But the Black Dragon Society continued to give energetic support to the nationalist cause in China. About 1907 it became particularly enthusiastic when Sun Yat-sen made it known that he was willing to give Japan a free hand in Manchuria and Mongolia in return for help for his revolutionary movement. Although the Japanese government was forced to ask Sun to leave the country (because the Chinese government had heard of the promise he made), the leaders of the Black Dragon Society were encouraged to press forward with their work in behalf of the Chinese revolutionary movement. In 1908 the society sponsored the publication of a Chinese journal, called the *Tōa Geppō* (East Asia Monthly), which was to provide the Chinese with more information about Japan and to contribute to the establishment of a closer relationship between the two countries. Then, in order to influence the Japanese government to assume a more favorable attitude toward the Chinese nationalist movement, an association called the *Yūrinkai*, was formed.[17] In 1911, sudden developments in southern China suggested that the revolution might succeed; consequently Uchida and other Japanese patriots stepped up their efforts to gain Japanese government backing. Saionji was then in power, however, and he was more cautious about taking action in China than General Katsura, the former Premier, had been. Uchida therefore found it necessary to go to Seoul for a talk with General Terauchi Seiki, the governor-general of Korea, who, Uchida thought, would exert the kind of influence that might tip the balance in favor of more positive aid for Sun Yat-sen. General Terauchi was not averse to extending Japan's interests in Manchuria and Mongolia, but he did not like the "republican" stamp of the Chinese nationalist movement. Uchida's argument on this point was that the movement was a logical product of the conditions prevailing in China and that the Japanese should make the most of the situation. But Terauchi could not be won over.[18]

Uchida, however, did obtain financial aid for the revolutionists. He heard, on his way to Korea, that Mitsui interests were selling supplies and ammunition to the Chinese government to help put down the revolution; he therefore sent off a telegram to Masuda Taka in the

Mitsui office in Tokyo, predicting that the revolutionary movement would be successful and asking that ammunition and supplies be sold also to Sun Yat-sen and his supporters. Masuda then went to Inouye Kaoru, a powerful figure in the oligarchy who had long worked closely with the Mitsui interests. Inouye pointed out that it would first be necessary to change the government's policy, and he specifically recommended that Masuda, in order to do this, confer with Katsura and Saionji. Uchida seems to have heard of these developments and to have sent word to his agents in China to have Sun Yat-sen and other revolutionary leaders telegraph Saionji, Katsura, Inouye, and other key figures concerning the successes and needs of the revolutionary party. The Chinese sent more than telegrams—they sent a mission. When it arrived in Tokyo, Uchida saw that the proper connections were made; and eventually the Chinese obtained a loan of 300,000 yen.[119]

The revolution was well along toward success in January, 1912, when, much to the disgust of Uchida and his agents, Sun Yat-sen suddenly decided to come to terms with Yuan Shih-kai, the most powerful figure in northern China and the man who on February 12, 1912, was named President of the new Republic. Without exception, the Japanese patriots condemned the union, claiming that Yuan was no friend of the revolutionary movement and that he would seize the first opportunity to destroy it. But even the most pro-Japanese of the Chinese leaders of the revolution were confident that Yuan was a changed man and that his assistance was needed. The Black Dragon Society agents themselves apparently realized that one of the basic reasons why the rebels came to terms with Yuan was that many Chinese had become convinced that the Japanese who were pouring into Shanghai, and who were claiming to be unselfish friends of the Revolution, were in reality agents of the Japanese government. They felt, too, that the Japanese government was planning to seize the opportunity, which these chaotic times offered, to gain a firmer hold over Manchuria and Mongolia.

Even after the union with Yuan Shih-kai, the Japanese nationalists continued to work with Chinese who had broken with Yuan; and by 1913 the Japanese detected promising developments, particularly after Sun came to Japan in 1913. Sun was sent as a representative of the Chinese Republic, but while in Japan he spent much of his time with Uchida, Tōyama, Inukai, and other Japanese nationalists who had supported his revolutionary movement. In speeches before Japanese gatherings, he gave Japan much credit for the success of his revolution and on one occasion stated:

"When I visited Europe and America some years ago, men of thought there feared that a revolution in China would give an incentive for the intervention of the foreign Powers and result in the dismemberment of the country and our national rights. They therefore advised me to withhold my hand from the undertaking. I did not take their advice, but threw in my lot with the Revolution, neither doubting nor fearing, because I was confident that assistance would be given to me in the accomplishment of my object. I undertook the work of Revolution relying upon the strong military force and faith of Japan, which I knew would prevent the European Powers and America from dividing the melon among themselves. With this confidence, I pushed on with the work of the Revolution, which had now been accomplished."[20]

Thenceforth Japanese patriots became even more determined to gain Japanese government support for Sun and his southern revolutionists, who were obviously becoming restive under Yuan Shih-kai. When fighting actually broke out between the North and the South, a propaganda program was started in Japan that was designed to arouse public opinion in favor of the South. At a banquet on June 3, 1913, Ozaki Yukio stated that, after all, 70 per cent of Japan's trade with China was with southern China. At the same meeting Ozaki also revealed that he had made a personal call on Foreign Minister Makino in an effort to change Makino's mind about the proper policy for the country to follow, and that Inukai had had an interview with the President for a similar purpose. A "China Study Group" was organized to sponsor rallies and lectures that would stir up public sentiment in behalf of the Southern cause.[21] At a meeting in July, the group passed this resolution: "The policy of the Japanese Empire towards China should aim first to secure supremacy of power in South Manchuria, to develop Inner Mongolia, to check any inclination of the foreign Powers towards the partitioning of the territory of China Proper, and to advance Japan's economic influence in South China."[22]

In September, 1913, Yuan Shih-kai moved against the Southern forces at Nanking; and when the city fell, Yuan's soldiers (under the command of Chang Tso-lin), who had come to believe that the opposition of the people of southern China was due chiefly to Japanese machinations, killed and manhandled Japanese soldiers and citizens found in the area. The "outrages" were immediately played up in the Japanese press, and persons who were associated with such groups as the China Study Group found the incident to be powerful ammunition for their publicity program in Japan. On the fourth of September, the Association of China Societies of Tokyo held a mass meeting at which huge crowds gathered in spite of police efforts to prevent the circulation of notices. On the speaker's stand was displayed a placard with this note: "The national prestige has collapsed, and our hearts are rent asunder. Our countrymen have been butchered, and the hair of our heads bristles with indignation." After hearing a few fanatical speeches, the crowd marched to the Foreign Office and sent in a deputation with the demand that all Foreign Office officials, because of their weak stand on the China issue, resign.[23] On the following day, Ōkuma Shigenobu, who was soon to be appointed Premier, was reported to have said that troops should be dispatched to China immediately to occupy key points, and that only after they had done so would he favor diplomatic negotiations.[24]

The Foreign Office bore the brunt of all the agitation because it had taken the position that it was not yet certain that the Japanese had been killed simply because they were Japanese, and it felt that it was not necessary to send more troops to China. The business world, too, seems to have taken a rather calm attitude toward the affair. The president of the Tokyo Chamber of Commerce stated that talk about sending troops to occupy Chinese territory would be taken "as an outburst of Japanese opportunist ambition" and would create among the Chinese people "permanent feelings of hatred toward Japan." But this moderation was more than countered by mass meetings and by a statement of the Minister of War (apparently without the knowledge of the Foreign Office) which concluded with the declaration: "Not a moment's delay can be permitted in settling the present question, and immediate measures must be taken for obtaining redress." The Association of China Societies, however, made specific recommendations for action: "We are convinced of the necessity of Japan occupying certain places which form the key to the existence of the Peking Government, and of sending troops to places which can be conveniently reached for the protection of Japanese residents, in order to maintain the national prestige of our Empire and of assuring permanent peace in China." The newspapers, too, became more outspoken. The Osaka *Mainichi* declared: "There is no room for the slightest delay on the part of Japan in taking action, and it is high time to make China feel the weight of a heavy iron axe."[25]

Additional heat was generated by the assassination of a Foreign

Office official who had been considered responsible for the "weak defense" of Japanese honour. The assassin, after waiting to find out whether or not his victim had really died, sat down on a large map of China and committed *hara-kiri*. He left a letter, which was later published in full, indicating that he murdered the Foreign Office official in order to "awaken the Foreign Office and the whole nation." He added: "The sacrifice of my life will compensate the country a million times for the loss the State has suffered . . . I will protect my country and pray for your blessing from my grave."[26] The papers played up every detail of the incident, and the Association of China Societies followed with more mass meetings, more resolutions, and more demonstrations before the Foreign Office.

Just how much these expressions of nationalist sentiment influenced government officials cannot be clearly established; but we do know that on September 10, 1913, five days after the assassination, the Japanese minister in China opened up negotiations with the Chinese, submitting demands that apologies be made, that the responsible general (Chang Tso-lin) be fired, and that adequate indemnities be paid.[27] While the negotiations were being carried on, the attacks upon the Japanese Foreign Office continued. The Association of China Societies, for example, adopted a resolution on the fifteenth which stated:

> The Government has made a mistake in opening the negotiations with China for redress. National prestige and national rights have been damaged, and the fundamental policy of dealing with China has been greatly hindered. The modest demand made will not fail to arouse the contempt of the Chinese officials and people, and also of the foreign Powers, and will lead to more trouble. We call upon this incompetent cabinet to resign without delay, as it is acting in opposition to the people's wish for the protection of the national interests.[28]

In the face of this public opposition the government was forced, or encouraged, to take more positive action, and in October, 1913, it sent an ultimatum to Yuan demanding financial compensation for the outrage against Japanese citizens, and apologies by the troops concerned. Yuan, apparently realizing the seriousness of the popular mood in Japan, complied with the demands. The Chinese agreed to pay an indemnity, to execute the principal murderers, to remove General Chang from his command, and to grant Japan a concession for the construction of five railway lines.[29]

During the remainder of 1913 and on into the following year continuous pressure was exerted on the Japanese government by nationalists who favored the adoption of a more "positive" policy toward China. The more aggressive associations demanded the resignation of the cabinet. They were therefore elated at the opportunities afforded by the scandal in the navy, uncovered early in 1914, which eventually led to the fall of the Yamamoto cabinet. The new Premier, Ōkuma Shigenobu, had long been an active supporter of constitutional government; but ever since the declaration of his "Ōkuma doctrine" in 1898 he had been recognized as a man who was alert to Japan's "opportunities" on the continent. It was expected that under his leadership the government would adopt a strong policy. One newspaper made the observation in the summer of 1914 that after the appointment of Ōkuma there had been "unmistakable signs of national energy," and that the people were confident that Japan would be able to hold her own in the international rivalries of the Far East.[30]

World War I and New National Opportunities

While Ōkuma was still Premier, war broke out in Europe, and in a matter of days, before there was any great popular demand for such a step, Japan joined in the fray. There had been some talk about the German danger to the peace of the Far East. The Osaka *Mainichi*, for example, had made reference to German capture and detention of neutral ships, and to German employment of neutrals for the building of defense works at Kiaochow.[31] There was also some comment about revenge for Germany's part in the Triple Intervention of 1895. But most of the papers seemed to look upon Japan's entrance into the war as a proper step in seizing what appeared to be an excellent opportunity to "solve the China problem." German power in the Pacific was not such a threat to Japan's security or interests as to stimulate strong nationalist feelings of the type that had prevailed during Japan's previous two wars. Soon after the war began, Dr. Miyake, editor of the famous nationalist journal *Nihon oyobi Nihonjin*, wrote that he was anxious about "a lack of seriousness" among the people, and urged that the Japanese "strain every nerve" in the prosecution of the war.[32] But at no time during the hostilities was there ever the national drive that characterized the attitude of the nation at the time of the Russo-Japanese War.

However, the war did offer to Japan another opportunity for expanding her interests on the continent—an opportunity that was much more promising than those presented previously by the chaotic conditions in China. Most people understood that the Western powers were in no position to resist or question Japan's moves in the Far East. Furthermore, Japanese nationalist leaders were encouraged by the fact that their government, under Ōkuma's hand, would be far more receptive to suggestions of positive action. It is therefore not surprising to find that members of the Black Dragon Society were soon devising plans for improving Japan's position on the continent. Three weeks after the surrender of Kiaochow, on November 29, 1914, Uchida Ryōhei presented to government officials a "Memorandum for a Solution of the China Problem." It stated:

Now is the most opportune moment for Japan quickly to solve the Chinese Question. Such an opportunity will not occur for hundreds of years to come. Not only is it Japan's divine duty to act now, but present conditions in China favour the execution of such a plan. We should by all means decide and act at once. If our authorities do not avail themselves of this rare opportunity, great difficulty will surely be encountered in the future in the settlement of the Chinese Question. Japan will be isolated from the European Powers after the war and will be regarded by them with envy and jealousy, just as Germany is now regarded. Is it not, then, a vital necessity for Japan to solve at this very moment the Chinese Question?[33]

Uchida felt that it was not wise to work through the Yuan regime. He proposed instead that efforts be made to induce the Chinese revolutionists and all other dissatisfied groups in China to rise up, that orders be given to the Japanese Army to move into China to restore order, and that a defensive alliance between the new government and Japan should be signed. Uchida also listed several points which he thought the treaty of alliance should include in order to assure Japan a predominant position in the internal and external affairs of China.

But those in favor of a more positive policy in China did not limit their activities to sending memoranda. In November, 1914, a mass meeting of more than a thousand men was held to discuss means of achieving this goal. Resolutions were passed, and a decision was reached to appoint a council of ten to consider further moves. The council then sent a committee of seven men to call on the Foreign Minister and press its views. When the Foreign Minister seemed rather unreceptive, many in the movement came out in open opposition to the cabinet, feeling that nothing could be done until the Ōkuma government was overthrown.[34]

Such pressure apparently had some effect on the government, for the notorious Twenty-one Demands were placed in the hands of the

Japanese minister to Peking on December 3, 1914, and were presented to the Chinese government on January 18, 1915. At the conference with Yuan Shih-kai when the demands were made, the Japanese minister pointed to the close contact that existed between Chinese revolutionists and certain "irresponsible" Japanese and hinted that unless the demands were accepted Yuan might find a revolution on his hands. He also pointed out that the Yuan regime was very unpopular in Japan and that acceptance of these demands would show Yuan's "friendly intentions."[35] There is a close resemblance between the demands made on China and the suggestions formulated by Uchida. The nationalists had every reason to be pleased with this development and to feel some satisfaction with the part they played in it. Their only objection was that the Japanese government had decided to deal with the Yuan regime.

In spite of the criticism of the government for compromising on some of the demands, Japanese nationals were greatly encouraged by the turn of events, and during the following months expansionism was in the air. Takekoshi Yosaburō, a historian and leading journalist of the day, urged that Japan extend her territories,[36] and one of the professors at the Kyoto Imperial University insisted that Japan should raise her sights to include the South Seas, as well as China.[37] There was more talk of the superiority of the yellow race, and an ambitious naval program was adopted. Toward the end of the year, Takekoshi even advocated that Japan take over the Dutch East Indies.[38] The feeling of national confidence was easily detected by foreigners who traveled in Japan in those days. Judge J. H. Gary, for example, in speaking of impressions which he had received during his recent trip to the Orient, said that the Japanese were

"highly intelligent, determined, adaptable, very industrious, and, above everything else, superbly loyal to their emperor and to their nation. The ordinary citizen lives for his country and is just as willing to die for it. There are no internal strifes; on the contrary, there is a harmonious whole. They present to the outside world a united front. This is as it ought to be in every nation. It gives solidarity of power that is invincible."[39]

Under the Terauchi cabinet, which was formed in October, 1916, there was a conscious effort by the government to be less hasty in expanding Japanese interests in China, for it was realized that the anti-Japanese sentiments aroused in China at the time of the Twenty-one Demands were not subsiding as quickly as had been expected. Furthermore, even England had become suspicious of Japan's intentions, and there were indications that American diplomats were doing all they could to oppose Japanese moves on the continent. Therefore, in anticipation of the postwar settlement, the Japanese government began to act more cautiously and to attempt to obtain some advance recognition of wartime gains. The new policy eased international tensions in the Far East, but the entrance of the United States and China into the war in the spring of 1917 probably was a more decisive factor in the rise of a more generous attitude in Japan toward foreign countries.

The good will was such that one journalist wrote about a loyalty higher than loyalty to the nation: "Patriotism must be strengthened," he said, "but in these times if a nation does not possess a moral spirit which is nobler than patriotism, it will not receive the respect of the world powers or have a civilization which is trusted by the powers."[40] And when the suggestion was first made that Japan send troops into Siberia, there were those who opposed such a venture on the grounds that helping Russia, against her wishes, would not yield the desired result and would further "widen the breach existing between the two countries."[41] By the summer of 1918 even America was held in high esteem. An editorial in the *Jiji* said: "The true greatness of America is its people. Their sincerity to their duty, their faith in the final victory of the righteous, and their courage in devoting everything for the cause of the Allies, are what have made America great and what have made the Allies grateful to America."[42]

The internationalist feelings of the Japanese public were moving to a point beyond anything favored by the Terauchi government. On various occasions, Terauchi spoke of his concern about the fad for democracy and urged officials to do their utmost to prevent the spread of these "dangerous ideas." Furthermore, the government found that in ordering troops into Siberia, and in supporting the Nishihara loans to China, it was being opposed by a large segment of the Japanese populace. The lack of enthusiasm for these foreign ventures was due, in part, to feelings of international good will, but it was also based upon opposition to Terauchi's "bureaucratic" government and to a growing discontent with the rising cost of living.

The high cost of living was associated with a remarkable wartime prosperity that was also a vital factor in the rise of more "confident" national attitudes. As a result of supplying markets formerly controlled by Europe and America, and as a result of filling Allied demands for war goods, Japan's foreign trade increased by about 300 per cent between 1914 and 1918. Furthermore, exports moved ahead of imports, so that Japan enjoyed a favorable balance of trade and became a creditor nation that was able now to make investments in China.[43] The investments were of such size and importance that American and European bankers became anxious about the advantage which Japanese financiers were gaining.

Just before the end of the war, Japan also had her first truly political-party cabinet, headed by Hara Kei, the first commoner to be appointed Premier of a Japanese cabinet. The political change was in part a product of the new interest in democratic principles, but it was also an expression of opposition to the Army-clan domination and an outgrowth of the social discontent that accompanied wartime inflation. But the change was also related to the more "neutral" attitude toward the conflict in China and to a general feeling of friendship toward Japan's victorious allies. Thus, in political developments too, there was strong evidence of widespread confidence in the strength and future of the Japanese nation.

⋄   ⋄   ⋄

The character of Japanese nationalism between 1905 and 1918 differed so greatly from the nationalism that had come before it, and that which followed it, that many will insist that there was no nationalism at all at this time. And indeed the popularity of naturalism, individualism, socialism and other movements and principles which were non-Japanese in origin and emphasis suggests that nationalism did not exert a powerful influence upon the thoughts and actions of the people. However, if we think of nationalism as basically a type of group loyalty, and if we disassociate the phenonemon from particular manifestations of it, we are more likely to see that the phenomenon did not disappear but rather took a different form. In the years between the end of the Russo-Japanese War and the end of World War I, Japan enjoyed what can be safely termed the most prosperous and secure period in her modern history. Fear and hatred of foreign enemies tended to be supplanted by pride in national accomplishments and by confidence in Japan's ability to become even more powerful.

The nationalist thought of the period, then, was not deeply grounded in feelings of inferiority and was not directly related to preparations for military conflict, but was focused rather upon the reasons for Japan's remarkable progress and the problem of what would assure further progress. The intellectual developments most clearly related to the first effort—the effort to explain Japan's success—was the rise of new interest in the study and consideration of *kokutai* (Japan's national entity). In most of the books, articles, and speeches on *kokutai*, we note an effort to define the nature and quality of the socioreligious-political structure that had emerged in Japan and had given the Japanese nation a unique and vital heritage. In these discussions, all the truly Japanese ethical standards, religious principles, and sociopolitical institutions were combined into a single structure called *kokutai*. It was felt that by understanding *kokutai* a Japanese could better understand and appreciate his nation's remarkable advances, gain greater confidence in further national growth, and receive inspiration to work more diligently toward the achievement of national goals.

But within a few years after the Russo-Japanese War, Japan's security and prosperity were bringing about social and religious changes that caused great concern among conservative intellectuals about the deterioration of family ties, the popular absorption in material gain, the interest of intellectuals in foreign ideas, and many other developments which seemed to spell ruin for Japan's traditional values. The National Morals movement arose from efforts to meet the danger. The movement was not so much a product of national pride as a product of national concern. Its leaders were not content with definitions—they wanted to reverse the trend toward a popular acceptance of individualism, materialism, socialism, and other nonnational principles and ideologies. The movement was a forerunner of the later, more energetic, state-supported drive to eliminate all the principles and concepts that are most characteristic of Western liberalism.

In spite of the energy with which these national movements were carried on, it is doubtful whether they were the dominant elements in the intellectual climate of the period, for the literature, art, and philosophy of the day were weighted heavily with works that were colored by foreign principles, standards, and interests. And yet it is submitted that even in these more nonnational developments there was still a strong sense of identification with the nation. In those years of confidence and prosperity, a man could become a credit to his nation by accomplishments in intellectual and artistic fields with a Western orientation.

In thought, then, nationalism was stronger than it would at first appear to be. National secret-society activity, however, was probably less significant as a manifestation of nationalism than is generally supposed, for the motivation behind this activity was obviously not purely national in character. In much of the activity it is easy to detect a healthy profit motive, and it is clear that in many cases the members of national societies were working with politicians who were seeking to improve their political position. The membership of the secret societies, as numerous as the societies were, included only a very small part of the population. It is true that at certain times the societies appeared to exert considerable influence upon government leaders and upon the press; but even in the most extreme cases there were other contributing factors which may have been more dominant. Furthermore, it is extremely doubtful whether the strong nationalist view of the societies, even when supported by the press, had any great influence upon the thoughts and actions of the great mass of the people.

The nationalism in Japan in this period, therefore, was beginning to take on a "confident" rather than a "fearful" character. It was now more like the nationalism that had emerged in France, England, and the United States. It was not primarily a product of foreign danger but a heritage of national achievement and a concomitant of confidence in the future progress of the nation.

NATIONAL RECONSTRUCTION

At the end of World War I it was clear to most thoughtful nationalists that the period of rapid commercial expansion had come
to an end. The Western powers had already shown themselves to be
suspicious of Japanese demands on China. And in the Siberian expedition the Americans had obviously been more disturbed about Japanese
territorial ambitions than about Russian Communist activities. At the
peace negotiations in Versailles some of the Western powers were certainly bent on resisting further Japanese advances and were even ready
to prevent Japan from gaining title to many of the concessions she had
already gained. The Four-Power Consortium and finally the Washington Disarmament Conference were merely two of the more noteworthy
developments in which the firmer attitude of Western countries was
shown. Furthermore, the Chinese, now that the war was over, were
more determined than ever to resist new Japanese encroachments—
anti-Japanese feelings rose to new heights after the announcement that
at Versailles the German rights and concessions in the Shantung Penin-

sula had been granted to Japan. But the tension in Japan's relations with the outside world was not sufficient to arouse among the Japanese people the kind of nationalism that had prevailed before the Russo-Japanese War, for in spite of Western rivalry and Chinese hatred, there was no immediate threat to Japan's security. However, Japan's postwar relations were associated with a break in her prosperous foreign trade and were therefore closely tied in with the economic and social upheaval that became the stimulant and the focus for subsequent nationalist energy.

Social Discontent

Because of Japan's serious deficiency in most of the important raw materials, and also because of a constant population problem, her economic growth, ever since she scrapped her isolation policy in 1865, has hinged upon the development of foreign trade. Because she found herself in competition with Western nations that were more advanced industrially, Japan relied heavily upon special commercial rights and privileges on the continent. As a direct result of two foreign wars—the Sino-Japanese War and the Russo-Japanese War—her commercial position was greatly strengthened. But the greatest advances were made, of course, during World War I, when hostilities in Europe gave her more freedom to exert political and military pressure in China and removed much of the Western competition for trade in Far Eastern markets.[1] However, with the end of the war the situation changed completely.

The first shock came from the decline in the demand for military goods. Almost immediately there was a sharp drop in the price of steel; thousands of industrial workers were thrown out of work, and many factories were forced to shut down. The Shantung controversy stimulated more Chinese boycotts against Japanese goods. Western merchants reëntered Far Eastern markets, and Western financiers once more showed an interest in making investments in China. In 1918, Japan had enjoyed 39.2 per cent of China's foreign trade; but in 1919 her share fell to 35.3 per cent, and in 1920 to 29.3 per cent. Finally, in the diplomatic field there were moves by Western powers, singly and in combination, which were aimed at preventing Japan from improving her commercial advantage. As a result of the operation of these factors, Japan's total export trade dropped from well over 4,000,000,000 yen in 1919 to less than 3,000,000,000 yen in 1921. The most serious aspect of the decline, however, was the disappearance of Japan's wartime favorable balance. In 1918 Japan exported more than she imported by about 300,000,000 yen; but as early as 1919 her imports exceeded her exports, and in 1921 the unfavorable balance reached a figure of more than 361,000,000 yen.[2] With the foreign credits Japan had gained during the war, she was able to make such extensive investments abroad that financiers in both the United States and England became concerned about their own financial prospects in China. But under the pressure of an unfavorable balance of trade, Japan lost the advantage she had previously gained.

Throughout the 1920's the trade situation failed to show any marked signs of improvement, in spite of energetic action by the government. In 1925 the total of the country's foreign trade was roughly equal to that of 1919, but the imports still exceeded exports by about 267,000,000 yen.[3] Thereafter the foreign trade situation continued to deteriorate, and finally, at the beginning of the world depression, Japan's exports were hit by what was probably the greatest single disaster in modern Japanese economic history. The collapse of the silk market hurt most. Ever since the early years of Japan's modernization program, silk had been the most profitable item in her foreign trade, not only because there was a great demand for silk, but because the production of silk was not dependent on imported raw materials. However, the depression in the United States brought a sudden decline in the demand for silk, and the Japanese exports went into a tail spin. In 1929 the exports had amounted to 2,149,000,000 yen; in 1930, however, they decreased to 1,470,000,000 yen, and in 1931 to 1,147,000,000 yen.This development, in an industrialized country with a shortage of raw materials and an expanding population, carried truly dynamic social implications and was therefore basic to subsequent trends in nationalism.

Although the depressed foreign trade was a major element in the serious condition of Japan's economy after World War I, other factors were operative. The government's failure to adopt sound financial policies, for example, had much to do with the inflationary trend that caused great hardship among the peasants, laborers, and salaried workers during the closing months of the war. In January, 1917, the wholesale price of one koku of rice was 16.37 yen, but in August of the following year it had soared to 39.18 yen.[4] In an effort to check the rise of rice prices, the Terauchi cabinet tried to restrict rice exports; but still prices continued to rise. On August 6, 1918, three hundred wives of fishermen in a village near the city of Toyama gathered to demand the sale of rice at a lower price. Soon a large crowd assembled and a riot ensued. Word of this spread to other areas and this led to similar riots in other parts of the country. In a ten-day period between the ninth and the nineteenth of August, riots raged in three major cities and in twenty-five different prefectures. In forty-two cities and towns, troops had to be used to restore order.[5]

Labor strikes, which caused even more anxiety among conservatives, also increased in both size and number at the end of the war. Since this development, too, was closely related to the rise in prices, and to a great lag in wages, it probably would have been less serious had wiser financial and labor policies been followed. The wholesale index (100 in 1900) rose in Tokyo from 234 in December, 1917, to 305 in September, 1918—an increase of 80 per cent in ten months. But in the same period, the wage index rose from 205 to 230—an increase of only 20 per cent.[6] Under these conditions, and in this period of wartime prosperity, the laborers began to organize and to carry out strikes in an effort to improve their living conditions. In 1913 there were only 47 labor disputes, affecting slightly more than 5,000 workers; but in 1918 there were 417 disputes, affecting more than 66,000 workers.[7] In a single strike at the Kawasaki dockyard in September, 1919, 16,000 laborers joined in the largest strike Japan had ever experienced. These disturbances caused more and more nationalists to feel that Japan's greatest need was for the removal of the causes of the disruption.

The direct action of peasants and laborers was indeed a threat to the status quo; but as the postwar depression began to take hold, workers became more anxious to keep their jobs than to obtain higher wages. Consequently there were fewer strikes, and the membership of labor unions declined. With the contraction of business, many small firms were forced into bankruptcy, and this gave the bigger companies excellent opportunities for consolidating their own position. In the rural areas, too, there was great distress, which affected not merely the peasants but also the small landholders. As a result of this general economic hardship, intellectuals began to search for solutions to Japan's social problems and soon were advocating principles and ideologies that were more disturbing to the conservative nationalists than strikes and riots. The nationalists were particularly disturbed about writers who supported programs that implied radical changes in Japan's traditional social structure—changes which the nationalists thought would not only threaten the position of those in power but would weaken the Japanese nation and retard its growth.

Subversive Thought

The persons who were considered by national conservatives to be most subversive were those who supported some foreign ideology. And the ideology which first gained great popularity in the postwar period was democracy. Although the movement did not become very popular until after the last months of the war—after the United States declared war on Germany in 1917—interest in democratic ideals had been growing for some time. The Allied propaganda to the effect that this war was to protect democracy from the evils of German militarism seems to have influenced many Japanese intellectuals. In January, 1916, Yoshino Sakuzo wrote an article on "The Principles of Constitutional Government and How to Perfect Them." He not only advocated acceptance of democratic principles of government but made specific suggestions for the best methods of implanting those principles in Japan. First, he said, it was essential to reform the election laws in order to give more people a voice in government. He then went on to advocate a reform of the House of Peers and the Privy Council, which were powerful institutions of privilege and were not responsible to the elected representatives of the people. Finally, he criticized militarism and imperialism because both were nondemocratic.[8] These were not new proposals, but since they were now made by a renowned and respected scholar in a period of growing discontent, they became popular subjects of debate. Clubs were organized to urge the adoption of the reforms suggested by Yoshino, and by 1918 the demand for universal manhood suffrage had become a dynamic political issue. In addition to supporting the proposals for reform, writers made increasingly virulent attacks against feudalists and bureaucratic practices; and the political parties marshaled their forces for an insistence upon the establishment of a government controlled by political parties instead of one dominated by the old feudal-military oligarchy.

It was in part a result of these various movements, and in part a result of the widespread social discontent that followed in the wake of the war, that the Hara cabinet was formed in September, 1918. Hara, the president of the majority party in the Diet, was the first commoner to be appointed Premier, and his was the first cabinet to be made up entirely—except for the Army and Navy ministers—of members of the majority party. This was very encouraging to those who had been influenced by Western liberal principles, and it served to stimulate further the drive for political reforms. But even though the opposition parties and most of the press took up the cry for universal manhood suffrage, Hara, under the influence of conservative elements in the government, refused to yield to the forces which had been largely responsible for his rise to power. In 1920 he dissolved the Diet, and in the general election that followed, his party gained additional strength. Hara interpreted the victory as an indication that the electorate was opposed to universal suffrage. Five years later, a law providing for universal manhood suffrage was passed; but by that time there were even more disturbing intellectual movements to convince the conservative political leaders that it was time to yield to popular demands for wider political representation.[9]

Until 1920 the new labor unions had been strongly influenced by democratic principles, and they had tended to place great confidence in the operation of representative institutions as the best means of advancing their cause. But with the failure of the Hara cabinet to yield to popular demands for universal manhood suffrage, labor leaders tended to become more interested in syndicalism, a movement that was then spreading throughout Europe. The syndicalist opposition to parliamentarianism met with a ready response in Japanese labor circles, and many labor leaders also accepted the syndicalist program of achieving social change by such direct-action tactics as general strikes. In the 1922 conference of one of the leading labor organizations the demand for universal suffrage was even deleted from the statement of principles. Also, in some of the labor disputes of the period, syndicalist tactics became prominent. But syndicalism came to be thought of as too unrealistic, and about 1923 it retreated before the advances of Communism, a movement that was considered to be a much more dangerous threat to the Japanese traditional order.[10]

In 1917 the labor movement was too weak to be greatly affected by the news of the Bolshevist revolution, and it was not until the end of 1920—after Hara had struck his blow against the further growth of representative government—that a few socialist leaders showed some interest in the movement. At that time, the Far Eastern Propaganda Section of the Comintern provided financial assistance for the establishment of a labor organization and a labor journal (*Rōdō Undō*) to propagate Communist principles in Japan. And after the second congress of the Comintern in August, 1920, Japanese Communists received even more help and encouragement, since the Comintern leaders were convinced that the Far East was a most promising area for the further advance of the Communist movement. At the third congress of the Comintern, in 1921, it was specifically declared that the Communist party must gain a foothold in Japan.[11] In July, 1922, the Japanese Communist party was organized, and in September it was formally recognized as the Japanese branch of the Comintern. By the following March it could boast of fourteen cells and fifty members; and with the current decline of syndicalism, Communist principles and tactics were reflected in the thoughts and actions of many labor leaders. At the time of the Tokyo earthquake in September, 1923, however, rumors were circulated that the fires had been started by Koreans and socialists, and the government took the opportunity to arrest many of the Communist leaders. The movement was seriously damaged by the arrests and also by a reëmergence, among laborers and intellectuals, of interest in representative institutions.[12]

Since the earthquake and fires of 1923 created an economic dislocation that may have been greater than that which prevailed in the immediate postwar years, conditions were even more conducive to the spread of social discontent. And yet it was just at this time that the most subversive movements weakened and that democratic principles of representative government moved to the fore. The shift seems to have been due primarily to the more enlightened policies adopted by the Kato cabinet in 1924. Although the cabinet was responsible for severe repressive measures against subversives, and although it was not a true political-party cabinet, it supported a universal manhood suffrage law and permitted laborers themselves to select representatives to the coming International Labor Conference. Under this "candy and whip" policy, the labor leaders and intellectuals veered back toward parliamentarianism. The leading labor federation (the Sō Dōmei) suddenly assumed a more coöperative attitude toward the government. In January, 1924, the central committee of the federation had decided to oppose the new government labor bill, since it would restrict the labor movement; but in August of the same year the same committee reversed its position and announced its support of the bill. In explaining the change of policy, the leaders of the Sō Dōmei pointed up the new developments which had occasioned the rise of a more moderate view among proletarian leaders and intellectuals: the earthquake disaster had revealed the weakness of labor among the masses; the revolutionary movement in Europe was subsiding; the Katō cabinet had decided to support a bill for universal manhood suffrage; and, finally, the government was taking more positive measures against subversive activity.[13] The Communist movement itself was influenced by the trend. Under the doctrinal leadership of Yamakawa Hitoshi, the party moved away from the "class struggle" emphasis toward what was called a "party dissolution" emphasis, or "Yamakawaism." Yamakawa believed that proletarian class consciousness in Japan was not sufficiently advanced to warrant a proletarian revolutionary program. He therefore advocated a plan of coöperating with all progressive groups in an effort to "develop" the masses. Yamakawaism came to dominate Communist activity; consequently party members began to work through progressive organizations and to support such popular causes as universal manhood suffrage. Finally, in March, 1924, the Communist party itself was dissolved.[14] After this there was a period of accelerated growth for the labor movement, and with the passage of the law providing universal manhood suffrage the next year a number of new proletarian parties were organized. Generally, laborers and peasants seemed to feel that representative institutions offered a truly hopeful medium for improving their living conditions and strengthening their hand in the affairs of government. However, the cabinet was beginning to take a more positive stand against radicalism, and the nationalist societies, too, were beginning to be more effective in their efforts to check the growth of the movements they considered to be subversive. Eventually these efforts were to become instrumental in the destruction of the new interest in representative institutions.

National Reconstruction

Since it was the "National Reconstruction" effort to check the growth of subversive tendencies within Japan that became the most characteristic form of nationalist activity after World War I, it seems proper to turn now to a consideration of the nature of the movement. As early as 1919, leaders of the old Black Dragon Society were shifting their attention from China to developments within Japan. They had become discouraged about the possibility of making further advances in China and were convinced that it was impossible for Japan to gain greater strength until her internal economic, social, and political situation had been stabilized. Therefore, within a few months after the war, the old program of supporting commercial expansion abroad tended to be overshadowed by a new program of opposing radicalism at home. At first the nationalists and their societies were fighting a far from even battle. The democratic, syndicalist, communist, and socialist movements were far more popular, among the mass of the people, than any nationalist program to uphold Japan's traditional ethical and moral principles. But the nationalists had strong weapons, and as Japan's internal and external affairs became more critical, they eventually marshaled powerful support for a compromise program which assured ultimate victory.

The nationalist activities after 1919 tended to move along two different lines. On the one hand there were those who opposed all expressions of discontent and all ideas and programs that favored any revision of Japan's traditional social and political order. This opposition took any form that promised results, including propaganda, bribery, threats, and assassination. The other type of nationalist activity was less reactionary, but was more effective in gaining popular support during the period of transition, for it supported a program of "reconstruction" that was designed to quiet discontent and at the same time preserve the basic elements of Japan's traditional institutions and principles.

Among the nationalist groups that channeled their efforts toward a direct and uncompromising opposition to any radical movement or ideology, the old established expansionist societies were important. But there were also new organizations, the most influential and significant of which was the *Dai Nihon Kokusui Kai* (Greater Japan National Essence Society). This was organized in 1919 by Tokonami Takejirō, Home Minister in the Hara cabinet, and it remained active until the end of the war in 1945. The platform of the society contained broad, high-sounding principles, such as: "We will guide the thinking of the Japanese people by glorifying reverence for the gods and worship of our ancestors."[15] But judging from the activities of the society and from the declarations of its leaders, it is obvious that the purpose was primarily to oppose the spread of radical thought and the growth of the labor movement. In the early 1920's the society's membership reached the 120,000 mark. Most of the members were unskilled and seasonal workers who did not have permanent positions and were highly dependent upon their foremen, labor bosses, and contractors—men who were also leaders of the society. Consequently, the society became an effective instrument for the suppression of strikes and other union activities, often by means of assassination and the destruction of property.[16]

But the economic and social upheaval of the postwar years produced peasant, labor, and intellectual movements which were far too virulent to be checked by such tactics. It was gradually realized by the more realistic nationalists, such as Ōkawa Shūmei, that any attempt to eradicate subversive activities would ultimately fail unless the attempt was geared to a program of social, economic, and political reform. Therefore, when it was learned that Kita Ikki, one of the Black Dragon Society members operating in China, had formulated a plan for the reform of the Japanese state, Ōkawa hastened to Shanghai to see the plan and to talk to Kita. He was ecstatic about what he found, for here was a national reconstruction program, not just another subversive internationalist ideology.[17]

Kita's book, *Nihon Kaizō Hōan Taikō* (An Outline Plan for the Reconstruction of the Japanese State), soon became the basic reference work for a number of societies that combined their opposition to subversive activities with a reform program which, it was felt, made more sense for Japan. The book therefore holds a key position in the rise of Japanese National Reconstructionism, but there were antecedents which should not be overlooked.

The spurt of socialist activity after the Russo-Japanese War came at a time when nationalism was still at a rather high pitch. But since socialism had been related with pacifism in Japanese minds, and since the military victory was a strong element in the current feelings of national pride, it was only logical that some socialists should be tempted to adjust socialist doctrines and programs to nationalist sympathies. One of the more prominent leaders of the movement was Yamamichi Aizan, who, as early as February, 1905, published a magazine, *Dokuritsu Hyōron* (Independent Criticism), that advocated the establishment of an "independent administration" by men who feared nothing but "the gods and their conscience."[18] What he had in mind was more clearly indicated when in the following August he founded Japan's first National Socialist party (*Kokka Shakai Tō*). In the party's statement of policy he demanded that the Japanese people unite with the sovereign "in the spirit of familial, filial relations" and that "through the power of the state they implement the principles of collective life." Also, the program of the new party stated that "since the Emperor of our country is in a sense a practitioner of socialism, we should restrict the wealthy and protect the laborers through the power of the Emperor."[19] It is significant that Kita Ikki, too, aimed at a union of nationalism and socialism. Ever since high school days, Kita had studied socialist literature, and at an early age he had contributed articles on socialism to various newspapers and magazines. In the midst of the postwar revival of socialism, however, he wrote a book entitled *Kokutai oyobi Junsei Shakai Shugi* (Japanese National Entity and Pure Socialism), which indicated that he had been influenced by the developments that were associated with the organization of the National Socialist party. The book was an attempt to integrate socialism with the unique institutions and principles of the Japanese people. But with the subsequent decline of socialism, the National Socialist movement also decayed. Kita joined the Black Dragon Society and went to China to take part in the Chinese revolutionary movement. Then, after World War I, when conditions in Japan seemed to require positive measures, Kita once more turned his attention to the social and political policies that he believed should be followed in Japan.[20]

The program that he formulated in his Outline Plan for the Reconstruction of the Japanese state (*Nihon Kaizō Hōan Taikō*)[21] was designed to meet fire with fire. The subversive forces at work in Japan were to be destroyed by a reconstruction that would alleviate the discontent on which the foreign ideologies were feeding, and that would preserve the essential features of the Japanese social order. Kita was opposed to both the revolutionists and the capitalists. No family, Kita wrote, should hold property in excess of 1,000,000 yen;[22] no landlord should possess land valued at more than 100,000 yen;[23] and no private industry should exceed an evaluation of 10,000,000 yen.[24] According to the Kita plan, any holding above these limits was to be seized by the state. The land taken from rich landowners—except for forests, and so forth— was to be sold to farmers who owned no land,[25] but the state was to retain control of confiscated industrial property.[26]

In justifying these measures, Kita took pains to point out that the ownership of private property was essential for the enjoyment and free activity of the individual.[27] He stated that the private ownership of industry stimulated economic activity and gave free play to the creative genius of the individual.[28] In fact, he declared that a society which did not stress the value of freedom and individualism had not yet emerged from the slavery of medieval times, and that any socialist ideology which did not respect private property was reflecting the attitudes of the "early communist ages."[29] Yet Kita was harsh in his criticism of an order that permitted excessive accumulations of capital. Such an "evil system," he said, placed too much economic and political power in the hands of a few individuals. If Japan is to avoid the disunity of modern China and the chaos of the United States, huge concentrations of capital must be confiscated.[30]

But for the carrying out of such a program, Kita placed no faith in class revolutions or in democratic processes. He favored a coup d'état, by an enlightened few, that would result in the seizure of political power from the corrupt and selfish old military, bureaucratic, financial, and political-party cliques. This power was then to be handed to the Emperor, who would proceed to implement the reconstruction program. At first, certain preparatory steps would have to be taken, such as the suspension of the Constitution, the declaration of martial law for a period of three years, the dissolution of the Diet, and the abolition of the peerage. To administer (for the Emperor) the reconstruction program, "great men" from all walks of life and from all parts of Japan were to be appointed to form a National Reconstruction cabinet. And under the cabinet there was to be a National Reconstruction Diet, elected in accordance with a new universal-suffrage law. But the Diet was only to deliberate on problems relating to the implementation of the program and was not to have the right to question basic policies of the reconstruction, as outlined by Kita and promulgated by the Emperor.[31] Various departments were to be set up to handle the expanded operations of the state. The Department of Navigation (Kōkai Shō), for example, was to use the ships taken from large capitalists to "fight for the supremacy of the seas," and the Department of Mining Industry (Kōgyō Shō) was to have the responsibility of developing the mineral resources of newly acquired territories.[32]

The implications of expansionism were not limited to details regarding the operation of the various departments of the newly organized government, for Kita was very much aware of the population pressure in Japan and was convinced that, although economic and social ills would be greatly alleviated by the carrying out of his program, it would still be necessary for Japan to obtain more land. In other words, he felt that the theory of a wider distribution of wealth, which he proposed for Japan, should also be applied, by force if necessary, on the international level. He maintained that there was a basic contradiction in the brand of Western socialism that sanctified proletarian movements but which condemned positive action by small nations as being aggressive and militaristic. More specifically, he wrote:

England is a powerful millionaire who has holdings over the entire world, and Russia is a huge landholder [with lands throughout] the northern half of the globe. So why doesn't Japan, which is an area made up of scattered island chains and which is in the position of a proletariat among nations, have the right to start a war, in the name of justice, in order to seize [possessions] from these monopolies? There are self-contradictions in the fundamental thoughts of those European and American socialists who approve of proletarian class struggle within a country but who consider international proletarian war as chauvinism or militarism.[33]

There was one other element of Kita's program to which attention should be called: the prominent part the military was to play in every phase of the program. The initial coup d'état was to be carried out principally by soldiers, and former servicemen were to be relied on for heading off any resistance the entrenched cliques might offer. It was explained that since the former servicemen, by performing military service, had carried out the highest duty to the Japanese nation, they would logically have a greater sense of loyalty to the nation. Also, Kita pointed out that many of them were farmers and laborers and that therefore, if their assistance was relied on, much of the confusion that had occurred in Germany and Russia would be avoided.[34] It was expected, then, that Kita's reconstruction program would be welcomed by military men, especially if and when the military should become dissatisfied with their status in Japan or with the policies followed by the government.

Until 1925, however, civilians were far more active than military men in the nationalist societies that accepted Kita's National Reconstruction program. Furthermore, during the period, the activity of such societies continued to be less prominent than that of societies engaged in an uncompromising opposition to all programs of social change. Also, the National Reconstruction societies, such as the *Yūzon Sha*, tended, until about 1925, to give more attention to the internal reform elements of Kita's reform program. On the subject of foreign policy the *Yūzon Sha* statement of 1920 reads as follows:

The Japanese people must become the vortex of a whirlwind which will liberate mankind. The Japanese nation is destined to revolutionize the world. The fulfillment of this ideal and the military reorganization of Japan are the work of the gods. We believe that our duty will not end with revolution or reformation of Japan alone, but we must be content to begin with the reform of our own nation because we have faith in the Japanese mission to free the universe.[35]

Thus, during the first half of the 1920's, the National Reconstruction movement remained comparatively weak; but thereafter, as foreign relations became more critical and the economic depression more severe, the National Reconstruction program became stronger and the militarist expansionist elements in Kita's program more prominent.

Crises

The flowering of the National Reconstruction movement after 1931 coincided with the rise of very critical conditions in both Japan's external and internal affairs. Although these conditions were interdependent developments, the character of Japan's economic growth made the foreign situation the more dominant, and helps to explain the reason for the appearance of the first ominous signs of crisis in Japan's relations with China. Since Japan's economy was so closely intertwined with China trade and was so dependent upon the preservation of special commercial privileges in China, the formulation and implementation of foreign policy was based on a careful consideration of relations with that country. From the time of the Russo-Japanese War until the end of World War I, Japan had experienced relatively little difficulty in her dealings with China; but the Chinese gradually became united in a common opposition to the special commercial rights enjoyed by foreign merchants. They had long resented the activity of foreigners (both European and Japanese); but with the Twenty-one Demands during the war, and the Japanese determination to take over German interests in Shantung after the war, there was a far more widespread and determined opposition to Japanese expansionism. And yet, after the establishment of the Hara cabinet in 1918, Japan adopted a more conciliatory policy, later known as the Shidehara policy, which resulted temporarily in better relations. Even after the Chinese Nationalists declared, at their first nation-wide convention held in January, 1924, that their primary aim was to eliminate unequal agreements with foreign countries, the Japanese stuck to the Shidehara policy, causing Chinese resentment to be directed principally at the British. But in 1925 and 1926, the Nationalists, under the leadership of Chiang Kai-shek, began to move northward, and fear was aroused in Japan that the whole of China would soon be under their control and that Japan's special position in Manchuria and Mongolia would be endangered. However, Foreign Minister Shidehara early in 1927 was still saying that it was the province of the Chinese themselves to decide who should govern China and what kind of a policy should be adopted. He insisted that no foreign power would ever succeed in imposing a political or social structure upon the Chinese people.[36]

When Chiang Kai-shek's armies moved into Nanking in February, 1927, many foreigners, including Japanese, were killed and injured, and foreign property was damaged. Both American and British ships responded with a bombardment of Nationalist positions, but not the Japanese. News of the incident, however, set off a great blast of criticism in Japan against a weak foreign policy that required Japanese citizens to submit to such humiliation. Then, in the next month, another incident broke out at Hankow, in which Japanese naval personnel were insulted. This set off another round of criticism, which, together with objections to the government's role in the current financial crisis, led to the establishment of a new cabinet with a more positive policy toward China.

There has been a tendency to trace much of Japan's expansionism of recent years back to this "positive policy" of the Tanaka cabinet that was formed on April 20, 1927. But careful reading of its official statements of policy, and a study of the action taken, will show that the Tanaka policy was very much like the Shidehara one, except that more emphasis was placed on the special nature of Japan's position in Manchuria and Mongolia, and that there was a stronger determination to "take emergency measures" to defend Japan's rights and interests.[37] But the Chinese Nationalist movement was now gathering momentum, and the economic situation in Japan was making it more urgent that the deterioration of the China trade be halted. Soon after January, 1928, Chiang Kai-shek initiated the Nationalist advance to the north. Tanaka again sent troops into Shantung to protect Japanese interests. Apparently no attempt was made to resist the northward advance of the Chinese troops; but fighting broke out between Chinese and Japanese soldiers at Tsinan, and the local Japanese commander (seemingly without instructions from home) issued an ultimatum to the Chinese which included the demand for a formal apology from Chiang Kai-shek. The Tsinan Incident led to a new outburst of anti-Japanese sentiment in China. Shigemitsu Mamoru, a Japanese Foreign Office official who later became minister to China, is undoubtedly correct in concluding that the Incident resulted in the destruction of all that had been accomplished under the Shidehara policy.[38] Then, a few days later, news began to spread that the assassination of Chang Tso-lin, the war lord of Manchuria, had been the result of a plot by Japanese army officers. To the Chinese this was more evidence of the aggressive intentions of the Japanese, and the boycotts of Japanese goods and anti-Japanese demonstrations began to multiply. Although one cannot escape the conclusion that this disastrous turn of events in the relations between the two countries was due not so much to an "aggressive" policy of the Tanaka cabinet as to irresponsible action by army officers in the field, Shigemitsu is certainly justified in condemning the cabinet for failing to reveal that the assassination of Chang Tso-lin was due to a plot concocted by a Colonel Kawamoto in the Japanese Kwantung Army. The facts, which were known at that time, were not made public until the Tokyo War Crimes Trial after the war.[39]

In 1928 negotiations were being carried on between Japan and China relative to the revision of China's unequal treaties, and Japan was showing more reluctance than other powers in agreeing to a restoration of tariff autonomy. But in this case too, Tanaka's cabinet apparently was not attempting to increase Japan's interests but was trying rather to prevent the surrender of rights which had been long held and which were considered essential for the preservation of the China trade. By December, 1928, Chang Hsüeh-liang, the new war lord of Manchuria, had placed himself under the Chinese Nationalist flag, making it clear that all negotiations with China would have a direct bearing upon Japan's position in Manchuria. Nevertheless, in the first few months of 1929, Japan yielded more of her rights, causing Japanese observers to feel that the future of Japanese trade was indeed dark. There was disagreement about whether this unfortunate situation had come about because Tanaka's policy had been too strong, or too weak, or merely inept; but all agreed that it had failed. Consequently a new cabinet was formed, with Shidehara once more serving as Foreign Minister.

Under Shidehara's supervision, agreements were reached in the spring of 1930 which restored tariff autonomy to China. These were followed by a short period of good feeling. But Chinese officials indicated that they would soon be renewing their efforts to force the Japanese to relinquish more of their special concessions in China. In the meantime, however, the world depression had swept in on Japan and had threatened the Japanese with an internal crisis that for a time at least was more immediate and real than the crisis that was developing in the relations with China.

After the collapse of Japan's silk trade—which was associated with a 30 per cent drop in exports in a one-year period—and the disastrous decline in the price of rice, agricultural districts were immediately thrown into an extremely desperate situation. Not long afterward the urban areas, too, felt the pinch. Unemployment increased, and many small business firms were forced into bankruptcy. In 1928 there had been only 397 labor strikes; but in 1929 the figure rose to 576, and in 1930 to 906.[40] Most people tended to blame these conditions upon the selfish, incompetent actions of the politicians in Tokyo and were ready to listen to any group or organization which could propose a creditable alternative course of action. The government was energetic in repressing those who were in any way supporting a revolutionary program, and the conservative nationalist activists stepped up their efforts to head off radicalism. However, it was young military officers influenced by reform programs such as those proposed by Kita Ikki that gradually emerged as the most dynamic political force of the day.[41]

Military Leadership of the Reconstruction Movement

The trend toward military leadership of the National Reconstruction movement was accelerated by the efforts of Ōkawa Shūmei. Ōkawa, who was a civilian, played a prominent role in the early stages of the movement, when participation was limited chiefly to civilians. But quite early, Ōkawa became an employee of the Army General Staff, and this enabled him to make important contacts within military circles. Furthermore, he soon became absorbed in the part of Kita's program that advocated a more equitable distribution of the world's territories and resources. As early as 1923 he insisted that it was Japan's mission to free Asia,[42] and in 1925 he wrote a book which pointed up the significance of war in world history, the inevitability of war between the East and the West, and Japan's sublime mission in world history. In the concluding chapter he wrote:

The history of the world indicates that the West and the East must be combined. However, this combination will not probably be completed in peace. . . . Before a new world appears, there must be a deadly fight between the powers of the West and the East. . . . This theory is realized in the American challenge to Japan. The strongest country in Asia is Japan and the strongest country that represents Europe is America. . . . These two countries are destined to fight. Only God knows when it will be. At any time, Japan might be summoned to fight. We must prepare all the time.[43]

Ōkawa was a man of action, and therefore a man whose ideas were akin to those of a soldier.

In 1926, Ōkawa was instrumental in the organization of the *Gyōchi Sha*, which, like its predecessor the *Yūzon Sha*, adopted many of the principles stressed in Kita's plan. In fact, Kita was an active member of the society. But now the military elements of Kita's program were accented. The society had a military section headed by a young military officer, Nishida Zei, who began to propagate the principles of the "reconstruction" program within the army and among the reserves.[44] In a book written in 1926, Ōkawa made a strong appeal to the military by developing the theme that in that day of moral degeneration only the soldier had retained the spirit and honor of the samurai;[45] he implied that therefore only the soldier could be relied upon to press forward with measures that would allow Japan to become the champion of the East in establishing a new world order.[46] A few years later, after the military had taken the lead in the National Socialist movement, the nationalist magazine *Ishin* made Ōkawa Shūmei, who was then in jail for his part in the attempted coup d'état of 1932, the subject of a whole issue. One of the articles, written by the former socialist Akamatsu Katsumaro, emphasized Ōkawa's great influence upon young military officers. Akamatsu even suggested that the work of Ōkawa had raised military influence to a point where the public had more confidence in soldiers than in political parties.[47]

In 1927, the year of the beginning of Japan's economic depression, a secret society of army officers, called the *Tenken Tō* (Heavenly Swords Society) became extremely active. The original statement of purposes declared that the society would attempt to bring about a fundamental reconstruction of Japan and awaken the nation to an understanding of its mission in the world. Instructions to members of the society declared that the army was the essence of national authority: "When you think of the importance of an army in a revolution, you will realize how important it is that we should league together in preparation for the coming revolution."[48] As to the plans for reconstruction, Kita's program was still the model, but the military were now taking the lead.

A similar society, the *Ōsui Kai*, was established in 1928 by young naval officers. The founder, Lieutenant Fuji Hitoshi, had come under the spell of National Reconstructionists some years earlier and was determined to spread the doctrine of Pan-Asianism among his fellow officers. The society's statement of principles ordered all members to "establish the Great Japanese Empire in conformity with the spirit of the foundation of Japan and to unify the world with morality and righteousness."[49] As the order suggests, far more weight was given to the expansion of Japan than to internal reform.

But as the world depression began to press in upon Japan, conditions became even more favorable for the growth of the National Reconstruction movement. The young officers, since most of them had come from rural families, were well aware of the economic distress that prevailed in agricultural communities. After 1929 they were therefore more ready than ever to listen to condemnations directed at party politicians, and more inclined to support proposals of direct-action tactics that would place the affairs of state directly in the hands of the military. However, as aroused as they were by economic distress, they were probably concerned more about the tendency of the government to cut down on military expenditures.

The Hamaguchi cabinet not only attempted to pare down military and naval estimates but obviously made a resolute effort to bring about an administrative reform that would weaken military control over non-military affairs. The attitude of the cabinet was made clear at the time of the London Naval Conference in March, 1930, when it decided to accept a compromise that was not acceptable to the Navy. Furthermore, in the face of Navy opposition the government ratified the treaty. The implications of this development were well understood by all military leaders, and thenceforth they tended to be even more irked by the political-party activities, which they considered to be arbitrary, selfish, and unpatriotic.

The effects of economic depression, the entrenchment policy, and finally the government's attack on the political power of the military combined to make Hamaguchi and his party extremely unpopular, not only among military men but among many civilians of various classes and occupations. The young officers who backed National Reconstruction programs were therefore encouraged to organize themselves for action, rather than for propaganda. And the civilian leaders, such as Ōkawa Shūmei, toured the country making lectures in support of their programs, demanding a "people's movement" that would oust the capitalists and the politicians and place political affairs in the hands of soldiers. The assassination of Hamaguchi in November, 1930, was indicative of the growing opposition to political-party government.[50]

In order to assume leadership of a movement which it was felt the times demanded, Lieutenant Colonel Hashimoto Kingorō and two other army officers organized a secret society in September, 1930, called the *Sakura Kai* (Cherry Blossom Society). The officers of the society were prepared to resort to the use of force, if necessary, to bring about the reconstruction of the Japanese state. The society's prospectus declared that the members could not stand the immoral behavior of the upper-class statesmen, the deterioration of the political parties, the capitalists' lack of understanding of the masses, the tendency of the press to confuse the minds of the people with no thought of the future of the state, the distress of the rural communities, unemployment, depression, the radicalism of various intellectual groups, the lack of patriotism among students, and the concentration of bureaucrats on protecting their positions. For all these unfortunate conditions the greedy politicians were assigned most of the blame, since, according to the same prospectus, they were not merely deceiving the people but were disregarding the wishes of the Emperor and were turning against the armed forces of the nation.[51] Unlike earlier national reconstruction societies, the Cherry Blossom Society turned immediately to devising plans for seizing control of the government by direct action. With the coöperation of Ōkawa Shūmei and others, in March, 1931, it plotted to assassinate key men in the government, force the resignation of the cabinet, and dictate the appointment of military men who would initiate the reconstruction of Japan. But at the last minute, high-level military officials who had been counted on to coöperate backed out, and the plot had to be called off.[52]

Having failed in this initial attempt to place the army in control of the government, the young officers of the Cherry Blossom Society, aware now that Japan's relations with China were causing widespread concern, decided to direct their efforts toward a basic "solution of the Manchurian problem." The Chinese had become determined to exercise sovereign rights over the area, and the Japanese Kwantung Army was determined to protect the interests and rights of Japanese subjects. The diplomats, according to Shigemitsu, who was in China at the time, were making substantial progress toward a diplomatic solution of major issues;[53] but members of the Cherry Blossom Society and a large part of the officers in the Kwantung Army—and of those in the War Department in Tokyo—were apparently convinced that the situation had reached a point where diplomacy was useless. Furthermore, there was a tendency in these circles to class diplomats with the greedy politicians, the *zaibatsu* (financial cliques), and the bureaucrats, whom they blamed for bringing Japan to its sorry state. It was therefore the Cherry Blossom Society type of "solution" that prevailed. A plot was hatched, with Hashimoto in a leading part, which was designed to give the Kwantung Army an excuse to seize direct control of Manchuria. The moves were opposed by most of the leading civilian officials in the government, and by the Emperor; but once the deed was committed, the civilian officials found themselves carried along in a current which they could not control.[54]

With the extension of Japanese army control over most of Manchuria and the outbreak of hostilities in Shanghai in January, 1932, the League of Nations and the United States resorted to a series of diplomatic steps which gradually created the impression in Japan that the Western nations, as well as China, were resisting Japan's "righteous mission" on the continent of Asia. There was once more a stirring of the type of nationalist sentiment that had prevailed in the years preceding and during the Russo-Japanese War.[55] Farmers, laborers, and even socialists, were more enthusiastic about performing military service. The attitude was reflected in various aspects of Japanese life, but particularly in politics.

The decisive, spectacular activities of the army in Manchuria seemed to capture the imagination and sympathy of most of the Japanese people. The political-party government, which was valiantly trying to bring the army into line, lost more of its prestige by revealing its ineffectiveness and by giving the impression of dragging its feet in this great national venture. Two months after the Incident, the Wakatsuki cabinet (with Shidehara still serving as Foreign Minister) resigned. If it had not been for the pressure exerted by Prince Saionji, political-party government probably would have come to an end then, rather than a few months later.[56]

The new upsurge of nationalist fervor led the proletarian parties to take a more definitely national position. One writer estimates that the two major proletarian parties lost one-third of their membership, after the Manchurian Incident, to the National Socialist movement. One faction of the most conservative of the parties, the *Shakai Minshu Tō*, broke off from the party and set up the Japan National Socialist party (*Nihon Kokka Shakai Tō*) under the leadership of a former socialist, Akamatsu Katsumaro. The platform carried the declaration that the party would work toward the establishment of a new Japan which would be founded in a spirit of unity among the people under the Emperor, and would be free of exploitation. More specifically, the members, by means of a people's movement, were to destroy money-power rule and perfect a government based upon the principles of the Imperial Way (*Kōdō*). Also, the party would attempt to bring about the destruction of capitalism by legal means and would guarantee adequate standards of living for the people by instituting a state-controlled economy. Finally, efforts would be made to bring about a "liberation of the Asian peoples in accordance with the principle of equal human rights and the principle of the equal distribution of natural resources."[57]

In spite of the efforts of political parties to take advantage of the rising tide of national sentiment, it was the various nationalist societies, working with or under the Army, that exercised the most influence in the political developments of the period. Many men who had formerly belonged to political parties now joined such societies, because they preferred direct-action tactics and "positive" programs to democratic processes. Thus, after the Manchurian Incident there was a new crop of nationalist societies, mostly with national reconstruction programs, and a whole new series of plots and assassinations; for in spite of the successes in Manchuria, military government devoted to the reconstruction had not yet been established at home.

One of the most prominent and active societies after the Manchurian Incident was the *Jimmu Kai* (Emperor Jimmu Society), headed by Ōkawa Shūmei. Although the society was considered to be the successor to the earlier *Gyōchi Sha* (also organized by Ōkawa), it assigned a more prominent position to militarists and received more generous financial support from businessmen. The *Jimmu Kai* soon claimed a membership of 30,000 and was engaged in a wide range of activities, including nation-wide lecture campaigns in support of National Socialist candidates seeking election to the Diet.[58] But its part in the coup d'état of May 15, 1932 (called the May Fifteenth Incident) was more important—members of the society assassinated Premier Inukai. Inukai had opposed the Army's policy of occupying Manchuria, and he still felt that representative institutions had real value. One week before the assassination, he made a speech at Yokohama in which he berated Fascism and praised democratic principles.[59] After his death a nonparty Premier was appointed—a step that marked the beginning of military dominance in the internal affairs of Japan. The men who participated in the plot were arrested and tried, but in the public eye they were considered brave patriots, doing their bit to bring about the reconstruction of Japan in accordance with the Imperial Way. Government officials are said to have received, in the course of the trial, more than 300,000 petitions for clemency. War Minister Araki, who was gaining the reputation for being the outstanding exponent of the Imperial Way movement, reported the receipt of a parcel which contained nine fingers and a petition stating that the nine donors were willing to give their lives if that would save the conspirators from punishment. After prolonged trials, in both military and civilian courts, the verdicts were finally announced. No death sentences were imposed. Ōkawa received the longest sentence, and after an appeal in 1935, it was reduced to five years.[60]

Although the young officers did not succeed in establishing the kind of regime they had envisaged, the Army itself was placed in a much stronger political position, and the government thereafter tended to adopt an even more uncompromising attitude in the management of foreign affairs. As a result of the Manchurian Incident and the outbreak of hostilities in Shanghai, the anti-Japanese feelings in China took on a very disturbing character; and experts in Chinese affairs, such as Shigemitsu, who was currently the Japanese minister to China, were helpless in the face of pressure for positive action.

The anti-Japanese sentiment in China, however, had relatively little effect upon the development of a more intense form of nationalism in Japan, for the Japanese did not fear Chinese opposition. There was merely a sense of national pride in the military victories against the "bandits" in Manchuria. But when the Western nations began to take a stiffer attitude toward Japan's advances, fears were aroused that the Western powers might join forces against Japan. This development presented an entirely different situation, and consequently, as Japan's relations with the West worsened, nationalism became more intense and began once more to take on a "fearful" character.

Even by the time of the May Fifteenth Incident in 1932, the Japanese were beginning to be disturbed by Secretary Stimson's notes and by the dispatch of the Lytton mission to investigate the Manchurian disturbance. Then, when the Lytton Report was made public and the Japanese government issued a statement to the effect that the report had passages that were "marked by omissions, inconsistencies and misapprehensions,"[61] public sentiment was stirred to a higher pitch of resentment against the unreasonableness and injustice of Western powers. Finally, when, on March 27, 1933, notice was given of Japan's decision to withdraw from the League, a strong nationalist wave swept over the country. Matsuoka Yōsuke, the Japanese representative to the League, was hailed as a great national hero because of his courageous stand against the selfish Western powers. It was at this time, too, that Japanese businessmen became excited about the tariff barriers that were being thrown up against Japanese goods. These moves were considered to be nearsighted and to be convincing evidence that the Western nations were bent on preventing Japan from obtaining her just due, in trade as well as in land and resources.

Relations between Japan and Russia were also more alarming, for the military campaigns in northern Manchuria definitely threatened Soviet interests in that area. Both the Japanese and the Russians, however, wished then to avoid an actual outbreak of hostilities. The Japanese promised to protect Soviet interests, and the Russians were extremely careful to remain neutral. But the Manchurian Incident had a powerful effect upon Russian estimates of the world situation, leading Molotov in December, 1931, to report to the Central Executive Committee that the Far Eastern conflict was "the most important problem of our foreign policy."[62] Not being in a position, militarily or economically, to resist the Japanese, the Russians showed a very conciliatory attitude. But at the same time, Soviet leaders began to prepare for the defense of their Siberian territory by stationing more troops in border areas and by adopting a new Five-Year Plan, which was focused upon the development of Far Eastern areas. Also, diplomatic relations with Nationalist China were resumed. On the Japanese side, too, actions were taken and thoughts were expressed which tended to aggravate the unfriendly relations between the two countries. After the May Fifteenth Incident of 1932, a new cabinet was formed in which General Araki Sadao, who only one month before had publicly advocated war with Russia, was appointed Minister of War.[63] Thenceforth, border disputes, railway incidents, and White Russian problems multiplied and became more difficult to handle.

By the summer of 1933, Japanese-Soviet relations had become so explosive that American military attachés in Tokyo predicted that war would break out between the two countries within two years.[64] In the midst of negotiations for the sale of the Chinese Eastern Railway to Manchukuo (the new name for the puppet state of Manchuria) seven Soviet officials of the railway were arrested in Harbin. The Union of

Soviet Socialist Republics claimed to have reliable information that the orders for the arrests had come from the Kwantung Army, and so broke off the railway negotiations. By this time the Tangku Truce had brought an end to Japanese army advances in China, and more officers were demanding a stronger policy toward Russia. One of Japan's leading diplomats, Shigemitsu, is said to have remarked, in October, 1933, that the Japanese Army seemed determined to attack Russia in 1935.[65] The lines were even more sharply drawn in November, 1933, when the U.S.S.R. and the United States opened up diplomatic relations with each other.[66]

But toward the end of 1933, after the bellicose General Araki was replaced by General Hayashi as War Minister, Russo-Japanese relations quieted down. Negotiations for the sale of the Chinese Eastern Railway were continued, and finally an agreement was reached in March, 1935. Also, after the spring of 1933 the United States, under the new Roosevelt administration, had taken a calmer attitude toward Japan's activities in Manchuria. There continued to be considerable anxiety about the possibility of Japanese isolation in a tempestous world; but Japan's relations with foreign nations were sufficiently calm to permit the leading national activists to turn their attention once more to the work of bringing about the reconstruction of the Japanese state.

The "Young Officer" Movement

Until about 1933 the direct-action tactics of army officers had been serving the interests of all the militarists, for such activities were gradually strengthening the hand of the Army in the internal and external affairs of the country. But thereafter, the radical aspects of the Young Officer movement caused increasing concern among the older, more conservative officers of both services.[67] There arose, therefore, a rather clear-cut cleavage within both the Army and the Navy. The so-called Young Officer group wanted to carry out a reorganization of society that would eliminate the power of the financial, political-party, and bureaucratic cliques so that Japan would have greater power for fulfilling her national mission. But the Control Group (*Tōseiha*) did not recognize the desirability of a drastic internal social-reform program, although it was in complete agreement with the Young Officers concerning the importance of giving the Army a more responsible role in the affairs of state. The Control Group held most of the high-level positions, nominally at least; but after 1933, men influenced by Imperial

Way (*Kōdō*) principles were beginning to work their way into positions of greater influence and responsibility.

In 1934 the War Ministry undertook to issue a series of pamphlets designed to gain greater popular support for the military position, and although most of the points of view expressed in the pamphlets were acceptable to all elements of the Army, one of the pamphlets reflected the views of the Young Officer group and therefore became a source of considerable controversy in both Army and civilian circles. The pamphlet, entitled *Kokubō no Hongi to Sono Kyōka no Teishō* (Principles of National Defense and Proposals for Strengthening Them), first emphasized the dangers inherent in the international situation and underlined the urgency of giving greater attention to national defense, but it did not adhere to the orthodox line in its discussion of the internal economic and political conditions. It took up the position that effective national defense was possible only with the elimination of poverty. Consequently, the pamphlet undertook to analyze the causes of poverty and to suggest concrete measures for improving the situation. Greater restrictions upon free competition and more government attention to measures that would "stabilize the people's livelihood" were suggested. It was argued that with more effective state control of production and distribution, not only could the living conditions of the people be improved but industrial production could be more easily adjusted to defense needs.[68] These radical thoughts, appearing in pamphlets published by the Army, were very disturbing, not only to the business world but to the Control Group within the Army. About the time this pamphlet appeared, and due in part to it, the ideological struggle within the Army became more intense, and it soon developed into a complex political interplay which broke out into the open in the Aizawa Incident in July, 1935.

The Control Group in the spring of 1935 began to reshuffle army posts in an effort to weaken the influence of the more radical Young Officers. The most important change was the removal of General Mazaki, a recognized leader of the Young Officer group (*Kōdōha*), from the position of inspector general of military education. The appointment of General Watanabe to the position gave the conservatives a stronger hold over the Army, and the Young Officers were furious. The reshuffle aroused the radicals to train their guns upon the conservative militarists, as well as upon the civilian financiers, bureaucrats, and politicians. A pamphlet was issued condemning the arbitrary action of the conservative generals. General Nagata, head of the Bureau of Military Affairs, was singled out for most of the criticism, for his office was considered to be the real center of military administration. In view of the heated invective that was thrown at him by the young nationalists, the news of his assassination did not greatly surprise those who were familiar with the situation. A Lieutenant Colonel Aizawa Saburo, an officer in the Young Officer group, became convinced that the cause of Reconstruction could not be advanced without the elimination of the hated Nagata. Aizawa felt, according to his own testimony, that conservative officers of the Army were allied with politicians, financiers, and bureaucrats in a concerted attempt to head off the Reconstruction movement. Thus, on August 11, 1935, Aizawa went to Tokyo to discuss the matter with like-minded patriots. He then went personally to Nagata to advise him to resign. General Nagata refused to comply with the "advice" and, furthermore, ordered Aizawa transferred to a post in Formosa. Before leaving for Formosa, however, Aizawa walked calmly into the War Ministry and murdered General Nagata. At the trial, the Colonel showed no signs of regret. He was merely humiliated that he had not been sufficiently adept with the sword to kill his victim instantly, and that he had not been sufficiently composed to pick up his hat before leaving the murder room.[60]

The incident created a tremendous sensation. The War Minister, General Hayashi, resigned; and other changes were made in a desperate attempt to quiet the Young Officer group, which, to a man, considered Colonel Aizawa a dedicated patriot. The conservative senior generals decided to proceed cautiously with the court-martial hearings, for they were aware that the occasion might serve to arouse even deeper and more widespread resentment against the senior officers of the army and their alleged allies. They decided to open the court-martial proceedings to the public and to give Aizawa complete freedom to present his case, apparently because they felt that to act quickly, or secretly, would create an even more explosive situation. Aizawa was permitted to criticize not only politicians, financiers, and bureaucrats but generals of the army who, he said, did not fully understand the critical conditions which prevailed in Japan. He spoke at great length about scandals and corruption in high places. The defense lawyer admitted the seriousness of murdering a senior officer but insisted that the "sincerity" of Aizawa's motives should be weighed carefully. The defense also made much of the thousands of letters and telegrams of sympathy that were coming in—many were read in court. It looked as though Aizawa was certain to come off with a light sentence. About all that conservative generals could do at the moment was to order the First Division at Tokyo—the division most deeply affected by Young Officer sentiment— to Manchuria.[70]

But the Young Officers apparently overplayed their hand. They decided upon another plot against those who were opposed to their reform program, and they felt they had to carry it out before the First Division left Tokyo. The result was the February Twenty-sixth Incident of 1936, the most ambitious of the conspiracies and the one that almost accomplished the kind of coup d'état Kita Ikki had outlined some seventeen years earlier. Martial law was declared, and General Mazaki was given an opportunity to state the case of the rebels. For a time the official army announcements reflected a certain sympathy for the ideas of the Young Officers. But in jockeying for position, the Young Officers gradually lost ground. In a few days the rebel noncommissioned officers surrendered, and all the major civilian conspirators were arrested. Eventually the Young Officer leaders either committed suicide or surrendered.[71]

The conservative senior officers were now in no mood to put up with such coddling as had taken place at the time of the Aizawa Incident. There were no public trials, which would have given the assassins a chance to gain public acclaim. Thirteen officers and four civilians were sentenced to death, and five officers were given life imprisonment. Kita Ikki and Nishida Zei, after a somewhat longer trial, received the death sentence and were executed on August 19, 1937. A new court-martial was convened for Colonel Aizawa, and he too was executed. By positive measures such as these the Control Group reëstablished its control over the Army. The entire National Reconstruction movement was severely damaged. Not only were many of its leaders lost, but many of the civilian reformers tended to lose confidence in military men as the natural leaders of the Reconstruction movement.

◇   ◇   ◇

The period between 1919 and 1936 seems to constitute a distinctly different stage in the development of Japanese nationalism—one in which nationalist energy was no longer directed primarily toward taking advantage of foreign opportunities but rather toward strengthening the nation from within, and one in which Japanese nationalism, once more, began to take on a "fearful" character. In this period there were two distinct phases, the one before 1931 and the one after that year. In both, the emphasis was upon internal reform that would strengthen the nation; but before 1931 the movement was propelled for the most part by civilians, and after 1931 by militarists.

During the civilian phase of National Reconstructionism, probably nationalism was at its lowest ebb in modern Japanese history, for internationalist interests tended to overshadow nationalist concerns. But as the economic situation began to deteriorate and social tensions to increase, intellectuals and patriots became more energetic in their search for ways to restore social harmony and economic prosperity. The story of nationalist development before 1931, then, is chiefly one of the formulation and support of various programs to save the nation from poverty and social strife. They ranged all the way from the simple use of force against undesirable changes to reforms which involved radical changes in the Japanese social structure. However, in each effort—by those who wished to serve the nation, rather than a class—the Imperial institution and the peculiar relationships embodied in *kokutai* were upheld.

In the militarist phase after 1931, reconstruction programs were altered, not only because the militarists were in power but because the crisis facing the nation was becoming a foreign, as well as an internal, crisis. The nationalist societies began to resort to direct-action tactics, both at home and abroad—tactics which accelerated the rise of the militarists to power and put further strain on the relations with foreign powers. Japanese nationalism began to revert to its classical form: that is, to be something guided and stimulated primarily from above, and to be focused more upon foreign danger than upon internal growth. Thus, the years of National Reconstruction were a transitional period in which nationalism was losing its "confident" character and was reverting once more to a "fearful" type.

10 ULTRANATIONALISM

At the time of the February Twenty-sixth Incident of 1936, tension in Japan's relations with China was building up once more. And in the next year a war broke out which did not come to an end until Japan's surrender to the Allied Powers in 1945. In those eight years the Japanese government constantly attempted to arouse the people to a greater awareness of the danger facing the nation, and to a deeper sense of loyalty to the Emperor. Political, religious, and educational institutions, as well as all forms of communication and all types of entertainment, were utilized in a broad "spiritual mobilization" program. Nationalism thus reached a level of development that has been identified—and with justification—as ultranationalism.

Foreign Crisis

Although internal affairs seemed to be the dominant concern of the nation from 1934 until after the February Twenty-sixth Incident of 1936, thereafter it was foreign relations that were the most disturbing.

As had been the case in most diplomatic crises since the Russo-Japanese War, the root of the difficulties lay in Japan's efforts to protect and advance her interests in China. Even in the period of relative calm after 1934, the Chinese Nationalist movement continued to gain strength, the Russian military power in Far Eastern areas was increasing, and England and the United States were displaying a firmer attitude toward Japanese expansion in Asia. But in the summer of 1935 the Japanese Kwantung Army again became restless and resorted to intrigues and political maneuvers which put further strain on relations with the countries that had already become aroused by the Manchurian Incident. General Doihara Kanji and other officers attached to the Japanese Kwantung Army, apparently without the approval of the home government, undertook to set up an autonomous state in northern China. Since the moves suggested expansion southward into China rather than northward against Russia, England immediately assumed a firmer attitude, for she had much at stake in China. At the time of the Manchurian Incident she had shown a disposition to coöperate with Japan, and even in 1934, on the occasion of the Hirota announcement of Japan's "Monroe Doctrine" for Asia, no change of attitude or policy was apparent. But when Japan denounced the Washington and London naval treaties, later in 1934, and when the Kwantung Army began to advance into northern China in the following year, British diplomats displayed real concern about Japan's intentions. In June, 1935, the British government announced that it would send its chief economic adviser, Sir Frederick Leith-Ross, to China. The Americans and the Japanese were also invited to send missions, but the officials in Tokyo understood the implications of the gesture and refused. After the arrival of the British mission in China, the Chinese Nationalist government undertook to nationalize silver, "with British assistance," and to stabilize China's currency. It was thus becoming clear that England was moving toward a policy of supporting China in order to check Japanese expansion.[1] The reaction in Japan, official and private, was extremely hostile and bitter. The Chinese were accused of selling their country to foreigners, and the British were denounced for their imperialistic policies. Fears of combined opposition from Western powers mounted, while the government made desperate efforts to come to some settlement with the Chinese. But the nationalist feeling in both China and Japan made such a settlement utterly impossible. No Chinese diplomat could have agreed to any special rights or privileges for Japan in Chinese territory, and no Japanese official would have dared to give up any of the rights or privileges already acquired on the continent.

The stronger resistance of the Chinese Nationalists, the apparent change of policy of the British, and the tendency of the Russians to be less conciliatory with regard to border disputes made the more thoughtful Japanese observers truly worried about the course of Japan's foreign relations. Within the armed services there was disagreement over just what policy should be adopted in dealing with this complicated situation. In general, however, most officers favored positive action and tended to be divided on whether to advance northward against the Russians, or southward into China and southeast Asia. The so-called Young Officer group, the group advocating radical social programs at home, was inclined to favor advancing against the Russians; but the conservative Control Group seemed to prefer expansion southward.[2] Therefore, after the February Twenty-sixth Incident of 1936, when the Control Group succeeded in reëstablishing its authority within the army, a foreign policy was formulated which was in accord with the views of those who proposed restraining the Russians and "solving the China problem." The foreign policy statement, agreed to on August 7, 1936, made it clear that the main objective was to secure Japan's position in China, while exercising great caution in all relations with Russia.[3] But many leaders were still sufficiently anxious about the Russian flank, and the loss of British support, to be quite ready to listen to German proposals for an alliance against Russia. The careful considerations of the Anti-Comintern Pact by the Privy Council reveals that the Japanese were convinced that such a pact would restrain Russia and therefore give Japan a freer hand in China.[4] Consequently, the Anti-Comintern Pact was signed on November 26, in spite of the fact that in the previous month Japan and Russia had come to an agreement on a five-year extension of the Japanese concession in Sakhalin, and on a new fisheries treaty.

The Anti-Comintern Pact, however, did not yield the desired results, for neither Russia nor China responded as expected.[5] Russia replied by refusing to sign the fisheries treaty that had been agreed upon earlier. And in spite of Japanese assurances that the pact was aimed only at the Comintern, the U.S.S.R. would agree to nothing more than a one-year renewal of the old fishing agreement. Border disputes also became more difficult to settle, and the Japanese began to suffer from Russian searches of Japanese vessels, from charges of espionage activities, and from complications arising out of dozens of minor incidents. Then in June, 1937, a border incident broke that threatened to get out of hand. Foreign Minister Hirota told the Diet that this "illicit invasion and occupation" of islands in the Amur River by the Russians was the most serious of the many border incidents that had occurred up to that time.[6]

The Anti-Comintern Pact also tended to draw various Chinese factions together against Japan, a development that was even more disturbing than the new attitude shown by Russia. Chiang Hsueh-liang, the former war lord of Manchuria who had retreated into northern China before the 1931 advances of the Japanese Kwantung Army, was anxious to join forces with any group that would help him in driving the Japanese from Manchuria. By the end of 1936 the Communists in northern China, who advocated an anti-Japanese policy, also had become quite active. Chiang and the Communists joined forces and, in December, 1936, succeeded at Sian in forcing Chiang Kai-shek to drop his campaign against the Communists and to assume leadership of a popular-front movement against Japan. Therefore, as the Japanese pushed their policy of "solving the China problem," various groups in China joined forces to resist such advances; this led to the development of an explosive situation that threatened at any moment to break out in open warfare. The explosion came in July, 1937, with the so-called Marco Polo Bridge Incident, which set off a war that did not end until eight years later.[7]

Impact on National Reconstruction

Just as the Manchurian Incident had caused most political organizations to move closer to a nationalist position, so the crisis of 1936–1937 led them to move even farther in the same direction. In 1931, the more radical proletarian organizations tended to drop internationalist elements in their programs in favor of something approximating National Reconstructionism; but after 1936 the National Reconstruction concepts were in turn revised to yield something which might be described as "social nationalism" (*shakai minshu shugi*), for nationalism obviously had come to overshadow socialism in even the most reform-conscious societies.

The programs of some organizations were not shifted so far from a reform emphasis as others, and there was a great variety of views on what method should be followed in implementing the revised policies. But in general, most groups tended, after 1936, to discard direct-action tactics, to rely less upon the military, to deëmphasize the effectiveness of leftist organizations, to favor unification of nationalist groups, and to recognize the desirability of stating all principles and aims in terms of national symbols. The nature and extent of the movements may be illustrated by describing briefly attempts made in 1936 to organize a nation-wide patriotic political party, an all-Japan patriotic labor union, a Japan patriotic peasant union, and a Japan patriotic youth association.

Several conferences sponsored by different groups were held with a view to establishing a new patriotic political party, since it was generally recognized that the strong action of the government against the Young Officers and their allies had made the pursuit of direct-action tactics unwise and the establishment of a patriotic political party essential. In May, 1936, representatives of some seventy organizations met to discuss the establishment of such a party. They decided to set up a Federation of Patriotic Organizations (*Zen Aikoku Dantai Tōitsu Remmei*), which, toward the end of the month, issued a statement that first praised Imperial rule and then expressed "for the sake of the Empire" the fear that the current cabinet was really doing nothing effective to solve the increasingly serious international problems or to check the activity of the "plutocrats, bureaucrats, party politicians and liberals who are running about madly in an attempt to strengthen their positions."[8] In its statement of principles the federation rejected liberalism, democracy, and capitalism. It also favored the establishment of a controlled economy based on the principle of Japanism (*Nihon shugi*) and the building of a single patriotic political party dedicated to service to the Emperor.[9]

Probably an even clearer indication of the new emphasis upon national ideals is seen in the attempt to organize an all-Japan patriotic labor organization. Those who had tried to organize a political party were hoping to gain the coöperation and support of all patriotic labor and peasant organizations, but many leaders of these organizations felt that it was necessary first to unify the various proletarian movements. In April, 1936, the representatives of several labor unions—with an estimated total membership of more than 100,000—met in an All-Japan Conference of Patriotic Labor Unions (*Aikoku Rōdō Kumiai Zenkoku Konwakai*) and decided upon a declaration that deplored materialistic trends which caused laborers to overlook the racial character and nationality of Japan. But now, the declaration continued, there has been an upsurge of Japanese spirit, and in the present crisis the laborers of

Japan must join hands in developing national industries, destroying communism and social democracy, reforming capitalism, and "clarifying our nationality." It also published a statement of principles, which urged a "brilliant rise of the Japanese Empire," the firm establishment of fair and just production relations, and the reformation of the capitalistic economic system by rational means. When this first meeting adjourned, all representatives, quite appropriately, went to worship at the Meiji Shrine.[10]

There was also a great drive to unite all patriotic peasant organizations. Several conferences were held in various areas, and the views expressed in most of them apparently were similar to those expressed by the labor conference mentioned above, but there were still traces of the agrarian ideas popularized seventeen years earlier by Gondō Seikyō. After stating that attempts should be made "to perfect an organization of village communities based upon the Japanese spirit," one group took a stand against Communism, class struggle, and monopoly capital. And finally statements were made in support of the "systematic development of productive power" and the organization of coöperative associations under government control.[11]

Of the various patriotic unification movements of 1936, the attempts to bring together all patriotic youth organizations probably had a more significant bearing upon the rise of nationalism. Several efforts were made to achieve unity among the many youth societies, but the one that attracted the most attention was the one made by Hashimoto Kingorō, that fiery founder of the Cherry Blossom Society. As has been indicated, Hashimoto was influenced somewhat by the ideas of Kita Ikki and was considered a member of the Young Officer group. Since he was implicated, in a minor way, in the February Twenty-sixth Incident of 1936, he was transferred to the reserve. But Hashimoto was too energetic to remain idle and soon was involved in plans for the building of a new political party of young men. He was still interested in change, but the nature of the change he now advocated was of a quite different type. Instead of "reconstruction" he now spoke of "renovation": "Our aim is renovation. In order to effect renovation, blood and enthusiasm are absolutely essential. The blood and enthusiasm are the possessions of young men. . . . To make young men become the framework of New Japan and to unite the whole strength, both tangible and intangible, of the Japanese race in our Emperor is the way to be loyal to our country. . . ."[12] But in order to "unite the whole strength of the Japanese race" and to achieve renovation, he felt that certain rather fundamental changes had to be made. The two-party political system, for example, should be scrapped, since these parties were working too closely with the financial interests. But such ideas did not disturb the government too much, for the organization of a huge youth society working toward the goal of spiritual renovation had a certain appeal to the conservative militarists who were then in power. But the emphasis upon a weakening of the "financial interests" was apparently too close to the old Young Officer view, and in 1937 Hashimoto was called back to active duty and his new party was subsequently dissolved.

To anticipate our story slightly, Hashimoto was again retired to inactive duty in 1939, and again he returned to the task of organizing the youth of the land. But the organization set up at that time was quite different. The society (the *Dai Nihon Sekisei Kai*) was not to work for internal reform but for a stronger national defense, Asiatic independence, and opposition to Great Britain. With a membership of more than five million and a very active program, including the publication of a magazine (*Tanjo Dai Nihon*), the society exerted great influence. Its program was now in tune with the desires of those in power, as is clearly seen from the fact that in 1940 the society was made an integral part, and Hashimoto an officer, of Japan's superparty, the Imperial Rule Assistance Association.

Kokutai Again

During and after World War I, when ideas of democracy, socialism, and communism were gaining popularity, *kokutai* (national entity) and the Imperial institution (the focus of *kokutai*) were not held in high esteem. As early as 1910 the famous "High Treason Case" revealed a shocking disrespect for the Emperor. Soon afterward, the historians became involved in a wordy dispute over the problem of the legitimacy of the Northern and Southern Imperial lines—a discussion that in earlier or later times would not have been permitted. Also, in 1911, Professor Minobe Tatsukichi published his lectures on the Constitution, in which he advanced the theory that the Emperor was an organ of the state. In those days the theory did not seem radical and was accepted by most legal scholars. Then, with the upsurge of interest in democratic ideals and institutions during the war, *kokutai* and the unique religious qualities of the Imperial institution were given even less attention, for parliamentarianism, universal suffrage, and political-party government had become the fad. Scholars even dared to write objective studies on the "age of the gods," clearing away some of the religious mystery surrounding the origin and rise of the Imperial family. The rumors of the sickness and incompetency of Emperor Taisho, followed in 1921 by the appointment of the Crown Prince as Regent, also weakened the prestige of the Imperial Household. Finally, the foreign trip of the Crown Prince, and also Prince Chichibu's study in England in 1923, did much to humanize the Imperial family. Thus, during the early 1920's, at the time of strong internationalist tendencies, the Emperor system, though still powerful, lost much of its religious character. The lowest point was probably reached at the end of 1923, when with the Toranomon Incident an attempt was made on the Regent's life.[13] Thereafter, however, the conservative forces reëmerged. Since the Emperor system (*Tennōsei*) became the focus for the revival of military authoritarianism, *kokutai* discussions once more became prominent, and the Emperor was again raised to a higher position.

It will be remembered that the Emperor was to head the various national reconstruction programs devised in the 1920's, and that the Young Officers carried on their activities under the banner of the Imperial Way (*Kōdō*). It was natural, then, for *kokutai* and Emperorism to regain popularity after the Manchurian Incident. While General Araki held the center of the stage with his fanatical declarations about the Imperial Way, educational, legal, historical, and literary thought reflected a greater appreciation of the traditional Emperor system. The more liberal theories, such as Minobe's organ theory, were thus subjected to attacks.

The Minobe Incident, which broke out in 1935, indicates the nature of the transition that was taking place. Since Minobe had rejected the theory of the Emperor's independent power and had stressed the rights of the Diet as a body made up of elected representatives of the people, he was condemned for not properly appreciating and understanding the Imperial Way. The charge was first openly made in the Diet by Etō Genkurō, who was a member of the Seiyūkai party and a reserve brigadier general. Then, on February 18, 1935, Kikuchi Takeo carried the attack to the House of Peers, to which Minobe himself had received an appointment. Minobe answered the charge to the satisfaction of most people in academic circles; but the newspapers took up the matter, and the problem was debated and discussed throughout the country. Although the Emperor and many of his closest advisers tended to take

Minobe's side, the problem was caught up in political rivalries and was carried along by the current wave of Emperorism. The Home Office had to ban Minobe's books and the Department of Education had to issue orders regarding the proper interpretation of *kokutai*. Still, the Army and various Reconstruction groups were not content, and the pressure on the cabinet increased. In October the government was forced to issue a statement clarifying its position on *kokutai*—emphasizing that it did not accept the Minobe interpretation. But the turmoil continued. Several Minobe sympathizers were forced to resign from their posts, and an attempt was even made upon Minobe's life.[14]

After the February Twenty-sixth Incident of 1936, when the radical Young Officer movement fell into disrepute and the Control Group (*Tōseiha*) came into power, moves to strengthen the Emperor's position were no longer limited to uncoördinated, spontaneous efforts by various nationalists and national groups, but took the form of a carefully considered, government-supported educational program. In the spring of 1937 the Department of Education published a book called *Kokutai no Hongi* (Principles of *Kokutai*) that provided an official interpretation for the guidance of teachers throughout the Japanese public school system. Some 300,000 copies were circulated, and instructions were issued directing that every effort be made to see that the Principles became the basis of Japanese education.

The first section of the book consists chiefly of a definition of *kokutai* and begins with these sentences:

The unbroken line of Emperors, receiving the Oracle of the Founder of the Nation, reign [*sic*] eternally over the Japanese Empire. This is our eternal and immutable national entity. Thus, founded on this great principle, all the people, united as one great family nation in heart and obeying the Imperial Will, enhance indeed the beautiful virtues of loyalty and filial piety. This is the glory of our national entity. This national entity is the eternal and unchanging basis of our nation and shines resplendent throughout our history.[15]

Subsequent chapters discuss the origin of the nation, the sacred virtues of the Emperor, and the cardinal duties of the Japanese subject. A final chapter shows how the virtues of the Emperor and the duties of the subject merge in *kokutai* to create "harmony and mutual fellowship" between sovereign and subject.[16]

The second section deals with the manifestations of *kokutai*. After a chapter on the peculiar character which *kokutai* has given to the development of Japanese history, attention is directed to its manifestations in the virtues of the Emperor, in the loyalty of the subject, in the divineness of the homeland, in the unique qualities of the Japanese people, and finally, in the religious rites and ceremonies that date from prehistoric times. In conclusion, the book asserts that in facing the critical problems that lie ahead, it is the mission of the Japanese people to create a new culture by "sublimating and assimilating foreign cultures" and by eliminating the individualistic qualities that had seeped into the country since the Meiji Restoration of 1868.[17] The basic doctrine of ultranationalism was here set forth by the government to serve as a guide for public education.

Spiritual Mobilization

Soon after the February Twenty-sixth Incident of 1936, the cabinet formulated a policy statement which, besides dealing with the subject of foreign relations, outlined a program of government action in the field of thought control.[18] It was stated that the government would set up a bureau of information to be responsible for the collection, evaluation, and dissemination of all information, both at home and abroad. Under this central bureau there were to be intelligence bureaus in each ministry, and each of these bureaus was to establish branches in every prefecture and in every "necessary" foreign country. Then, in order that the information network might utilize and control all organizations that could be of assistance in directing the thoughts and attitudes of the people, all the political, social, cultural, religious, labor, youth, and business organizations were to be encouraged, and if necessary forced, to unite into a single, powerful body. A similar unity was to be fostered among Japanese groups abroad. Furthermore, a national body was to be set up in each of the following fields of communication and entertainment: press, radio, moving pictures, publication, drama, music, and art.

After outlining this integrated organizational structure, the statement then proceeded to set forth principles to be followed in the collection of intelligence and in the dissemination of information and propaganda. Regarding domestic propaganda, "thought education" was placed at the head of the list, although the preservation of health, restrictions on consumption, and the increase of production were also given high priority. In "thought education" attention was first directed to the schools. Various methods were to be followed to "guide the staffs of various schools and research institutes so that they would conduct propaganda on their own initiative, but in accordance with the policy of the authorities." The statement then outlined principles for the supervision and control of newspapers, radiobroadcasts, magazines, books, pamphlets, posters, manifestos, mottoes, motion pictures, plays, concerts, records, painting, photography, sculpture, the fine arts, exhibitions, and lectures. Detailed policies were outlined also for foreign propaganda.

Although Japan was not yet involved in war, the conservative militarists who were then in power began immediately to implement certain aspects of the program. In July, 1936, the Bureau of Information (*Jōhō Bu*) was established.[19] Its purpose, according to an article in one of its own publications, was to provide "accurate information on internal and external affairs"; but later on in the same article it was explained that "the basic purpose of internal publicity in Japan is to unite all members of the nation in one spirit and promote the consolidation of their spiritual life."[20] Within a year, and after the start of the China Incident, the work of the bureau assumed new importance; consequently the bureau was enlarged and reorganized, and was given even greater power. Ten special advisers were appointed, one each for the fields of newspapers, magazines, radiobroadcasts, theater arts, motion pictures, and so forth.

Under the pressure for greater spiritual unity, the schools had to make appropriate revisions in their curricula and in their teacher-training programs. In 1936 various steps were taken to place the educational system in line with the government's policy—the publication of the book on the "Principles of *Kokutai*" in 1937 was merely one of the more significant steps. More drastic reforms had to be adopted in subsequent months, for the war with China had broken out, and the rulers were determined to keep the national feelings of the people at a high pitch. Efforts in this direction were particularly noteworthy after the summer of 1938, when those in authority came round to the view that the Chinese conflict was not to be settled easily and that a far more determined effort was required. It was then that the Konoye cabinet was "reconstructed" in order to bring in men who would be better able to give momentum and direction to a drive against the dangers threatening the future of Japan. General Araki was appointed Minister of Education, and with his usual enthusiasm and energy he set to work directing education toward spiritual goals. By public speeches and departmental instructions he emphasized the importance of spiritual and moral education. In June, 1938, he sent an order to all school officials, which stated:

Now is a time when we must bear clearly in mind the true significance of the present situation, manifest the ideal underlying the founding of our Empire, assimilate the culture of the East and the West with lofty aspirations, and endeavor to establish a new order of peace on earth. With a glorious national structure to begin with, the people should work all the harder toward promoting the spirit of loyalty to the Emperor and service to the country. The whole nation must unite and go forward to master the situation.[21]

One part of the government's program to stir up a greater sense of loyalty took the form of support of a movement for the "spiritual mobilization of the nation." The movement, under government auspices, was first initiated in September, 1937, but it was not pushed very energetically at first, for there was widespread confidence that the hostilities would soon be brought to a succesful conclusion. But, as has been noted, the Incident looked more serious after 1938; and eventually, in April, 1939, the government adopted new measures for strengthening and expanding the "spiritual mobilization" movement. As explained by the Bureau of Information, these measures were essential because: "With the development of a new phase of the [China] Affair in which long-term activities for spiritual as well as material construction have to be carried out in the midst of the most complicated, strained international relations, further enlightenment on the essential nature of the current emergency and new emphasis in the policies and programme of this important movement have been felt by its leaders and the Government."[22] The points to be emphasized were clearly outlined: Japan had a mission to construct a "New Order in East Asia"; nothing short of the destruction of the Nationalist government of China and the completion of the New Order would suffice to settle the conflict with China; Japan must show an "irrevocable national determination" to eliminate any interference with Japan's mission; and, in order to implement the project, national defenses must be strengthened all along the line. Under this program, thought control became far more effective, for it was no longer limited primarily to censorship and other negative forms of control but was extended to the actual direction of thoughts and feelings. Japanese nationals were not merely kept from expressing certain thoughts and sentiments but were told repeatedly and through various channels what views and beliefs they should hold on all major national issues.

In carrying out "spiritual mobilization," State Shinto and the publication system were of course relied on, but gradually all communication channels and all types of entertainment were used. Since Japan had become one of the most literate countries in the world, and since her people were avid readers, much attention was given to the control of the publication of newspapers, books, and magazines. One editorial writer testified after the war that on numerous occasions between 1935 and the outbreak of the Pacific War in December, 1941, he had written articles favoring a settlement of the China dispute, proposing peace, questioning Japan's right to rule China, and criticizing Japanese military aggression. All his writings on these subjects, he said, were written in a manner calculated not to be offensive to governmental policy. However, whenever he indicated any displeasure with governmental policy, he received visits from the military police and civil police, who warned him not to write on such subjects again.[23] Another witness claimed that, after 1939, censorship of the press became so strict that the *Asahi,* one of the leading Tokyo newspapers, set up a special censorship bureau to see to it that the numerous Home Ministry bans were properly respected.[24] A large number of news articles and stories were foisted upon the newspaper and magazine publishers, and an increasingly large number of books were published directly by various government agencies. The Army and the Department of Education were particularly active in this field. In January, 1941, according to a postwar affidavit by Itō Nobumi, who had been president of the Board of Information (successor of the Bureau of Information), all publishers in the country were organized into the Japan Publishers' Association, all book distributors were organized into the Japanese Book and Magazine Distributors Corporation, and all newspapers into the Japanese Newspaper League. Ito pointed out, too, that it was customary for each of these associations to consult with the president of the Board of Information before choosing their officials. These arrangements, explained Ito, "resulted in complete government control of all information media included in their respective groups."[25]

Radiobroadcasts were probably just as effective as publications in influencing the Japanese mind, for radiobroadcasting was controlled and operated by the government, and almost every household in the nation had a radio that was used extensively. After 1936 all programs were closely censored and were placed under the supervision of the Bureau of Information. The news, of course, contained only those items and those slants approved by the authorities. After the outbreak of the

China Incident in 1937, the programs were more carefully planned in order to provide a more effective means of channeling the thoughts of the populace along approved lines. In January, 1938, a ten-minute period beginning at 7:30 P.M., a time with an extremely high listener rate, was taken over by the government. On this program, officials made statements, explanations, and appeals of various types. As a Bureau of Information magazine stated a few months later, "The radio has thus become an important organ for uniting the nation." But radio's contribution to "spiritual mobilization" was not limited to this government program. Some broadcasts were beamed to Korea, Formosa, Manchukuo, and China in order to bring the peoples in those areas closer together under Japanese leadership. Entertainment programs were also geared to the work of creating greater national solidarity. As the Bureau of Information's official publication put it:

Entertainment programs now being broadcast bear close connection to the current situation. Certain programs offer numbers inspiring bravery and courage among the people. Others provide dramas and other entertainment features in which are interwoven the objectives of the National Spiritual Mobilization movement. To enhance the national spirit and raise the morale of the people, simple and popular broadcasts of *naniwabushi, biwa* music and *gidayu*, of stories concerning the activities of Japanese soldiers, inspiring anecdotes concerning patriotic people on the home front, historical tales of loyalty and bravery in ancient and modern times, and of other educational material commendable in the light of promotion of the Japanese spirit are regularly given.[26]

The government considered radiobroadcasting so important in its "publicity and information" program that it made special attempts to increase the number of set owners. Radios were given away in some of the poorer villages, and the subscription and registration fees were cancelled for large families and for those with men at the front. Although in 1938 in Japan only 53.1 persons in each 1,000 owned radios, as compared with 206.5 in the United States, the size of the Japanese families and the extensive use of the radios probably served to make radiobroadcasting in Japan almost as important, as a means of communication, as in the United States. It was therefore extremely valuable as a means of carrying out "spiritual mobilization."[27]

By 1938 the motion-picture industry had become very active in Japan and was filming between five hundred and six hundred pictures a year. Japan was thus near the top in world production. The number of theaters, however, was not so impressive; according to an investigation made in February, 1938, there were 1,765 motion-picture theaters in the country—one theater for every 40,000 persons. But the theaters were well attended—in 1937 there were more than 200,000,000 paid admissions. In March, 1939, the Diet enacted the Motion-Picture Law which was the first important effort of the Japanese government to use moving pictures as an instrument of national policy. There had been certain controls, including censorship of finished films; but with the enactment of this law the government assumed direct control over the production and distribution of all films. It required that scenarios be submitted for approval in advance of production, and it assumed the right to control the distribution of films. Even for the establishment and construction of theaters, licenses were required, and certain "designated pictures" had to be shown by all theaters.[28] "Competent ministers" were obligated to recommend pictures that would contribute to the "advancement of national culture."[29] A motion-picture producer stated before the Military Tribunal at the end of the war that after the law was passed, it was impossible to obtain Japanese productions that were not ultranationalistic or militaristic.[30] As the foreign situation became more critical, the motion-picture industry was even more thoroughly integrated into the government's thought program. American pictures, which were very popular with the movie-going public, were shown less frequently, especially after 1940 when it was ordered that no picture which was not approved by the Ministry of Education could be shown in Japan. Many "Japanese-spirit" films were produced by the War Ministry itself, such as the one entitled "Japan in Time of Emergency," which, by depicting the critical nature of Japan's foreign relations, underlined the dangers facing the nation and thus aroused the people to a firmer determination to be loyal and unselfish citizens.[31] This picture, like many others of the same type, was shown not only in theaters throughout the country but in most of the schools. Some pictures—the "Holy War," for example—played up Japan's mission to rescue China; others were centered on the glorification of military life, on Emperor worship, or on the superiority of Japan and her divine mission.[32] By the end of the 1930's the Japanese had become great movie-goers, and thus such films undoubtedly exerted considerable influence upon a large segment of the Japanese population.

Other means of disseminating information were not overlooked, although the channels already mentioned were of the greatest interest to the government. Music, especially martial music, was deemed to be very effective in stirring people to a greater sense of their duty to the nation, and it was easy for a foreign observer in Japan in the years before the war to detect a prevalence of such tunes. But there was little evidence of the government's hand in this trend—it was apparently only another manifestation of the more intense feeling of nationalism. The same holds true for the stage, where a larger proportion of the plays shown were those that accented the self-sacrificing behavior of loyal Japanese subjects. However, after the outbreak of the China Incident in 1937, even the old art of *Kamishibai* (illustrated stories by candy vendors) favored nationalistic stories that were distributed by the government. The president of the Japanese *Kamishibai* Association later testified that after July, 1941, one of the most widely used stories, entitled, "Japan Is Now Fighting," represented the United States and England as being responsible for the China War.[33]

It is impossible to measure the degree to which the government's "spiritual mobilization" program influenced public thinking. The literature, art, and news of the period gives evidence that the nation was overwhelmed by nationalist thoughts and feelings; but it has been pointed out that no other type of expression was permitted. Foreigners who resided in Japan at that time, felt that the sentiments of most of the Japanese people were in accord with those expressed in the newspapers, over the radio, and in the movies. The academic world was undoubtedly more discriminating. At least one postwar scholar of Japanese nationalism has stressed the point that the intellectuals did not play an important role in the nationalist trend.[34] And yet the number of historical, philosophical, and social studies dealing with the Japanese spirit was considerable. A bibliography of "Japanese-spirit studies," compiled in 1938, lists 37 books published in 1928, 80 in 1932, and 111 in 1938.[35]

The "New National Structure" Movement

The outbreak of war in Europe in 1939 temporarily eased the tension in Japan's foreign relations. Since Germany had come to terms with Russia, it appeared that Japan might be able to arrive at some working agreement with the Colossus of the North. Furthermore, it was obvious that England would be so thoroughly occupied in Europe that she could not interfere with Japan's activities in Asia. In the light of these developments, Japanese leaders were somewhat optimistic about profiting from the war as they had profited from World War I. But no hasty action was to be taken, for it was thought best to wait and see whether the Germans were going to succeed in their military venture. The situation seemed to clarify itself when in May, 1940, the Germans swept into Holland, Belgium, and France. Within a few weeks those nations succumbed to German military power and Great Britain herself was placed in serious danger. This turn of events completely altered the situation in the Far East, and it seemed obvious to many that Japan was now presented with tempting opportunities for further continental expansion. Immediately, Japan demanded that France cease sending supplies to China through Indo-China, and that she permit the Japanese to keep military observers there. Japan was prepared to use force if the demands were not accepted. The French yielded. Not long afterward, Arita, the Foreign Minister, outlined the doctrine of Greater East Asia by which Japan was to be the "stabilizing force" of eastern Asia. But in spite of the energy shown by the Yonai cabinet in making use of new opportunities, the militarists were still dissatisfied and the Yonai cabinet was forced to resign. Prince Konoye then became Premier, on July 22, 1940, and he appointed Matsuoka Yosuke as his Foreign Minister and General Tōjō as his War Minister. On July 26 and 27, the cabinet reached an agreement on basic principles of foreign policy. The government was, first of all, to be firm with the United States, the only power that was in a position to offer any opposition to Japanese moves in Asia. Also it was decided to come to terms with Russia, work more closely with Germany and Italy, and adopt a stronger policy in French Indo-China and Indonesia. Foreign Minister Matsuoka said: "I have always said that the mission of Japan is to proclaim and demonstrate *kōdō* [the Imperial Way] throughout the world. . . . Accordingly, the immediate aim of our foreign policy at present is to establish, in accordance with the lofty spirit of *kōdō*, a great East Asian chain of common prosperity with the Japan-Manchukuo-China group as one of the links."[36] The more positive policy of the government was reflected in the writings of private journalists, who broke into print with plans and speculation concerning the establishment of a New Order in East Asia. A professor of the Tokyo Imperial University wrote in August, 1940, that "the Japanese race, which is fighting for the New East Asia order, should be regarded also as charged with the mission of fighting for a new order in the Pacific."[37]

The decision to draw closer to Germany was a most crucial development in Japanese history, not only because it led to a new crisis in foreign relations but also because it was associated with the adoption of political, economic, and educational policies which accelerated the rise of Japanese nationalism to a more fanatical level. Although the decision to work more closely with Germany was not made until after Germany's startling military victories in Europe, it was by no means made on the spur of the moment. Ever since the Franco-Prussian War, Japan had thought highly of German military science, and in the modernization of the Japanese army, German influence was strong. Then, as Japan turned against the liberalism of France, England, and the United States, it was realized that the political, philosophical, and educational concepts of Germany were more to the liking of the Japanese ruling classes. Consequently, the Constitution followed a German pattern, and German philosophy and educational principles gained tremendous popularity. After 1895, when Germany joined Russia and France in the Triple Intervention, Japanese enthusiasm for German science and culture was somewhat dampened. And yet, even while Japan was fighting against Germany in World War I, there were several writers who saw that the two countries faced similar handicaps as a result of lagging behind western Europe and America in industrial development. After the war, when Japan's economic crisis worsened, she found herself moving along paths that were parallel to those followed in Germany. The National Reconstruction movement in Japan was not dissimilar to National Socialism in Germany. Both countries began to resort to direct-action tactics to improve their international positions about the same time, and both soon found themselves faced with a common foe, the U.S.S.R. and the Communist International. Then came the signing of the Anti-Comintern Pact, in 1936, and the strengthening of cultural and political ties.

As Germany continued her program of freeing herself from "the shackles of the Versailles system," Hitler and his diplomatic officials, in January, 1938, came to favor revising the pact in a manner that would bring Japan and Germany closer together—this time against the British.[38] Japan, in following her policy of expanding southward, was running into more difficulties with England, but the Navy and certain moderate civilian elements objected to an alliance with Germany which might precipitate war. However, the Japanese Army, by diplomatic efforts outside Foreign Office channels, gradually succeeded in causing the government to favor such an alliance. An agreement might have been reached in 1939 had not Germany suddenly signed the

German-Russian Pact and, by destroying what value the Anti-Comintern Pact had had as a restraining force on Russia, temporarily killed Japanese interest in a stronger alliance.

After the German victories in June, 1940, the Japanese Army once more looked with favor upon the idea of an alliance with Germany, feeling that this would give Japan the freedom that was needed to settle the China war. The Germans, however, no longer felt the need of Japanese support and therefore were not enthusiastic about the proposals. But in September, the battle of Britain began to look less hopeful for Germany. Hitler and his diplomats therefore returned to the idea of an alliance with Japan. Both countries felt that advantages could be derived from joining forces in an attempt to hasten the defeat of England and to prevent the entry of the United States into the war. An alliance, it was felt, would give Germany greater freedom to prosecute the war against England, and give Japan greater freedom to finish off the China Incident and to expand into southeastern Asia. American assistance to England, in these months, and American resistance to Japan's moves in French Indo-China made both Germany and Japan more anxious to neutralize American power. The Japanese Navy obviously understood the dangers involved but was overruled by Matsuoka and the Army. At a meeting of the Privy Council, several officials indicated that they considered the prevention of a Japanese-American war to be a fundamental aim of the pact.[39] The final decision, reached on September 26, may have been hastened by the American order prohibiting further shipments of scrap iron to Japan. Again, however, the Tripartite Pact, like the Anti-Comintern Pact before it, did not yield the expected results, for the Americans considered the pact a threat and immediately placed the Selective Service Act into effect, stepped up war production, and increased lend-lease aid to England. The Tripartite Pact, then, marked the rise of a more serious situation in Japan's foreign relations, stirring up a new external pressure that aroused more intense feelings of nationalism. But the signing of the pact was also accompanied by political, social, and educational developments within Japan which can be appropriately described as steps toward the establishment of a totalitarian state—leading to a social situation that was more conducive to the rise of ultranationalism.

The internal reorganization programs that accompanied the drive for a closer tie-in with Germany were popularized by a slogan demanding the establishment of a New National Structure (Shin Taisei). The movement was related to the earlier demands for a single political party. Ever since the rise of the militarists to power in 1931 and 1932 there had been strong demands for a single party that would replace the "weak, selfish, and corrupt" political parties. The movement gained momentum after the February Twenty-sixth Incident of 1936 when Prince Konoye's name came to be mentioned more frequently as the logical leader of such a party.

In the spring of 1940, Konoye seemed more sympathetic with the views of those who were behind the movement, although the views varied considerably. There were some who were interested in a new party as a means of increasing military control over all governmental affairs. There were others who thought of another Nazi party. Some apparently saw the proposed party as a means of instituting the kind of reforms advocated by the National Reconstructionists. And then there were high-ranking civilian advisers to the Emperor who considered it as a most promising instrument for checking the spread of military control over nonmilitary affairs. Strangely enough, each group seemed to consider Konoye a logical and acceptable leader for the new single party. Of course, his noble birth and the well-known fact that he had long been the protégé of Prince Saionji, the most influential adviser to the Emperor, gave him tremendous prestige; in addition, his desire to get along with everyone apparently gave the impression that he was sympathetic with each of the divergent views. It seems, however, that he was primarily interested in preserving at least a modicum of power for civilian officials, and that he was somewhat sympathetic with the Young Officers of the Army and their desire for internal reforms. But he also gave the conservative elements in the Army, as well as the Nazi-oriented nationalists, reason to believe that he was on their side, leaving no question about who should lead the new party.

Konoye resigned his position as president of the Privy Council to free himself for heading the movement, and the established political parties also hastened to disband in order to assure themselves a position of prominence in the new body. But soon after the organization of the Konoye cabinet in July, 1940, the New National Structure movement took on a more definitely national coloring. Prominent figures were talking about an organization that was more inclusive and more Japanese that a single totalitarian party of the Nazi type. Kuhara Fusanosuke, a wealthy businessman, was one of the more influential men pressing for the construction of such a system.⁴⁰ He favored a structure based on the whole of the people and functioning in support of, and in coöperation with, the Emperor—a structure that would encompass all groups, classes, and activities of the Japanese nation, not just the elected representatives to the Diet.⁴¹ Prince Konoye, in his address before the first session of the Preparatory Committee for establishing the New National Structure in August, 1940, said: "The New National Structure movement aims at superseding the old party politics postulated upon liberalism. It is essentially national, all-embracing and public-spirited in character. It aims at the concentration and unification of the nation's entire powers. Its activities extend to the whole life of the nation."⁴² Obviously, the Prince had shifted ground under the impact of the nation-oriented movement.

In spite of the Prince's original desire to use the New National Structure movement as a means of controlling the Army, it was the Army that was soon taking the lead in organizational efforts. And the Army was intent upon building a structure that was truly totalitarian—that is, one that would bring all political, economic, and cultural activities of the nation under direct control of the government. But as the nature of the Army's plan became known and understood, powerful forces became arrayed against it. At the forefront of the opposition stood the financiers and the industrialists who could not consent to a development which would threaten the profit system. They immediately branded the movement as communistic and marshaled their forces to prevent the establishment of such a structure. The bureaucrats, politicians, and certain segments of the Army also gravitated into the opposition camp; and in a short time, compromises had to be made which resulted in the establishment of a National Structure that fell far short of what had been originally planned by the more ambitious military leaders.⁴³

The New National Structure, which did emerge in October, 1940, had a most impressive title: Imperial Rule Assistance Association (*Taisei Yokusan Kai*). It was announced as an organ in which all activities—cultural, labor, youth, business, and political—were to be centered. A headquarters with numerous bureaus and divisions was set up in Tokyo, and branch offices were established in every district, city, town, village, and ward in the land. But in reality the association had been so pared down by compromises that it was nothing more than a huge propaganda agency. To be sure, there were large organizations, affiliated with the Imperial Rule Assistance Association, that brought together all labor, agricultural, and youth organizations in the nation. But these, too, existed primarily as instruments of ideological control. In other words, the association was little more than another powerful instrument for carrying out the mobilization of the Japanese spirit. Konoye himself said, in an interview with the press on October 4, that the New National Structure movement was in essence a movement for the clarification of *kokutai.*" Again, the Prince had shifted ground; but this time it was because of resistance from those who objected to the type of totalitarian control which the Army was demanding in the summer and fall of 1940. After 1940 there were several reorganizations of the Imperial Rule Assistance Association; and although it never took on the character of a powerful superparty (as similar organizations did in Germany and Russia), it was made into an extremely efficient medium for further stimulating the development of nationalist sympathies.

While Japan was joining hands with Germany and Italy and organizing a New National Structure, nationalist thought was focused on the slogan: "A new order in Greater East Asia." It was a basic element in the Tripartite Pact of September, 1940. Article 2 stipulated that "Germany and Italy recognize and respect the leadership of Japan in the establishment of a new order in Greater East Asia." The entire movement for the establishment of the New National Structure was thought of as a necessary first step in preparing the nation for assuming the responsibilities entailed in setting up the new order in Greater East Asia. But nationalist thought after the summer of 1940 was also more definitely directed *against* Western exploitation and *against* Western liberalism—not merely *toward* strengthening the Japanese spirit. As the psychologists would put it, nationalism was now characterized more by negative identification than by positive identification.

The new orientation in nationalist thought can be seen in all forms of expression. But for an illustration of the nature and strength of the movement, let us turn to the emphasis in the new educational reforms that were adopted in the spring of 1941. As an integral part of the New National Structure movement the educational system, too, was reorganized. The primary schools thereafter were to be called national schools (*kokumin gakkō,*) and education was to be compulsory for eight years, rather than six. But of greater significance was the fact that the curriculum was to be revised in order that all educational activities should glorify the principles of the Imperial Way, foster the national spirit, and strengthen "faith in the national policy." Furthermore, all students were to be made familiar with the general situation in eastern Asia so that they would become conscious of Japan's position and responsibilities. Approximately a third of the curriculum was given over to such national training. The basic course was to be aimed at

clarifying the essence of national polity, fostering the national spirit and making the pupils conscious of their duties to the Empire, by improving their knowledge of the morals, language, history and geography of Japan. The pupils must be induced to appreciate the happiness of being born in the Empire; they must be trained to live in piety and in devoted service to the public. Pupils must be made to understand that the national spirit is based on the aspiration of the Empire, which is to go on developing forever. Further, they must be taught not only to understand that the history and geography have fostered a national character, but to strive to create and develop the unique culture of Japan.

The general situation of East Asia in particular and the world in general must be laid before the pupils in an effort to qualify them as future members of a great nation. The national, or civic, course must be taught the pupils in close coordination with the other courses, by means of reference to politics, economics, national defences and maritime affairs.

An even clearer indication of the emphasis, however, is to be found in a textbook prepared by the Department of Education and published in the spring of 1941. The book, called *Shimmin no Michi* (The Way of the Subject), was designed, according to the preface, to contribute toward the destruction of the self-centered and utilitarian ideas that had seeped into Japan from the West, and toward clarifying the Way of the Subject—a way which was based, first of all, upon service to the state.

The first part of the book outlines the development and expansion of the Western powers. "Their march into all parts of the world paved the way for their subsequent world domination politically, economically, and culturally and led them to act freely as they pleased, fashioning them to believe that they alone were justified in their outrageous behavior." After asserting that these Western powers moved from region to region, enslaving the people and exploiting the resources, *The Way of the Subject* declares that the wars of the last century were caused by Western aggression and emphasizes the inevitability of the disintegration of the old order. "The thoughts that have formed the foundation of the Western civilization since the early period of the modern age," the book continues, "are individualism, liberalism, materialism, and so on. These thoughts regard the strong preying on the weak as reasonable, unstintedly [*sic*] promote epicurean desires, seek a highly expanded material life, and stimulate the competition for acquiring colonies and securing trade, thereby leading the world to a veritable hell of fighting and bloodshed. . . ." This virulent expansionism and these selfish, materialistic concepts are leading to world collapse, according to the book, and the only way to prevent this collapse is for Japan to undertake the "construction of a new world order based on moral principles." The loyal subject is then told that Japan has already moved quite far in that direction; that, beginning with the Russo-Japanese War, Japan was beginning to construct a new world order; and that with the Manchurian Incident of 1931 there was "a violent outburst of Japanese national life" which reflected the spirit of the "Empire-founding." By these moves, Japan, it was taught, had already stirred hopes in the hearts of all Asiatic peoples that they would be freed from the "shackles and bondage of Europe and America."

The Way of the Subject emphasized that the greatest obstacle which Japan continuously faced was opposition from the rapacious Western powers, who had been trying to strengthen their position at the expense of the weak, and to "obstruct Japan's continental development." Because of this opposition, Japan was forced to withdraw from the League of Nations, and then to engage in fighting with the Chinese, because the Chinese did not understand what the Western powers were up to and tended to rely upon them rather than upon Japan. It was emphasized that Japan's aims were pure, and that what she wanted most of all was "to enlighten China, to strengthen Sino-Japanese unity, and to realize coexistence and coprosperity, thereby building up a new order in East Asia and contributing to the consummation of world peace."

In charting the course ahead, *The Way of the Subject* asserted that the signing of the Tripartite Pact and the "disposal of the China Affair" were merely stepping stones, and that the ultimate goal was "the elimination of the evils of European and American influences in East Asia." A start had been made, the book stated, but henceforth the road would be rugged, since "A group of liberalistic and democratic nations standing for the maintenance of the *status quo* is uniting" to prevent Japan from realizing her ambition. Consequently, "commonplace determination will not suffice for the great task of causing world humanity to seek stabilization. A quick reform and strengthening of various domestic structures are necessary for the country to break through this difficult situation." Ever since the period of westernization which followed the Meiji Restoration, the Japanese mind has become more and more polluted with the "luxurious and frivolous tendencies that spread over the country." To be sure, the Manchurian "Incident" and the China "Affair" have led to some improvement; but the situation now, says the book, calls for national solidarity "permitting no temporizing mind." More specifically, the situation calls for the establishment of a "highly geared and centralized defense state and the strengthening of a total national war framework." And "unless a country is systematized even in time of peace, so that the total war of the state and the people is constantly concentrated on the objective of the country, and the highest capacities displayed, the country is predestined to be deposed before taking up arms."

At the base of this national solidarity lies *kokutai*. And a vital element of *kokutai* is the service by the subject in accordance with ancient principles of loyalty and filial piety. "The first prerequisite of filial piety is to fulfill the duty of subjects of guarding and maintaining the Imperial Throne in observance of the bequeathed will of their ancestors. . . . Unless men offer their lives and sink their desires for money and fame, they cannot render their unswerving services to the state and place it in a secure position in time of emergency, thereby answering the Imperial Will."

The final section of the book consists mainly of concrete suggestions of ways in which the principles set forth above can be practiced by all Japanese people in all walks of life and at all ages. Great attention is given to the family, for it is considered a link between the past and the present, as well as a link between the individual and the state: "Our country's being a Family-State does not mean that the state is formed by families but that the state is a family in itself, and individual families exist with the state as their source." In the family, then, the spirit of filial piety and ancestor worship are to be emphasized. But in all occupations of life, people must be aware that they are first of all serving the Emperor, and that therefore they should be concerned more with production than with profit. "The cardinal point of practising the Way of the Imperial Subject lies in that each person no matter what occupation he may be engaged in, perform his duties being clearly conscious of his role in the national life, rejecting egoistic and utilitarian ideas, and by realizing now the bequeathed Way of the ancestors in which they rendered devoted service to the state." The book concludes on this note: "This is the very moment that the Japanese nation should thoroughly understand the fundamental character of the Empire, eliminate selfish and utilitarian ideas, enhance national morals of service to the state as prior to all, base keen insight into the international situation, and fulfill the duty of the people with indomitable will, and unflinching determination, thereby diffusing the glorious and great principles of the Japanese empire to the world."

The goals of Japanese education being thus set forth in unmistakable terms, and the whole educational system being geared to a more energetic striving toward such goals, it is no wonder that American educators participating in the postwar reform program should describe the system as "education for war." American educational ideals of independent thought and objective criticism were not merely unacceptable; they were considered subversive, and were condemned.

The War in the Pacific

Upon the conclusion of the Tripartite Pact in September, 1940, Germany proposed that efforts be made to bring Soviet Russia into the alliance and that Japan try to reach an understanding with the United States. If Russia could be brought into the alliance, the Axis bloc would be truly formidable; and if a Japanese-American understanding could be reached, both Germany and Japan would presumably have a freer hand in coping with their respective wars.[45]

Matsuoka, Japan's current Foreign Minister, was more energetic and more successful in his negotiations with Russia than with the United States.[46] As early as October, 1940, the Russian Foreign Office was approached on the subject; but it was in February of the following year that Matsuoka really put his heart into the project, for by that time Germany was pressing for an attack on Singapore. Matsuoka went to Berlin in March, 1941, and while there, he apparently was kept in the dark regarding German plans for an attack on Russia. Ribbentrop hinted that a Japanese-Russian neutrality pact "probably would not altogether fit into the framework of the present situation,"[47] but Matsuoka still went to Moscow. He had no difficulty in getting Stalin and Molotov to agree to a neutrality pact, and on April 13, 1941, it was signed. In June, two more agreements were reached which gave both countries greater freedom for action on other fronts—the Russians for resisting the expected German attack, and the Japanese for advancing into southeastern Asia to cut off assistance to Chiang Kai-shek. When Germany did attack Russia on June 22, there were Japanese in high places (including Matsuoka) who thought that Japan should aid Germany against Russia; but at an Imperial Conference held on July 2 it was decided that Japan should remain neutral in the Russo-German War, and that she should concentrate on efforts in China and southeastern Asia.[48]

In attempting to smooth out relations with the United States, the Japanese failed utterly.[49] Negotiations were opened informally sometime in December, 1940; and by April, 1941, formal conversations were held in Washington between Secretary of State Hull and Ambassador Nomura. When Matsuoka returned from his European tour, during which he had signed the Russo-Japanese neutrality pact, he found his Foreign Office quite enthusiastic about the advances that were being made in Japanese-American negotiations. But Matsuoka was not pleased. He considered these moves a betrayal of Germany, and apparently resisted attempts to follow up the initial gains.[50]

The outbreak of war between Russia and Germany in June caused many officials in the Japanese government to feel that it was even more necessary that America and Japan come to terms. But still Matsuoka held back, maintaining that such an agreement would weaken the pact, and insisted that Japan instead join Germany in an attack on Russia. After the Imperial Conference of July 2, 1941, in which it was decided that Japan would remain neutral in the Russo-German War and press for a solution of the China problem,[51] Matsuoka still would not yield to demands for an improvement of relations with the United States. Even the Army, at this time, favored such an effort; and a cabinet reorganization followed, in which Matsuoka was replaced by Admiral Toyoda.

But American-Japanese relations had already reached a very critical point. For with each step the Japanese took into French Indo-China— and they took several after the Imperial Conference of July 2—the United States took a firmer stand, finally deciding to freeze all Japanese assets. In the face of this stronger American attitude, the Japanese militarists gradually became less enthusiastic about efforts to patch up relations with the United States, for they were determined to proceed at all costs with the plans of cutting off all assistance to Chiang Kai-shek from the south.[52] Konoye and other civilian and naval leaders, however, felt that an improvement in American relations was more important than a move southward. In order to resolve this internal disagreement on foreign policy, another Imperial Conference was held on September 6, 1941. In this it was decided that Japan should do her utmost to gain by diplomatic methods American and British acquiescence in Japan's requirements—which included cutting off aid to Nationalist China— and that if these diplomatic efforts did not show any promise by October, then Japan should resort to war. The Emperor himself took a positive stand in favor of doing everything possible to settle the difficulties by diplomatic means.[53]

But at the base of the diplomatic impasse there were three American demands which had to be faced: that the policy of equal commercial opportunity for all nations in China be respected; that Japan disassociate herself from the Axis alliance; and that Japanese troops be withdrawn from China. Konoye was convinced that these demands did not constitute a hopeless barrier to the achievement of an understanding, for Japan had already decided to abide by the open-door policy, and he was certain that oral assurances about Japan's relations with Germany would satisfy the United States. On the third issue, however, there were truly serious difficulties, for the Army was becoming more obdurate in its refusal to retreat a single step. Konoye tried his best to convince General Tōjō, who was then War Minister, that it was of utmost importance to avoid war with the United States. At the famous Ogikubo Conference of October 12, 1941, Konoye proposed that the Army agree to make a "nominal" concession: "You can appear to be doing what America wants, and in reality have the same thing as occupation." But Tōjō would not budge, and reportedly replied in these terms: "If we give in to America now, there will be no end to her repressive policy. You say that evacuation means yielding in name only. But, it would greatly discourage our men. I absolutely disagree with you."[54] At the close of the conference, Tōjō insisted that the negotiations be discontinued. In the face of this attitude, Konoye resigned on October 16. He was replaced by Tōjō himself. Thereafter relations with the United States deteriorated rapidly, and the military-controlled Japanese government began harnessing all the nation's energy for extending the four-year old "Incident" by a declaration of war against the United States and Britain.

It was not merely the Army, however, that was showing a stiffer attitude toward the United States, for after July, 1940, nearly all editors, writers, and public speakers were moving in the same direction. The central theme of their discussions was that the United States was responsible for what was called the ABCD (American, British, Chinese, and Dutch) encirclement. After the Tōjō cabinet came into power in October, writers became particularly outspoken, charging the United

States with attempting to dominate the Pacific and demanding that the government meet the situation with an iron will. One newspaper, for example, stated that:

What America wants is time to complete her preparations for a Pacific war; what Japan loses in the course of time is a large quantity of embargoed goods which cannot be obtained elsewhere and also her relative strategical superiority and her credit with the Western powers. America has everything to gain and nothing to lose; Japan has everything to lose and nothing to gain. America has arbitrarily taken advantage of time to strengthen the encirclement of Japan with no sacrifice; Japan has exposed herself to disdain by placing three months in the opponents' hands. Such has been the conspicuous reality of the American-Japanese negotiations since America's freezing of Japanese assets. There are limits to patience; over-patience is cowardice and will lead to defeat.[55]

Businessmen would logically have taken a more moderate view; but at a general meeting of the Japan Chamber of Commerce and Industry, held on November 14, 1941, the president of the organization said that although the hostile powers were free to underestimate Japan's actual power, it was absolutely intolerable that, under such a mistaken observation, they should proceed to obstruct Japan's work of establishing a New Order in East Asia and to menace the right of Japan and other east Asian countries to live. The "crafty" measures of the powers to blockade Japan economically by freezing Japanese assets, he said, could not be tolerated for a moment. "It is, therefore, earnestly to be desired that the government pursue the fixed national policy resolutely." The president concluded by saying that "all Chambers of Commerce and Industry throughout the country are ready to do everything in their power to support the Government in its attempt to break through the crisis."[56]

The attack on Pearl Harbor was apparently the kind of action desired. The Imperial rescript, which announced the declaration of war against Britain and the United States, was enthusiastically received. Of course the thought-control machinery would not have permitted open criticism, but the ecstatic outbursts of the press suggest far more than mere conformity with governmental regulations. The *Chūgai Shōgyō*, for example, stated: "We have now a rare opportunity of manifesting our glorious national polity, and the spirit of our race."[57] And the Tokyo *Nichi Nichi* declared: "With a flash of the sabre, the Japanese air forces, Army and Navy are already scoring great successes, and American and British bases in the Pacific are being crushed one by one. This is a war of emancipation of East Asia, a war of reconstruction of East Asia. Look, the ominous clouds that have been hanging low over the Pacific are being cleared away and brightness is appearing over the horizon."[58]

The actual outbreak of war was welcome news, but the reports of tremendous victories against the armed forces of the United States and England were far more exhilarating. The writers could not remain calm about the unbelievable sinkings of American and British battleships and the occupation of island bases throughout the Pacific. In January, 1942, one man wrote that although Colonel Frank Knox had often spoken of the "unbeaten tradition" of his country's fleet, "that glorious tradition has been shattered by the debacle in Hawaii where the proud standard of the American Navy was furled and shrouded in the black infamy of the greatest defeat in the history of world navies."[59]

The Japanese forces, however, moved on to even greater victories, including the capture of Singapore in February, the occupation of the Dutch East Indies in March, and the surrender of Bataan in April. Throughout the country, great victory celebrations were held, and public figures and writers could not refrain from indulging in outbursts of national pride. Tōjō and others were constantly warning the nation against overoptimism, but in the face of the succession of victories on all fronts there were few who could worry about the future. In these early months of the war, Japan's leading English newspaper carried an article on Japanese nationalism by a Japanese patriot which indicates something of the strength of the national feelings at the time:

Nationalism is already a religion in Japan, whereas in Western countries any ism has but a relative position in the minds of the people, like nationalism against internationalism, capitalism against communism, and so forth. Nationalism in Japan is something greater and more important than an ism. It is a national religion, and therefore, occupies an absolute position in the minds of the masses. . . . If necessary for the preservation of our State, we are ready to lay down our lives any moment for it is the most sacred of all treasures we have in this world. . . .[60]

After the summer of 1942, however, Japan's remarkable victories came to an end. The United States was putting up a stronger resistance. Japan's attempts to occupy Port Moresby and Midway Island were blocked, and the Americans began to make slow advances in Guadalcanal. By the end of 1942, the more thoughtful Japanese observers saw that the tide was beginning to turn. Throughout 1943 and the first part of 1944, the United States armed forces were advancing slowly from the east and from the southeast. These advances could not be entirely hidden from the public; consequently the government was forced to exert itself, on all levels, in an attempt to strengthen the nation for a showdown.

The government first concentrated upon a further strengthening of the New National Structure, the building of which had been started in the summer of 1940. By the election of April, 1942, remarkably successful attempts were made to see that only government-"designated" candidates were elected to the Diet. Also the Imperial Rule Assistance Association was streamlined and was integrated more closely with the administrative operations of the government. But probably the largest share of the government's efforts was concentrated on the consolidation of Japan's position in the large areas recently occupied. An important step was the establishment in October, 1942, of the Greater East Asia Ministry, an organ that was to assume full responsibility for achieving economic, political, and ideological unity in Greater East Asia. The establishment of the new ministry, however, not only marked the beginning of a more intensive drive to consolidate Japan's position but also marked the rise of a more advanced stage of military control. In high-level conferences before the war, only the Navy and Foreign Office officials offered any significant resistance to Army efforts to obtain control and to carry out its policies. With the retreat of the Navy at the Ogikubo Conference in October, 1941, only the Foreign Office resistance was left. But after the establishment of the Greater East Asia Ministry in 1942, the position of the Foreign Office was further weakened. Indeed, the Foreign Minister, Togo, was so disturbed by the development that he withdrew from the cabinet.

In the spring of 1943, the Japanese military authorities tried desperately to win the east Asian peoples over to an acceptance of the principles and aims which had aroused the deep sense of mission among the Japanese people. A tremendous amount of money and energy was expended on propaganda in each of the areas, and in addition, concrete measures were taken to assure greater coöperation and "understanding." Early in 1942, Japan agreed to give up (to the Wang government) many of the concessions she had enjoyed in China. In August, the independence of Burma was recognized, and soon afterward a treaty was signed with Thailand (Siam). Later, "independence" was granted to the Philippines, and an alliance was signed with the Wang government of China. There was also much talk of the possibility of a new independent government for India. The culmination of the drive for Greater East Asian unity came, however, with the signing of the Joint Declaration of Greater East Asia Nations in November, 1943. This declaration of joint determination to free Asia from the domination of Europe and America was represented as East Asia's answer to the Atlantic Charter. The declaration was said to be an expression of the spontaneous will of all nations in Asia, and the Atlantic Charter was belittled as an effort of a few to perpetuate an unjust order that was for the exclusive benefit of the Anglo-Saxon powers.[61]

The degree to which Japan's propaganda affected the thinking of Asian peoples bears directly upon the nature and course of intellectual currents in Asia, but it falls outside the scope of this study. Apart from the effect of the propaganda on other Asian peoples, it is clear that the Greater East Asian movement helped to arouse among the Japanese an even deeper sense of mission. It seemed to add substance to the doctrine that this was a holy war, aimed at creating a new world order in which peace would prevail and in which each nation would gain its "proper place." The Greater East Asia movement, and particularly the concrete measures to give Chinese, Burmese, and Filipinos political independence, seemed to provide proof that this was not a war to acquire territory and riches for Japan, but a war to free Asia from the clutches of the greedy Western powers. Throughout 1943, in particular, much was written and said about establishing the new order in Greater East Asia. The breadth and depth of the Japanese feelings are suggested in a book by a young Japanese journalist, Fujii Tatsuki, who had lived twenty-five years in the United States, but who had gone to Singapore in 1939 to work on a Japanese-owned English newspaper. At the beginning of the war, Fujii was interned by the British, but after the fall of Singapore he returned to his newspaper work in Shonan (the new Japanese name for Singapore). In the epilogue to the book, which he wrote in 1943, he said:

On the war front, I have talked with the soldiers. They fight with the same conviction and determination to rid East Asia, once and for all, of insidious Anglo-American influences. In the Southern Regions, I have seen the ideal of the Greater East Asia Co-Prosperity Sphere in action, have witnessed Overseas Chinese, Filipinos, Indonesians, Indians and Burmese willingly cooperate with the Japanese authorities. Japan has set the lead for the rest of East Asia's millions in this Greater East Asia War—which sounds the death-knell of Anglo-American imperialism and the battlecry for the liberated Asiatics. . . . These are indeed critical days for Japan for in common with the rest of East Asia the future happiness of millions is at stake. To be working in the midst of this titanic struggle is the greatest experience of all.[62]

In the autumn of 1943, as Japan admitted the withdrawal of her troops from Attu, and with the beginning of the American counter-offensive in the Gilberts, the government began to stress the importance of greater production. There is evidence to show that from the first many experts realized that the outcome of the war might well hinge on whether or not Japan could develop her productive capacity to a point where the American industrial potential could be equalled. In February, 1943, Tōjō asked for special powers to expand industrial production, and thereafter the government gained more nearly complete control over all aspects of the nation's economic activities. But still there was strong competition between the military services for materials and goods, and there arose serious duplications and rivalries that seemed to retard industrial expansion. But a more serious cause for alarm was the heavy loss of merchant shipping as a result of American submarine attacks. Therefore, in spite of optimistic reports in the press, there was real anxiety about the relatively slight increase in the manufacture of critical military equipment and supplies. To improve the situation, another new ministry was set up in September, 1943: the Munitions Industry, which was headed by General Tōjō himself. The Imperial Rule Assistance Association already had done much to mobilize all labor resources, including women and school children; but now the Munitions Industry initiated a drive to achieve an even greater rationalization of industrial effort.

The concentration on production was only one aspect of a general settling down to a long war, for as the American counterattack moved from the Gilberts to the Marshalls and into New Britain and up the coast of New Guinea, even the Japanese press began to say that the enemy's fighting spirit must not be made light of.[63] Finally, when the Americans moved into the Marianas in June, 1944, it was agreed that "the enemy is quite desperate. ... This is the supreme moment in which the people behind the lines must concentrate their total energy on the war to crush the enemy."[64] But in spite of concentration and spirited fighting, Saipan fell in July. It was recognized as a disaster, and Tōjō found that he could not resist demands—primarily from the Navy—that he resign. A leading newspaper, the *Asahi*, concluded that with the enemy now in occupation of Saipan, it was quite clear that the next step would be to carry out air raids on Japan in order to destroy production and to break Japanese morale. "The raids will not be the farcical things as those on northern Kyushu were. We must be prepared

232   NATIONALISM IN JAPAN

for continuous, unremitting attacks on a huge scale. Moreover, the possibility of enemy fleets approaching our shores has grown with the extension of the enemy's airpower over the Pacific. . . ."[65]

After the fall of Saipan, the American counterattack gathered momentum. Within a short time, other islands were taken by the Americans; bombing raids on the mainland of Japan were carried out regularly; landings were made in the Philippines; and finally, in the great naval battle of the Philippines, the Japanese navy lost its offensive power. Although the naval defeat was not revealed to the Japanese public at the time, it was realized that the situation had become really serious. It was in these trying months that the Japanese people began to hear about the suicide attacks of their patriotic young men, and about the strong defense that was put up by Japanese soldiers on islands in the Pacific. It was made clear that the Japanese civilians on many of the islands chose to jump from cliffs and into the ocean rather than become prisoners of the hated Americans. Some of the suicides may have been due, in part at least, to the belief that the Japanese, if captured, would have to suffer tortures more horrible than death, for the Japanese press was giving much space to the cruelty of the enemy. In December, 1943, strong accusations were made against the Americans for sinking the Japanese hospital ship *Buenos Aires Maru;*[66] and in the following August one newspaper made this comment: "If one considers the atrocities which they [the Americans] have committed against the American Indians, the Negroes and the Chinese, one is amazed at their presumption in wearing the mask of civilization. . . . However, the atrocities and inhuman actions perpetrated against the officers and men of the Imperial Forces since the outbreak of the War of Greater East Asia, in utter disregard of international war laws, surpass all former acts of bestiality."[67] It still must be recognized that the spirit shown by the Japanese soldiers, as well as by the civilians, indicated a patriotism that was, with reason, termed fanatical. The spirit of the Japanese was remarked upon in the American press, and many of our most astute observers began to feel that this fanatical nationalism would force the Japanese to fight to the bitter end, making is unlikely that surrender would come until the islands had been invaded and completely conquered.

After the landing of American forces in Okinawa in April, 1945, another cabinet was formed, and the new Premier, Admiral Suzuki, declared that "the enemy shall only take Japan over my dead body."[68] The cabinet was considered to be impotent and the situation hopeless; yet, as one writer later stated, "The Japanese nation felt that it would have to fight to the very end." This feeling, he said, arose from "the nation's love of the Emperor and of the soil of Japan."[69] There were only a few who had the will or the energy to criticize their superiors, although continuous large-scale bombing attacks showed that victory was impossible. Even after the collapse of Germany in June, the dropping of the atomic bomb on Hiroshima, and the declaration of war by Russia on the following day, most Japanese still were determined to fight on to a final battle. The Imperial rescript of August 15 announcing the acceptance of the terms of the Potsdam Declaration seems to have taken most of the people by surprise. They fully expected the message to be a plea for a final effort to defend the homeland, not an announcement of surrender. One nationalist records the reaction as follows:

> The Imperial Rescript shocked the people more than did the appearance of the atomic bomb. This was because, although they did suffer from the lack of food and other means of maintaining a sustenance and although they were completely worn out with the fear of air raids, yet they were willing to fight to the last soldier if the Emperor so commanded. The feeling which the nation had at that time was one that transcended all consideration of the good or bad of such a resistance or the possibility of fighting to the last. The entire nation had deep within its heart an almost unbearable resentment and hatred against the dictatorship of the military and the high-handedness of the bureaucrats. Yet, just because of that, the nation had not hoped for defeat. At the news of the unconditional surrender, some people were dumbstruck into senselessness, others were roused to overpowering indignation. But what man, born a Japanese, could oppose the words of the Emperor which had been spoken in tears? The entire nation in solemnity, tears brimming in their hearts, submitted obediently to the command to surrender.[70]

◇   ◇   ◇

One of the most significant features of the post-1936 brand of nationalism was that the ruling classes once more became the propelling force of the movement. In the early stages of modern nationalism which preceded the Russo-Japanese War, the rulers had taken the lead in generating feelings of national unity and loyalty; but after World War I, when the principal danger to the nation came from within the nation itself, rather than from the outside, the persons who advocated social reforms in national terms were the ones who became the most influential. In the period between 1919 and 1936 there were indications that nationalism might become a people's movement—that is, one pressed by the common man and geared to popular demands for reform. But as the foreign crisis became more serious, the ruling groups once more gained control of the movement and began to direct it into channels more to their liking.

It should be remembered, however, that the national socialist movement before 1936 was, for very cogent reasons, acceptable also to the conservative ruling groups. In the first place, the movement was serving to weaken the appeal of Communism and other nonnational ideologies which seemed to threaten the established order. In the second place, the national socialists were constantly pointing to military men as the logical leaders of the reform movement, thereby making an appeal to the senior men in the Army and Navy who had lost much of their influence in the affairs of government. And finally, the movement aroused deeper feelings of national unity, a development the value of which any member of the ruling class was quick to see. Until about 1932, then, the conservative advisers to the Emperor were by no means opposed to the reformist character of the nationalist movement. After the February Twenty-sixth Incident of 1936, however, it was the conservative element in the Army that assumed direct control over the course of nationalist thought, for conditions had changed and social reform—even of a national variety—no longer served, so far as the rulers were concerned, a useful political function.

As early as 1932, the conservatives had begun to be disturbed about the Young Officer movement. When the radical Army pamphlet was published in 1934 suggesting basic alterations of the Japanese social and political order, and when assassination plots by nationalist societies began to look more like well-organized rebellions, high-ranking government officials saw that National Socialism, as well as Communism and Western democratic ideas, had to go. The National Reconstruction movement not only was a danger to the traditional order, but it no longer was needed as a means of weakening Communism and other internationalist ideologies, since those subversive forces were being effectively suppressed by the police. Also, the reëmergence of the military to a position of dominance in political affairs after the Manchurian Incident destroyed much of the old enthusiasm for National Reconstruction emphasis upon military leadership. And finally, there was now a far more effectual means of stimulating national feelings in the form of an emphasis upon the danger which Japan faced at the hands of "aggressive" foreign powers.

The resumption of ruling-class control over the course of nationalist thought meant, first of all, that the attention of the nation was no longer to be directed to nationalist goals merely through the activities of individual nationalists and nationalist societies. Now the whole nation was to be subjected continuously to the influence of nationalist propaganda disseminated through various public channels and by means of all public-information and entertainment media. The state shrines, the schools, and the police system were far more centralized and standardized than they had been in earlier days. They were therefore more effective than ever as instruments of ideological control and stimulation. In addition, by 1936, there were revolutionary developments in the field of communication and entertainment which gave to the government powerful new weapons for its ideological program.

Even the press, which had been rather difficult to bring into line in earlier periods, was not only more responsive to government policies but carried more influence with the public, since Japan, because of the increase in the number of newspapers, magazines, and books published, had become one of the most print-conscious nations in the world. The greatest changes, however, had come as a result of the development of radiobroadcasting and moving pictures. Radios had been developed first and, under government control, had become so popular that a very large part of the families of the nation after 1936 were regularly subjected to direct appeals by government agencies of thought control. Moving pictures were possibly as important as radios, for although not as many people saw movies as listened to radios, the pictures probably made a deeper impression. And again the government was not slow to mobilize this entertainment medium for the Spiritual Mobilization program. When we consider, too, the efforts of the government to associate all labor, agricultural, and youth societies of the nation with its Imperial Rule Assistance Association, it no longer seems so remarkable that in an eight-year war the Japanese government should have been so successful in stirring up national sentiments of a fanatical and ultranationalistic character.

With nationalism now being directed by the government, it was natural that thought which implied basic changes in the status quo should be looked upon with disfavor. The nationalist thought which was acceptable was that which emphasized the value—and even the divine qualities—of traditional institutions, principles, and standards. *Kokutai* (that "national entity" which encompassed all the social relationships, standards of conduct, and institutions peculiar to Japan) and the Emperor institution (the divine, hereditary head of the State Shinto

Cult and the father of the Japanese state-family) were therefore the center of the thought that dealt with the nation itself. But after 1936, enemies of the nation received the greatest emphasis in nationalist thought, for Japan was facing a serious crisis in her foreign relations, and the leaders apparently understood quite well that a keen awareness of foreign danger was far more likely to create the kind of national unity that they desired.

But there was still another characteristic of foreign-oriented nationalist thought and activity which makes the post-1936 period particularly significant: the attention given to the Japanese mission of establish-in a new order in East Asia. (The Pacific War, in fact, was officially designated by the Japanese as the Greater East Asia War.) This mission meant that each Japanese national was not merely fighting for the protection of his homeland against the aggressive actions of powerful enemies but was fighting to free Asian peoples from the domination and exploitation of Western nations. The Greater East Asia mission added to national service a noble, unselfish element which was indeed impelling.

The post-1936 ultranationalism, then, was in large part a government-propelled movement which engendered feelings that included a powerful sense of mission and also a strong fear of foreign enemies, since every information and entertainment medium in the land was constantly drawing attention to both. Fear was undoubtedly the more active ingredient in the mixture. The news and other propaganda efforts were constantly pointing up the injustice of Anglo-Saxon attitudes and policies toward Japan. The ABCD encirclement and the subversive quality of Anglo-Saxon ideas were given so strong a play that each Japanese tended to fear for the future of his nation and to blame this sad state of affairs upon the selfish, greedy British and Americans. Nationalism had indeed assumed a virulent form.

11 NEW NATIONALISM

The Imperial rescript of August 15, 1945, brought Japan's eight-year war to an end and destroyed all meaning in the people's determination to sacrifice their lives fighting for the Emperor. The old "suicide attack" mood was suddenly replaced by a mood of "coöperation"—one of the most remarkable developments in Japanese history. Clearly, the suddenness and completeness of the shift were indicative of the peculiar character of Japanese nationalism. When it was pointed out that henceforth the best interests of the nation lay in a new direction, the people moved in that direction with the same unity of purpose as had marked their wartime activities. Peace was accompanied also by a collapse of the thought-control machinery; and the reality of the occupation, at first at least, did not justify the old fears and was not so powerful a stimulant to nationalism as the earlier fear of defeat had been. Furthermore, the Occupation reforms struck deeply at the roots of the institutional support of ultranationalist thought. Japan therefore came to enjoy one of the most internationalist-minded periods of her modern history. Nationalism was still present, but in a new form. However, as the world situation became more intense, the Allied Powers showed less concern over the possible revival of Japanese ultranationalism. Each of the "two worlds" adopted policies designed to gain Japanese nationalist support for its attempt to attract Japan, with her great industrial and military potential, into its camp. Under these conditions the classical type of Japanese nationalism has begun to reëmerge as a strong sociointellectual force.

Surrender

At seven o'clock on the morning of August 15, 1945, Radio Tokyo went on the air with an announcement that at noon the Emperor would speak personally to the nation. It was a sensational announcement, for the Emperor had never spoken over the radio before, and only a few people had ever heard his voice. He was not expected to say anything important—probably just make another plea for greater determination to defeat the enemy—but at noon most of the people were glued to their radios. As it turned out, they were overwhelmed more by what the Emperor said than by the fact that he was saying it, since he announced in effect that the government had decided to accept the terms of the Potsdam Declaration, one article of which called for "unconditional surrender." Being fully determined to fight to the end, the Japanese could not believe that their government had decided to surrender before the Imperial Army had tested its strength against the enemy and before the nation had proved that it enjoyed divine protection from foreign invasion. In some communities, those who accepted the Imperial rescript at its face value were condemned for being unpatriotic. It was obvious to most that either the Imperial rescript was not the Emperor's or pressure had been brought to bear on him by self-seeking advisers.

The radio soon carried other announcements and speeches, however, which convinced most people that the government and the Emperor had really decided upon surrender. At the same time it was explained, in many ways and by many high-ranking officials, that this did not mean annihilation of the Japanese nation, but rather a critical juncture at which all loyal Japanese people would have to "endure the unendurable and suffer the insufferable" in order to advance the interests of the nation by winning the peace rather than winning the war. The Imperial rescript itself had declared that Japan was "to continue as one family from generation to generation, ever firm in its faith of the unperishable-ness of its sacred land . . ." A cabinet proclamation warned:

The people must be concerned now with the defense of the national structure. There must be no internal strife over already past facts to allow others to take advantage and there must be nothing done lightly in the heat of emotion to cause the world to lose trust in the country. . . . The government . . . will fight all hardships and always conform with the Imperial Will, absolutely to recover the national prestige and answer the will of our ancestors.[1]

And the Premier, Prince Higashikuni, in announcing the policies that would guide his cabinet, explained that in coöperating wholeheartedly with the occupying forces every Japanese would be serving the best interests of the nation: "When the whole Empire unites as one and advances overcoming the present difficulty in perfect order and unity, in full observance of the Imperial Wishes, the whole world will be surprised at the greatness of Japan's polity, transcending victory and defeat. It is at this time of difficulty and adverse fortune that the true value of our polity will be revealed."[2] Other Imperial Princes too were called upon to carry the Emperor's orders to the soldiers on the continent. Gradually, most of the nation, including even the soldiers far from home who had not yet met with defeat at the hands of the enemy, were brought into line.

In spite of the Imperial rescript and the emphasis upon a different national goal, there were some, particularly in the armed services, who were convinced for a time that the Emperor was being misled and that the nation should fight on rather than surrender. It is reported that War Minister Anami "prostrated himself in tears" before the Emperor and appealed to him to change his decision. Some say that when the Emperor refused to budge from his position, Anami considered a military coup d'état. But instead, he committed suicide, leaving a note which explained that in this way he wished to apologize for his "grave offense."[3] Between the time of the decision to surrender on August 15 and the broadcasting of the Imperial rescript on the following day, a group of staff officers of the army instigated a plot to seize control of the government in an effort to assure a continuance of the war. They were unable to gain the backing of the highest army officials, but they felt certain that they would obtain the support of the rank and file of the army. Several government offices were invaded; the homes of some officials who refused to coöperate were burned; and the Japan Broadcasting Company was seized. But the insurrectionists met more opposition than had been expected. On the following morning, the leaders, seeing that the plot was collapsing, committed suicide.[4]

Even after the Emperor had broadcast his memorable Imperial rescript on August 15, there were some manifestations of resistance to the fateful decision. Certain suicide squads of the Navy Air Corps dropped leaflets that urged the people not to surrender, stating that the Imperial rescript was a forgery. Posters and handbills charged that the Emperor had been misguided. A platoon of soldiers, brought into Tokyo from Ibaraki, revolted, and there were other cases of organized resistance. But none was large. Most of the uprisings came to an end as a result of influence exerted by high-ranking officers, for the movements lacked both leadership and popular support—unmistakable evidence that the new decision, announced by the Emperor in convincing terms of national self-interest, was accepted by the great mass of the Japanese people. The strong social pressures and the weight of authority, which had long been characteristics of Japanese social relationships, were sufficient to bring all dissident groups into line. By the time the first advance units of the occupation forces arrived on August 28, 1945—just two weeks after the decision to surrender had been made —the Japanese people, at all levels and in all walks of life, had come round to an amazingly widespread acceptance of the new policy to substitute coöperation for war.

Still, there was no feeling of joy about this turn of events, for the public had been preoccupied too long with the horrors and dangers expected from domination by a foreign power. The organized thought-control machinery had aroused a fearful apprehension of what the occupation would mean for the Japanese individual and for traditional Japanese institutions and principles. Wild rumors, sensational news, and even official statements in the two-week interval between the decision to surrender and the beginning of the occupation tended to strengthen expectations of cruel and inhuman treatment from occupation troops. "Many mothers," said one writer, "were unwilling to risk their daughters' safety in view of wartime propaganda and rumors about the general uncouthness and even bestiality of Allied troops."[5] Residents of coastal cities therefore fled to the country or to the mountains, and many of those who remained at home dared not venture forth from their houses after Allied soldiers began to land.

Before the arrival of the occupation forces much happened to weaken the nationalist urge, as well as to direct it along different lines. In the first place, the entire thought-control machinery was stopped, in anticipation of directives from the Occupation authorities. Realizing that the Occupation authorities would soon turn their attention on all organizations and individuals that had been responsible for whipping up enthusiasm for Japan's aggressive program of foreign expansion, the various government agencies concerned with the control and dissemination of information broke off their operations. Radio programs and newspapers, taking their cue from the Imperial rescript on "enduring the unendurable and suffering what is insufferable," dropped the anti-British, anti-American line. This meant that the propelling force behind subsequent changes in the course of Japanese nationalism, for a time at least, was to be outside the realm of governmental control.

Furthermore, the announcement of surrender was followed immediately by an economic, political, and social deterioration that constituted a reversal of the trend toward social unity—a trend which had been a basic force in the growth of Japanese nationalism. Ever since the Manchurian Incident, the government, as it came under the control of the Army, had been directing an ever larger proportion of the productive power of the nation into fields that would provide the greatest possible support for the war effort. But months of bombing had wrought havoc in all fields of communication and had resulted in serious damage to many industries. The sudden cessation of war, under conditions of defeat, also created greater economic dislocation. The government, too, was badly shaken. The great sprawling bureaucracy was unable to make quick adjustments to the new situation. Many bureaus and offices no longer had a job to do; others had to adopt drastic policy changes. Of course, there were new tasks that did not fall within the jurisdiction of any of the established organs of government. The confusion and disorganization was further augmented by fears which led thousands to flee from the cities in order to avoid the horrors that were expected to come in the wake of occupation. In general, surrender was accompanied by developments that, other things being equal, would have led to a weakening of the spirit of nationalism—in spite of the fact that Japan was facing actual occupation by enemy troops, not merely the fear of such a possibility.

Occupation

The landing of the American troops met with almost no opposition, merely apprehension and confusion. Russell Brines, one of the American correspondents on the scene, wrote that on his first day in Tokyo even the passengers on the trains scurried out of the sight of the American military uniforms, and "only an occasional pedestrian peeped from behind buildings."⁶ But in a few days the Japanese came to realize that the warsick American soldiers were for the most part a decent and friendly lot. GI's were generous with candy and cigarettes, and, as Brines reports, "They returned dozens of lost children to distracted parents, rushed sick strangers to hospitals and saved many accident victims."⁷ This behavior, together with the realization that the war was over, created widespread feelings of relief. The people emerged from their hideouts, and children flocked to any American uniform in the hopes of obtaining a stick of gum, a piece of candy, or just to say "Her-ro" and "Gooddo by." The country's "collective sigh" was a powerful antidote to the old, ultranationalist urge. Of course, the official policy of coöperation had already been accepted, but now it was being accepted enthusiastically. The Imperial rescript had pointed out a new path for the national effort; but the friendly, generous, and humane attitude of the occupation troops made the first appreciable dent in the old ultranationalist behavior pattern and raised doubts about the validity of the old anti-Western propaganda. Concern and unselfish sacrifice for the nation was now giving way before interest in, and a certain liking for, the former enemy.

One of the first tasks to be performed by the Occupation authorities was to disarm the troops and to disband the army and navy. The Potsdam Declaration had stipulated this requirement; consequently the government and people offered no resistance, permitting demilitarization to be carried out efficiently and expeditiously. The dissolution of the armed forces had an important bearing upon the future direction of Japanese nationalism, since militarism had been a basic ingredient of Japan's aggressive brand of nationalism. With the defeat of the armed forces and their subsequent demobilization, the political influence of the militarists was destroyed, and thus room was left for the rise of new political elements. Whatever these elements might be, they would be civilian and would therefore be less likely to follow policies that would lead to the reëmergence of aggressive nationalism.

Moral Demilitarization

The next major task of the Occupation was to bring about "moral demilitarization." Occupation policies had been drawn up before the war was over, while *banzai* raids, *kamikaze* attacks, and other manifestations of fanatical loyalty were still fresh in the memory of everyone. It was natural, then, that the representatives of the Allied Powers, in stating their terms of surrender in 1945, should demand that there "be eliminated for all time the authority and influence of those who have deceived and misled the people of Japan into embarking on world conquest, for we insist that a new order of peace, security and justice will be impossible until irresponsible militarism is driven from the world."[8] Even before the work of demobilizing the army and navy had been completed, General MacArthur initiated the first step toward "moral demilitarization" by directing the Japanese government "to issue necessary orders to prevent the dissemination of news, through newspapers, radio broadcasting or other means of publication, which fails to adhere to the truth or which disturbs public tranquility." Restrictions upon freedom of speech were to be kept to an absolute minimum.[9] The directive was followed up by more specific orders prohibiting any "direct or indirect control of newspapers and news agencies" by the Japanese government, and requiring the abrogation of all laws and regulations which provided the legal basis for such control.[10] Most of the agencies had already dropped much of their wartime propaganda effort, but General MacArthur's directives struck at the roots of the entire control structure and made it certain that, during the period of the occupation at least, the government would be unable to resume its efforts to direct the thinking of the Japanese people.

In October, 1945, an even more positive step was adopted in an effort to carry out the policy of eliminating ultranationalism and militarism. Japanese authorities were ordered to prohibit the teaching of militaristic and ultranationalistic ideologies and were required to remove all active exponents of militarism and ultranationalism from the schools. The implementation of the order was to be followed by the establishment of an educational program based upon the principles of democracy, individualism, and freedom.[11] But the school system had been used so exclusively for "spiritual training" in accordance with the principles of Shintoism and Confucianism that a strict enforcement of the directive would have left the schools almost without textbooks or teachers. Consequently, the actual screening of teachers did not get under way until some seven months later, and the Education Ministry was allowed to use wartime textbooks after the most undesirable portions had been deleted by "inking out, cutting, pasting pages together, and similar devices." The work of preparing new textbooks with a more sympathetic attitude toward liberal principles of the West was started, but the results of the effort were not felt until several months later.[12]

On December 15, 1945, a historic directive of General MacArthur abolished all government sponsorship, support, control, and dissemination of the State Shinto doctrines. The directive cited several reasons why the "disestablishment of State Shinto" was desirable; but undoubtedly the most cogent reason, as far as the Occupation was concerned, was that it would "prevent a reoccurrence of the perversion of Shinto theory and beliefs into militaristic and ultranationalistic propaganda designed to delude the Japanese people and lead them into wars of aggression." The directive was very broad. It ordered that no government official or employee was to take part in the spread of Shinto teachings, that Shinto institutions and priests were to receive no public funds, that all government agencies for the control and support of Shinto were to be abolished, that the teaching of Shinto doctrines in the schools was to cease, and that the shrines were to be prohibited from propagating militaristic and ultranationalistic doctrines. In other words, the "State" was to be removed from State Shinto, placing the cult on equal footing with all other religions and all other sects of Shinto. Thereafter, Shinto priests were to refrain from teaching militaristic and ultranationalistic doctrines, which, according to the directive, included: (1) the doctrine that the Emperor is superior to the heads of other states because of divine ancestry; (2) the doctrine that the Japanese people are superior to other people because of divine origin; (3) the doctrine that Japan is superior to other lands because of divine origins; and (4) the doctrines that tend "to delude the Japanese people into embarking upon wars of aggression or to glorify the use of force as an instrument for the settlement of disputes with other peoples."[13] By this directive General MacArthur legally disassociated the old Sun Cult from the affairs of state[14] and ordered the exponents of the cult to cease teaching the ultranationalistic doctrines that had been so dynamic a stimulant to nationalism.

Still another important step taken by the Occupation to complete the separation of the state from the old State Shinto cult, was to require the Emperor himself to make a statement denying his divinity. In the Imperial rescript of January 1, 1946,[15] the Emperor declared: "The ties between us and our people have always stood upon mutual trust and affection. They do not depend upon mere legends and myths. They are not predicated on the false conception that the Emperor is divine and that the Japanese people are superior to other races and fated to rule the world."[16] Together with the December directive, which ordered the "disestablishment" of State Shinto, the rescript seemed to complete the process of making the Sun Cult a purely private faith. Such moves alone did not destroy the importance of the cult as a vital factor in the lives of the Japanese people, but they did remove from the hands of the rulers of Japan, temporarily at least, a powerful weapon for stirring up the nation into a new frenzy of national solidarity.

The Occupation authorities had been quick to destroy the thought-control structure, to adopt a reëducation program, and to attack State Shinto, but they moved somewhat more slowly in carrying out the policy of removing from positions of responsibility—that is, "purging"—"active exponents of militarism and militant nationalism" and of dissolving all ultranationalistic or militaristic societies and institutions.[17] Available evidence suggests that there was no unanimity of opinion among Occupation personnel as to the advisability of expediting the implementation of this part of the Occupation policy. Already there were some, especially Major General Charles Willoughby, chief of the Military Intelligence Section, who opposed drastic steps of this type on the ground that they would weaken Japan as a potential ally in the coming struggle with Russia. But there were others, notably Brigadier General Courtney Whitney, chief of the Government Section, who favored a strict interpretation, and a careful implementation, of the basic policy. Finally, General MacArthur sided with General Whitney; and the Japanese government was ordered on January 4, 1946, to take the necessary steps to carry out the "purge" of ultranationalist leaders and the dissolution of ultranationalist societies.[18]

The purge directive required the Japanese government "to remove from public office and exclude from government service" all persons who had been "active exponents of militaristic nationalism or influential members of ultranationalistic or terroristic societies." Specific categories of persons to be affected were set up, and a "catchall" clause was added that covered all who "by speech, writing or action" had shown themselves to be active exponents of militant nationalism."[19] The directive was described by General Whitney as "blasting from their entrenched positions in the command posts of the government all those who planned, started and directed the war, and those who enslaved and beat the Japanese into abject submission and who hoped to do the same with the whole world."[20] It took the Japanese government several weeks to make the necessary preparations for issuing the implementing ordinances; but by April 10, 1946, when the first postwar election was held, so many influential leaders had fallen under the purge that the political world was thrown into a state of confusion. The cabinet itself was disrupted, for Premier Shidehara had appointed men who had held positions of influence during the war and who therefore fell under the terms of the purge directive. Within the Diet a large proportion of the members were made ineligible for government service. The Liberal party gained additional strength from the shake-up and from the subsequent election; but the leader of the party, Hatoyama, was himself purged, since he had not only served as Minister of Education between 1931 and 1934 and was "responsible for stifling freedom of speech in the schools by means of mass dismissals and arrests of teachers," but had participated in the forced dissolution of farm-labor bodies and had applauded Hitler's regimentation of labor.[21] After pressing the purge against government officials, the "catchall" clause was implemented so that writers, publishers, and businessmen were removed from positions of influence. Leading officials in some 103 newspapers and news agencies, 221 book and magazine publishing houses, 12 motion-picture and theatrical companies, 6 broadcasting companies, and 5 information agencies were purged. This particular phase of the program inflicted a telling blow against the agencies that had been most useful to the government in arousing national loyalties during and before the war. But the purge was also extended to the entire public school system and to local officials throughout the land.[22]

The purge program created a stir in many areas of Japanese life, but it is easy to overstate its effect upon the course of national thought. It is true that the purge was carried out in a period in which nationalism was relatively calm, and yet there were several forces and conditions, outside the operation of the purge program, which help to explain that development. Many prominent exponents of aggressive nationalism were removed from positions of influence and responsibility; but in many cases the removal was merely nominal, and in others the men removed were replaced by others who held similar views and convictions. The entire movement undoubtedly facilitated the Occupation effort to foster the growth of democracy; but it is highly doubtful whether it alone contributed much toward the destruction of ultranationalism.

The dissolution of ultranationalist societies did not attract so much attention as the purge program, and it probably contributed less to "moral demobilization." Many of the more aggressive, terroristic societies were dissolved even before the January 4 directive[23] was issued; and the situation prevailing after the war was so different that many societies would logically have been reorganized, even if there had been no Occupation directive. Some which had programs that seemed to be valid under the new situation merely underwent formal reorganization, and some probably went underground. The work of ferreting out evasions of the dissolution directive was mainly the responsibility of the G-2 Section, and that section, it will be remembered, was unenthusiastic about the whole program. As early as 1948, if not earlier, there were reports that some of the ultranationalist societies were helping G-2 investigators to gain information about the activities of Communist organizations. Thus, one cannot escape the conclusion that the directive requiring the dissolution of ultranationalistic societies was only a minor, though spectacular, feature of the decline in the influence of nationalist societies. The democratization program was probably far more significant, since it did much to undermine the political and legal structure which made possible the authoritarian manipulation of national sentiments.

Democratization

Under the terms of the Potsdam Declaration the Occupation was obligated to see that the Japanese government removed all "obstacles to the revival and strengthening of democratic tendencies among the Japanese people."[24] In the first few months of the occupation, General MacArthur and his staff were concerned primarily with demilitarization; but as early as September, 1945, Prince Higashikuni, the Premier, was informed that the Supreme Commander of the Allied Powers (SCAP) considered a revision of the old Constitution to be a matter of first importance.[25] In the light of Japan's traditional structure, and the government's determination to preserve the essential features of that structure, it was natural that the first official steps toward revision were taken by the Emperor himself: he appointed Prince Konoye to assume responsibility for drafting the necessary revisions. But in October, 1945, after the establishment of the Shidehara cabinet, the government set up the so-called Matsumoto committee to take over the task. The committee's most serious problem was how to revise the Constitution in a way that would preserve the *kokutai* (national entity) and at the same time satisfy the demands of the Allied Powers. Any revision based upon the assumption that sovereignty rested with the people, and that the rule of law should prevail over the rule of persons, would automatically run counter to the time-honored sovereignty of the Emperor.[26] The Matsumoto committee finally agreed to a draft that came down on the side of tradition. As the committee itself explained: "Considering the fact that Japan has been reigned over by a line of Emperors unbroken from the very beginning of our national history, there is no room for doubt that an overwhelming majority of our people are strongly desirous of retaining the system. That is the reason why the draft revision proposes to maintain a system wherein the Emperor exercises sovereign power. . . ."[27] General MacArthur and his staff could not accept revisions that left the basic nature of the Japanese state unchanged. Feeling that the Japanese people were in sympathy with privately drafted revisions which placed sovereignty squarely in the hands of the people, General MacArthur finally decided to have his own Government Section draft a constitution that would embody the principles he considered important and that would serve as "the most effective method of instructing the Japanese government on the nature and application of these principles." Seven days later, the SCAP draft was completed, and on February 13, General Whitney presented it to officials of the Japanese government, telling them

that there was no compulsion upon them to take further action but that the Supreme Commander was determined that the constitutional issue should be brought before the people well in advance of the general election and that they should have full opportunity to discuss freely and freely express their will on constitutional reform. Failing action by the Cabinet, General Mac-Arthur was prepared to lay the issue before the people himself.[28]

The rejection of the Matsumoto draft and the presentation of the SCAP "guide" was received in Japanese government circles with a "distinct sense of shock." Officials tried valiantly to get SCAP to retreat from its position; but when those efforts failed, a conference was held before the Emperor. He recommended the acceptance of a "thorough-going revision, even to the point of depriving the Emperor himself of all political authority."[29] A few days later, a final draft was published; it included, as Article 1, the following statement: "The Emperor shall be the symbol of the state and the unity of the people, deriving his position from the sovereign will of the people."[30] The Japanese government officials having accepted the principle of popular sovereignty, relatively little difficulty was experienced in reaching agreement on other matters, such as the formulation of a bill of rights, the establishment of a diet with broad powers, the provision for a cabinet that was responsible to the diet, and the organization of a judiciary "with power to determine the constitutionality of any law, order, regulation or official act."[31]

Once the truly liberal constitution was accepted, other reforms followed rapidly. The legal system was overhauled in order to implement principles set forth in the bill of rights, especially those included in this clause: "With regard to choice of spouse, property rights, inheritance, choice of domicile, divorce and other matters pertaining to marriage and the family, laws shall be enacted from the standpoint of individual dignity and the essential equality of the sexes."[32] The civil service system was reorganized in an effort to destroy the "feudalistic bureaucracy" and facilitate the development of a "modern" system of civil service administration.[33] Even local government was refashioned to allow the people to participate in, and exercise control over, local affairs. Executive and legislative functions on the local level were removed from the complete and direct control of the central government and placed in the hands of officials elected locally.[34] The police system, which "permitted such brutally outrageous violations of personal liberties, individual dignity and fundamental human rights" was drastically changed to facilitate "the flowering of the local government" and the "quickening of the . . . independence of spirit which alone can guarantee the continued development of democracy in Japan."[35] In the field of education, reforms were adopted which removed much of the centralized control and made the system more responsible to popular, rather than state, needs. And in economic affairs steps were taken to destroy the monopolistic power held by a few financial cliques (zaibatsu), not only because they were considered to have been working closely with the military and the ultranationalists in directing the efforts of the country toward aggressive expansion, but because it was felt that a destruction of this monopolistic power was essential for the healthy growth of democracy.

The momentum of the democratization process reached its highest peak in 1947 when, after the first general election under the new constitution, the Social Democrats won the largest number of seats in the Diet, and Katayama Tetsu (president of the Social Democratic party) was chosen Premier. The Social Democrats had gained tremendous support from the labor and peasant unions that had mushroomed since the end of the war; it was therefore obvious that the new cabinet would have to pay some heed to the demands of the workers and peasants. To the discomfort of the conservative parties, the Social Democrats began to talk about the nationalization of the coal industry, since the low output of coal was recognized as one of the most serious obstacles to the economic rehabilitation of the country. But in the face of the economic effects of inflation and the political pressure of conservative political elements, the Katayama cabinet did not last long. The revival of conservative power, the obvious lack of political consciousness among the common people, the prevalence of bossism, and the continuing power and influence of other authoritarian institutions and practices caused much skepticism about democratization; and yet, seen in the light of Japanese historical perspective, it cannot be denied that new attitudes were arising in Japan which were giving an entirely different character to Japanese nationalist thought.

A People's Nationalism

With the announcement of surrender, the rulers had tried to focus subsequent nationalist thinking on coöperation with the Occupation as the best means of assuring the preservation of the essential character of the Japanese national polity. But coöperation with the Occupation and an enthusiastic reception of the reform programs were at first not so much products of a desire to preserve Japan's traditional order as they were products of a popular desire to capture the secret of Western power. The surrender had reawakened the old feelings of inferiority, and there was therefore a revival of the old urge to learn as much as possible about the West. The urge was so strong that, as in the early Meiji period, there was a tendency to accept things Western merely because they were Western. This did not mean that nationalism was dead. It meant merely that there was a kind of desperate searching for new sources of strength *for the Japanese people* and a determination to show the West that the Japanese still had qualities and abilities that entitled them to a respectable position in the society of nations.

The policies announced by the Shidehara cabinet in October, 1945, reflected this broader national interest. Shidehara declared that his new cabinet intended to follow the principles outlined in the Charter Oath of 1868, which had set the tone for the process of westernization of the 1870's.[36] The policy received even higher sanction in January, 1946, when the Emperor himself reproclaimed the oath in his famous "The Emperor is not divine" rescript. After quoting in full the original oath, he said:

The [Charter Oath] is evident in its significance and high in its ideals. We wish to make this oath anew and restore the country to stand on its own feet again. We have to reaffirm the principles embodied in the charter and proceed unflinchingly toward elimination of misguided practices of the past and, keeping in close touch with the desires of the people, we will construct a new Japan through thoroughly being pacific, the officials and the people alike obtaining rich culture and advancing the standard of living of the people.[37]

Although nationalist thought and energy were once more moving along lines that had been followed in the Meiji period, there were major differences. In the first place, the identification of the people with their nation, after 1945, was far deeper and broader than in the earlier period. An industrial revolution, a centralized educational system, a highly developed complex of communication media, a series of military victories, and finally a disastrous defeat could not but result in a group solidarity (even with the disappearance of thought-control) that was of a far higher order than the solidarity that had existed in the 1870's. In those early years, national loyalties had not worked down into the lower reaches of the Japanese society; but after 1945 it was in those very strata of society that the main strength of nationalist aspirations lay. Although the officials, the businessmen, and the intelligentsia may have begun, after V-J Day, to associate themselves with a supranational society, the concerns of the great mass of the people did not go beyond a concern for the strength and weakness of the Japanese people.

Still another difference was that after 1945 the nationalist tune was no longer being called by the rulers in response merely to *state* needs, but was being called principally by the ruled, who were concerned more directly with the needs of the *people*. The removal of the thought-control structure and the weakening of the authoritarian system by democratic reforms made it possible for the newly organized peasant and labor groups to express their views and aspirations. Consequently, the center of gravity of national thought tended to shift to a lower level in Japanese society. The great mass of the people were now beginning to express national sentiments in their own terms. This provided a distinctly different tone to nationalist thought, because the people were in direct conflict with the ruling classes on at least one very important matter—the problem of improving the standard of living.

It is a well-established fact that one of the key factors in Japan's remarkable commercial and industrial expansion during the last one hundred years has been the availibility of a large pool of cheap and controllable labor which made production cheaper, commerce more profitable, and the accumulation of wealth more rapid. Japan's businessmen and government officials (as well as that great economist Thorstein Veblen) understood quite well the significance of this advantage and were therefore consistent in their efforts to check the growth of agrarian and labor movements. But it was not merely considerations of profit that led them to follow this policy, for considerations of the welfare of the Japanese state led them to the same conclusions. With a scarcity of national resources and overpopulation, it was impossible, they claimed, for Japan to achieve economic growth except by the expansion of foreign trade. In other words, an ingrown economic development, with the farmers and laborers at home becoming the major consumers, was impossible, because large amounts of food, as well as raw materials for industrial activity, had to be imported. And to gain credits to pay for these imports much had to be exported. Since the lack of resources and the pressure of population were more serious than ever after the war, it was not surprising to find that the rulers and businessmen of Japan were still fearful of the growth of labor and agrarian movements and that their idea of what was good for Japan was still centered on the preservation of the traditional national structure, traditional morals, and traditional social relationships. They were not enthusiastic about many aspects of the reform program, and in many ways they exerted themselves to check the growth and influence of movements that aimed at broadening the base of political power and widening the distribution of economic wealth. The most straightforward statement of what might be termed conservative policy with regard to the matter of improving living standards is found in a statement of a political society (the *Tōa Remmei Kai*) which was headed by the famous military figure Ishihara Kanji. The statement, formulated soon after the surrender, was in the form of instructions to members of the society on how to act under the Occupation. After outlining the importance of doing everything possible to show that Japan had become democratic and antimilitaristic, it stated that the immediate objective in domestic affairs was to hold down the standard of living of the people and to uphold the ideal of simple living.[38] But generally the policy has not been stated so baldly, being concealed in pleas on behalf of the preservation of the essential character of *kokutai*.

The people as a whole, however, have been concerned less about *kokutai* than about raising their standard of living. Eight years of continuous war, ending in a highly destructive series of bombing attacks on many of the industrial centers of the country, had disrupted the economy and made life extremely miserable. Immediately after the announcement of surrender there were other developments that aggravated the situation. Since most of Japan's production had been in the field of military industry, and since all such production was suddenly halted at the time of the surrender, the economic dislocation was terrific. Panic was avoided only because the government followed a spending program which temporarily alleviated the situation; but this government spending marked the beginning of one of history's most vicious inflationary trends. On the day of surrender there were approximately thirty billion yen worth of Bank of Japan notes in circulation, but by the end of that same month the figure had risen to forty-two billion. At a time of very low production there was an orgy of buying which caused prices to skyrocket. People who depended on savings, fixed wages, or salaries were therefore faced with an increasingly oppressive condition. The Occupation ordered the government to cease the payment of military pensions, to abolish wartime subsidy contracts, and to assess taxes on excess war profits. But the gains that were made from complying with these orders were more than offset by new government operations, many of which were required by the Occupation itself. By the end of January, 1946, there were more than fifty-eight billion yen worth of Bank of Japan notes in circulation—nearly twice as many as on the day of surrender. As a result, prices rose so sharply that by June, 1947, black-market prices were from fifty to seventy times as high as prewar prices. And even with the remarkable growth of the labor movement, and its success in obtaining wage increases, wages were still only about thirty-seven times as high as before the war. The lag, of course, was an important factor in the discontent that prevailed in the cities.[39]

In addition to inflation, the contact with Occupation personnel undoubtedly added to the dissatisfaction of the common man, for it seemed that every American soldier had an unlimited amount of money to spend. The presence of large numbers of troops, even in the most out-of-the-way places, was a constant reminder to the people that their own living conditions were indeed distressing. The American moving pictures had a similar effect. The influx of American films after the war and their repeated portrayal of the luxurious life abroad increased the feelings of discontent and the demand—from the bottom of society up, rather than from the top down—for a better life. Conversations with men and women in any circle, as well as a perusal of current books, magazines, and newspapers, revealed that it was this demand for a better life that was the basic aspiration of the people.

The growth of the labor movement after the end of the war was probably the most significant manifestation of this national aspiration. Quite early, the Occupation ordered the Japanese government to promulgate a labor-union law and a labor-standards law. These laws gave the workers a new freedom to organize, and by the end of 1947, twenty-eight thousand labor unions with a membership of more than six million had been organized. The unions not only negotiated for higher wages and better working conditions but soon became interested in politics. By 1947 they had become an extremely powerful political force. It was mainly the support of labor groups that enabled the Social Democrats to gain a plurality in the election of 1947. For many reasons, the labor movement is undoubtedly the most significant social phenomenon of the postwar period. And until 1948 at least, it was moving in harmony with the dominant concern of the Japanese people: the desire for a higher standard of living.

The labor movement received most of its support from those who were convinced that the demand for a higher standard of living could be best achieved by direct pressure on employers for higher wages and better working conditions, and by demands on the government for a wider distribution of wealth through socialization. But there continued to be a strong feeling that a positive solution of the problem lay in greater mastery of the technical achievements of the West. In fact, many still felt that the war had been lost primarily because of technological inferiority. Members of the Occupation whose task it was to acquaint the Japanese with new Western books and magazines found that the greatest demand was for scientific literature. The whole trend toward westernization was in a sense a response to this feeling about the importance of technological advancement as a means of improving living conditions.

But there were also many who still held to the old argument that because of Japan's lack of natural resources and overpopulation, neither socialization nor technological advances would provide a basic solution to Japan's economic problems. These people insisted that the revival and development of foreign trade were the prime requisites of economic recovery. The force of the argument was undoubtedly more apparent to government officials and businessmen, and more to their liking, than it was to the common people. Even the common people, however, could not but be influenced by the traditional theory, which was very logical, and which at the same time had provided a convincing rationale for expansionism. But in the field of foreign trade, Japan was at the mercy of Allied Powers, and as long as the Powers were preoccupied with destroying Japan's ability to embark upon aggressive war, little coöperation could be expected. By 1948, however, the international situation had changed sufficiently to bring about a definite revision in Occupation policy—a change which led the Allied Powers to give serious thought to Japan's economic needs and to adopt measures which had a direct bearing not only upon economic trends but upon the course of national thought.

Rehabilitation

The shift in Occupation policy, which began to take definite shape in 1948, was closely associated with the rise of the "cold war" and with the succession of Communist victories in China. These developments tended to alter the attitude of Americans toward Japan. There was less talk of preventing the reëmergence of Japanese expansionism and more emphasis upon the importance of strengthening the country as a bulwark against the further spread of Communism. To those who favored a reorientation of Occupation policy it was obvious that Japan would serve as an effective bulwark only if she were provided with a modicum of economic well-being. Self-sufficiency was recognized as desirable not only on military grounds but on ideological grounds.

In the early years of the Occupation, while the Allied Powers were still agreed upon the desirability of preventing the reëmergence of Japan as an aggressive power, General MacArthur took the stand that economic problems lay outside the sphere of his responsibility. By 1947 he and his advisers were becoming acutely aware of the explosive character of the economic situation, and of its implications for the occupation and for the international position of the free world. The first reaction was to recommend the conclusion of a peace treaty and the withdrawal of occupation forces in order to give Japan greater freedom to handle her economic problems and to avoid the possibility of her blaming the occupation for her continued economic distress. But when the Allies failed to agree upon procedures for the peace negotiations, and when it became clear that the economic problems had to be faced, there was a gradual shift of policy, which gave the highest priority to economic rehabilitation.

In January, 1948, Secretary Royall made a statement in San Francisco to the effect that the United States should help Japan get back on her feet economically so that she could serve as a stronger defense against Communist aggression. The view that the statement indicated an official acceptance of a shift in policy was substantiated two months later by the Strike report, which recommended a drastic revision of reparations demands. The Draper report, published in May, 1948, was an even clearer indication of the American determination to come to grips with the Japanese economic problem.

The new policy revision meant first of all that some of the earlier programs had to be played down or dropped. Those reëxamined first were those that tended to increase Japan's economic burdens or to add to the further dislocation of her economy. Reparations was an obvious case in point, and after the Strike report there were signs of a more liberal attitude. Eventually the United States decided not to demand reparations for itself, and to attempt to keep the demands of other Allies to a minimum. After 1948 the deconcentration of economic power also was viewed with greater distaste, for an increasingly large number of influential political figures in America, as well as in Japan, were opposing this "socialistic" program which, they claimed, was disrupting the Japanese economy and making recovery more difficult. Under this pressure the Occupation hastened to shorten the list of companies that were to be affected by "deconcentration," and in the summer of 1949 General MacArthur announced that the program was "completed." But the Occupation officials did not rest content with these negative measures. In rapid succession, various financial, tax, trade, and industrial experts were invited to Japan to give advice and to outline programs that would speed up economic recovery. The most significant help, however, came in the form of large grants of money that would permit Japan to buy the materials and machinery necessary for reviving her export industries. By the last half of 1948 there were signs that Japan's trade was coming to life.

But in 1948, Japan was still being plagued by inflation. The circulation of Bank of Japan notes increased from 220,000,000,000 yen to 360,000,000,000 in that one year, and prices rose in the same period by another 50 per cent. But because of good rice crops and larger imports of food and materials from America, living conditions improved; the new conservative Yoshida cabinet was therefore enabled, with Occupation help and prodding, to take effective measures against inflation. In 1949 the government budget was balanced, the new exchange rate of 360 yen per dollar was maintained, and, chiefly because of General MacArthur's famous letter of July, 1948, stating that government workers did not have the right to strike against the government, wages were stabilized. Economists felt that the inflationary trend had been checked and that Japan was now really moving toward economic rehabilitation.[40] With these developments the popular discontent about low living standards was somewhat alleviated, and the people were therefore more responsive to another national concern: political independence.

Political Independence

The actual outbreak of hostilities in Korea in the summer of 1950, and the later entry of Communist China into the fray, marked the rise of a truly critical situation in the Far East. It caused the free nations among the Allied Powers to take even more positive measures to support the economic rehabilitation of Japan; but it also made them aware that political independence would have to be granted if Japan was to gain the kind of strength, and to provide the kind of support, that was so sorely needed by the free nations.

Very soon after the outbreak of hostilities, the State Department of the United States asked John Foster Dulles to work out with representatives of the Allied Powers an acceptable peace treaty with Japan. Both the United States and the United Kingdom were sufficiently impressed with the urgency of the matter to agree that a treaty should be negotiated, even if the approval of the U.S.S.R. could not be gained. After months of involved negotiations, Dulles succeeded in formulating a draft which, with special defense treaties for the Philippines, New Zealand, and Australia, was acceptable to most of the Allied Powers, except those within the so-called Communist bloc. Many Asiatic nations were not so enthusiastic about Japanese independence as was the United States. India and Burma refused to participate in the Peace Conference or to sign the treaty, and others were displeased with certain aspects of the settlement. But for Japan it was a step toward liberation from foreign occupation. The loss of the Ryukyu and Bonin Islands, and the agreement to permit the stationing of American troops in Japan after the signing of the peace treaty, left some feelings of dissatisfaction. But most felt that under the circumstances and for the time being these undesirable features were a cheap price to pay for the return of political independence.

The Korean war and the peace settlement, however, aroused strong fears in large segments of the population that Japan was being drawn again into the vortex of another military conflict. The restrictions and hardships of many years of militarism and war were still fresh in the minds of most people, and although they had been subjected for years to indoctrination on the dangers inherent in Communist expansion (which was now getting pretty close to home), there was still widespread determination to avoid embroilment in another war, and especially to avoid fighting the battles of another country.

Comments by leading political and military figures in the United States strengthened the fear that Japanese independence was merely a prelude to rearmament. The establishment of the National Police Reserve of 75,000 men soon after the outbreak of the Korean war was associated in Japanese minds with the new American interest in a peace treaty. When in October, 1950, the Chinese armies marched to the support of the North Koreans, there was even more talk in the United States about strengthening Japan as a bulwark against the further spread of Communism. But although Communism was now a greater threat, the Japanese seemed to be more determined than ever to avoid involvement in war. The clause in the new constitution outlawing war as a means of settling international disputes was defended more earnestly, and many political groups vied with each other in insisting that rearmament was unconstitutional, expensive, and generally undesirable.

But as the war in Korea dragged on, and as the achievement of political independence became a certainty, there was a tendency for the public to revise its views on the subject of rearmament. A Yomiuri public-opinion poll, taken in January, 1952, showed that 57.9 per cent of the people favored the establishment of an army once the peace treaty was placed into effect, whereas in August, 1950, only 38.9 per cent had expressed such a view.[41] By February, 1952, the government felt that public opinion had shifted sufficiently to permit the announcement of a plan to strengthen the defense organization. But the move was criticized sharply by opposition parties, the press, and various political societies, since most people feared that the government was leading the country back to militarism. In general, rearmament was recognized as a necessity, but as a necessary evil which had to be watched carefully. The Communists, the left wing of the Socialist party, and many university students were so afraid of the implications of rearmament that they opposed it altogether.

The Communists were against rearmament because they were following the line that the United States was making Japan a tool for its aggressive policies and that therefore the Japanese should not play into the hands of Americans by building an army for their use.[42] The left-wing Socialists took the stand that Japan could not afford an army, that the money could be better used for social betterment, and that in this atomic age the old-type armies were useless anyway.[43] The students claimed that the old politicians and senior military officers were insisting upon rearmament in utter disregard of the fact that it would be the young people of the country who would be carrying the guns and doing the fighting. They pointed out that although it was an ideal of the nation to protect the lives of its people, the present government seemed to be bent upon throwing away lives by its program of supporting the building of an army that would be sent, on American orders, into Korea, Manchuria, or even China.[44]

The majority of the people, however, have now come round to the belief that some rearmament is required in order to fulfill properly the minimum tasks and responsibilities of an independent nation. But even those who are most articulate in the support of rearmament are careful to emphasize that it is necessary only because of the threat of Communist aggression, and that it is only for defensive purposes. Even former Colonel Tsuji Masanobu, a famous strategist and one of the most outspoken supporters of rearmament, insists that what he has in mind is a small force that would keep any future world war from engulfing Japan. To be specific, he feels that if Japan had ten divisions, the U.S.S.R. would not be able to invade Japan with less than thirty divisions, which, he says, not even the great Russia would be able to spare for such a project. He goes along with Nehru in believing that it is not necessary, or desirable, to accept the thesis that it is impossible for Asia to maintain an independent position in the "two world" struggle. He absolutely rejects the idea of using Japanese troops to fight for Americans or of permitting Asians to fight against Asians upon orders from America. Finally, he states that "rearmament does not mean the revival of the old defeated army, but the rebuilding of a new army, in reality as well as in name," which would be "imbued with the spontaneous activity of youth who are burning with love for their homeland." He writes: "By rearmament we will be coming to the aid, through the state, of those who were cast adrift and who became the victims of war, and we will also be moving together toward the achievement of liberation from the horrors of war."[45]

Thus, the current rearmament discussions are bound up with that basic national desire for true political independence. Those who feel that a new army could not possibly be independent are against rearmament, and those who do support rearmament insist that Japan can and must be certain that the new army protect Japan, not merely serve some foreign power. The signing of the peace treaty has been welcomed as a great national achievement, but it has made the people excessively sensitive about any possible restrictions on, or dangers to, their autonomy.[46]

Political Struggle for Nationalist Support

Every political group in Japan is aware of the force and significance of the basic national desires for greater economic well-being and political independence. In the programs of each group, high priority is given to the policies that promise freedom from poverty and resistance to foreign domination. Each group, whether radical or conservative, points out and condemns the forces, conditions, or enemies that it believes were the cause of its internal weaknesses or external dangers.

The Communist doctrine has traditionally stressed internationalist ideals; but the Japanese Communist party in each successive revision of its program since 1945 has attempted to make a stronger appeal for nationalist support. Even in the earliest policy pronouncements after the war, the party played down the old thesis of abolishing the Emperor system to the extent of advocating that the matter be left to the decision of the people.[47] Until 1950, the Japanese Communist party adopted the strategy of being a party that was "likable" and that favored a "peaceful revolution." The program stressed a "united democratic front" for the "solution of the national economic crisis,"[48] and under these policies the party grew. By 1949 it had a registered membership of about 100,000 and had 35 seats in the Diet. Also, it has been estimated that 40 per cent of the university students were supporting the party program and that there were more than 3,000,000 sympathizers.[49] But after the Communist victory in China and the signing of the Sino-Soviet treaty, there was a drastic shift which marked a return to a more "positive" policy—one with an even broader, more direct, national appeal. Nozaka, who had formulated the earlier "likable" policy, was condemned in January, 1950, by the official Cominform organ for being not only antidemocratic and antisocialist but also antipatriotic and anti-Japanese.[50] The "likable" policy thus was dropped, and gradually the party turned to more militant policies and tactics. In a draft of "The Fundamental Tasks of the Japanese Communist Party in the Coming Revolution," published in May, 1950, the liberation from foreign danger came first in the new outline of the party's goals:

[There must be a] liberation of the people from the control of international monopoly capital. This means complete opposition to the colonization and militarization of Japan so that national independence might be achieved. It means also opposition to war so that world peace may be insured. To attain the above, the following demands must be made:
(1) An overall peace in accordance with the Potsdam Declaration and the reestablishment of Japan's sovereignty.
(2) The speedy withdrawal of all occupation troops after conclusion of a peace treaty.
(3) Opposition to war and to the colonization and militarization of Japan. . . .[51]

The completion of the "bourgeois democratic revolution" was placed in a position of secondary importance. The guns were now trained first upon the "American imperialists," and next upon the "traitorous monopoly capitalists."

On the day after the outbreak of the Korean war, about which the Japanese Communists seem to have had advance notice, the Japanese Communist party organ, *Akahata* (The Red Flag), took the line that the North Koreans had been attacked. Two weeks later there were reports of sabotage in Japan, and the Communist leaders disappeared underground. When the United States moved to work out a peace treaty with Japan, the efforts were described by the Japanese Communist party as a "trampling on [Japan's] ardent desire for independence. . . . We [Japanese] seek freedom, independence and peace. We 80,000,000 Japanese do not want to become slaves of a foreign country. Our national land has been covered by a network of military bases. Our industries and lives have been destroyed. And our national pride has been completely trampled on. . . ."[52] Stalin himself added his blessing to the nationalist appeal in his New Year's message to the Japanese people in January, 1952, when he said that he hoped for the freedom and happiness of the people of Japan and for their success in winning *complete independence.* In the May Day Incident (1952), Communists attracted world-wide attention by their terroristic acts against American lives and property; and at the time of the general elections in October, 1952, their campaign revolved around charges that the Americans were using and exploiting the Japanese nation. The Communist newspaper published maps showing the location of American installations in Japan and attempted to arouse nationalist feelings against Americans by printing cartoons that placed the American GI, in his relations with Japanese girls, in the worst possible light.[53] Like the conservative "rightists," the Communists are not merely responding to the nationalist demands for a better way of life and for a truly independent nation but are now moving forward with an energetic program designed to whip up fears of foreign—that is, American—domination and exploitation. The Communists, in other words, are now turning to the very tactics that Japan's militarists used earlier to arouse among the people a fanatical support for their expansionist drive. Judging from the present program of the Communists and from their policies elsewhere, it is logical to assume that if they gain the upper hand in Japan, they will use all information, education, and entertainment media—just as the conservative ultranationalists did—to arouse deep fears of foreign danger in order to gain greater strength for their regime and for their programs. It seems clear that in the future the Communist party will continue its efforts to stir up anti-American sentiment as a means of capturing the power of nationalism for its cause.

The Socialists too, in both the right- and the left-wing sections of the party, are making a strong bid for nationalist support by advocating a broad program of reforms designed to improve the standard of living of the people as a whole, and by favoring measures and policies which they feel will be most effective in assuring a real and meaningful independence for the Japanese nation. They are making their appeals directly to the peasants, laborers, and intellectuals—the groups in which nationalist power is based. But, unlike the Communists, they believe that their programs can be achieved by peaceful, nonrevolutionary tactics, and they do not feel impelled to bolster their appeal with charges of exploitation against the Anglo-Saxon nations. Further-more, since they have confidence in representative institutions, and since they aim to gain nationalist support by following a program aimed to satisfy the nationalist aspirations of the great mass of the people, they feel no need for—and they definitely oppose—authoritarian thought-control tactics. But as the two-world struggle becomes more intense, the calm, peaceful internal program and the more strictly neutral attitude toward foreign powers have placed the party at a disadvantage. The tendency for people to gravitate to the anti-Soviet and anti-American extremes—the process currently tabbed as "polar-ization"—has somewhat weakened the Socialists' attempt to gain na-tionalist support for their program.

The more conservative political parties are also adjusting their pro-grams and policies in order to head off nationalist opposition. But being conservative, they do not favor the socialistic principles of the Communists and the Socialists, preferring to point up the internal and external dangers to the nation arising out of the growth of Com-munism at home and abroad. However, they also recognize the impor-tance of the popular demand for real political independence and therefore take pains to show that although they fear Russia more than the United States, they have not become the tools of American foreign policy. But in addition to paying considerable attention to the basic national demands of the people, the liberal parties—including the Liberal (*Jiyū Tō*), the Democratic (*Minshu Tō*), and the Progressive (*Kaishin Tō*)—have also shown themselves to be receptive to, if not actually in favor of, a resumption of some form of thought control, particularly in the field of "moral education."

The democratic reforms, the removal of the old police restrictions, the various Western fads, and what might be called the "postwar fever" have all contributed to a general breakdown of traditional patterns of conduct, particularly among young people in urban areas. The trend is most disturbing to the older, more conservative members of Japanese society. There has been much talk, among these groups, of a great moral vacuum. And as Japan has moved closer toward independence, the demand for moral education has become louder. In the fall of 1951 even the Minister of Education felt that the time had come to take some official action. As a trial balloon, he let it be known that he planned to circulate a "moral code," after the peace was signed, for use as a guide for public education. As pointed out in an excellent article by R. P. Dore, the code was quite different from the old Imperial rescript. Clauses concerning the "dignity of the individual personality" preceded those on the family, society, and the state. But there was still a definite traditional flavor. The basic pattern of social relationships was not one between equals but between superior and inferior, and the state still appeared as something of a "metaphysical entity."[54] But the response of the country discouraged the minister, for the time being at least, from pressing for the adoption of his guide. The *Yomiuri* carried this editorial comment: "Our sense of democratic morality constrains us to oppose [the Moral Code] firmly. [The Minister's] system is similar to the ethical teachings of Confucius. . . . When [the Minister] proceeds to adore the Emperor, his moral code turns into a new version of the Imperial Rescript on Education."[55] All but one of the newspapers took a similar stand, and the matter was dropped. But it is significant that a high official in the Liberal party government should have made such a move. To many persons, this trial balloon, together with official efforts to revive interest in Shintoism and the Emperor institution, suggests that the conservative political groups of the country would welcome a revival of government efforts to channel nationalist ideas and feelings. In general, then, the conservative political parties and their supporters appear to be less responsive to the national aspiration for a better way of life but are careful to place themselves on the side of true political independence for Japan—even independence from American control. They appear to be most enthusiastic in pointing out the dangers—internal and external—of Communism, and they are beginning to show an inclination to use all possible thought media as vehicles for a revival of traditional authoritarian values. If these conservatives continue to retain control of the government, and if international relations continue to be critical, it seems logical to assume that the conservative parties would adopt more of the prewar ultra-nationalist techniques in order to direct the power of nationalism into lines more to their liking.

In addition to the political groups that operate through the representative institutions, there are many nationalist societies which favor extraparty political tactics and are therefore closely associated with what appears to be the rise of a new trend toward a revival of the earlier, more classical type of Japanese nationalist activity. Nationalism is still generating somewhat spontaneously among the people as a whole; but a number of close observers detect ominous signs of renewed activity in behalf of Emperorism and *kokutai*, as opposed to efforts to meet the popular demands for a better way of life and for true political independence.

The hundreds of nationalist societies that have cropped up since the war are not unlike their earlier counterparts. Their programs and activities, like those of the earlier societies, are presented as manifestations of a selfless love of the fatherland (*sokoku*). Traditional institutions, principles, and relationships are upheld, and radical changes, such as those advocated by the Communists, are condemned. The societies also tend to relate their love of country with Pan-Asianism, advancing the thesis that the Asian people can "liberate" themselves only by working together. Finally, these groups generally reject the principles of democratic representation—in fact, if not in word—and favor direct action and the exercise of personal influence. The members of the organizations, for the most part, consider themselves to be a select group, and they are bound together by close ties of personal loyalty. Consequently, most societies are identified with some influential leader who exercises strong authoritarian control over their policies and activities.

At this early date in the resurgence of "rightest" activity, it is difficult to identify the most significant developments. But, as before the war, it appears that the strongest movements are again centered in either the Tohoku or the Kyushu district. Kyushu, the island nearest the Asiatic continent, has been the home of many of the most powerful rightist societies ever since the founding of the *Genyōsha* Society more than seventy years ago. Later, the Black Dragon Society (*Kokuryūkai*), probably the most influential of the rightist organizations during the first two decades of the twentieth century, was also primarily a Kyushu product. And now that many of the nationalist leaders have been "depurged," there are indications that a strong combination of "patriots" of the Black Dragon Society tradition is being formed, it is rumored, under the leadership of Ogata Taketora, currently Minister without Portfolio in the Yoshida cabinet and said to be the successor to Hirota Koki, the leading figure in the Black Dragon Society during the 1930's and Premier after the February Twenty-sixth Incident of 1936. As yet the group apparently has not been organized formally; but in view of the importance of the traditions of leadership and personal loyalty, it is obvious that considerable influence can be exterted without formal organization.

Of the many societies that were organized in Kyushu after the war, the one which has probably received the most publicity is the *Nihon Kakumei Kikuhata Dōshi Kai* (Japan Revolutionary Chrysanthemum Flag Society). Although the society has been weakened by internal dissension and will probably fade away in due time, an outline of the major items in its program will serve to suggest the nature of the ideas and principles that characterize rightist activity in the area. In a general statement of principles, formulated in 1947, the society committed itself to the support of (1) the maintenance of the Emperor system and the establishment of democracy; (2) the complete destruction of the Communist party and the establishment of constitutional government; (3) construction of a permanently neutral state; and (4) strict enforcement of the terms of the Potsdam Declaration. But later there was a split in the society, and a group under the leadership of another man revised the original program so as to incorporate two other programs that have become popular among the "rightists": support of the "Asian peoples' movement" and stabilization of the national life. In this later revision there was no mention of democracy. Instead, the society was to work for the construction of a noble (*koki*) society.[56]

Rightist movements in the Tōhoku area (the northeastern part of the main island of Honshu) reflect a greater interest in the living conditions of the people, for that area has long been noted for its agrarian distress. The climate there is more severe and the once-a-year rice crops are poor. Some of Japan's most powerful rightist movements have come out of the Tōhoku area. The new developments of the last few years suggest that the area will continue to be the base for some of the stronger societies. The one that seems to top the list at the moment is the *Tōa Remmei*, a society originally organized in 1942 with that colorful military figure Ishihara Kanji at its head.

Quite early, Ishihara came to believe in what has been called the East Asia Federation Doctrine; this still stands at the center of the *Tōa Remmei* principles and exerts a strong influence upon the programs of many of the current national societies. The doctrine seems to rest on the conviction that there will soon be a "final" world war in which the peoples of eastern Asia should fight together, rather than against each other. Therefore, at the time of the Manchurian Incident in 1931, Ishihara became one of the most energetic exponents of the idea that an independent government should be set up in Manchuria which would serve as the first step toward the construction of an East

Asia Federation. The plan was to establish a government based on the principles of the Kingly Way (Ōdō), and once this was in operation, to attempt to draw China into the federation. Ishihara was therefore quite insistent that Japan avoid war with China. He felt that Japan should agree to withdraw all troops from China, if Chiang Kai-shek would recognize the new Manchurian government. Then, with a growing understanding of mutual problems, the peoples of the East Asia Federation, Ishihara believed, would be prepared to offer strong resistance against the further spread of Communism. In pressing this program, Ishihara eventually came into conflict with Tōjō himself; and after the war, Ishihara and his followers were inclined to place most of the blame for the defeat of Japan on Tōjō and his group, since they had caused Japan to become involved in fighting a war against other Asian people.

At the beginning of the occupation period the *Tōa Remmei* reformulated its program to fit the new situation, but the old East Asia Federation doctrine still remained the focus of the new program. The society set up headquarters on a farm called the Nighiyama Farm in Yamagata Prefecture, and for a time its activities were limited to popularizing improved farming methods, and similar projects. But at the time of the dissolution of the ultranationalist societies, Ishihara was convinced that his East Asia Federation doctrine would meet with the approval of Occupation authorities; he therefore wrote to General MacArthur explaining the society's program. But Ishihara died in 1949, and for a time his movement was centered in an organization called the *Kyōwa Kai*—the same name as that of an organization in Manchuria which later became the model for the Imperial Rule Assistance Association. The *Kyōwa Kai* published a newspaper, the *Kyōwa*, which expressed a deep concern about the poverty and social maladjustments of the day and supported the East Asia Federation idea. The paper condemned "those influential men in politics, economics, and religion who are housed in four-storied bank buildings and who indulge in Turkish baths."[57] It also declared that

at a time when we have become the wives and concubines of others and are trying to snatch moments of relief, the prosperity of Japan is the prosperity of a beggar; and the safety of the country is nothing more than the safety which leaves others with the right of choice. What can we do? We can work for the self-determination of the people (*minzoku joketsu*), for the mutual respect of peoples' states (*minzoku kokka no sōgo sonju*) and for the principle of noninterference in the internal affairs [of other states] (*naisei fu-kanshō*).[58]

In 1949 a political party, the *Kyōwa Tō*, was organized by the same group. The platform stated:

On the principle of [preserving] peace and saving the nation, and with a burning conviction, we hereby resolutely organize the Kyowa party and raise the first voice for a new life. Our party is not a so-called capitalistic party; nor is it communistic. We rather wish to carry out the principle of democratic control through a peoples' organization which, centered around the Emperor, would be geared to the higher world view. In economics we would particularly make each person use his own unique abilities by emphasizing the three principles of national development, coöperative development and individual development. We would construct an ideal society in which there would be a unity of agriculture based upon a harmonization of nature and science. And we would also carry out a complete construction of a national life. In regard to our ideal state we would realize most completely the lofty lines of Marx, who would have wiped out all exploitation by preserving a rich cultural life for all the people by utilizing all excess productive power.[59]

In recent months the *Kyōwa Kai* has resumed its old name, *Tōa Remmei*, and another colorful military figure, former Colonel Tsuji Masanobu, seems to be rising to a position of preëminence in the movement. Tsuji, who gained fame during the war as a brilliant military strategist, achieved further fame after the war by successfully avoiding arrest by the British, who had listed him as a war criminal. For three years he roamed about in China, and returned to Japan only after the War Crimes trials had come to an end. He then immediately broke into print with a detailed account of his experiences in China[60] and began to air his views about the importance of coöperation by all Asian peoples and the urgency of the reëstablishment of a new-type army in Japan.[61] Tsuji's election to the Diet in October, 1952, by a heavy majority[62] provides further proof of his popularity. One cannot help noting the similarity between the socialist-nationalist synthesis of the *Tōa Remmei* movement and the characteristic features of the National Reconstruction movement which was so powerful in the 1930's. It is not beyond the realm of possibility that the *Tōa Remmei* will be the forerunner of another "*Jimmu Kai*," with less socialism and more nationalism.

The so-called "rightist" movement is still comparatively weak and formless; but as Japan moves closer to rearmament, and as the old ultranationalist leaders regain freedom of action (when "depurged"), it seems likely, if international relations continue to be critical, that the nationalist societies will become stronger and that they will be a truly significant agency for redirecting nationalist sentiments along classical lines: that is, primarily *against* enemies of the state, rather than *for* the economic, political, and cultural growth of the nation.

"Neutralism"

Because of the Korean war, American economic aid, and postwar rehabilitation programs have brought to Japan a certain degree of economic prosperity, and also because the Peace Treaty has provided the Japanese with at least the form of political independence, the people as a whole seem to be giving more attention to international affairs and to Japan's role therein. It is only logical, therefore, that many are being taken in by the Communist emphasis upon American exploitation, that many are being aroused by the conservative opposition to Communist expansion, and that many are also influenced by the rightist tendency to support Pan-Asianism and oppose both Russia and the West.

Anti-Communist sentiment is undoubtedly more widespread than anti-Americanism. To appreciate fully the appeal of anti-Communist program it must be borne in mind that Japan has been concerned with Russian expansion for centuries. She fought one of her bloodiest wars to prevent Russian domination of Manchuria and Korea in 1904–1905, and for twenty years before V-J Day the Japanese people were constantly reminded of the Communist danger. Furthermore, the Japanese will not soon forget that the U.S.S.R. attacked them when they were down—that only after Japan had asked the U.S.S.R. to intercede for her with the United States to stop the war, only after the Japanese Navy had been destroyed, and only after the atomic bombs had been dropped did Russia declare war on Japan.[63] The reluctance of the Russians to return Japanese prisoners from Siberian camps was irritating. And finally, the outbreak of war in Korea has been a sharp reminder that Communist expansion is real and near. Within Japan the recent terroristic activities of the Japanese Communist party have also provided a clear object lesson on what Communism means. Thus the rightist programs have a strong appeal among a large number of people, and the popular response serves to encourage the government and the conservative political groups to be even more positive in their efforts to stamp out the movement.

The anti-Communist sentiment is in part anti-Russian, for the relationship between Russian Communism and Japanese Communism is apparent to all. The orientation in Communism to which the Japanese prisoners of war in Siberia were subjected, the radio propaganda programs beamed to Japan, and the extensive activities of the Russian "diplomatic" agents in Japan have also served to show that it is the Russians who are ultimately responsible for the spread of Communism, not only in Japan but in China and Korea as well.

The anti-Communist feelings are also somewhat anti-Korean, for it is well established that a large part of the active Communists in Japan are Koreans. For decades the Korean minority has been made the scapegoat for one misfortune after another—including the fires that followed the great Tokyo earthquake of 1923—but since World War II, the Korean assumption of special rights and privileges, particularly in and around Kobe and Osaka, has caused the Japanese to be even more suspicious of the Koreans. Now that the Koreans obviously constitute a dominant element in the Communist party, more attention and more irate feelings are directed toward this minority group. But the anti-Korean sentiment is somewhat negated by a more dominant element in conservative nationalist thought: Pan-Asianism. Not only the *Tōa Remmei,* but many other rightist societies give Pan-Asianism a prominent place in their platforms, and this doctrine dictates that the Japanese shall work together with all Asians in order that all may be "liberated" from the domination of foreign (Western) powers.

However, Pan-Asianism has a more direct bearing upon Japan's attitude toward the Chinese than on her attitude toward the Koreans. In spite of the fact that the Chinese are now under a Communist government, many of the most conservative and reactionary leaders in Japan seem to feel that somehow it is still possible for the Chinese and the Japanese to work together. Undoubtedly the firmness of the conviction is based in part upon the realization that economic recovery of Japan will be difficult, if not impossible, unless she gains access to Chinese markets and raw materials. Therefore, with regard to the Chinese, Pan-Asianism seems to have cancelled out any hatred which might have been engendered in the Korean war. In a real sense, then, Pan-Asianism has weakened the anti-Chinese sentiments that would logically have emerged from Japanese antipathy to Communism.

Anti-American feelings have become a popular subject of discussion in recent months, for the Communist propaganda against America is apparently having some effect. As one Japanese writer indicated in a recent article, anti-American sentiment used to be considered the monopoly of Communists and their fellow travelers, but now such feelings seem to be spreading into other segments of the Japanese society, for charges against the Americans are meeting with a rather sympathetic response from conservatives and moderates, as well as from radicals.

The Communist line that Japan is being exploited by American capitalists and that she is being used as an advance base for an ambitious program of American expansion can be noted in the thinking of student and minority groups; but anti-American sentiment cannot be explained in terms of Communist propaganda alone. A basic factor is to be found in a general reaction to seven years of occupation that was chiefly American, and to seven years of drastic educational, political, economic, and religious reforms that in general followed American patterns. For a time there was great enthusiasm for the occupation and the reforms, since they provided a happy alternative to continued war, and since they seemed to offer new sources of strength for the nation. But the occupation and its reforms did not supply a substitute for the old sense of national mission with which the Japanese had been completely absorbed before 1945. Christian missionaries resumed their work with great energy in 1945, and the tremendous increase in the number of conversions suggested that Christian convictions might fill the moral vacuum that came in the wake of defeat. But in spite of the growth of the Christian movement, only about one per cent of the population has become associated with the Christian church. And it is doubtful whether this small part of the population is nearly so ardent in its support of Christian ideals as was the nation in its wartime support of the national mission. Under these circumstances it is understandable that the Japanese people should begin to lose their enthusiasm for the "American" reform program, and that they should begin to look back once more to their own traditional values and ideals.

In addition to the general reaction against the American occupation and the American-engineered reforms, there are a number of specific complaints against American policies, actions, and attitudes, which have had an uneven effect upon different sections of the population but which *in toto* have served to accelerate the rise of anti-American sentiments. With the early basic policy to "demilitarize" Japan and to see to it that Japan "never again becomes a menace to the United States or to the peace and security of the world,"[84] the Japanese have never had any quarrel. Even the second primary objective, the establishment "of a peaceful and responsible government which will respect the rights of other states, and which will support the objectives of the

United States as reflected in the ideals and principles of the Charter of the United Nations"⁸⁵ was accepted with remarkable equanimity, if not outright enthusiasm. But when, after 1948, there began to emerge another policy, one of building up Japan into a strong bulwark against the further spread of Communism, there emerged certain inconsistencies of policy which troubled many of the most pro-American and democratic-minded people. Under the earlier policy, for example, successful attempts were made to encourage the development of a strong labor-union movement, to break up the monopolistic economy power of the *zaibatsu* (financial cliques), to decentralize police control, and to write into the new constitution a declaration that the "maintenance of land, sea, and air forces . . . will never be authorized."⁸⁶ But under the operation of the post-1948 policy to build up a strong Japan, steps were taken by the Japanese government (with Occupation support) to limit the right of unions to strike, to "complete" (or break off) the deconcentration of economic power, to revert once more to greater centralization of police control, and to rebuild a Japanese military force. This change in direction was consistent in terms of American security, for the earlier policy was meant to destroy the threat of Japanese expansionism, whereas the later policy was meant to destroy the threat of Russian expansionism. But for the Japanese, the change tended to bring disillusionment and even suspicion. The ideals of democracy and peace had a strong humanitarian appeal. They were enthusiastically embraced by many Japanese; and Americans, for the most part, were held in high esteem for their role in introducing democratic ideals and processes into Japan. But when the Americans began to support measures that undermined the very movements which they had introduced earlier under the banner of democracy, there was great consternation. People began to wonder whether their American teachers really believed in the ideals that they had been teaching. The suspicion was the greater because the Japanese were not so disturbed as were the Americans about the danger of Communism. Probably the severest blow of all came when General MacArthur, who had praised the new constitution in glowing terms, suggested that the clause outlawing war might have to be revised. Even the economic aid given by the United States after 1948 and the achievement of political independence in 1952 probably strengthened rather than weakened the conviction that, after all, American policy was geared to American interests rather than American ideals.

Undoubtedly, the behavior of individual Americans in Japan has also served to increase the antipathy of Japanese toward Americans. As was pointed out earlier, the behavior of American soldiers in the beginning stages of the occupation was much better than the Japanese had been led to expect. But as the occupation wore on, the wartime veterans were gradually replaced by new recruits who were not nearly so well disciplined and who, in general, were much rougher in their treatment of the former enemies. Under the circumstances, it is surprising that the incidents were not more numerous than they were; but still they were more numerous and more serious than we in the United States, depending upon the usual press coverage, realized. And of course even the smallest incident created a deep impression upon a sensitive people smarting from the impact of national defeat.

But it was probably attitudes of superiority that cut deepest. The GI's and the American civilians in the Occupation could not but be affected by the victory of their nation. They were confident and self-sufficient. They took pride in the obvious superiority of their mechanical know-how, and it was not long before these attitudes were reflected in their treatment of the Japanese. The Japanese understood that this reaction was natural, but they still cringed before implications of inferiority. It is quite possible that, in such a frame of mind, many Japanese may even begin to look upon some of the terms of the recent administrative agreement as a revival of the old extraterritoriality privileges enjoyed by Westerners in the nineteenth century.[67]

Expressions of anti-American sentiments vary greatly in type and intensity. It is generally believed that the intellectuals have been affected least of all by the trend; nevertheless many of them now prefer to travel and study in Europe rather than in America.[68] Also, the conservative leaders in government and business have not been influenced much by the movement; but this may be due more to a realization of Japan's dependence upon American economic and military aid than to any special feelings of friendship for the American people. Even this group shows some impatience with the American refusal to recognize Communist China, since the refusal complicates the revival of trade with the continent; and they are also disturbed about American resistance to Japanese trade expansion in North America.[69] Those who are less concerned about the protection of their position and their property are most influenced by anti-American sentiments. They are the ones who yield most readily to resentment or hatred against policy changes, against superior, overbearing, unjust treatment by Americans. It is they who are most likely to be taken in by the Communist propaganda.

In spite of the unmistakable evidence of the rise of an anti-American movement, it must be admitted that the feelings have not reached the degree of hatred which prevailed in prewar and wartime years. Americans who have resided in Japan continuously since the end of the war but who are not familiar with the prewar situation are inclined to be somewhat disturbed by the recent trends. For those who remember the fanatical outbursts of prewar years, however, the present manifestations of anti-American feeling seem quite mild. The American attitude toward Japan, for one thing, is now characterized by friendliness rather than suspicion; and furthermore, the Japanese government is not now pursuing a policy of stimulating stronger loyalty to the state by arousing opposition to the policies and principles followed by Western countries. Nevertheless, even relatively weak feelings of anti-Americanism are serious and complicate our attempts to gain the support of the Japanese for a common cause. The movement is potentially dangerous for the free world. If it should continue to grow and Communism should succeed in identifying itself with the movement, the force of nationalism could be directed against the United States and against its effort to protect the free world from Communism.

The Pan-Asian element of the rightist programs is associated, in an inverse relationship, with opposition to all non-Asian peoples. And since there are indications that the rightist movement will continue to grow, particularly if Japan rearms and if the international situation remains critical, there is some justification for expecting a certain merging of the radical opposition to America with the conservative opposition to Russia. Within the Japanese Communist party there are elements that have rejected Russian dictatorship of policy, and among the conservatives there are those who are particularly irked by indications that America may now turn to a policy of curtailing foreign aid and protecting competing American businesses by raising trade barriers. If Russian and American foreign policies should long run counter to Japanese national sensibilities, and if the Japanese should gain enough strength to assume a more independent attitude, it is not inconceivable that under the prodding of various rightist movements the Japanese should once more take up the cause of Pan-Asianism with enthusiasm and thereby weld their anti-Russian and anti-American feelings into something like the old sentiment of opposition to all non-Asian foreigners. It is in this connection that neutralism, and talk of an Asian "third force" become particularly significant.

✧   ✧   ✧

The character of postwar nationalism in Japan differs so drastically from the ultranationalism of prewar and wartime years that observers are tempted to conclude that the phenomenon has disappeared. But to adopt such a conclusion is to misunderstand the basic nature of nationalism and to overlook the possibility of its resurgence in a form which would again threaten the peace and security of the world.

In studying the attitudes and feelings of the Japanese people since V-J Day, we can readily see that it was not the sense of loyalty to the nation that was changed, but rather the expressions and manifestations of that loyalty. Under conditions of defeat, the old patterns of thought and action no longer made sense in terms of service to the nation. And, furthermore, under the Occupation and its reforms, the government was unable to carry on with its old thought-control program. Consequently, nationalist thought not only was molded into new ways of serving the nation but became a spontaneous product of popular interests, not primarily a product of officially controlled propaganda.

The new nationalism that emerged after the war was, therefore, more closely geared to the concerns of the common people. With these as a focus, aspirations for a better way of life for all Japanese became the central theme. The improvement of living standards, moreover, was considered to be principally a Japanese problem and was not tied up with antiforeign feelings. In part this was due to a reaction against hatreds engendered by a particularly energetic propaganda program that had begun several years earlier, but it was also due to the surprisingly considerate behavior of the Occupation personnel and to the rise of some very acute, internal, postwar economic problems. For a time the solution of the economic problems and the improvement of living conditions were considered primarily Japanese problems. Instead of blaming the situation on foreigners, the Japanese turned their attention to modernization and to internal reforms that would yield a more equitable distribution of economic wealth and political power. The new nationalism was remarkably free of antiforeign feelings—in fact, there was a strong upsurge of internationalism. Nationalist feelings, strangely enough, were characterized more by confidence than by fear, even though Japan had just been defeated in war.

After the collapse of the Chinese Nationalist regime there was so radical a change in international relations in the Far East that Occupation policy was revised. This revision had repercussions throughout Japanese society and altered the character of nationalist thought. As the Occupation adjusted its program to the cold war, the people became more conscious of world affairs and more concerned about Japan's international position. Thus they gradually grew more anxious to achieve political independence.

When the Korean war broke out, the United States became so anxious to obtain assistance in dealing with the crisis that officials soon turned to the possibility of gaining the support of Japan. It was then that Mr. Dulles was given the responsibility for arranging the Peace Treaty. The prospect of regaining political independence was, of course, most gratifying to all Japanese nationals, but under the circumstances, they could not escape the fear that the Peace Treaty would not give them true independence. In fact, there arose a general concern lest in gaining nominal independence they would be associating themselves more closely with the United States and possibly committing themselves to military support of American foreign policy.

The negotiations for a peace treaty, therefore, led to a new shift in national interests, not only because the Japanese found themselves drifting into the vortex of another world conflict but also because the economic distress in Japan had been alleviated somewhat by orders from the Americans for supplies and services used in the Korean war. The shift, however, was not simply toward interest in true political independence; it was also toward the old concern with foreign dangers. Internal problems began to assume a position of less importance, and there was a tendency for Japanese nationalism, once more, to be directed outward rather than inward.

The feeling of foreign danger has not yet crystallized. Many Japanese are convinced that the danger is primarily from Russia, and others are equally certain that the danger is from America. Not a few Japanese, however, feel that Japan is in danger from both quarters, and they stress the importance of returning to the traditional way of life and of associating Japan with a Pan-Asian movement as the best possible means of strengthening the nation.

Both inside and outside the country, determined efforts are being made to harness the power of nationalism. Within the country, the conservative groups seem to enjoy the advantage at the moment; but socialist and Communist groups have powerful weapons, and they have by no means conceded the fight. Externally, the free world seems to have the edge; but again, the Communists, with their great stronghold on the Asiatic continent, are in an excellent bargaining position and are showing no signs of retreat. They are making their bid not merely through high-powered, well-integrated propaganda programs designed to appeal to nationalist sympathies, but are relating that effort to a broadly conceived plan of economic, political, and military development which, if realized, will leave the Japanese no alternative but to seek nationalist growth within the Communist orbit.

The struggle to harness the power of Japanese nationalism has not destroyed the new nationalism. Even though there is more antiforeign sentiment than there was in 1946, and even though there is a tendency for the people to revert to traditional values and ideals, the dominant aspirations of the Japanese people are still for a better way of life and for a true political independence—not the destruction of foreign enemies. It is also clear that their interest in international coöperation, and particularly in the development of the United Nations, may very well outweigh their preoccupation with purely national interests. The reactionary trend and the antiforeign attitudes are by no means central to the intellectual atmosphere of the day—they are merely clearly discernible movements which have to be watched closely and must be taken into careful consideration by all who are concerned about and responsible for the formulation and implementation of our Asian foreign policy. A review of Japan's history during the last three decades shows how potent the force of nationalism became—even driving the nation to adopt policies and to take steps that ran counter to its own best interests, for nationalism was charged with an emotionalism that left no room for the adoption of measures dictated solely by reason. It is therefore of vital concern to all those who support the ideals of freedom and peace to see to it that Japan's new nationalism does not merge with the Communist advance and does not revert once more to the old emotional ultranationalism that was based on fear and that was whipped up to fanatical heights by a government bent on the achievement of state goals by the use of force against foreign enemies.

Notes

ABBREVIATIONS USED IN THE NOTES

CJ   *Contemporary Japan*

FEQ   *Far Eastern Quarterly*

HJAS   *Harvard Journal of Asiatic Studies*

IMTFE   International Military Tribunal of the Far East

IPS   International Prosecution Section

JHM   Japanese Home Ministry

JWC   *Japan Weekly Chronicle*

JWM   *Japan Weekly Mail*

SCAP   Supreme Commander of the Allied Powers

TASJ   *Transactions of the Asiatic Society of Japan*

NOTES FOR CHAPTER 1: INTRODUCTION

¹ *Historical Evolution of Modern Nationalism,* by Carleton Hayes, is still our best analysis of nationalism. But certain valuable points have been made in more recent studies. Hans Kohn, for example, in his introduction to *The Idea of Nationalism: A Study in Its Origins and Background,* has contributed much to our understanding of the subject. The social scientists, particularly those in the new field of social psychology, are doing valuable work in certain areas. One of the more promising projects is being carried out at the Institute for Social Research in Oslo on "The Dynamics of National Attitudes," and some particularly helpful and stimulating ideas have been presented by C. Bay in "The Theoretical Preparation of a Research Project on Nationalist Attitudes," a paper read at the World Congress of Sociology and Political Science (held at Zurich in 1950) and published in the *International Social Science Bulletin* in 1951.

² Cf., for example, Popper, *The Open Society and Its Enemies.*

³ Kroeber, *Anthropology,* pp. 743–744.

⁴ King, *Some Elements of National Solidarity,* p. 13.

⁵ Trewartha, *Japan: A Physical, Cultural and Regional Geography,* p. 213.

⁶ For an excellent study of the cult, see Buchanan, "Inari: Its Origin, Development and Nature," *TASJ,* 2d Ser., Vol. XII. See also Rabbitt, "Rice in the Life of the Japanese People," *TASJ,* 2d Ser., XIX, 187–257.

⁷ Trewartha, *op. cit.,* p. 245.

⁸ Von Engeln, *Inheriting the Earth; or, the Geographical Factor in National Development,* p. 9.

⁹ Harata Atsutane, *Zoku Shindō Taii* (The Great Principles of Shinto), *Shintō Daijiten* (Tokyo, 1937), I, 399; trans. in D. C. Holtom, *Modern Japan and Shinto Nationalism* (rev. ed.; University of Chicago Press, 1947), p. 16.

¹⁰ Bernard Joseph emphasizes the importance of this element in *Nationality, Its Nature and Problems,* p. 55.

¹¹ Sansom, *An Historical Grammar of Japan,* p. 1.

¹² Joseph, *op. cit.,* p. 74.

NOTES FOR CHAPTER 2: NATIONAL CONSCIOUSNESS

¹ The most recent study, the work of four scholars, is Wakamori Tarō, ed., *Kokka no Seisei* (Formation of the [Japanese] State), Vol. I of *Shin Nihon Shi Taikei* (New Outline History of Japan). Two of the more widely discussed books are Fujima Seidai's *Nihon Kodai Kokka* (The Ancient Japanese State) and Inouye Mitsusada's *Nihon Kodai Shi no Sho Mondai* (Problems in Ancient Japanese History). There is also an interesting study in English: Gerard Groot, "An Essay on Early Japanese History," *TASJ,* 3d Ser., I, 24–46.

² Support for this conclusion can be found even in Chinese annals: Emperor Yūraku (A.D. 456–479), in a note to the Emperor of China, speaks of extensive conquests to the east, to the west, and across the sea (in Korea) on the north. *Sung-shu i-man ch'uan,* quoted in Wakamori, *op. cit.,* p. 160.

[3] *Ibid.*, pp. 157–158.

[4] *Nihongi*, chap. 22, Suiko, 13th year, 4th month, 3d day, *Kokushi Taikei*, I, 377; trans. in Aston, "Nihongi, Chronicles of Japan from the Earliest Times to A.D. 697," *Transactions and Proceedings of the Japan Society, London*, Vol. II, Suppl. I, p. 129.

[5] *Ibid.*

[6] Spae, in his *Ito Jinsai, a Philosopher, Educator and Sinologist of the Tokugawa Period*, states (p. 18): ". . . except for Article II (enjoining reverence to the Three Precious Things, *Sampo*) and Article X (against anger), which are of Buddhist content; the other fifteen Articles quote, more or less verbally, passages from the different fundamental books of Confucianism then in vogue at the capital, or at least are inspired by them."

[7] In emphasizing the point that Prince Shotoku was attempting to strengthen the state, Akiyama in his *History of Nippon* (p. 71) points out that the Prince wrote three history books with these titles: *Tennō-ki* (History of the Emperor), *Kokuki* (History of the State), and *Omitakara-no-Hongi* (History of the People).

[8] *Sui Shu*, "Wa-Kuo" (Japanese Section of the History of the Sui Dynasty), trans. in Tsunoda and Goodrich, *Japan in the Chinese Dynastic Histories*, p. 32. This phrase does not appear in Japanese chronicles.

[9] Kiyohara, *Nihon Dōtoku Shi* (History of Japanese Morals), p. 159. Motoori, the famous eighteenth-century nationalist, was not merely pleased at the Japanese insistence upon equality, he was irked that the Chinese Emperor was offended. Motoori felt that the Japanese Emperor should have started the note like this: "The Heavenly Emperor notifies the King of Go," and implies that the Emperor might have done just this had he not been interested in obtaining certain favors; James Murdoch, *A History of Japan*, III, 488.

[10] Fairbank, "The Imperial Tradition in Japan and in Europe," *Far Eastern Leaflets*, Nos. 1–6, pp. 20–22.

[11] Akiyama, *op. cit.*, p. 73. Also see Miller, "An Historical Study of the Higher Administrative Officials of the Council of State in Japan in the Eighth Century A.D."

[12] Reischauer, *Early Japanese History (c. 40 B.C.—A.D. 1167)*, Part A, pp. 151–152.

[13] If the date of 712 is not accepted—and many do not accept it—the oldest history becomes the *Nihongi* (Chronicles of Japan), which was completed in A.D. 720.

[14] Aston, *op. cit.*, p. iv.

[15] Akiyama, *op. cit.*, p. 73.

[16] Reischauer, *op. cit.*, Part A, p. 207.

[17] Brown, *Money Economy in Medieval Japan*, pp. 3–10.

[18] Nippon Gakujutsu Shinkōkai, *The Manyōshū: One Thousand Poems Selected and Translated from the Japanese* (Tokyo: Iwanami Shoten, 1940), p. 83.

[19] Cf. Aston, *A History of Japanese Literature*, pp. 53–130.

[20] Brinkley, *A History of the Japanese People from the Earliest Times to the End of the Meiji Era*, p. 345.

[21] Cf. Brown, *op. cit.*, pp. 10–15.

[22] Anesaki, *History of Japanese Religion with Special Reference to the Social Life of the Nation*; Eliot, *Japanese Buddhism*.

²³ Shūhō, *Zenrin Kokuhō Ki,* in *Shiseki Shuran,* XXI, Sec. 14, pp. 25–26; trans. (quite freely but adequately) in Kuno, *Japanese Expansion on the Asiatic Continent,* I, 246–247.

²⁴ Akiyama, *op. cit.,* p. 161.

²⁵ Trans. in Anesaki, *Nichiren the Buddhist Prophet,* pp. 57–58.

²⁶ "Kaimoku Sho" (Opening the Eyes), in *Nichiren Shōnin Zenshū* (Complete Works of Saint Nichiren), I, 126; trans. in Anesaki, *op. cit.,* p. 73. Anesaki explains that "the Pillar means the supporter, the lordship; the Eyes, the mastership; and the Great Vessel, the giver of life, the fatherhood."

²⁷ Trans. in Anesaki, *op. cit.,* p. 110.

²⁸ *Ibid.,* p. 126.

²⁹ Nichiren to Lord Toki, 22d day, 10th moon, 1281, *ibid.,* p. 127.

³⁰ Brown, "The Japanese Tokusei of 1297," *HJAS,* XII, 188–206.

³¹ Kiyohara, *op. cit.,* p. 270.

³² *Ibid.,* p. 264.

²³ *Ming Shih,* "Jih-pen Chuan" (History of Ming, Japanese Section), quoted in Kimiya, *Nisshi Kōtsū Shi* (History of Japanese-Chinese Relations), II, 274; trans. in Kuno, *op. cit.,* I, 84.

³⁴ Ming Shih, "Jih-pen Chuan," in Kimiya, *op. cit.,* II, 280–281; trans. in Kuno, *op. cit.,* I, 256–257.

³⁵ *Zenrin Kokuhō Ki,* II, 42–43; in *Shiseki Shūran,* XXI; trans. in Kuno, *op. cit.,* I, 280–281.

³⁶ Kuno, *op. cit.,* I, 105.

³⁷ Tsuji, *Kaigai Kōtsū Shiwa* (Historical Account of Communications with Nations beyond the Seas), pp. 313–316.

NOTES FOR CHAPTER 3: ARTICULATE NATIONAL CONSCIOUSNESS

[1] Brown, *Money Economy in Medieval Japan,* pp. 33–97.

[2] Brown, "Impact of Firearms on Japanese Warfare, 1543–98," *FEQ,* VIII (1948), 236–239.

[3] *Ibid.,* p. 246.

[4] *Ibid.,* pp. 247–249.

[5] Brown, *Money Economy,* pp. 90–93.

[6] Cf. Boxer, *The Christian Century in Japan, 1549–1650.*

[7] *Ibid.,* pp. 91–136.

[8] Sansom, *The Western World and Japan,* p. 176.

[9] Boxer, *op. cit.,* pp. 308–361.

[10] *Ibid.,* pp. 362–374.

[11] *Ibid.,* p. 385.

[12] Sansom, *op. cit.,* pp. 199–200.

[13] *Ibid.,* p. 177.

[14] Boxer, *op. cit.,* pp. 382–383.

[15] Tokutomi, *Kinsei Nihon Kokumin Shi* (Modern History of the Japanese People), XIII, 147.

[16] *Ibid.,* XIII, 125; trans. in Sadler, *The Maker of Modern Japan,* p. 373.

[17] Kiyohara, *Nihon Dōtoku Shi,* p. 358.

[18] *Ibid.,* p. 359.

[19] Murdoch, *A History of Japan,* III, 143.

[20] Kiyohara, *op. cit.,* p. 362.

[21] *Ibid.,* pp. 370–372.

[22] Itō Jinsai (1627–1705) and Ogiu Sorai (1666–1728). But these men, too, were more interested in classical Confucianism, and Ogiu tended even to place Japan in a position of inferiority, because of his high regard for the Chinese sages. For an excellent study of Itō see Spae, *Itō Jinsai*.

[23] Sadler, *A Short History of Japan*, App. VI, p. 335.

[24] Nitobe's work on *Bushido, the Soul of Japan* remains the best-known secondary work in English on the subject, but the interpretations are somewhat idealized. A more accurate picture would be gained by a reading of the play about the Forty-seven Ronin, written in the eighteenth century and translated in Inouye, *Chushingura, or Forty-seven Ronin*.

[25] Trans. in Sadler, *op. cit.*, p. 335.

[26] This student, Asami Keisai (1652–1711), went much further than Yamazaki in his reaction to Confucianism. He attacked Confucian scholars who looked up to China and slighted their own country, asserting that the term Central Kingdom (*Chūkoku*) should not be used for China alone. In his book *Seiken Igen* he made a strong plea for loyal service to the Emperor. Consequently, in the eighteenth century, when the Royalist movement became stronger, this book was a source of great inspiration. Kiyohara, *op. cit.*, pp. 363–364.

[27] *Ibid.*, pp. 373–374.

[28] Ihara Yoshi, *Tokugawa Jidai Tsūshi* (History of the Tokugawa Era) (Tokyo: Daidokan, 1912), p. 292; trans. in Kuno, *Japanese Expansion on the Asiatic Continent*, II, 139.

[29] Kiyohara, *op. cit.*, p. 406.

[30] Trans. in Satow, "The Revival of Pure Shin-Tau," *TASJ*, III, Part 1, App., p. 14.

[31] *Ibid.*

[32] *Ibid.*, p. 13.

[33] *Ibid.*, p. 37.

[34] *Ibid.*, p. 30.

[35] Murdoch, *op. cit.*, III, 409.

[36] Tokutomi, *op. cit.*, XXII, 112–422.

[37] *Ibid.*, XXII, 423–500.

[38] Murdoch, *op. cit.*, III, 417.

NOTES FOR CHAPTER 4: EMPERORISM AND ANTIFOREIGNISM

[1] Ramming, *Reisen Schiffbruchiger Japaner im XVII. Jahrhundert*, p. 71.

[2] Hayashi Shihi, *San Koku Tsūran* (A Survey of the Three Countries [Hokkaido, Korea, and Ryukyu]), trans. into French by J. Klaproth in *San Kokf Tsou Ran To Sets, ou aperçu general des Trois Royaumes* (Paris and London, 1832). Hayashi also wrote the *Kaikoku Heidan* (Military Discussion of a Maritime Nation), in 1791.

[3] Honda's book was called *Keisei Hisaku* (Secret Administrative Plans). Cf. Tokutomi, *Kinsei Nihon Kokumin Shi*, XXV, 84–89; and Sansom, *The Western World and Japan*, p. 232.

[4] Kuno, *Japanese Expansion on the Asiatic Continent*, II, 235–237.

[5] Kuiper, "Some Notes on the Foreign Relations of Japan in the Early Napoleonic Period (1798–1805)," *TASJ*, 2d Ser., I, 55–82.

[6] Aston, "Russian Descents in Saghalien and Itorup in the Years 1806 and 1807," *TASJ*, 1st Ser., I, 79–84.

[7] Tokutomi, *op. cit.*, XXV, 336–344; Kuno, *op. cit.*, II, 232–233.

284 NOTES

8 Tokutomi, *op. cit.*, XXV, 345–352; Kuno, *op. cit.*, II, 233–234.

9 Hirata Atsutane, *Chishima Shiranami* (White Waves of the Kuriles), quoted in Satow, "The Revival of Pure Shin-Tau," *TASJ*, III, Part 1, App., p. 37.

10 Trans. in Murdoch, *A History of Japan*, III, 491.

11 *Ibid.*, III, 492.

12 Tokutomi, *op. cit.*, XXV, 363–376; W. G. Aston, "H.M.S. *Phaeton* at Nagasaki in 1808" *TASJ*, VII, 323–336.

13 Golovnin, *Narrative of My Captivity in Japan, during the Years 1811, 1812 and 1813*, I, 276.

14 Trans. in Murdoch, *op. cit.*, III, 58.

15 Tsuchiya, *Nihon Kokubō Kokka Kensetsu no Shiteki Kōsatsu* (A Historical Consideration of the Establishment of the Japanese Defense State), p. 91.

16 Murdoch, *op. cit.*, III, 453–455.

17 Takano Nagahide, *Yume Monogatari* (Dream Stories), trans. in D. C. Greene, "Osada's Life of Takano Nagahide," *TASJ*, XLI, Part 3, p. 424.

18 Trans. in Murdoch, *op. cit.*, III, 530.

19 Sansom, *The Western World and Japan*, pp. 249–252.

20 *Shōzan Zenshū* (Collected Works of [Sakuma] Shōzan), I, 89, 91, 97–98; trans. in Sansom, *op. cit.*, p. 255.

21 *Shōzan Zenshū*, I, 97–98, trans. in Sansom, *op. cit.*, p. 254.

22 Terry, "Sakuma Shōzan and His Seiken-Roku," p. 19.

23 Sakamaki, "Japan and the United States, 1790–1853," *TASJ*, 2d Ser., XVIII, 4–20.

24 *Ibid.*, pp. 30–36.

25 Cf. Hawks, *Narrative of the Expedition of an American Squadron to the China Seas and Japan, 1852, 1853 and 1854*.

26 Satow, trans., *Japan 1853–1864, or, Genji Yume Monogatari*, p. 4.

27 *Ibid.*, p. 6.

28 *Ibid.*, pp. 7–8. (Italics mine.)

29 Yoshida Shōin, *Yushu Roku* (Record of a Dark-Room Prisoner), outlined in H. E. Coleman, "The Life of Shōin Yoshida," *TASJ*, XLV, Part 1, p. 161.

30 Satow, trans., *op. cit.*, p. 9.

31 Smith, "The Introduction of Western Industry to Japan during the Last Years of the Tokugawa Period," *HJAS*, XI, 130–152.

32 Terry, *op. cit.*, p. 69.

33 Cf. Harris, *The Complete Journal of Townsend Harris, First American Consul General and Minister to Japan*.

34 Satow, trans., *op. cit.*, pp. 19–20. (Italics mine.)

35 Treat, *Diplomatic Relations between the United States and Japan, 1853–1895*, I, 89–90; Sansom, *op. cit.*, p. 297.

36 Treat, *op. cit.*, I, 90–98.

37 Satoh, *Agitated Japan: The Life of Baron Ii Kamon-no-Kami Naosuke*, pp. 137–138, 140.

38 Satow, trans., *Kinsei Shiriaku: A History of Japan from the Visit of Commodore Perry in 1853 to the Capture of Hakodate by the Mikado's Forces in 1869*, p. 20.

39 *Ibid.*, pp. 24–25.

40 Satow, *Japan 1853–1864*, pp. 44–45.

41 *Ibid.*, p. 48.

42 *Ibid.*, p. 49.

43 *Ibid.*, p. 48.

[44] Treat, *op. cit.*, I, 178.
[45] *Ibid.*, I, 181.
[46] *Ibid.*
[47] *Ibid.*, I, 184–188.
[48] *Ibid.*, I, 162.
[49] *Ibid.*, I, 169–180.
[50] *Ibid.*, I, 189–190.
[51] *Ibid.*, I, 359–360.
[52] Satow, *Kinsei Shiriaku*, pp. 71–72.
[53] *Ibid.*, p. 73.
[54] Treat, *op. cit.*, I, 398.
[55] *Ibid.*, I, 402–406.
[56] Trans. in Ike, *The Beginnings of Political Democracy in Japan*, p. 34.
[57] Cf. Nihon Keizai Shi Kenkyūjo (Japanese Economic History Research Institute), ed., *Bakumatsu Keizai Shi Kenkyū* (Studies in Late Tokugawa Economic History).
[58] See Fairbank and Teng, "On the Ch'ing Tributary System," *HJAS*, VI, 135–246; Nelson, *Korea and the Old Orders in Eastern Asia*.

NOTES FOR CHAPTER 5: NATIONAL REFORMS

[1] Imperial Oath, 3d month, 1858, *Dajōkan Nisshi*, I, 9; trans. in McLaren, ed., "Japanese Government Documents," *TASJ*, XLII, Part 1, p. 8. (Italics mine.)
[2] Chōshū-Satsuma-Hizen-Tosa Memorial, 23d day, 1st month, 1869, *Dajōkan Nisshi*, III, 24–25; trans. in McLaren, *op. cit.*, pp. 31–32. (Italics mine.)
[3] Cf. McLaren, *A Political History of Japan during the Meiji Era, 1867–1912*, pp. 15–152.
[4] Imperial Rescript on the Abolition of the Han, 14th day, 7th month, 1871, *Dajōkan Nisshi*, VI, 11–12; trans. in McLaren, ed., "Japanese Government Documents," pp. 32–33. (Italics mine.)
[5] The tax reform is carefully analyzed in Norman, *Japan's Emergence as a Modern State; Political and Economic Problems of the Meiji Period*, pp. 134–144.
[6] Studied in Kublin, "The 'Modern' Army of Early Meiji Japan," *FEQ*, IX, 20–41.
[7] Field Marshal Prince Yamagata, "The Japanese Army," in Ōkuma, comp., *Fifty Years of New Japan (Kaikoku Gojunen Shi)*, I, 209.
[8] Emperor Meiji's Imperial Rescript to Soldiers and Sailors, Jan. 4, 1882, trans. in Lory, *Japan's Military Masters*, App., pp. 239–245.
[9] See Smith, "The Introduction of Western Industry to Japan during the Last Years of the Tokugawa Period," *HJAS*, XI, 130–152.
[10] Allen, *A Short Economic History of Modern Japan, 1867–1937*, pp. 26–41, and Norman, *op. cit.*, pp. 104–135.
[11] Osuga, "The Establishment of State Shinto and the Buddhist Opposition in the Early Meiji Period," pp. 54–65.
[12] Ishin Shiryō Hensan Kai (Association for the Compilation of Restoration Historical Materials), comp., *Ishin Shi* (History of the Restoration), V, 472–474.
[13] Imperial Rescript, 3d day, 1st month, 1870, *Dajōkan Nisshi*, IV, 1; trans. in Kono, "Kannagara no Michi: The Meaning of Kannagara," *Monumenta Nipponica*, Vol. III, No. 2 (1940), p. 25.

[14] Toyoda, *Nihon Shūkyō Seidō Shi no Kenkyū* (Studies in the Institutional History of the Japanese Religion), pp. 196–215.

[15] Order trans. in Anesaki, *History of Japanese Religion*, p. 335.

[16] Toyoda, *op. cit.*, pp. 228–241.

[17] Charter Oath, June, 1868, trans. in McLaren, "Japanese Government Documents," 8. (Italics mine.)

[18] Kikuchi, *Japanese Education*, pp. 67–70.

[19] Chamberlain, *Things Japanese*, p. 180.

[20] Kikuchi, *op. cit.*, p. 70.

[21] Mori, *Education in Japan*, p. lvi.

[22] Kikuchi, *op. cit.*, p. 333.

[23] As translated in an unpublished manuscript lent to me by Warren Smith. (Italics mine.)

[24] *Japan Year Book, 1905*, p. 183. The population had increased from 37,000,-000 in 1883 to more than 41,000,000 in 1893; *ibid.*, p. 14.

[25] Kawabe, *The Press and Politics in Japan*, pp. 44–47.

[26] *Ibid.*, p. 62.

[27] *Ibid.*, p. 71. (Italics mine.)

[28] Quoted in Sansom, *The Western World and Japan*, p. 398.

[29] *Ibid.*, pp. 412–415. Feldman, "The Meiji Political Novel: A Brief Survey," *FEQ*, IX, 245–255.

[30] Sansom, *op. cit.*, pp. 382–386.

NOTES FOR CHAPTER 6: PRESERVATION OF "NATIONAL ESSENCE"

[1] Kiyohara, *Meiji Jidai Shisō Shi* (History of Thought in the Meiji Era), pp. 135–136.

[2] In 1881 a Shinto society, the *Shintō Kyodō Shoku*, was organized, which, under the leadership of Arisugawa Teruhito Shinnō (1835–1895), became an important agency for popularizing Shinto of the Sun Cult variety. "Arisugawa no Miya Teruhito-Shinnō Gojiseki" (Deeds of Prince Teruhito-Shinnō Arisugawa), *Kokugakuin Zasshi*, Vol. XLII, No. 2 (1936), pp. 1–23, summarized in unpublished manuscript by Warren Smith.

[3] The translation of the Constitution can be found in a number of publications, including Ōkuma, *Fifty Years of New Japan*, II, App. A, 579–589.

[4] Ito, *Commentaries on the Constitution of the Empire of Japan*, p. 7.

[5] Education Minister Instructions to School Inspectors, 1881, quoted in Marquis Kimmochi Saionji, "National Education in the Meiji Era," *in* Ōkuma, *op. cit.*, II, 164.

[6] Translation available in many publications, including General Headquarters SCAP, *Education in the New Japan*, II, Part 1, App. D, 76.

[7] This edict is in the *Nihon Shoki*, chap. 25, 3d year, 4th month, 29th day of Emperor Kotoku's reign, *Kokushi Taikei*, I, 443–444; trans. in Aston, "Nihongi," *Transactions and Proceedings of the Japan Society*, London, Vol. II, Suppl. 1, p. 226.

[8] Quoted in Kiyohara, *op. cit.*, pp. 137–140.

[9] Takada Shinji, *Nihon Jukyō Shi* (History of Japanese Confucianism) (Tokyo: Chijin Shokan, 1941), pp. 262–264.

[10] SCAP, *Education in the New Japan*, II, 76.

[11] Quoted in Kiyohara, *op. cit.*, pp. 131–132.

[12] Mary Fenollosa, Preface to E. F. Fenollosa, *Epochs of Chinese and Japanese Art*, I, xv–xvii.

[13] *Shigaku Zasshi,* Vol. I, No. 1 (1889), p. 4.

[14] Inouye Tetsujirō, *Kyōiku to Shūkyō to no Shōtotsu* (Conflict between Edu-cation and Religion), quoted in Kiyohara, *op. cit.,* pp. 160–161.

[15] *Ibid.,* p. 165.

[16] *Yoshida Shōin Zenshū* (Complete Works of Yoshida Shōin), I, 596; trans. in Kuno, *Japanese Expansion on the Asiatic Continent,* II, 352–353.

[17] A translation of this note is found in Dennett, *Americans in Eastern Asia,* p. 435.

[18] Cf. Ike, "Triumph of the Peace Party in Japan in 1873," *FEQ,* II, 286–295.

[19] Stead, ed., *Japan by the Japanese,* p. 166.

[20] The United States encouraged the Japanese to undertake the Formosan expedition in order to induce them "to separate themselves as far as possible from the exclusive policy of the Chinese, and to adopt the progressive policy of free commercial and social intercourse with other powers." Hamilton Fish to Charles De Long, Dec. 30, 1872, *Foreign Relations of the United States* (1873), p. 568.

[21] Norman, "The Genyosha: A Study in the Origins of Japanese Imperialism," *Pacific Affairs,* XVII, 276.

[22] Tsiang, "Sino-Japanese Diplomatic Relations, 1870–1894," *Chinese Social and Political Science Review,* XVII, 105.

[23] Norman, *op. cit.,* p. 272.

[24] Arthur Doily, *The New Far East* (5th ed., London, 1904), pp. 33–35, quoted in Pollard, "Dynamics of Japanese Imperialism," *Pacific Historical Review,* VIII, 29.

[25] McLaren, *A Political History of Japan during the Meiji Era, 1867–1912,* p. 225.

[26] Spinks, "Origin of Japanese Interests in Manchuria," *FEQ,* II, 264–266; Treat, "The Cause of the Sino-Japanese War, 1894," *Pacific Historical Review,* VIII, 149–157.

[27] *JWM,* Jan. 6, 1894.

[28] *JWM,* Jan. 13, 1894.

[29] Quoted in Treat, *op. cit.,* p. 153.

[30] *JWM,* June 16, 1894.

[31] *Ibid.*

[32] *JWM,* Aug. 25, 1894.

[33] *JWM,* Sept. 15, 1894.

[34] *JWM,* Oct. 20, 1894.

[35] *JWM,* Nov. 10, 1894.

[36] *JWM,* Jan. 8, 1895.

[37] *Ibid.*

[38] *JWM,* Feb. 2, 1895.

[39] *JWM,* Feb. 16, 1895.

[40] *JWM,* Mar. 2, 1895.

[41] *JWM,* Mar. 23, 1895.

[42] *JWM,* Apr. 20, 1895.

[43] *JWM,* Apr. 27, 1895.

NOTES FOR CHAPTER 7: JAPANISM

[1] *JWM,* May 25, 1895.

[2] Osaka *Asahi,* quoted in *JWM,* Feb. 22, 1896.

³ The first issue included a statement of policy which indicated that the editors would attempt to arouse a deeper understanding of Japanese history and literature, *Kokugakuin Zasshi*, November, 1894.

⁴ In July, 1895, the *Nihonjin* was also reorganized and a new statement of policy was formulated. *Nihonjin*, I, 1–2.

⁵ For the society's policy statement of May 10, 1896, see Kiyohara, *Meiji Jidai Shisō Shi*, p. 185.

⁶ A member of the *Dai Nihon Kyōkai* took this line in his reply to a declaration made by the Christian-supported *Nihon Shūkyō Sha*. Kiyohara, *op. cit.*, p. 185.

⁷ *Ibid.*, p. 193.

⁸ Kimura Takatarō, "Nihon Shugi wo Sansu," *Taiyō*, June, 1897, quoted in Kiyohara, *op. cit.*, p. 194.

⁹ Kiyohara, *op. cit.*, p. 195.

¹⁰ "Waga Kokutai to Shin Hanto," *Taiyō*, November, 1897, quoted in Kiyohara, *op. cit.*, pp. 194–195.

¹¹ *Hōchi Shimbun*, quoted in *JWM*, Apr. 9, 1898.

¹² *JWM*, May 14 and 21, 1898.

¹³ Jansen, "The Japanese and the Chinese Revolutionary Movement, 1895–1915," p. 82.

¹⁴ *Ibid.*, pp. 83–84.

¹⁵ Holtom, *Modern Japan and Shinto Nationalism*, p. 76.

¹⁶ Kimura Takatarō, *Yaso-kyō Kōnin Kahi Ron* (Against the Official Recognition of Christianity), quoted in Kiyohara, *op. cit.*, pp. 210–211.

¹⁷ *JWM*, Sept. 16, 1899.

¹⁸ *JWM*, Dec. 23, 1899.

¹⁹ Kuzu, *Tōa Senkaku Shishi Kiden* (Biographical Memoirs of Pioneer East Asian Patriots), I, 706–708.

²⁰ *Ibid.*, I, 679.

²¹ Kinoshita, *Nihon Fuashizumu Shi* (History of Japanese Fascism), I, 8.

²² For summaries of Japanese press comments on the Alliance, see *JWM*, Feb. 22, Mar. 1, and Mar. 8, 1902.

²³ Kuzu, *op. cit.*, I, 686–688.

²⁴ *Ibid.*, I, 736.

²⁵ Resolution of Aug. 9, 1903, quoted in Kuzu, *op. cit.*, I, 715.

²⁶ *Ibid.*, I, 717.

²⁷ *JWM*, Jan. 2, 1904.

²⁸ *JWM*, Jan. 16, 1904.

²⁹ *JWM*, Jan. 23, 1904.

³⁰ *JWM*, Jan. 16, 1904.

³¹ *Ibid.*

³² *JWM*, Apr. 9, 1904.

³³ Henry Dyer, *Dai Nippon, the Britain of the East* (London, 1904), quoted in *JWM*, Dec. 31, 1904.

³⁴ *JWM*, Oct., 1904.

³⁵ Quoted in *JWM*, Dec. 10, 1904.

³⁶ Viscount Watanabe Kunio, "Tōzai Bummei no Shokusetsu-chi" (The Junction of Oriental and Western Cultures), *Taiyō*, January, 1905, reviewed in *JWM*, Jan. 28, 1905.

³⁷ Ōkuma Shigenobu, "Mankan Keiei Shoken" (My Views on the Development of Manchuria and Korea), *Taiyō*, May, 1905, pp. 33–37.

[38] *JWM*, June 17, 1905.
[39] *Taiyō*, summarized in *JWM*, June 24, 1905.
[40] *Taiyō*, July, 1905, summarized in *JWM*, July 22, 1905.
[41] *Nihon Teikoku Dai Nijū Yon Tokei Nenkan* (24th [1905] Statistical Annual of the Japanese Empire), table 250, p. 401.
[42] Allen, *A Short Economic History of Modern Japan*, table xx, p. 178.
[43] *Ibid.*, tables xiv–xvii, pp. 174–177. Horie, *Nihon Keizai Shi* (Economic History of Japan), pp. 241–244. Ōuchi Hyoe, "Keizai" (Economics), in Yanaihara, ed., *Gendai Nihon Kōshi* (Brief History of Modern Japan), I, 180–184.
[44] Cf. Ike, *The Beginnings of Political Democracy in Japan.*

NOTES FOR CHAPTER 8: NATIONAL CONFIDENCE

[1] *JWM*, Sept. 2, 1905.
[2] The reaction to the peace terms is described in some detail in McLaren, *A Political History of Japan*, pp. 299–300.
[3] *Ibid.*, p. 294.
[4] Otsuka, H., "The Nation's Mental Depression," *Taiyō*, December, 1905, summarized in *JWM*, Jan. 27, 1906.
[5] *British and Foreign State Papers, 1904–1905*, p. 137.
[6] Roy Hidemichi Akagi, *Japan's Foreign Relations, 1542–1936: A Short History* (Tokyo: Hokuseido Press, 1936), p. 272.
[7] G. Nye Steiger, *A History of the Far East* (Boston: Ginn, 1944), p. 726.
[8] Kajinishi, *Nihon Keizai Shi* (Economic History of Japan), pp. 185–195. Ōuchi, "Keizai," in Yanaihara, ed., *Gendai Nihon Koshi*, pp. 184–206. Horie, *Nihon Keizai Shi*, pp. 245–251. Allen, *A Short Economic History of Modern Japan*, pp. 73–89.
[9] Kiyohara, *Meiji Jidai Shisō Shi*, p. 271.
[10] Hasegawa Tenkei, *Jizen Shugi* (Naturalism), quoted in Kiyohara, *op. cit.*, pp. 274–275.
[11] Akamatsu, *Nihon Shakai Undō Shi* (History of the Socialist Movement in Japan), pp. 96–130.
[12] Kiyohara, *Meiji Jidai Shisō Shi*, pp. 317–322.
[13] Kiyohara, *Nihon Dōtoku Shi*, pp. 732–756.
[14] Quoted in *JWM*, Feb. 23, 1907.
[15] U. S. Dept. of State, *Foreign Relations of the United States, 1906*, Part I, pp. 171–172.
[16] A. Whitney Griswold, *The Far Eastern Policy of the United States* (New York: Harcourt, Brace, 1938), 129.
[17] Kuzu, *Tōa Senkaku Shishi Kiden*, II, 435–439.
[18] *Ibid.*, pp. 439–441.
[19] *Ibid.*, pp. 441–446.
[20] *JWC*, Feb. 27, 1913.
[21] *JWC*, Sept. 11, 1913.
[22] *JWC*, June 19, 1913.
[23] *JWC*, July 10, 1913.
[24] Osaka *Mainichi*, Sept. 5, 1913.
[25] *JWC*, Sept. 11, 1913.
[26] *JWC*, Sept. 18, 1913.
[27] *Ibid.*
[28] *JWC*, Sept. 25, 1913.

[20] Details about the railroad concessions are included in Kuzu, *Nisshi Kōshō Gaishi* (Private History of Relations between China and Japan) II, 62–63.
[30] *JWM*, July 18, 1914.
[31] *JWC*, Aug. 13, 1914.
[32] Summarized in *JWC*, Aug. 27, 1914.
[33] U. S. Dept. of State, *Foreign Relations of the United States, 1915*, p. 134. Japanese text of the entire document is in Ōtsu Junichiro, *Dai Nihon Kensei Shi* (Tokyo: Hobunkan, 1927–1928), VII, 491–503.
[34] Kuzu, *Tōa Senkaku Shishi Kiden*, II, 573.
[35] "Part of the conversation during the interview on January 18, 1915, between the Japanese Minister, Dr. Hioki, and President Yuan Shih-kai," Enclosure 1 of P. S. Reinsch to Secretary of State, May 4, 1915, U. S. Dept. of State, *Foreign Relations of the United States, 1915*, p. 132.
[36] *Japan Magazine*, March, 1916, pp. 687–688. Another article by Takekoshi, in the January issue of *Yuben*, "Japan's Sea Policy" (summarized in *JWC*, Jan. 20, 1916) advocated expansion southward.
[37] Kambe, "Problem of National Expansion," *Japan Magazine*, August, 1916, p. 203. In the June issue of *Taiyō*, Dr. Kambe wrote about his recent trip to Formosa: "Now that Japan is regarded as the one best fitted for leadership among the Oriental races, the people of Formosa, Korea, and even of China, should do all in their power to aid her in the task of amalgamation and aggrandisement, as it is their only hope of becoming independent of the white races." Summarized in *Japan Magazine*, p. 253.
[38] Takekoshi Yosaburo, *Toho Jiron*, summarized in "Current Japanese Thought," *Japan Magazine*, November, 1916, pp. 434–435.
[39] *JWM*, Nov. 25, 1916.
[40] *Jitsugyō no Nihon*, July 15, 1917.
[41] *JWC*, Sept. 6, 1917.
[42] Summarized in *Japan Advertiser*, July 12, 1918.
[43] Kajinishi, *op. cit.*, table 17, p. 219.

NOTES FOR CHAPTER 9: NATIONAL RECONSTRUCTION

[1] See Yamasaki and Ogawa, *The Effect of World War upon Commerce and Industry of Japan*, and Ōuchi Hyoe, "Keizai," in Yanaihara, ed., *Gendai Nihon Kōshi*, I, 206–225.
[2] Kajinishi, *Nihon Keizai Shi*, table 17, p. 219.
[3] *Ibid.*
[4] Honda, *Nihon Shakai Undō Shi Gaisetsu* (Outline History of Japanese Social Movements), p. 66.
[5] See Shinobu, *Taishō Seiji Shi* (Political History of Taisho), II, 539–693.
[6] Honda, *op. cit.*, pp. 64–65.
[7] *Ibid.*, p. 70. See Shinobu, *op. cit.*, III, 687–753.
[8] *Chūō Kōron*, January, 1916; quoted in Honda, *op. cit.*, p. 65.
[9] The political struggle for universal suffrage is discussed in some detail in Shinobu, *op. cit.*, III, 853–901.
[10] Honda, *op. cit.*, pp. 75–77.
[11] Swearingen and Langer, *Red Flag in Japan*, pp. 11–12.
[12] Honda, *op. cit.*, pp. 92–99.
[13] *Ibid.*, pp. 82–83.
[14] *Ibid.*, pp. 98–99.

[15] Kinoshita, *Nihon Fuashizumu Shi*, I, 18.

[16] *Ibid.*, I, 18–19. Tanin and Yohan, *Militarism and Fascism in Japan*, pp. 75–77.

[17] Tanaka, *Nihon Fuashizumu no Genryū* (Origins of Japanese Fascism), pp. 223–234. Kinoshita, *op. cit.*, I, 42–43.

[18] Tanaka, *op. cit.*, p. 27.

[19] *Ibid.*, p. 56.

[20] *Ibid.*, pp. 24–212.

[21] Kita's book was first mimeographed. Several hundred copies were circulated secretly among members and friends of the *Yuzon Sha* in 1919; but in January, 1920, publication and distribution of the book was banned. The second printing came in May, 1923, after enough deletions and revisions were made to satisfy government censors. There were new printings in 1926, 1928, and 1932. Since World War II the work has been republished in the revived *Nihon oyobi Nihonjin*, Vol. III, No. 10 (August, 1952), pp. 124–156, and Vol. III, No. 11 (September, 1952), pp. 91–125.

[22] Kita, *Nihon Kaizō Hōan Taikō*, in *Nihon oyobi Nihonjin*, Vol. III, No. 10, p. 136.

[23] *Ibid.*, p. 140.

[24] *Ibid.*, p. 145.

[25] *Ibid.*, p. 142.

[26] *Ibid.*, pp. 145–151.

[27] *Ibid.*, p. 141.

[28] *Ibid.*, p. 145.

[29] *Ibid.*, p. 137.

[30] *Ibid.*, p. 146.

[31] *Ibid.*, pp. 130–136.

[32] *Ibid.*, p. 149.

[33] *Nihon oyobi Nihonjin*, Vol. III, No. 11, p. 118.

[34] *Ibid.*, Vol. III, No. 10, p. 139.

[35] *Ōtakebi*, July, 1920, quoted in JHM, Bureau of Policy Affairs, Section for the Maintenance of Public Peace, "Nihon Kakushin Undō Hiroku" (Secret Record of Japanese Reform Movements), 1938, MS in SCAP, IPS Doc. No. 12, p. 13.

[36] Iwabuchi, *Sekai Gojūnen Shi* (Fifty Years of World History), pp. 297–308. Robert Phillip Multhauf, "A Study of Japan's Diplomatic Relations with China, 1922–1932" (unpublished M.A. thesis, University of California, Berkeley, 1950.

[37] Iwabuchi, *op. cit.*, p. 310.

[38] Shigemitsu, *Shōwa no Dōran* (Confusion of the Showa Era), I, 35.

[39] *Ibid.*, I, 36–41.

[40] Honda, *op. cit.*, pp. 89–90.

[41] For an excellent survey of the Young Officer movement, see Wald, "The Young Officers Movement in Japan, *ca.* 1925–1937: Ideology and Actions."

[42] Ōkawa, *Fukkō Ajia no Sho Mondai* (Various Problems Relative to the Revival of Asia).

[43] Ōkawa, *Ajia, Yōroppa, Nihon* (Asia, Europe, and Japan), p. 82; trans in "Analyses," IPS Doc. No. 684, pp. 3–4.

[44] Kinoshita, *op. cit.*, I, 70.

[45] Ōkawa Shūmei, *Nihon oyobi Nihonjin no Michi* (The Way of the Japanese and of Japan) (Tokyo, 1930), p. 102.

[46] *Ibid.,* pp. 142–143.

[47] Akamatsu Katsumaro, "A Sketch of Mr. Okawa Ishin" (1934), "Analyses," IPS Doc. No. 686.

[48] JHM, "Nihon Kakushin Undō Hiroku," p. 29; trans. in Wald, *op. cit.,* p. 31.

[49] JHM, *op. cit.,* p. 56; trans. in Wald, *op. cit.,* p. 40.

[50] Iwabuchi, *op. cit.,* pp. 313–315.

[51] Kinoshita, *op. cit.,* I, 103–107.

[52] After the war, General Ugaki swore under oath before the International Military Tribunal for the Far East that it was he who had called off the coup d'état, and that because of this and his part in reducing the size of the army at an earlier date, he was unable to get a general to serve as War Minister when he tried to set up a cabinet in 1937. Ugaki Kazushige Affidavit, June 15, 1946, IMTFE Exhibit No. 163. Marquis Kido was well aware of the nature of the plot, "Kido Kōin Nikki," Aug. 7, Aug. 12, and Sept. 9, 1931.

[53] Shigemitsu, *op. cit.,* I, 50–57.

[54] Shidehara, who was Foreign Minister at the time, and Wakatsuki, the Premier, both testified that they made every effort to control the army but failed. Shidehara Kijurō Affidavit, June 17, 1946, IMTFE Exhibit No. 156 and Wakatsuki Reijirō Affidavit, June 18, 1946, IMTFE Exhibit No. 162. Other affidavits by leading officials at the time add further support to this conclusion. Cf. Harada, *Saionji Kō to Seikyoku,* II, 61–107.

[55] Ikuta Chōkō, "Fuashizumu to Kokuminsei" (Fascism and the Disposition of the People), *Chūō Kōron,* April, 1932, p. 53.

[56] Yoshino Sakuzō, "Fascism in Japan," *CJ,* September, 1932, pp. 186–190.

[57] Honda, *op. cit.,* p. 154.

[58] Kinoshita, *op. cit.,* I, 135–139.

[59] Inukai Ken [son of the Premier] Affidavit, June 16, 1946, IMTFE Exhibit, No. 161.

[60] Wald, *op. cit.,* pp. 126–138.

[61] "Observations on the Report of the Commission of Enquiry Appointed by the Resolution of December 10, 1931, of the Council of the League of Nations Made Public by the Foreign Office, November 21, 1932," *CJ,* March, 1933, p. 717.

[62] Moore, *Soviet Far Eastern Policy, 1931–1945,* p. 10.

[63] May 3, 1932. Harada, *op. cit.,* II, 273.

[64] Grew, *Ten Years in Japan,* p. 98.

[65] Harada, *op. cit.,* II, 155.

[66] Grew, *op. cit.,* p. 108.

[67] Wald, *op. cit.,* pp. 139–181.

[68] *Ibid.,* pp. 159–162.

[69] *Ibid.,* pp. 173–175.

[70] *Ibid.,* pp. 175–181.

[71] *Ibid.,* pp. 182–218. The part that Kita Ikki and his protégé, Nishida Zei, played in the incident has been discussed in a postwar article by Iwabuchi Tatsuo: "Kita Ikki to Nishida Zei" (Kita Ikki and Nishida Zei), *Chūō Kōron,* March, 1950, pp. 127–139. Iwabuchi has also written an article on the incident itself: "Ni-ni-roku Jiken no Boppatsu" (Outbreak of the February Twenty-sixth Incident), *Chūō Kōron,* July, 1946.

NOTES FOR CHAPTER 10: ULTRANATIONALISM

[1] Friedman, *British Relations with China: 1931–1939*, pp. 18–67.

[2] July 1, 1936. Harada, *Saionji Kō to Seikyoku*, V, 103.

[3] Five-Minister Decisions on Basic National Policy, Aug. 7, 1936, IMTFE Exhibit No. 216.

[4] "Report of Privy Council Investigation Committee," Nov. 20, 1936, IMTFE Exhibits Nos. 479 and 484. Cf. Ikle, "Japanese-German Relations, 1936–1940."

[5] For Japanese-Russian relations at this time, see Domingsil, "Soviet-Japanese Relations, 1931–1937," and Shirley, "Japan's Foreign Policy toward Russia, 1931–1945."

[6] Hirota Koki, Address to the Diet, July 27, 1937, IMTFE Exhibit No. 2497.

[7] Cf. Selle, *Donald of China*, and Bisson, *Japan in China*.

[8] *Zen Aikoku Dantai Tōitsu Remmi* declaration, May 29, 1936, in Kinoshita, *Nihon Kokka Shugi Undō Shi* (History of Japanese Nationalist Movements), II, 472.

[9] *Ibid.*, II, 473.

[10] *Ibid.*, II, 478–483.

[11] *Ibid.*, V, 492–498.

[12] Hashimoto Kingorō, "Seinen Shoshi ni Tsugu" (A Message to Young Men), *Taiyō Dai Nihon* (Dec. 17, 1936), trans. in IMTFE Exhibit No. 675-A.

[13] Kondō Tadayoshi *et al.*, eds., *Gendai Shisō Kenkyū Hen* (Compilation of Studies in Modern Thought), in *Gendai Bungaku Sōsetsu* (General Survey of Modern Culture), III, 14–16.

[14] For a rather careful survey of the incident see Yabe, *Konoye Fumimaro Den* (Biography of Konoye Fumimaro), I, 296–299.

[15] Gauntlett, trans., *Kokutai no Hongi: Cardinal Principles of the National Entity of Japan*, p. 59.

[16] *Ibid.*, pp. 59–104.

[17] *Ibid.*, pp. 105–183.

[18] "The Outline of Program Concerning the Execution of Intelligence and Propaganda Activities," May 20, 1936, IMTFE Exhibit No. 151.

[19] Ito Nobufumi Affidavit, June 1, 1946, IMTFE Exhibit No. 142.

[20] Bureau of Information, Prime Minister's Department, "On Publicity and Information," Tokyo *Gazette*, October, 1937, pp. 6–7.

[21] Instruction from Minister of Education, June 29, 1938, IMTFE Exhibit No. 138.

[22] Bureau of Information, Prime Minister's Department, "Concerning National Spiritual Mobilization," Tokyo *Gazette*, June, 1939, pp. 27–29.

[23] Suzuki Tomin Affidavit, June 17, 1946, IMTFE Exhibit No. 150.

[24] Ogata Taketora Affidavit, June 15, 1946, IMTFE Exhibit No. 146.

[25] Ito Nobufumi Affidavit, June 1, 1946, IMTFE Exhibit No. 142.

[26] Department of Communications "Broadcasting in the Current Emergency," Tokyo *Gazette*, November, 1938, pp. 7–8.

[27] *Ibid.*, pp. 8–10.

[28] Cabinet Information Bureau, "Motion Pictures in Japan," Tokyo *Gazette*, October, 1939, pp. 133–142.

[29] Motion-Picture Censorship Law, Apr. 5, 1939, IMTFE Exhibit No. 155.

[30] Nakai Kimbei Affidavit, June 15, 1946, IMTFE Exhibit No. 147.

[31] Scenario of film *Hyōji Nihon* (Japan in Time of Emergency), produced in June, 1933, IMTFE Exhibit No. 148-A.

[32] Nakai Kimbei Affidavit, June 15, 1946, IMTFE Exhibit No. 147.

[33] Saki Akio Affidavit, June 15, 1946, IMTFE Exhibit No. 144. The text of "Japan is Now Fighting," trans. in IMTFE Exhibit No. 145.

[34] Maruyama Masao, "Nihon Fuashizumu no Shisō to Undō (Japanese Fascist Thoughts and Movements), in *Tōyō Bunka Kōza*, No. 2 (1948), p. 151.

[35] "Nihon Seishin Kenkyū ni Kansuru Bunken" (Bibliography of Japanese Spiritual Studies), *Shisō Kenkyū*, March, 1939, pp. 61–94.

[36] Statement of August 1, 1940, published under the title "On Fundamental National Policies," Tokyo *Gazette*, September, 1940, pp. 89–91.

[37] Kamikawa Hikomatsu, "New Order in the Pacific is Vital Problem Concerning Japan," *Nippon Hyōron*, August, 1940, trans. in *Contemporary Opinion on Current Topics*, July 25, 1940, p. 6.

[38] See Ikle, *op. cit.*

[39] Minutes of the Privy Council Committee on the Tripartite Treaty, Sept. 26, 1940, IMTFE Exhiibt No. 1030.

[40] Ozaki Hotsumi, "The New National Structure," *CJ*, October, 1940, p. 1285.

[41] Kuhara Fusunosuke, "The Basis for a Single Party," *CJ*, July, 1940, pp. 813–814.

[42] *CJ*, October, 1940, pp. 1366–1369.

[43] Yabe, *op. cit.*, II, 197–199.

[44] *Ibid.*, II, 199.

[45] Iwabuchi, *Sekai Gojūnen Shi*, p. 349.

[46] See Ikle, *op. cit.*, and William L. Langer and S. Everett Gleason, *The Undeclared War, 1940–1941* (New York: Harper, 1953), pp. 464–493.

[47] Memorandum of Ribbentrop-Matsuoka conversation, Mar. 27, 1941, U. S. State Department, *Nazi-Soviet Relations, 1939–1941* (New York: Didier, 1948), pp. 289–298.

[48] Resolution of the Imperial Conference, July 2, 1941, IMTFE Proceedings, 6567. One clause reads: "Japan will continue the disposition of the Chinese Incident, and will step up the southward advance in order to establish for herself a basis for self-existence and self-defense."

[49] Cf. Feis, *The Road to Pearl Harbor*.

[50] Iwabuchi, *op. cit.*, p. 350.

[51] Cf. Ikle, *op. cit.*

[52] Iwabuchi, *op. cit.*, p. 352.

[53] *Ibid.*, pp. 353–357.

[54] *Ibid.*, p. 359.

[55] Miyako *Shimbun*, Nov. 4, 1941.

[56] *Japan Chronicle*, Nov. 23, 1941.

[57] Quoted in *Japan Times and Advertiser*, Dec. 9, 1941.

[58] *Ibid.*

[59] Ito Masanori, "Japan's Victory in Historical Light," *CJ*, January, 1942, p. 47.

[60] Kazan Kayahara, "Japanese Possess Highest Form of Nationalism, Unique in World," *Japan Times and Advertiser*, Mar. 22, 1942.

[61] From a statement made at the first anniversary of the Joint Declaration, *Nippon Times*, Nov. 7, 1944.

[62] Fujii, *Singapore Assignment*, pp. 121–122.

[63] *Asahi Shimbun*, Dec. 27, 1943.

[64] *Asahi Shimbun*, quoted in *Nippon Times*, June 6, 1944.

[65] *Asahi Shimbun,* July 19, 1944, trans. in part in *Nippon Times,* July 20, 1944.

[66] Tokyo *Shimbun,* reviewed in *Nippon Times,* Dec. 21, 1943.

[67] *Nippon Sangyō Keizai,* Aug. 5, 1944, trans. in *Nippon Times,* Aug. 6, 1944.

[68] Kodama, *I Was Defeated,* p. 157.

[69] *Ibid.,* p. 158.

[70] *Ibid.,* pp. 171–172.

NOTES FOR CHAPTER 11: NEW NATIONALISM

[1] *Nippon Times,* Aug. 19, 1945.

[2] *Ibid.*

[3] Details of General Anami's suicide were revealed later by Lt. Col. Takeshita Masehiko, who was with General Anami at the time, in a special issue of the *Gungei Shunju.* Quoted at length in *Nippon Times,* Aug. 15, 1952.

[4] Kato, *The Lost War,* pp. 241–244.

[5] *Ibid.,* p. 252.

[6] Brines, MacArthur's Japan, p. 26.

[7] *Ibid.,* p. 28.

[8] "Proclamation Defining Terms for Japanese Surrender" (the Potsdam Declaration), July 26, 1945, U. S. State Dept., *Occupation of Japan,* p. 54.

[9] SCAP Instruction No. 16, Sept. 10, 1945, *Political Reorientation of Japan,* II, 460. It should be noted, however, that in the same instruction the Occupation laid down restrictions of its own: "Subjects which cannot be discussed include Allied troop movements which have not been officially released, false or destructive criticism of the Allied Powers, and rumors."

[10] SCAP Instruction No. 93, Oct. 4, 1945, *Political Reorientation of Japan,* II, 463.

[11] "Administration of the Educational System of Japan," Adjutant General Directive 350, Oct. 22, 1945, published in Civil Information and Education Section, General Headquarters, SCAP, *Education in the New Japan,* II, Appendix B, Part 1, pp. 26–28.

[12] SCAP, *Education in the New Japan,* I, 138.

[13] SCAP Instruction No. 448, Dec. 15, 1945, *Political Reorientation of Japan,* II, 467–469.

[14] After the "disestablishment of State Shinto" directive, neighborhood associations (*tonarigumi*) continued to collect funds for the support of Shinto shrines and for certain Shinto activities. To remedy the situation, the Education Ministry instructed the prefectures, on Aug. 12, 1946, that the neighborhood associations were to be considered as public bodies, and that therefore their support of Shinto was illegal. SCAP Civil Information and Education Section, *Religions in Japan,* p. 131.

[15] Mark Gayn, in the Jan. 6, 1946, entry of his diary, reported that the first draft of the Imperial rescript was written in the office of General Dyke, chief of the Civil Information and Education Section. *Japan Diary,* p. 95.

[16] SCAP, *Political Reorientation of Japan,* II, 470.

[17] "United States Initial Post-Surrender Policy for Japan," Aug. 29, 1945, *ibid.,* II, 423.

[18] Dec. 20, 1946, Gayn, *op. cit.,* pp. 42–43. This view has been corroborated by men who were participating in the occupation at the time.

[19] "Removal and Exclusion of Undesirable Personnel from Public Office," SCAP Instruction No. 550, Jan. 4, 1946, SCAP, *Political Reorientation of Japan,* II, 482–488.

[20] SCAP press release, Jan. 4, 1946, *ibid.*, p. 489.

[21] "Removal and Exclusion from Public Office of Diet Members," May 3, 1946, *ibid.*, pp. 494–495.

[22] *Ibid.*, I, 8–81.

[23] "Abolition of Certain Political Parties, Associations, Societies and Other Organizations," SCAP Instruction No. 548, Jan. 4, 1946, *ibid.*, II, 479–481.

[24] "Potsdam Declaration," July 26, 1945, *ibid.*, II, 413.

[25] *Ibid.*, I, 91.

[26] Legislative Bureau of the Cabinet, "Interpretation of the New Constitution," Nov. 3, 1946, *ibid.*, I, 93.

[27] "General Explanation of the Constitutional Revision Drafted by the Government," *ibid.*, II, 619.

[28] SCAP, *Political Reorientation of Japan*, I, 105.

[29] *Ibid.*, I, 106.

[30] *Ibid.*, II, 671.

[31] *Ibid.*, II, 671–677.

[32] *Ibid.*, II, 672.

[33] *Ibid.*, I, 252.

[34] *Ibid.*, I, 273–284.

[35] *Ibid.*, I, 295.

[36] *Nippon Times*, Oct. 11, 1945.

[37] SCAP, *Political Reorientation of Japan*, II, 470.

[38] Costello, *Democracy vs. Feudalism in Post-War Japan*, pp. 99–101.

[39] Ōuchi Hyoe, "Keizai" (Economics), in Yanaihara, *Gendai Nihon Kōshi*, I, 254–259.

[40] *Ibid.*, pp. 259–268.

[41] *Yomiuri*, Feb. 8, 1952, trans. in U. S. State Dept., "Japanese Press Summary," Feb. 8, 1952.

[42] *Zenei*, February, 1952, trans. in U. S. State Dept., "Japanese Press Translations," Mar. 7, 1952.

[43] Tsuji, *Jiei Chūritsu* (Self-Defense [and] Neutrality), p. 195.

[44] *Ibid.*, pp. 193–195, and *Jiji*, Feb. 17, 1952, trans. in U. S. State Dept. "Japanese Press Summary," Feb. 18, 1952.

[45] Tsuji, *op. cit.*, pp. 195–200.

[46] *Asahi*, Feb. 14, 1952, U. S. State Dept., "Japanese Press Summary," Feb. 14, 1952.

[47] J. P. Napier, *A Survey of the Japan Communist Party* (Tokyo: *Nippon Times*, 1952), p. 12.

[48] *Ibid.*, p. 13.

[49] Rodger Swearingen, "Communist Strength in Japan," *Nippon Times*, Aug. 10, 1952.

[50] *Ibid.*

[51] "Research Project on Japanese Communism," Harvard University Russian Research Center Doc. No. 5, p. 12.

[52] *Zenei*, February, 1952, trans. in U. S. State Dept., "Japanese Press Summary," Mar. 7, 1952.

[53] Scalapino, "Japan and the General Elections," *Far Eastern Survey*, Oct. 29, 1952, p. 154.

[54] Dore, "The Ethics of the New Japan," *Pacific Affairs*, XXV (June, 1952), 147–159.

[55] *Yomiuri*, as quoted in *Nippon Times*, Nov. 20, 1951.

[56] Kinoshita, "Shinsei Uyoku Undō wo Tsuku, Nihonban 'Nashiyonarizum' no Me Kae" (Rise of a New Right-Wing Movement; the Sprouting of a Japanese-Type Nationalism), *Kaizō*, October, 1951, pp. 76–77.

[57] *Ibid.*, p. 74.

[58] *Ibid.*, p. 75.

[59] *Ibid.*

[60] Tsuji, *Underground Escape.*

[61] Tsuji, *Jiei Chūritsu.*

[62] Scalapino, *op. cit.*, p. 154.

[63] Kawai, *"Mokusatsu,* Japan's Response to the Potsdam Declaration," *Pacific Historical Review*, XIX, 409–413.

[64] "United States Initial Post-Surrender Policy for Japan," Aug. 24, 1945, U. S. State Dept., *Occupation of Japan, Policy and Progress*, p. 74.

[65] *Ibid.*, p. 74.

[66] *Ibid.*, p. 119.

[67] Takeuchi, "Basic Issues in Japan's Foreign Policy," *Far Eastern Survey*, Nov. 19, 1952, p. 164.

[68] Ōya Soichi, "Sonnō Jōi to Sonso Jōbei" ("Revere the Emperor and Expel the Barbarians" and "Revere the U.S.S.R. and Expel the Americans"), *Kaizō*, July, 1952, pp. 106–111, trans. in *Nippon Times*, July 15, 1952.

[69] Takeuchi, *op. cit.*, pp. 165–166.

Bibliography

Bibliography

The breadth and depth of nationalism in Japan, particularly in the last sixty years, gives some relevance to almost every Japanese book, poem, order, letter, newspaper, or play ever written; to every picture painted; to every song sung; and to every movie or radio program presented. And since the Japanese have a remarkable propensity for collecting, have preserved a vast quantity of historical materials, and have become one of the greatest publishing and reading peoples of the world, the compilation of a complete bibliography of Japanese nationalism is utterly impossible. This bibliography is merely a listing of the more important sources that I used—but did not always exhaustively exploit—in making this preliminary study. I have added a few notes that may be of help to those wishing to probe deeper into the problem.

Unpublished Document Collections

In Japan there are many important collections of unpublished source materials which contain information relating to the rise of Japanese nationalism. They can be found in public libraries, ministerial archives, Buddhist temples, and private storehouses. The collections listed here are the significant ones available in the United States.

International Military Tribunal for the Far East (IMTFE) materials. Mimeographed copy in the University of California Library. Approximately 150,000 pp.

> In connection with the long trial (1945–1948) of Japanese war criminals, a tremendous amount of evidence, written and oral, was presented to the International Military Tribunal for the Far East. Since the indictment was extremely broad, the evidence covered a wide range of historical events and problems for the period 1928 to 1945. A large part of the official "Proceedings" (48,412 pages of mimeographed material) consists of the oral testimony of some 419 Japanese officials and the depositions and affidavits of 779 others; but the most valuable historical material is found in the 4,336 documents which were accepted by the Tribunal as "Exhibits" (about 50,000 pages of mimeographed material). These Exhibits include treaties, agreements, conventions, Imperial ordinances, Imperial rescripts, Foreign Office documents, military reports, Home Office analyses, personnel records of the accused (28 high-ranking Japanese officials), maps, and statistical reports. Use of the material has been facilitated by a number of indexes prepared by the International Prosecution Section. See Delmer M. Brown, "Recent Japanese Political and Historical Materials," *American Political Science Review*, XLIII (October, 1949), 1010–1017.

International Prosecution Section documents. Microfilm copy in the Library of Congress. 94 reels.

> When the International Military Tribunal for the Far East was established, General Douglas MacArthur set up a section in his headquarters to handle the prosecution of the Japanese war criminals. The section, called the International Prosecution Section (IPS), had a large staff which accumulated, evaluated, and translated a mass of documentary material. But only a very small percentage (probably less than one per cent) was submitted to the Tribunal as evidence. The major part, therefore, was not included in the IMTFE materials. The basic collection, however, was kept intact by the Occupation, and recently selections from it (approximately 90,000 frames) were microfilmed. The negative has been deposited with the Library of Congress. Among the IPS documents are such notable items as the secret report of Japanese "Renovation" movements prepared by the Home Office in 1938. There are also minutes of Privy Council meetings, police reports, and the diary of Kido Kōichi (as yet unpublished). The IPS also prepared indexes of these materials, and it mimeographed "Analyses" of the documents (about 3,500 pages). A copy of the "Analyses" has been presented to the University of California library. The Library of Congress is preparing an index to the IPS documents in its microfilm collection.

Japanese Foreign Office documents. Microfilm copy in the Library of Congress. More than 2,000 reels.

> Although a large part of the prewar and wartime files of the Japanese Foreign Office was burned or otherwise intentionally destroyed by Japanese individuals at the time of surrender, the remainder of the collection is intact. The Library of Congress and the State Department in 1949 jointly undertook to microfilm a substantial portion of the material dating from about 1890 to 1945. In addition to the usual telegrams, notes, and instructions, there are a number of special reports and studies of a wide range of problems in Japan's foreign relations. The Library of Congress is preparing an index to these documents.

Published Document Collections

In Japanese

The Japanese have published more than 2,000 collections of historical materials in the last 100 years. For the most recent list of published collections see *Zōtei Zenshū Sōsho Kakaku Sōran, Meiji Shonen-Shōwa Nijū Nen* 増訂全集叢書價格總覽　明治初年一昭和二十年　(Revised Price List of Collections, 1868–1945), compiled jointly by Kawashima Gosaburō 川島五三郎　and Yagi Toshio 八木敏夫 (Tokyo: Nihon Kosho Tsūshin Sha, 1947). Listed below are only the collections that could be used with profit by those who wish to proceed further with the study of modern Japanese nationalism.

Dai Nihon Ishin Shiryō 大日本維新史料 (Historical Materials of the Restoration of Greater Japan). Compiled by the Ishin Shiryō

Hensan Kai 維 新 史 料 編 纂 會 . 19 vols. completed. Tokyo, 1939–.

In 1889 an association was established for the purpose of compiling and publishing historical materials dealing with political developments in the years immediately preceding and following the Restoration of 1868. In 1911 the project was taken over by the government. The Ishin Shiryō Hensan Kai (The Society for the Compilation of Restoration Historical Materials) was set up under the Department of Education. A committee of scholars was selected to collect and edit documents pertaining to the years 1846–1871. The period was divided into five sections, and each section was assigned to a subcommittee. Although 19 volumes have appeared, the project is far from complete.

Dai Nihon Shiryō 大日本史料 (Historical Materials of Greater Japan). Compiled and published by the Tokyo Teikoku Daigaku Bungakubu Shiryō Hensanbu 東 京 帝 國 大 學 文 學 部 史 料 編 纂 部 . 171 vols. completed by 1951. Tokyo, 1901–.

This compilation and publication project was started early in the nineteenth century by Hanawa Hokiichi 塙 保 己 一 (1746–1821), and was later taken over by the Historical Compilation Bureau of the Tokyo Imperial University. The collection was designed to include all important documents from A.D. 887, the last year covered by the *Rikkokushi* 六 國 史 (Six National Histories) down to the Meiji Restoration of 1868. Twelve sections were planned, one for each major historical period, and a group of scholars was made responsible for the collecting and editing of the documents for each section. The documents are presented topically and in chronological order. In spite of the large number of volumes that have been completed, less than 10 per cent of the years have been covered.

Ishin Nisshi 維 新 日 誌 (Restoration Gazette). Compiled by Hashimoto Hiroshi 橋 本 博 . 10 vols. Tokyo, 1932–1933.

This contains, among other items, the *Dajōkan Nisshi* 太 政 官 日 誌 (Journal of the Grand Council), which includes official orders, decrees, and notices for the period 1868–1878. The *Dajōkan Nisshi* was the predecessor of the present official gazette, *Kampō* (cited below).

Kampō 官 報 (Official Gazette). Published by the Naikaku Insatsu Kyoku 內 閣 印 刷 局 . Tokyo, 1883–.

This is the major source for governmental pronouncements of various types, including Imperial ordinances, laws, regulations, and notices. A supplement, the *Kampō Gōgai*, contains the proceedings of both houses of the Diet. The *Kampō* is indexed monthly, and the index is published as a supplement to one of the issues of the following month. For a time during the occupation the *Kampō* was translated into English. It is only one of many government publications. For a list, by ministry, of the publications in any given quarter, see the *Kanchō Kankō Tosho Mokuroku* 官 廳 刊 行 圖 書 目 錄 (Catalogue of Government Publications), published by the Naikaku Insatsu Kyoku since 1927.

Koji Ruien 古 事 類 苑 (Encyclopedia of Historical Materials). Compiled by Jingū Shichō 神宮司廳. 60 vols. Popular ed., Tokyo: Koji Ruien Kankō Kai, 1933–1936.

> The compilation of this remarkable encyclopedia of source materials was started by the Japanese Department of Education in 1879. The work was at first directed by the Confucian scholar Nishimura Shigeki; it was subsequently taken over by various agencies, and the encyclopedia was finally completed in 1914. It was organized under thirty subjects, and these in turn were subdivided. The material under each heading was placed in chronological order and was prefaced by a concise, valuable summary. Several sections have material touching upon the subject of nationalism. Vols. 6 to 11, for example, consist of material on Shinto rites; Vols. 33 to 35, religion; and Vols. 37 to 39, literature. Vol. 60 is an index.

In English

McLaren, Walter Wallace, ed. "Japanese Government Documents," *Transactions of the Asiatic Society of Japan*, XLII, Part 1 (1914).

> English translations of several key documents of the post-Restoration period are included.

Supreme Commander of the Allied Powers, Civil Information and Education Section. *Education in the New Japan*. 2 vols. Tokyo, 1948.

> The more important directives and laws pertaining to the Occupation's educational reforms are published in Vol. 2.

———. *Religions in Japan*. Tokyo, 1948.

Supreme Commander of the Allied Powers, Government Section. *Political Reorientation of Japan*. 2 vols. (Report for September, 1945, to September, 1948.)

> The more important laws and directives dealing with the Occupation's political reforms are published in Vol. 2.

United States Department of State. *Occupation of Japan, Policy and Progress*. Far Eastern Series 17.

> This volume includes documents pertaining to Occupation policy and early Occupation reforms.

Chronicles, Diaries, and Memoirs

A vast amount of material in this category has been published, and there is much in manuscript form. A useful guide for the pre-Restoration (1868) material is the *Nihon Shiseki Nempyō* 日本史籍年表 (List of Japanese Historical Works in Chronological Order), compiled by Koizumi Yasujirō 小泉安次郎 (rev. ed., Tokyo: Yoshikawa Kōbun Kan, 1911). This gives only titles, but by turning to Hirose Bin's 廣瀬敏 *Nihon Sōsho Sakuin* 日本叢書索引 (An Index of Japanese Collections) (Tokyo: Musashino Shoin, 1939), one can determine whether a work has been published, and if so, the place of publication. Also, for short explanations about the major chronicles, the following will be helpful: Samura Hachirō 佐 村 八 郎 , *Zōtei Kokusho Kaidai* 增 訂 國 書 解 題 (rev. and enlarged ed. of the "Annotations on Historical Works"), (4th ed., Tokyo, 1926), 2 vols. The major pre-Restoration chronicles and histories have been published in Taguchi Ukichi 田 口 卯 吉, ed., *Kokushi Taikei* 國 史 大 系 (Selected Japanese Historical Works) (Tokyo: Keizai Zasshi Sha, 1897–1901), 17 vols. The titles listed below are some of the more important post-Restoration diaries and memoirs by leading political figures and by foreign diplomats and observers.

UNPUBLISHED DIARY

Kido Kōichi 木 戸 幸 一 diary. Photostatic copy of the original MS, in the University of California Library.

> Since Kido held a number of high offices after 1930, including the position of Lord Keeper of the Privy ·Seal, his diary is a revealing record of the high-level political conferences held and decisions made in the decade immediately preceding World War II. A large part of the diary was translated at the time of the War Crimes Trial; apparently the only parts available 'in the United States at the present time are those covering three or four years of the 1930's, microfilms of which are in the University of California Library, Berkeley. Several items were also translated and accepted by the International Military Tribunal as exhibits.

PUBLISHED CHRONICLES, DIARIES, AND MEMOIRS

In Japanese

Fukuzawa Yukichi 福 澤 諭 吉 . *Fukuō Jiden* 福 翁 自 傳 (Autobiography of Fukuzawa Yukichi. Tokyo, 1898.

> The original autobiography is included in *Fukuzawa Zenshū* 福 澤 全 集 (Complete Collection of Fukuzawa's Works) (Tokyo: Kokumin Tosho Kabushiki Kaisha, 1925–1926), Vol. 6; it is translated by Kiyooka Eiichi in *Autobiography of Fukuzawa Yukichi* (Tokyo, 1934). Papers not included in *Fukuzawa Zenshū* were published in *Zoku Fukuzawa Zenshū* 續 福 澤 全 集 (Supplement to Complete Collection of Fukuzawa's Works) (Tokyo: Iwanami Shoten, 1933–1934).

Hara Keiichirō 原 奎 一 郎, ed. *Hara Kei Nikki* 原 敬 日 記 (Diary of Hara Kei). 9 vols. Tokyo, 1950–1952.

Harada Kumao 原 田 熊 雄 . *Saionji Kō to Seikyoku* 西 園 寺 公 と 政 局 (Prince Saionji and the Political Situation). 9 vols. Tokyo: Iwanami Shoten, 1950–1952.

> This title does not indicate clearly the true nature or full worth of the work. Those familiar with the IMTFE materials know it as the "Harada-Saionji Memoirs" which came to light at the time of the Tokyo War Crimes Trial. The Tribunal singled out these memoirs in its final statement: "The special position of Prince Saionji as the last of the Genro provoked full and candid disclosure to him through his secretary Harada. Harada's long period of

service to the Genro in this special task of obtaining information from the very highest functionaries of the Government and the Army and Navy is a test of his reliability and discretion . . . the Tribunal is satisfied that these are the original memoranda as are dictated by Harada and edited by Saionji. To the extent to which they are relevant, the Tribunal considers them helpful and reliable contemporary evidence of the matters recorded." U. S. War Dept., *Judgment of the International Military Tribunal for the Far East* (Washington, 1948), Part A, p. 22.

Iwakura Kō Kyūseki Hozon Kai 岩 倉 公 舊 蹟 保 存 會, ed. *Iwakura Kō Jikki* 岩 倉 公 實 記 (Papers of Prince Iwakura). 3 vols. Tokyo, 1927.

Kido Kōin 木 戶 孝 允. *Kido Kōin Nikki* 木 戶 孝 允 日 記 (Diary of Kido Kōin). 3 vols. Tokyo, 1932–1933.

Kiheitai Nikki 奇 兵 隊 日 記 (Diary of the Kiheitai). 4 vols. Tokyo: Nihon Shiseki Kyōkai, 1918.

Ōkubo Toshimichi 大 久 保 利 通. *Ōkubo Toshimichi Nikki* 大 久 保 利 通 日 記(Diary of Ōkubo Toshimichi). 2 vols. Tokyo: Nihon Shiseki Kyōkai, 1927.

Ozaki Yukio 尾 崎 行 雄. *Gakudō Kaiko Roku* 咢 堂 回 顧 錄 (Memoirs of Ozaki). 2 vols. Tokyo, 1951.

Shigemitsu Mamoru 重 光 葵. *Shōwa no Dōran* 昭 和 の 動 亂 (Confusion of the Shōwa Era). 2 vols. Tokyo: Chūō Kōron Sha, 1952.

In Western Languages

Alcock, Sir Rutherford. *The Capital of the Tycoon: A Narrative of Three Years' Residence in Japan.* 2 vols. New York, 1863.

Aston, William G. "Nihongi, Chronicles of Japan from the Earliest Times to A.D. 697," *Transactions and Proceedings of the Japan Society, London,* II (1896), Supplement 1.

Gayn, Mark. *Japan Diary.* New York: Sloane, 1948.

Golovnin, Vasilii Mikhailovich. *Narrative of My Captivity in Japan, during the Years 1811, 1812 and 1813.* London, 1818.

Grew, Joseph C. *Ten Years in Japan: A Contemporary Record Drawn from the Diaries and Private and Official Papers of Joseph C. Grew, United States Ambassador to Japan, 1932–1942.* New York: Simon and Schuster, 1944.

Harris, Townsend. *The Complete Journal of Townsend Harris, First American Consul General and Minister to Japan.* Ed. by Mario Emilio Cosenza. New York: Doubleday, 1930.

Hawks, Francis L. *Narrative of the Expedition of an American Squadron to the China Seas and Japan, 1852, 1853 and 1854, under the Command of Commodore M. C. Perry, United States Navy, by Order of the Government of the United States.* 3 vols. Washington, 1856.

Heco, Joseph. *The Narrative of a Japanese; What He Has Seen and the People He Has Met in the Course of the Last Forty Years*. Ed. by James Murdoch. 2 vols. Yokohama, 1894.

Satoh, Henry. *Agitated Japan: The Life of Baron Ii Kamon-no-Kami Naosuke (based on the Kaikoku Shimatsu of Shimada Saburo)*. New York, 1896.

Satow, Sir Ernest Mason. *A Diplomat in Japan: The Inner History of the Critical Years in the Evolution of Japan When the Ports Were Opened and the Monarchy Restored, Recorded by a Diplomat Who Took an Active Part in the Events of the Time; with an Account of His Personal Experiences during That Period*. London: Seeley, 1921.

Satow, Sir Ernest Mason, trans. *Japan 1853–1864, or, Genji Yume Monogatari*. Tokyo, 1905.

———. *Kinsei Shiriaku: A History of Japan from the Visit of Commodore Perry in 1853 to the Capture of Hakodate by the Mikado's Forces in 1869*. Yokohama, 1873.

Tsunoda, Ryusaku, trans., and L. Carrington Goodrich, ed. *Japan in the Chinese Dynastic Histories: Later Han through Ming Dynasties*. South Pasadena: Perkins Asiatic Monographs, No. 2, 1951.

Works by Nationalists and National Societies

There is a vast amount of nationalist literature, particularly for the period 1930–1945. The Investigation Section of the Japanese Foreign Office compiled a list in *Kokkashugi ni Kansuru Bunken Mokuroku* 國 家 主 義 ニ 關 ス ル 文 獻 目 錄 (Catalogue of Literature on Nationalism) in 1935. Although the bibliography includes little more than the titles, the many works listed make it a sizable book. The major collections and the more significant books published in the twentieth century are listed here.

COLLECTIONS

Dai Nihon Shisō Zenshū 大 日 本 思 想 全 集 (Collection of Intellectual Works of Greater Japan). Ed. by Uemura Katsumi 上 村 勝 彌 . 18 vols. Tokyo: Dai Nihon Shisō Zenshū Kankō Kai, 1932–1934.
This includes the works of some 56 different Tokugawa writers: Dutch scholars, Confucianists, students of classical Japan (*kokugakusha*) 國 學 者 , and others. It contains major works by Kumazawa Banzan 熊 澤 蕃 山 , Yamaga Sokō 山 鹿 素 行 , Yamazaki Anzai 山 崎 暗 齋 , Satō Nobuhiro 佐 藤 信 ' 淵 , Kamo Mabuchi 賀 茂 眞 淵 , Motoori Norinaga 本 居 宣 長 , Hirata Atsutane 平田篤胤 Honda Toshiaki 本 田 利 秋 , Sugita Gempaku 杉 田 玄 白 , Takenouchi Shikibu 竹 內 式 部 , Yoshida Shōin 吉 田 松 陰 , Sakuma Shōzan 佐 久 間 象 山 , Hashimoto Sanai 橋 本 左 內 , and others.

Kokka Kaizō Ronsaku Shū 國家改造論策集 (Collection of Theories and Plans for the Reconstruction of the State). Ed. by Japanese Home Ministry, Keiho Kyoku Hoan Ka 警保局保安課 Tokyo: Kōdō Kai Shuppan Bu, 1934.

> This has major nationalist writings of the National Reconstruction variety. Books by Kita Ikki 北 一 輝 and Tachibana Kōsaburō 橘 孝 三 郎, as well as proclamations by leading nationalist societies are included.

Meiji Bunka Zenshū 明治文化全集 (Collection of Meiji Cultural Works). Ed. by Yoshino Sakuzō 吉野作造. 24 vols. Tokyo: Nihon Hyōron Sha, 1928–1930.

> Each volume in this collection includes selected works in particular fields. Vol. 1 (The Imperial Household), Vol. 10 (Education), Vol. 11 (Religion), Vol. 12 (Literature and the Arts), and Vol. 15 (Thought) contain works relating to nationalism.

Nichiren Shōnin Zenshū 日蓮聖人全集 (Complete Works of Saint Nichiren). Ed. by Suzuki Sōtarō 鈴木莊太郎. 7 vols. Tokyo, 1925.

Nihon Kokusui Zensho 日本國粹全書 (Collection of Works on Japanese National Essence). Ed. by Nihon Kokusui Zensho Kankō Kai 日本國粹全書刊行會. 24 vols. Tokyo: Nihon Kokusui Zensho Kankō Kai, 1915–1918.

Nihon Seishin Bunka Taikei 日本精神文化大系 (Selected Works in Japanese Spiritual Culture). Ed. by Fujita Tokutarō 藤田德太郎 *et al.* 10 vols. Tokyo: Kinseidō, 1934–1938.

> Each volume contains the major "spiritual" work of a particular period; the second volume, for example, is for what is called the Yamato 大和時代 era.

Shōnan Ikō 小楠遺稿 (Papers of Yokoi Shōnan). Ed. by Yokoi Tokio 横井時雄. Tokyo, 1888.

Shōzan Zenshū 象山全集 (Complete Works of [Sakuma] Shōzan). 2 vols. Tokyo: Shinano Mainichi Shimbunsha, 1934.

Yoshida Shōin Zenshū 吉田松陰全集 (Complete Works of Yoshida Shōin). Ed. by Yamaguchi-ken Kyōiku Kai 山口縣教育會. 10 vols. Tokyo: Iwanami Shoten, 1934–1936.

SEPARATE WORKS

Gondō Seikyō 權藤成卿. *Jichi Mimpan* 自治民範 (Model of Self-Government). Written in 1919. Tokyo: Heibon Sha, 1947 [last ed. known to me].

Japanese Education Ministry. *Shimmin no Michi* 臣民の道 (The Way of the Subject). 1941.

> Translated in part in Otto D. Tolischus, *Tokyo Record*, 1943 (see below).

————. *Kokutai no Hongi* 國 體 の 本 義 (Principles of National Entity). Published in 1937.

English translation by John Owen Gauntlett published in 1949 (see below).

Japanese War Ministry. *Kokubō no Hongi to Sono Kyōka no Teishō* 國防の本義と其強化の提唱 (Principles of National Defense and Proposals for Strengthening Them). Published as a pamphlet in 1934.

Reprinted in *Kokka Kaizō Ronsaku Shū*, pp. 663–685.

Kita Ikki 北 一 輝. *Kokutai Ron oyobi Junsei Shakai Shugi* 國 體 論 及 純 正 社 會 主 義 (Japanese National Entity and Pure Socialism). Written in 1906.

Discussed at length in Tanaka Sōgorō, *Nihon Fuashizumu no Genryū* (cited below), pp. 24–113.

————. *Nihon Kokka Kaizō Hōan Taikō* 日 本 國 家 改 造 法 案 大 綱 (Outline Plan for the Reconstruction of the Japanese State). Written in 1919. Last published in *Nihon oyobi Nihonjin* 日 本 及 日 本 人 (Japan and the Japanese), Vol. III, No. 10 (August, 1952), pp. 128–156, and Vol. III, No. 11 (September, 1952), pp. 92–132.

————. *Shina Kakumei Gaishi* 支 那 革 命 外 史 (Private History of Chinese Revolution). First published in 1921. Tokyo: Seiki Shobō, 1940 [last ed. known to me].

Kodama, Yoshio. *I Was Defeated.* Tokyo: Asian, 1951.

Kuzu Yoshihisa 葛 生 能 久. *Tōa Senkaku Shishi Kiden* 東 亞 先 覺 志 士 記 傳 (Biographical Memoirs of Pioneer East Asian Patriots). 3 vols. Tokyo: Kokuryū Kai, 1933.

————. *Nisshi Kōshō Gaishi* 日 支 交 涉 外 史 (Private History of Relations between China and Japan). 2 vols. Tokyo: Kokuryū Kai, 1939.

Masaki Hiroshi 正 木 ひ ろ し *et al.* *Konnichi no Aikoku Shin, Hiyumanizumu no Tachiba kara* 今 日 の 愛 國 心, ヒ ュ ー マ ニ ズ ム の 立 場 か ら (Present-Day Patriotism, from the Point of View of Humanism). Tokyo: Sankeisha, 1952.

Ōkawa Shūmei 大 川 周 明. *Fukkō Ajia no Sho Mondai* 復 興 亞 細 亞 の 諸 問 題 (Various Problems Relative to the Revival of Asia). Tokyo: Daitōkaku, 1922; rev. ed., 1939.

————. *Ajia, Yōroppa, Nihon* 亞 細 亞, 歐 羅 巴, 日 本 (Asia, Europe, and Japan). Tokyo, 1925.

————. *Nihon Seishin Kenkyū* 日 本 精 神 研 究 (Study of the Japanese Spirit). Tokyo, 1927; 118th ed., 1942.

————. *Nihon oyobi Nihonjin no Michi* 日 本 及 日 本 人 の 道 (The Way of the Japanese and of Japan). Rev. ed., Tokyo: Gyochi Sha, 1930.

————. *Nihon teki Genkō* 日 本 的 言 行 (Japanese Words and Deeds). Tokyo, 1930.

————. *Nihon Nisen Roppyaku Nen Shi* 日 本 二 千 六 百 年 史 (Two Thousand Six Hundred Years of Japanese History). Tokyo, 1939.

Tsuji Masanobu 辻 政信. *Jiei Chūritsu* 自 衞 中 立 (Self-Defense [and] Neutrality). Tokyo: Atō Shobō, 1952.

————. *Underground Escape.* Tokyo: Robert Booth and Taro Fukuda, 1952.

Newspapers and Magazines

The most comprehensive collection of nationalist ephemeral material in the United States is at the Hoover War Library, Stanford University. Only newspapers and magazines used in making this study are included in the following list.

In Japanese

Asahi Shimbun 朝 日 新 聞 (Morning Sun Newspaper). 1878–.

Chūō Kōron 中 央 公 論 (Central Review). 1916–.

Jitsugyō no Nihon 實 業 の 日 本 (Industrial Japan). 1897–.

Kokugakuin Zasshi 國 學 院 雜 誌 (Magazine of Institute of National Studies). 1894–.

Miyako Shimbun 都 新 聞 (Capitol Newspaper). 1946–.

Nihon oyobi Nihonjin 日 本 及 日 本 人 (Japan and the Japanese). 1905–.

Nihonjin 日 本 人 (Japanese). 1888–1905.

Taiyō 太 陽 (Sun). 1894–.

Zen'ei 前 衞 (Advance Guard). 1946–.

In English

Contemporary Japan. 1932–.

Contemporary Opinion on Current Topics. 1938–1940.

The Japan Advertiser. 1932–1940.

Japan Magazine. 1910–1939.

Japan Times and Advertiser. 1940–1941.

Japan Weekly Chronicle. 1920–1941.

Japan Weekly Mail. 1888–1916.

"Japanese Press Summary." Daily summaries made by American Embassy in Japan since 1951. (Mimeographed.)

Nippon Times. 1942–.

Osaka *Mainichi.* 1938–.

Tokyo *Gazette.* 1937–1941.

Monographs and Special Studies

The only Japanese writers who have given serious thought to the subject of Japanese nationalism are Maruyama Masao, Kinoshita Hanji,

Tsukui Tatsuo, and Kada Tetsuji. Maruyama's work has been of the greatest help, for he has made some very penetrating studies, particularly in his theoretical analyses based on comparisons between nationalism in Japan and nationalism in other parts of the world. Kinoshita Hanji, in his various works, has supplied a mass of detailed information about the development of nationalist societies. Tsukui has studied the growth of nationalism in its relationship to the history of socialism in Japan. Kada Tetsuji is the only one to make a broad historical analysis of the type attempted here; but he wrote early, covered only the development since Meiji, and was too close to the phenomenon to view it very objectively. There is one excellent study in English, by D. C. Holtom, on State Shinto, a very vital element in modern Japanese nationalism.

The works that have been of particular value to me in making this study are marked with an asterisk.

In Japanese

Fujima Seidai 藤 間 生 大 . *Nihon Kodai Kokka* 日 本 古 代 國 家 (The Ancient Japanese State). Tokyo: Itō Shoten, 1949.

Inouye Mitsusada 井 上 光 貞 . *Nihon Kodai Shi no Sho Mondai* 日 本 古 代 史 の 諸 問 題(Problems in Ancient Japanese History). Tokyo: Shiansha, 1949.

Ishin Shiryō Hensan Kai 維 新 史 料 編 纂 會 , comp. *Ishin Shi* 維 新 史 (History of the Restoration). 2d ed., Tokyo: Meiji Shoin, 1942. 6 vols.

Iwabuchi Tatsuo 岩淵辰雄 . "Kita Ikki to Nishida Zei" 北 一輝と西田 税 (Kita Ikki and Nishida Zei), *Chūō Kōron,* March, 1950, pp. 127–139.

*———. *Sekai Gojūnen Shi* 世 界 五 十 年 史 (Fifty Years of World History). Tokyo: Shuppan Kabushiki Kaisha, 1945.

*Kada Tetsuji 加 田 哲 二 . *Nihon Kokka Shugi no Hatten* 日 本 國 家 主 義 の 發 展 (Development of Japanese Nationalism). Tokyo: Keio Shobō, 1938; rev. ed., 1940.

Kimiya Yasuhiko 來 宮 泰 彦 . *Nisshi Kōtsū Shi* 日 支 交 通 史 (History of Japanese-Chinese Relations). 2 vols. Tokyo: Kanazashi Hōryūdō, 1928.

*Kinoshita Hanji 木 下 半 治 . "Shinsei Uyoku Undō wo Tsuku, Nihon-ban 'Nashonarizumu' no Mebae" 新 生 右 翼 運 動 を 衝 く 日 本 版 ' ナ シ ョ ナ リ ズ ム ' の 芽 生 え (Rise of a New Right-Wing Movement; the Sprouting of a Japanese-type Nationalism), *Kaizō,* October, 1951, pp. 71–79.

*———. *Nihon Kokka Shugi Undō Shi* 日 本 國 家 主 義 運 動 史

(History of Japanese Nationalist Movements). 2 vols. Tokyo: Iwasaki Shoten, 1952.

> This study appeared originally in 1936 under the title of *Nihon Fashizumu* 日本ファシズム (Japanese Fascism). A revised version was published in 1940 entitled *Nihon Kokka Shugi Undō Shi*. When the War Crimes Trial began, this work was translated into English by the Occupation, but it was not published. In 1949 Kinoshita issued another revised version, *Nihon Fashizumu Shi* 日本ファシズム史 (History of Japanese Fascism), which was to be the first volume of a two-volume study. But when the second volume was finished, the first was republished and both appeared under the old title *Nihon Kokka Shugi Undō Shi*.

*Kiyohara Sadao 清原貞雄. *Nihon Dōtoku Shi* 日本道德史 (History of Japanese Morals). Tokyo: Chūbunkan Shoten, 1930. A revised edition was published in 1937.

―――. *Meiji Jidai Shisō Shi* 明治時代思想史 (History of Thought in the Meiji Era). Tokyo: Daitōkaku, 1921.

Kondō Tadayoshi 近藤忠義 *et al.*, eds. *Gendai Shisō Kenkyū Hen* 現代思想研究篇 (Compilation of Studies in Modern Thought). Vol 3 of *Gendai Bungaku Sōsetsu* 現代文學總說 (General Survey of Modern Culture). Tokyo: Gakutōsha, 1952.

*Maruyama Masao 丸山眞男. "Nihon Fashizumu no Shisō to Undō" 日本ファシズムの思想と運動 (Japanese Fascist Thoughts and Movements). One of four studies in *Sonjō Shisō to Zettai Shugi* 尊攘思想と絶對主義 (Absolutism and "Revere-the-Emperor: Expel the Barbarian" Thought). Tokyo: Hakujitsu Shoin, 1948. Pp. 97–184.

―――. "Meiji Kokka no Shisō" 明治國家の思想 (The Thought of the Meiji State). One of a series of studies in a volume edited by the Rekishigaku Kenkyūkai, 歴史學研究會, *Nihon Shakai no Shiteki Kyūmei* 日本社會の史的究明 (Historical Studies of Japanese Society). Tokyo: Iwanami Shoten, 1949. Pp. 181–236.

―――. "Nihon ni okeru Nashonarizumu, Sono Shisō teki Haikei" 日本に於けるナショナリズム，其思想的背景 (Intellectual Background of Nationalism in Japan). *Chūō Kōron*, January, 1951, pp. 295–304.

Nihon Keizai Shi Kenkyūjo 日本經濟史研究所 (Japanese Economic History Research Institute), ed. *Bakumatsu Keizai Shi Kenkyū* 幕末經濟史研究 (Studies in Late Tokugawa Economic History). Tokyo: Yuhikaku, 1935.

"Nihon Seishin Kenkyū ni kansuru Bunken" 日本精神研究に關する文獻 (Bibliography of Japanese Spiritual Studies), *Shisō Kenkyū*, March, 1939, pp. 61–94.

Ōya Sōichi 大宅壯一 "Sonnō Jōi to Sonso Jōbei" 尊皇攘夷と尊ソ攘米 ("Revere the Emperor and Expel the Barbarians," and "Revere the U.S.S.R. and Expel the Americans"), *Kaizo*, July, 1952, pp. 106–111; trans. in *Nippon Times*, July 15, 1952.

Shinobu Seisaburō 信 夫 清 三 郎 . *Meiji Seiji Shi* 明 治 政 治 史 (Political History of Meiji). Tokyo: Kōbundo, 1950.

————. *Kindai Nihon Gaikō Shi* 近 代 日 本 外 交 史 (Diplomatic History of Modern Japan). 2d ed., Tokyo: Kenshin Sha, 1949.

————. *Taishō Seiji Shi* 大 正 政 治 史 (Political History of Taisho). 4 vols. Tokyo: Kawaide Shobō, 1951–1952.

Tanaka Sōgorō 田 中 惣 五 郎 . *Nihon Fuashizumu no Genryū* 日 本 フ ァ シ ズ ム の 源 流 (Origins of Japanese Fascism). Tokyo: Haku-yōsha, 1949.

Tōyama Shigeki 遠 山 茂 樹 . *Meiji Ishin* 明 治 維 新 (Meiji Restoration). 3d ed., Tokyo: Iwanami Shoten, 1952.

Toyoda Takeshi 豐 田 武 . *Nihon Shūkyō Seido Shi no Kenkyū* 日 本 宗 教 制 度 史 の 研 究 (Studies in the Institutional History of Japanese Religion). Tokyo: Koseikaku, 1938.

Tsuchiya Takao 土 屋 喬 雄 . *Nihon Kokubō Kokka Kensetsu no Shiteki Kōsatsu* 日 本 國 防 國 家 建 設 の 史 的 考 察 (A Historical Consideration of the Establishment of the Japanese Defense State). Tokyo: Kagaku Shugi Kōjō Sha, 1942.

Tsuji Zennosuke 辻 善 之 助 . *Kaigai Kōtsū Shiwa* 海 外 交 通 史 話 (Historical Account of Communications with Nations beyond the Seas). Tokyo: Naigai Shoseki, 1930.

Tsukui Tatsuo 津 久 井 龍 雄 . *Nihon Shugi Undō no Riron to Jissen* 日 本 主 義 運 動 の 理 論 と 實 踐 (Theory and Practice of the Japanism Movement). Tokyo: Kensetsu Sha, 1935.

*————. *Uyoku* 右 翼 (Right Wing). Tokyo: Shōwa Shobō, 1952.

Wakamori Tarō 和 歌 森 太 郎 , ed. *Kokka no Seisei* 國 家 の 生 成 (Formation of the [Japanese] State). Vol. 1 of *Shin Nihon Shi Taikei* 新 日 本 史 大 系 (New Outline History of Japan). 6 vols. Tokyo: Asakura Shoten, 1952.

*Yabe Sadaji 矢 部 貞 治 . *Konoye Fumimaro Den* 近 衞 文 麿 傳 (Biography of Konoye Fumimaro). 2 vols. Tokyo: Kōbundō, 1952.

Yanaihara Tadao 矢 內 原 忠 雄 , ed. *Gendai Nihon Shōshi* 現 代 日 本 小 史 (Brief History of Modern Japan). 2 vols. Tokyo: Misuzu Shobō, 1952.

In Western Languages

Akiyama Kenzō. *The History of Nippon.* Tokyo: Kokusai Bunka Shin-kōkai, 1941.

Anesaki, Masaharu. *Nichiren, the Buddhist Prophet.* Cambridge: Harvard University Press, 1916.

Aston, William G. "Russian Descents in Saghalien and Itorup in the Years 1806 and 1807," *Transactions of the Asiatic Society of Japan,* I (1874), 79–84.

Bay, C. "The Theoretical Preparation of a Research Project on Nationalist Attitudes," *International Social Science Bulletin,* Vol. III, No. 2 (Summer, 1951), pp. 244–246.

Bisson, Thomas Arthur. *Japan in China.* New York: Macmillan, 1938.

Boxer, C. R. *The Christian Century in Japan, 1549–1650.* Berkeley and Los Angeles: University of California Press, 1951.

Brines, Russell. *MacArthur's Japan.* New York: Lippincott, 1948.

Brown, Delmer M. "Impact of Firearms on Japanese Warfare, 1543–98," *Far Eastern Quarterly,* VIII (May, 1948), 236–253.

———. "The Japanese Tokusei of 1297," *Harvard Journal of Asiatic Studies,* XII (June, 1949), 188–206.

———. *Money Economy in Medieval Japan.* New Haven: Far Eastern Monograph Series, Vol. I (1951).

Buchanan, D. C. "Inari: Its Origin, Development and Nature," *Transactions of the Asiatic Society of Japan,* 2d Series, XII (December, 1935).

Chamberlain, Basil Hall. *Things Japanese, Being Notes on Various Subjects Connected with Japan for the Use of Travellers and Others.* 4th ed., rev., London: John Murray, 1902.

Coleman, Horace E. "The Life of Shōin Yoshida," *Transactions of the Asiatic Society of Japan,* XLV (1917), Part 1, pp. 119–188.

Costello, William. *Democracy vs. Feudalism in Post-War Japan.* Tokyo: Itagaki Shoten, 1948.

Dennett, Tyler. *Americans in Eastern Asia: A Critical Study of the Policy of the United States with Reference to China, Japan and Korea in the 19th Century.* 2d ed., New York: Barnes & Noble, 1941.

Domingsil, Filomeno. "Soviet-Japanese Relations, 1931–1937." Unpublished M.A. thesis, University of California, Berkeley, 1937.

Dore, R. P. "The Ethics of the New Japan," *Pacific Affairs,* XXV (June, 1952), 147–159.

Fairbank, John K. "The Imperial Tradition in Japan and in Europe," *Far Eastern Leaflets* (Washington: American Council of Learned Societies, 1942), Nos. 1–6, pp. 20–22.

Fairbank, John K., and S. U. Teng. "On the Ch'ing Tributary System," *Harvard Journal of Asiatic Studies,* VI (June, 1941), 135–246.

Feis, Herbert. *The Road to Pearl Harbor: The Coming of the War between the United States and Japan.* Princeton University Press, 1950.

Feldman, Horace Z. "The Meiji Political Novel: A Brief Survey," *Far Eastern Quarterly,* IX (May, 1950), 245–255.

Friedman, Irving. *British Relations with China: 1931-1939.* New York: Institute of Pacific Relations, 1940.

Fujii, Tatsuki. *Singapore Assignment.* Tokyo: Nippon Times, 1943.

Gauntlett, John Owen, trans. *Kokutai no Hongi: Cardinal Principles of the National Entity of Japan.* Cambridge: Harvard University Press, 1949.

Greene, D. C. "Osada's Life of Takano Nagahide," *Transactions of the Asiatic Society of Japan,* XLI, Part 3 (August, 1913), 424.

Groot, Gerard. "An Essay on Early Japanese History," *Transactions of the Asiatic Society of Japan,* 3d Series, I (December, 1948), 24–26.

Hayes, Carlton. *Historical Evolution of Modern Nationalism.* New York: R. R. Smith, 1931.

Ike, Nobutaka. *The Beginnings of Political Democracy in Japan.* Baltimore: Johns Hopkins Press, 1950.

Ito, Hirobumi, Prince. *Commentaries on the Constitution of the Empire of Japan.* Trans. by Count Miyuji Ito. 3d ed., Tokyo: Chū-ō Daigaku, 1931.

Ito, Masanori. "Japan's Victory in Historical Light," *Contemporary Japan,* IX (January, 1942), pp. 37–47.

*Jansen, Marius B. "The Japanese and the Chinese Revolutionary Movement, 1895–1915," Unpublished Ph.D. dissertation, Harvard University, 1950.

Joseph, Bernard. *Nationality, Its Nature and Problems.* New Haven: Yale University Press, 1929.

Kato, Masuo. *The Lost War: A Japanese Reporter's Inside Story.* New York: Knopf, 1946.

Kawabe, Kisaburō. *The Press and Politics in Japan: A Study of the Relation between the Newspaper and the Political Development of Modern Japan.* University of Chicago Press, 1921.

Kawai, Kazuo. "Mokusatsu, Japan's Response to the Potsdam Declaration," *Pacific Historical Review,* XIX, (November, 1950), 409–413.

Kikuchi, Dairoku. *Japanese Education.* London, 1909.

King, James Clement. *Some Elements of National Solidarity.* University of Chicago Press, 1935.

Kohn, Hans. *The Idea of Nationalism: A Study in Its Origins and Background.* New York: Macmillan, 1944.

Kono, Shōzō. "Kannagara no Michi: The Meaning of Kannagara," *Monumenta Nipponica,* Vol. III, No. 2 (1940), pp. 9–31.

Kroeber, A. L. *Anthropology: Race, Language, Culture, Psychology, Prehistory.* Rev. ed., New York: Harcourt, Brace, 1948.

Kublin, Hyman. "The 'Modern' Army of Early Meiji Japan," *Far Eastern Quarterly,* IX (November, 1949), 20–41.

Kuhara, Fusanosuke. "The Basis for a Single Party," *Contemporary Japan,* IX (July, 1940), pp. 813–814.

Kuiper, J. Feenstra. "Some Notes on the Foreign Relations of Japan in the Early Napoleonic Period (1798–1805)," *Transactions of the Asiatic Society of Japan,* 2d Series, I (December, 1924), 55–82.

Langer, William L., and S. Everett Gleason. *The Undeclared War, 1940–1941.* New York: Harper, 1953.

Lory, Hillis. *Japan's Military Masters.* New York: Viking Press, 1943.

McLaren, Walter Wallace. *A Political History of Japan during the Meiji Era, 1867–1912.* New York: Scribner, 1916.

Miller, Richard James. "An Historical Study of the Higher Administrative Officials of the Council of State in Japan in the Eighth Century A.D." Unpublished M.A. thesis, University of California, Berkeley, 1947.

Moore, Harriet Lucy. *Soviet Far Eastern Policy, 1931–1945.* Princeton University Press, 1945.

Mori, Arinori. *Education in Japan: A Series of Letters Addressed by Prominent Americans to Arinori Mori.* New York, 1873.

Nelson, Melvin Frederick. *Korea and the Old Orders in Eastern Asia.* Baton Rouge: Louisiana State University Press, 1945.

Nitobe, Inazo. *Bushido, the Soul of Japan: An Exposition of Japanese Thought.* 10th ed., New York: Putnam, 1905.

Norman, E. Herbert. *Japan's Emergence as a Modern State; Political and Economic Problems of the Meiji Period.* New York: Institute of Pacific Relations, 1940.

———. "The Genyosha: A Study in the Origins of Japanese Imperialism," *Pacific Affairs,* XVII (September, 1944), 261–284.

Ōkuma, Shigenobu, comp. *Fifty Years of New Japan (Kaikoku Gojunen Shi).* 2 vols. London: Smith, Elder, 1910.

Osuga, William Makoto. "The Establishment of State Shinto and the Buddhist Opposition in the Early Meiji Period." Unpublished M.A. thesis, University of California, Berkeley, 1947.

Ozaki, Hotsumi. "The New National Structure," *Contemporary Japan,* VIII (October, 1940), 1285.

Pollard, Robert T. "Dynamics of Japanese Imperialism," *Pacific Historical Review,* VIII (March, 1939), 5–35.

Popper, Karl Raimund. *The Open Society and Its Enemies.* Princeton University Press, 1950.

Rabbitt, James A. "Rice in the Cultural Life of the Japanese People," *Transactions of the Asiatic Society of Japan,* 2d Series, XIX (December, 1940), 187–258.

Ramming, Martin. *Reisen Schiffbruchiger Japaner im XVII. Jahrhundert.* Berlin, 1931.

Sadler, A. L. *The Maker of Modern Japan.* London: Allen & Unwin, 1937.

Sakamaki, Shunzo. "Japan and the United States, 1790–1853," *Transactions of the Asiatic Society of Japan,* 2d Series, XVIII (December, 1939), 4–20.

Sansom, George B. *An Historical Grammar of Japan.* Oxford: Clarendon Press, 1928.

Satow, Sir Ernest Mason. "The Revival of Pure Shin-Tau," *Transactions of the Asiatic Society of Japan,* III (1883), Part 1 [reprint of 1875], Appendix.

Scalapino, Robert A. *Democracy and the Party Movement in Prewar Japan: The Failure of the First Attempt.* Berkeley and Los Angeles: University of California Press, 1953.

———. "Japan and the General Elections." *Far Eastern Survey,* Oct. 29, 1952, p. 154.

Selle, Earl Robert. *Donald of China.* New York: Harper, 1948.

Shirley, James Robert. "Japan's Foreign Policy toward Russia, 1931–1945." Unpublished M.A. thesis, University of California, Berkeley, 1952.

Smith, Thomas C. "The Introduction of Western Industry to Japan during the Last Years of the Tokugawa Period," *Harvard Journal of Asiatic Studies,* XI (June, 1948), 130–152.

Spae, Joseph John. *Ito Jinsai, a Philosopher, Educator and Sinologist of The Tokugawa Period.* Monumenta Serica Monograph XII. Peiping, 1948.

Spinks, Charles Nelson. "Origins of Japanese Interests in Manchuria," *Far Eastern Quarterly,* II (May, 1943), 264–266.

Stead, Alfred, ed. *Japan by the Japanese: A Survey by Its Highest Authorities.* New York: Dodd; London: Heinemann, 1904.

Swearingen, Rodger, and Paul Langer. *Red Flag in Japan, International Communism in Action, 1919–1951.* Cambridge: Harvard University Press, 1952.

Takeuchi, Tatsuji. "Basic Issues in Japan's Foreign Policy," *Far Eastern Survey,* Nov. 19, 1952, pp. 161–166.

Tanin, O., and E. Yohan. *Militarism and Fascism in Japan.* New York, International Publishers, 1934.

Terry, Charles S. "Saguma Shōzan and His Seiken-Roku." Unpublished M.A. thesis, Columbia University, 1950(?).

Tolischus, Otto D. *Tokyo Record.* New York: Reynal & Hitchcock, 1943. Appendix I.

Treat, Payson J. "The Cause of the Sino-Japanese War, 1894," *Pacific Historical Review,* VIII (June, 1939), 149–157.

————. *Diplomatic Relations between the United States and Japan, 1853–1895.* Stanford University Press, 1932.

Trewartha, Glenn Thomas. *Japan: A Physical, Cultural and Regional Geography.* Madison: University of Wisconsin Press, 1945.

Tsiang, T. F. "Sino-Japanese Diplomatic Relations, 1870–1894," *Chinese Social and Political Science Review,* XVI (April, 1933), 1–106.

Von Engeln, O. D. *Inheriting the Earth; or, the Geographical Factor in National Development.* New York: Macmillan, 1922.

*Wald, Royal Jules. "The Young Officers Movement in Japan, *ca.* 1925–1937: Ideology and Actions." Unpublished Ph.D. dissertation, University of California, Berkeley, 1949.

Yamasaki, K., and G. Ogawa. *The Effect of World War upon Commerce and Industry of Japan.* New Haven: Yale University Press, 1929.

General Works

In Japanese

Akamatsu Katsumaro 赤 松 克 麿 . *Nihon Shakai Undō Shi* 日本社會 運動史 (History of the Socialist Movement in Japan). Tokyo: Iwanami Shoten, 1952.

Honda Takeo 本 多 武 雄 . *Nihon Shakai Undō Shi Gaisetsu* 日 本 社會運動史概說 (Outline History of Japanese Social Movements). Tokyo: Tatebana Shobō, 1952.

Horie Yasuzō 堀 江 保 藏 . *Nihon Keizai Shi* 日 本 經 濟 史 (Economic History of Japan). Tokyo: Tōyō Shokan, 1949.

Kajinishi Mitsuhaya 楫 西 光 速 . *Nihon Keizai Shi* 日 本 經 濟 史 (Economic History of Japan). Tokyo: Ochanomizu Shobō, 1952.

Tokutomi Iichirō 德 富 猪 一 郎 . *Kinsei Nihon Kokumin Shi* 近 世 日 本 國 民 史 (Modern History of the Japanese People). 50 vols. Tokyo: Meiji Shoin, 1934–1936.

In Western Languages

Allen, George C. *A Short Economic History of Modern Japan, 1867–1937.* London: Allen & Unwin, 1946.

Anesaki, Masaharu. *History of Japanese Religion with Special Reference to the Social Life of the Nation.* London: Kegan Paul, 1930.

Aston, William G. *A History of Japanese Literature.* New York: Appleton-Century, 1937.

Brinkley, Frank. *A History of the Japanese People from the Earliest Times to the End of the Meiji Era.* New York: Encyclopaedia Britannica, 1915.

Eliot, Sir Charles Norton Edgecumbe. *Japanese Buddhism.* London: Arnold, 1935.

Fenollosa, Ernest F. *Epochs of Chinese and Japanese Art: An Outline History of East Asiatic Design.* 2 vols. New ed., New York: Stokes, 1913.

Kuno, Yoshi Saburō. *Japanese Expansion on the Asiatic Continent: A Study in the History of Japan with Special Reference to Her International Relations with China, Korea, and Russia.* 2 vols. Berkeley: University of California Press, 1937–1940.

Murdoch, James. *A History of Japan.* 3 vols. London: Kegan Paul, 1923–1926.

Reischauer, Robert Karl. *Early Japanese History (c. 40 B.C.–A.D. 1167).* 2 vols. Princeton University Press, 1937.

Sadler, A. L. *A Short History of Japan.* Sydney and London: Angus & Robertson, 1946.

Sansom, George B. *The Western World and Japan: A Study in the Interaction of European and Asiatic Cultures.* New York: Knopf, 1951.

Index

Index

ABCD (American, British, Chinese, Dutch) encirclement: America blamed for, 227; affects nationalism, 237

Abe Isō, socialist writer, 153

Aikoku Rōdō Kumiai Zenkoku Konwakai (All-Japan Conference of Patriotic Labor Unions): nationalist societies unite in, 204–205

Ainu: in Japanese racial make-up, 7; Emishi probable ancestors of, 11; uprisings, 20

Aizawa, Lieutenant Colonel Saburō, opposes conservatives, 197–198

Akamatsu Katsumaro, leader of Japan National Socialist party, 191–192

Alcock, Sir Rutherford: against Chōshū, 85; guesses reason for samurai antiforeignism, 89

America. *See* United States

Anami, General Korechika, objects to surrender, 240

Ando family, succession disputes, 30

Anglo-Japanese Treaty, strengthens Japanese position, 139–140

Ansei, Great Persecution of, attempt to check *Sonnō* movement, 80

Anti-Comintern Pact: against Russia, 202; opposed, 202–203; signed, 217

Antiforeignism: rejection of relations with Western nations, 42–47; reaction against Confucianism, 52–58; focused on Russians, 62–66, 131–147; on British, 66–72, 171–237; on Americans, 72–75, 171–237; "Revere the Emperor! Expel the Barbarians!" movement, 76–87; almost disappears, 87–88, 148–170, 238–256; analysis of, 89–90; reflected in modernization, 91–111; in birth of modern nationalism, 112–129; reëmerges, 256–278

Aoki Bunzo, early Dutch scholar, 57

Araki, General Sadao, exponent of Imperial Way, 193–195, 207; promotes spiritual education, 210–215

Arita Hachirō, Foreign Minister, outlines doctrine of Greater East Asia, 216

Ashikaga Bakufu. *See* Japan, Ashikaga Bakufu

Ashikaga Takauji, emperors chosen by, rule at Kyoto, 31

Ashikaga Yoshimitsu: settles succession dispute, 32; "King of Japan," 34

Ashikaga Yoshimochi, rejects tributary relationship, 34

Ashikaga Yoshinori, reëstablishes tributary relationship, 34–35

Ashikaga Yoshiteru, strengthens castle, 40

Association of China Societies of Tokyo, opposes government stand on China issue, 162, 163

Azuchi-Momoyama era. *See* Japan, Azuchi-Momoyama era

Bakufu. *See* Japan, Kamakura era, Ashikaga era, and Tokugawa Bakufu

Biddle, Commodore, denied trading privileges, 73

Black Dragon Society. See *Kokuryūkai*

Boxer rebellion, effect of, on relations bet. Japan and Russia, 138–139

Brinkley, Captain Francis, on Japanese spirit, 127

British. *See* England

Buddhism: introduction of, 8; in Seventeen-Article Constitution, 12; supported by Soga, 13; merged with Shinto, 17; supported by Nara government, 17–18; stimulus for economic growth, 19; centrifugal force, 20; Reformation, 24–25; Nichiren sect, 27–29; attempts to suppress, 101; compromise with Shinto, 102–103

Bureau of Information. See *Jōhō Bu*

Burma: independence recognized, 230; refuses to sign Japanese Peace Treaty, 258

Bushidō (warrior code): Yamaga Sokō on, 54; conduces to loyalty to Emperor, 98; role of, in education, 105; success in Russo-Japanese War attributed to, 142–143

Canton: center of foreign trade, 23; trade with America, 72

Chang Tso-lin: outrages Japanese, 161–163; assassinated, 186

Chiang Hsüeh-liang: joins Chinese Nationalists, 186; leads popular front against Japan, 203

Ch'angan, model for Nara, 16

Charter Oath. *See* Imperial Oath

Cherry Blossom Society. See *Sakura Kai*

Chiang Kai-shek, clashes with Japanese, 184-185, 200

China

Sui dynasty: united China, 11–12

T'ang dynasty: defeats Yamato armies in Korea, 12, 15–16; decline of, 20

Sung dynasty: overseas trade, 23

Ming dynasty: diplomatic relations with Japan severed, 33; Japanese piracy, 33–35; Japanese tributary relationship, 34–35; export of copper coins, 34–35; export of raw silk, 42

Ching dynasty: Anglo-Chinese War, 70–71; second treaty settlement, 77; conflict with Japan, 125–130; Treaty of Shimonoseki, 129; concessions to Japan, 136; recognition of Japan's position in Korea, 152; activities of Japanese nationalists, 158–164

Republican era: Japanese nationalists outraged, 161–163; Twenty-one Demands, 165–166; opposition to Japanese expansion, 171–172; strained relations with Japan, 184–187; attacks at Nanking, 185; tariff autonomy from Japan, 185–186; anti-Japanese feelings, 193; Japan's autonomous state, 201

Communist regime: victories and Occupation policy in Japan, 256; supports North Korea, 259

China Study Group, backs China's southern cause, 161

Chinese Imperial idea: Yamato leaders affected by, 14; Hideyoshi influenced by, 47

Chōshū clan: adopts Western military methods, 76; backs Imperial Court, 81–83; attacks Western warships, 83–84; attacked by Western naval force, 85; position at Imperial Court, 85; negotiates agreement with Western powers, 85–86; receives support from Satsuma, 86; Bakufu expedition, 86; lands handed over to Emperor, 94–95; provides troops for Imperial Guard, 95

Christianity: introduced by Jesuits, 42; considered subversive, 42–44; and trade, 43; Japanese persecute followers of, 44–46; books about, banned, 46–47; feared chiefly by Bakufu, 47; movable-type printing used in spreading, 49; opposed by Shintoists, 119–120; adjustment of, to "Japanism," 133; prohibited in schools, 137; attacked, 137–138

Classical Japanese scholars. See *Kokugakusha*

Code of Education: promulgated, 104; revised, 105

Communist party: Far Eastern Propaganda Section of Comintern, 176; Japanese party organized, 177; government repression of, 177; Yamakawaism, 178; effect of Communist victories in China, 256; opposes rearmament, 260; seeks nationalist support, 261–263; positive policy of, 262; terroristic acts of, 263, 269; target of nationalist society, 267; sentiment against, 270–271; relationship bet. Russian and Japanese parties, 270–271; anti-Americanism of, 271–272 Confucianism: principles of, in Seventeen-Article Constitution, 12–13; Teishu school of, 51–52; contributions of, to *kokutai* movement, 52; Kumazawa Banzan, 53; Yamaga Sokō, 53–54; Kamo Mabuchi, 55–56; Motoori Norinaga, 56–58; given less support by Tokugawa Bakufu, 57–58; Hirata Atsutane, 65; opposition to Dutch scholars, 70; antiforeignism, 90; in national education, 104–106; *Shibun Gakkai*, society for promotion of, 106, 117; in Imperial Rescript on Education, 118; propagated, 118–119

Conservative political parties: bid for nationalist support, 264; moral education, 264-265; Shintoism, 265

Constitution: gift of Emperor, 115; revised, 248–250; Emperor symbol of state, 249; cabinet responsible to Diet, 250

Control Group. See *Tōseiha*

Customs and manners, reflect national interests, 110

Dai Nihon Kokusui Kai (Greater Japan National Essence Society), for conservative nationalism, 179–180

Dai Nihon Kyōkai (Greater Japan Education Society): supports Imperial Rescript on Education, 133; "Japanism," 134

Dai Nihon Shi (Great History of Japan), compiled by Mito school, 54–55

Dajōkan Nisshi (Journal of the Grand Council), official gazette, 107

Democracy: early development of, 98–99, 175–176; target of secret-society activity, 192–193; weakened by New National Structure movement, 218–219; basis of new education, 244–245; Occupation policy, 244–250; opposed by new nationalist societies, 266

Doihara, General Kanji, sets up autonomous state in China, 201.

Dōkyō, tries to become emperor, 18

Dore, R. P., on "Moral Code," 264–265

Dosō (pawnshops), origin and development of, 24

Draper report, revision of Occupation policy, 257

Dulles, John Foster, drafts peace treaty, 258–259, 277

Dun, Edwin, notes aggressive spirit, 127

Dutch: traders not missionaries, 44; restricted to Nagasaki, 44; share monopoly of Japanese foreign trade, 46; books on Christianity banned, 46–47; position in Formosa, 48; steam sloop fired on, 84; warship at Osaka, 87

Dutch scholars (rangakusha): Aoki Bunzo, 57; for Western military techniques, 70; opposed by Confucian scholars, 70; for Western methods of production, administration, and education, 70–72; for lifting of trade ban, 74–75; Sakuma Shōzan, 92

Dyer, Henry, on Japanese patriotism, 142

East Asia Common Cultural Society. See Tōa Dōbun Kai

Education: Imperial Oath, 94; assistance from America, 104; "urgent state necessity," 104–105; military training, 105; Confucian versus liberal ideals, 105–106; loyalty, 106; literacy, 106; philosophy, 208–209; spiritual mobilization, 209–215; reorganization, 221–222; Shimmin no Michi, 222–225; militaristic and ultranationalistic ideologies prohibited, 244–245; decentralization, 250

Emishi: resistance to Yamato, 11; uprising, 14

Emperor: hereditary head of state, 8; message to Chinese Emperor, 13; Taika reforms, 15; supports Buddhism, 15, 17–18; Kojiki compiled by order of, 16–17; position of, firmly established, 19; under Shogun, 22–23; removed by Kamakura Bakufu, 23; asks for protection against Mongols, 27; Go-Daigo, 31–32, 55; position strengthened by Jinnō Shōtōki, 32; poverty of, 35; descent from Sun Goddess ridiculed, 57; descent from Sun Goddess glorified, 65–66; attitude of Bakufu toward, 81; orders Chōshū and Shimazu to stabilize country, 81; orders expulsion of foreigners, 83; ratifies treaties, 87; Restoration of, 87–88; Yoshida Shōin for, 93; Imperial Oath, 94; orders abolishment of clans, 95–96; issues Rescript to Soldiers and Sailors, 98; rescript on Shinto missionary program, 102; endorses book on Confucianism, 106; and Constitution, 115; issues Rescript on Education, 115–116; Kōdō, 117, 192, 207, 221; supported by Saigō Takamori, 123; revered by Genyōsha, 123–124; sends message to Admiral Tōgō, 143; issues rescript against "evils of the time," 152; elevated by kokutai, 206–209; favors diplomatic settlement, 227; issues rescript on surrender, 234, 239; denies divinity, 245–246; status of, in revised constitution, 248–249; symbol of state, 249; reproclaims Imperial Oath, 252; Japanese Communist party attitude toward, 261; supported by "Moral Code," 265; Emperor system upheld by nationalist society, 267. See also Imperial Court, etc.

Emperor Jimmu Society. See Jimmu Kai

England: early trade bet. Japan and, 44; Vancouver expedition, 66; Phaeton incident, 66–67; Dutch accusation against, 67; British supplies seized by Japanese, 67; Anglo-Chinese War, 69; Crimean War, 75–76; warships enter Japanese ports, 76; British reaction to Imperial order expelling foreigners, 83; British ships sent to Chōshū, 84; admiral sends ultimatum to Bakufu, 84; ultimatum to Satsuma and retaliation, 85; displays force, 86-87; supports Japan against Russia, 134–136; Anglo-Japanese Treaty, 139–140, 151; fears closing of "open door" in Manchuria, 157; suspicious of Japanese intentions, 167; strengthens China, 201; target of proposed alliance, 217–

England—*Continued*
218; outbreak of war with Japan, 228–229

Expansionism: early manifestations of, 63–64; Yoshida Shōin on, 121; demands for Japanese invasion of Korea, 121–122; Formosa expedition, 122–123; Satsuma rebellion, 123; secret societies, 123–124; in government circles, 124–125; opposed by Itō Hirobumi and Inouye Kaoru, 125; war on China, 126–128; noted by foreign observers, 127; stirred by success in war, 127–128; aroused by resentment against Russia, 134–135; directed toward China, 136; quickened by Ōkuma support, 136–137; gains momentum from victory against Russia, 156; focus shifted from Korea to Manchuria, 156–157; from Manchuria to China, 158; Kita Ikki's program of, 182–183; Ōkawa Shūmei's policy of, 187–188; replaces internal reform, 188–191; conflict over direction of, 202. *See also* Greater East Asia movement

February Twenty-sixth Incident: Young Officers versus Control Group, 198; shift in national reconstruction program, 203–204

Formosa: conquest of, by the Dutch, 48; seizure of, advocated, 75; Japanese expedition to, 122-123

France: resents Imperial order expelling foreigners from Japan, 83; steamboat fired upon by Chōshū, 84; admiral seeks reprisal, 84; Triple Intervention, 131; sphere of interest in China, 157; defeat of, by Germany 216

French Indo-China, America resists Japanese advances in, 218

Fuji, Lieutenant Hitoshi, forms *Ōsui Kai*, 188–189

Fujiwara, Seikwa, of Teishu School of Confucianism, 51

Fukoku Kyōhei (Rich Country! Strong Army!), slogan, 92–93, 99

Fukuzawa Yukichi, simplifies written Japanese, 107

Gamō Kumpei, investigates Imperial tombs, 59

Gary, Judge J. H., on Japanese national confidence, 166

Genji Monogatari (Tales of Genji), Heian prose, 21

Genyōsha: organization and policies of, 123–124; influence of, 124–125

Germany: Triple Intervention, 131, 217; World War I, 164–165; victories arouse optimism among Japanese, 216–225; Anti-Comintern Pact, 217; Tripartite Pact, 217-218, 225; Matsuoka negotiations, 225–226; collapse, 234

Go-Daigo, Emperor: resists Kamakura Bakufu, 30–31; *de facto* power, 31; sets up Southern Court, 31

Gondō Seikyō, agrarian reform program of, 205

Great Reforms: adoption of, 14–15; influence of T'ang power on, 15–16; culmination of, in Nara era, 16–20

Greater East Asia Ministry, 230, 231

Greater East Asia movement: doctrine outlined, 216; Tripartite Pact, 221; Joint Declaration of Greater East Asian Nations, 230–231; Japanese mission, 231

Gyogi, adjusts Buddhism to Shintoism, 18

Hara Kei: heads first political party cabinet, 168; resists demands for universal manhood suffrage, 176

Harris, Townsend, negotiates treaty bet. U.S. and Japan, 77

Hashimoto, Lieutenant Colonel Kingorō: a founder of *Sakura Kai*, 190; plots Japanese control of Manchuria, 190–191; plans political party of young men, 205–206; organizes nationalistic youth society, 206

Hayashi Razan: supports Teishu school of Confucianism, 51; on *kokutai*, 51–52

Hayashi Shihei, advocates seizure of Yezo, 63

Hideyoshi: in control of precious metals, 38, 41; ally of Ieyasu, 40; pioneer in castle construction, 40; orders Jesuits to leave Japan, 43; campaign of, into Korea, 47; demands submission of Philippines, 48

Higashikuni, Prince Naruhiko: policies of, 240; drafts revision of constitution, 248

Hirado, foreign trade permitted in, 44

Hirata Atsutane: strengthens Shinto, 65-66; on divine descent of Japanese people, 66

Hirayama Kōzō, suggests organization of national army, 65

Hirota Kōki, Foreign Minister: announces "Monroe Doctrine" for Asia, 201; on Russian border incidents, 203

Hitler, Adolf: on closer Germany-Japan ties, 217; on idea of alliance with Japan, 218; regimentation of labor applauded by Hatoyama, 247

Holtom, Dr. D. C., scholar of Shinto, 9

Honda Toshiaki, advocates seizure of Yezo and Kamchatka, 63

Ieyasu: ally of Hideyoshi, 40; proscribes Christianity, 42–43; respects Imperial Court, 47; starts *sankin kōtai* system, 49–50

Ii Naosuke: favors foreign treaties 78; assassinated, 79–80

Imperial Conference: on Russo-German War, 226; on relations with the U.S. and Britain, 226–227

Imperial Court: Seventeen-Article Constitution, 12–13; Great Reforms, 12–30; cultural center, 20–21; loss of political power to Kamakura Bakufu, 22; in open struggle with Bakufu, 23; nominal position of preëminence, 23; power of, under Go-Daigo, 30–31; two Imperial Courts, 31-32; position strengthened by *Jinnō Shōtōki*, 32; loss of prestige, 35; proper respect paid to, by Hideyoshi and Nobunaga, 47; scholarly pursuits, 50; Yamazaki Anzai, 52–53; reactions against Confucian studies, 53, 57–58; Kamo Mabuchi, 55–56; center of movement against Bakufu, 58–59, 78; subjected to greater control, 59–60; treated more leniently, 60; refuses approval of foreign treaties, 77–78; receives support from Chōshū and Satsuma, 81; independent action, 81–82; Meiji Restoration, 87–88; moved to Tokyo, 101; supports *Shibun Gakkai*, 117

Imperial Oath: Meiji policy, 94; revived, 251–252

Imperial Rescript on Education: issued, 115–116; glorified, 133; "Moral Code," 265

Imperial Rescript to Soldiers and Sailors, 98

Imperial Rule Assistance Association. See *Taisei Yokusan Kai*

Imperial Way. See *Kōdō*

Inouye Kaoru: opposes expansionist policy, 125; influences Mistsui, 160; coöperates with nationalists in China, 160

Inouye Tetsujirō: attacks Christianity, 120, 138; on *kokutai*, 154–155; popularizes National Morals movement, 155

Ise Shrine: Sun Goddess enshrined at, 18; revived interest in, 35

I-shan, attempts to persuade Japanese to submit to Mongols, 27

Ishihara Kanji: heads political party, 253; heads *Tōa Remmei*, 267; theories and activities of, 267–268; conflict with Tōjō, 268; seeks approval of Occupation, 268

Ishin Gakkai (Society for Restoring Learning), popularizes Shinto, 116–117

Itagaki Taisuke, head of *Genyōsha*, 124

Itō, Prince Hirobumi: student of Yoshida Shōin, 93; author of Constitution, 93; opposes expansion, 125; invited to join *Nichiro Kyōkai*, 140; leads *Seiyūkai*, 146

Itō Nobumi, president of Board of Information, 212

Japan

Nara era (710–784): permanent capital, 16; myths and traditions recorded, 16; political centralization, 17; Buddhism officially supported, 17–18; doctrinal adjustment between Buddhism and Shintoism, 18; *Tōdaiji*, 18; economic prosperity, 19; literary and artistic achievements, 19–20

Heian era (794–1192): political and economic deterioration, 20; classical period of Japanese literature, 21; seeds of feudalism, 21

Kamakura Bakufu (1192–1333): centralization, 22; struggle with Imperial Court, 22–23; Chinese political theory, 23; gold in Mutsu, 23; pawnshops and bills of exchange, 24; Buddhist Reformation, 24; Mongol invasions, 25–30; economic deterioration, 29–30; political chaos, 30–31

Ashikaga Bakufu (1338–1573): established, 31–32; lack of political stability, 31–32; Imperial Court, 32; tributary relationship with Ming China, 33–35; power of Imperial

Japan—*Continued*

Court usurped, 35; arts encouraged, 35–36

Azuchi-Momoyama era (1582–1600): Portuguese arrival, 37; political centralization, 38; economic growth, 38–42; Christianity introduced, 42; Christianity considered subversive, 42–44; Imperial Court, 47

Tokugawa Bakufu (1600–1867): loose federation, 43; fears Portuguese and Spaniards, 43–44; persecutes Christians, 44–45; restricts foreign trade, 44–46; fears *ronin,* 45; Shimabara rebellion, 46; political unity overstated, 47–48; Spaniards in Philippines, Dutch in Formosa, 48; communications improved, 49; contacts between clans, 49; *sankin kōtai,* 49–50; *rōnin* plot of 1651; scholarly pursuits, 50–51; Confucian scholars, 57–58, 60; political and economic deterioration, 58; *Sonnō* movement, 59–60, 60–65; relations with Russians resisted, 64; tighter seclusion policy, 67; economic deterioration, 68; uprisings, 68–69; reforms, 69–70; revises seclusion policy, 69–70; reaction of, to Perry's visit, 73–75; stirs up opposition, 76–78; makes compromise with Imperial Court, 78; "Revere the Emperor! Down with the Bakufu!" slogan, 80; Chōshū and Satsuma support Imperial Court, 81; demands of Emperor, 82; demands from Western powers, 82–87; expedition against Chōshū, 86; relinquishes control, 87–88

Meiji government (1868–1912), representative principles, 93; lands from Satsuma, Chōshū, Tosa, and Hizen, 94; representative institutions, 95; Imperial Guard, 95; clans abolished, 95–96; modern tax system, 96–97; national army, 97–98; opposition from declassed *samurai,* 97–98; economic development and military needs, 99–100; Sun Cult a state religion, 101–103; Shinto missionary program, 103; educational reform, 103–106; revision of unequal treaties, 112, 125–127; Constitution, 115; Imperial Rescript on Education, 115–116; outlying islands, 122–123; Korea, 122–123; Satsuma rebellion, 123; Sino-Japanese War,

126–128; peace treaty, 129; Triple Intervention, 131; extraterritorial privileges removed, 137; Anglo-Japanese Treaty, 139–140; Russo-Japanese War, 142–144; Portsmouth Treaty, 149; diplomacy, 151, 157–158

Taishō era (1912–1926): utlimatum to Yuan Shih-kai, 163; Okuma policy, 164–166; memorandum from Uchida Ryōhei, 165; Twenty-one Demands on China, 165–177; postwar attitude of foreign powers, 166–167; wartime prosperity, 167–168; political party cabinet, 168; postwar depression, 171–174; universal manhood suffrage, 176; action against subversives, 177; democratic processes supported, 177–178

Shōwa era (1926–): strained relations with China, 184–187; "Monroe Doctrine" for Asia, 201; Washington and London Naval treaties, 201; British policy, 201–202; closer relationship with Germany, 202–203; thought control, 209–215; new foreign policy, 216; Tōjō ministry, 227; industrial production, 232; surrender, 239–242; deterioration, 242; occupation, 242–243; thought-control structure removed, 244; teaching of ultranationalist ideologies prohibited, 244–245; government sponsorship of state Shinto abolished, 245; Emperor derives divinity, 245–246; exponents of militarism "purged," 246–247; ultranationalist societies dissolved, 248; new constitution drafted, 248–250; legal system reformed, 250; legal status of women raised, 250; decentralization, 250; economic deterioration, 255; labor reform, 255; economic rehabilitation, 256–258; peace treaty, 258–259

Japan Communist party, dissolved, 178

Japan Revolutionary Chrysanthemum Flag Society. See *Nihon Kakumei Kikuhata Dōshi Kai*

Japanese army: organized by Yamagata, 97–98; ready for continental operations, 98; victorious against China, 127–129; victorious against Russia, 142–144; force in Japanese politics, 145–146; criticized, 175; role in Kita

Ikki's reform program, 183; leadership of national reconstruction movement, 187–195; irritated by London Naval Conference, 189; success, 191; conflict between Young Officer Group and Control Group, 195–198; reconstruction programs, 199; question of expansion, 202; forces government to take more positive policy, 216–225; Imperial Rule Assistance Association, 220–221; opposes efforts to improve relations with America, 226–227; dominates government, 230; disarmament, 243; revival of, 259–261

Japanese language: unifying medium, 7–8; writing, 19, 21; more popular written forms, 24; interest in classical writings, 55–56; revolutionary changes in written style, 106–107; popular literature and press, 107–110

Japanese Morals Society. See *Nihon Kōdō Kai*

Japanese music, and nationalist sentiments, 214–215

Japanese "National Essence" movement: early development, 113–114; and Shintoism, 114–117; and Confucianism, 117–119; influence on art, history, and religion, 119–120

Japanese navy, resists army pressure, 218

Japanese newspapers: early development of, 107; circulation and national crisis, 107–108; oppose government, 108–109; censored, 108; help national unity, 109; controlled, 211–212

Japanese Religions Society. See *Nihon Shūkyō Sha*

Japanese-Russian Society. See *Nichiro Kyōkai*

Japanese Socialist party. See *Nihon Shakai Tō*

Japanism. See *Nihon Shugi*

Jimmu, Emperor, link between Sun Goddess and emperors, 16–17

Jimmu Kai (Emperor Jimmu Society): activities of, 192; and *Tōa Remmei*, 269

Jingikan (Shinto Department): Taika reform, 15; Meiji era, 101; replaced by *Kyōbushō* (Religious Department), 102–203

Jinnō Shōtōki (On the Legitimacy of the Imperial Line), early work in nationalist literature, 32

Jōhō Bu (Bureau of Information): establishment and purpose of, 210; controls channels of information, 210; thought-control activities of, 211–214

Joint Declaration of Greater East Asia Nations, Asian nations under Japanese leadership, 230–231

Kaesen (bills of exchange), expanded use of, 24

Kagoshima: British seize supplies from, 67; British attack, 85

Kajin no Kigū (Chance Meeting with a Beautiful Woman), patriotic novel, 109–110

Kamchatka, seizure of, advocated, 63, 75, 121

Kamikaze (Divine Wind): repels Mongols, 26; imprint upon intellectual history, 26–27

Kamishibai (illustrated stories by candy venders), controlled, 215

Kamo Mabuchi, classical Japanese studies, 55–56

Katayama Sen, socialist writer, 153

Katayama Tetsu: reform program of, 250–251; loses support, 251

Katō Hiroyuki, on *kokutai*, 154–155

Keikoku Bidan (The Saga of a Classical Country), patriotic novel, 109

Kikuchi Takeo, attacks Monobe, 207–208

Kimura Takatarō: supports "Japanism," 133–134; opposes Christianity, 137–138

Kita Ikki: plan for reform of Japan, 180–184; national reconstruction societies, 183–184; program revised, 187; death of, 198

Kitabatake Chikafusa: supports Go-Daigo, 30; author of *Jinnō Shōtōki*, 32

Kōdō (Imperial Way): early use of term, 117; *Nihon Kokka Shakai Tō* advocates government based on, 192; Young Officer group, 207; New National Structure Movement, 221

Kōdōha (Young Officer group): advocates reorganization of social structure, 195; pamphlets on reform, 196; angered by removal of General Mazaki, 196–197; aroused by Aizawa Incident, 197; responsible for February Twenty-sixth Incident, 198, supplanted by the *Tōseiha*, 198; favors advancing against Russia, 202; conflict with *Tōseiha*, 235

Kogakuha (Classical School of Confucianism), 53–54

Kojiki: compilation and purpose, 16–17; Motoori Norinaga recommends study of, 56

Kojikiden (Commentary on Kojiki), by Motoori Norinaga, 56

Kokka: early use of word, 10; applied to Yamato, 11; Seventeen-Article Constitution, 13; declaration of *Nihon Kokkyō Daidō Sha,* 114

Kokubō no Hongi to Sono Kyōka no Teishō (Principles of National Defense and Proposals for Strengthening Them), controversial army pamphlet, 196

Kokubunji (provincial temple), established by Imperial decree, 18

Kokugakuin Zasshi (Magazine for the Institute of Japanese Studies), outlet for "Japanism" thought, 133

Kokugakusha (Japanese classical scholars): Kamo Mabuchi and Motoori Norinaga, 55–56

Kokumin Dōtoku Gairon (An Outline of National Morals), by Inouye Tetsujirō, 155

Kokumin Dōtoku Undō (National Morals Movement): reaction against foreign ideologies, 155; reaction to Western liberalism, 169

Kokuryūkai (Black Dragon Society): to extend Japanese influence on Manchuria, 139–141; activities in Korea and Manchuria, 156–157; attention shifted to China, 158–159; revises plans, 165; from expansion to internal reform, 178–179; a Kyushu product, 266

Kokuryūkai Kaihō (Journal of the Black Dragon Society), influence of, 139

Kokutai (national entity): religious significance of, 8; word used in *Jinnō Shōtōki,* 32; supported by Fujiwara Seikwa, 51; strengthened by Confucian emphasis on loyalty, 52; Christianity not in accord with, 138; success of Japan attributed to, 154–155, 169; national reconstructionists uphold, 199; loses favor, 206; regains it, 207; interpretation of, 208, 209, 221; *Shimmin no Michi* on, 224; preservation of, in new constitution, 249; less attention given to, 254; new interest in, 265–266

Kokutai no Hongi (Principles of Kokutai), philosophy of education, 207–208

Kokutai oyobi Junsei Shakai Shugi (Japanese National Entity and Pure Socialism), by Kita Ikki, 181

Konkōmyō Sutra, *Tōdaiji* doctrine, 18

Konoye, Prince Fumimaro: cabinet of, reconstructed, 210; foreign policy of, 216; resigns presidency of the Privy Council, 219; leader in New National Structure movement, 219–220; stresses essence of *Kokutai,* 221; favors improvement of relations with the U.S., 226; takes part in Ogikubo Conference, 227; revises constitution, 248

Korea: Chinese conquests and influence in, 12, 15–16; priests and immigrants from, in Japan; Japanese withdrawal from, 16; new Japanese interest in, 75; Japan attempts to strengthen control over, 121–213; invasion crisis, 127; Japanese modernization resented, 132; turns to Russia, 132; Japanese position recognized, 151; civil war, 258–260; anti-Korean feeling in Japan, 271

Kotoku Denjirō, leader of anarchist plot, 153

Kroeber, A. L., on cultural lag in Japan, 6

Kublai Khan: attempts to invade Japan, 26–27; later plans to conquer Japan, 27

Kuhara Fusanosuke, advocates Imperial Rule Assistance Association, 219–220

Kumaso, resist Yamato, 11

Kumazawa Banzan: of Oyōmei school of Confucianism, 53; places Japan above China and India, 53

Kusunoki Masashige, in *Dai Nihon Shi,* 55

Kyōbushō (Religious Department), establishment of, 103

Kyōwa Kai, and *Tōa Remmei,* 268–269

Kyōwa Tō, formation and platform of, 269

Kyushu: home of the Kumaso, 11; grandson of Sun Goddess arrives in, 17; military operations in, 24; center of new rightest movements, 266. *See also* Shimabara rebellion.

Labor: strikes after World War I, 174; syndicalism, 176; Communism, 176–177; democracy, 177–178; strikes, 187; unions more nationalistic, 204–205; expansion of unions, 255

Laxman expedition, purpose and effect of, 63–64

Sekisho (checking stations), contacts between clans, 49

Sesshū, landscape painter, 35

Seventeen-Article Constitution: compilation, 12; political significance, 13

Shibun Gakkai (Society for the Study of Confucian Culture), 106, 117

Shidehara Kijūrō: foreign policy, 184–185; agreements with China, 186; cabinet of, and "purge," 247; follows principles of Imperial Oath, 251–252

Shigaku Zasshi (Historical Journal), national focus, 19

Shigemitsu Mamoru: Tsinan Incident, 185–186; opposed by militarists, 190; pressed for positive action, 193; on Japanese army determination to attack Russia, 195

Shimabara rebellion: *rōnin*, 45–46; apostatized Christians, 46; local injustices, 46; Bakufu discontinues plans for conquering Philippines, 48

Shimazu Izumi: reports to Imperial Court, 81; ordered by Emperor to stabilize country, 81

Shimmin no Michi (The Way of the Subject), about duties and responsibilities of Japanese, 222–225

Shimonoseki, Treaty of, 129

Shin Taisei (New National Structure): background, 215–218; a single-party movement, 219; Konoye leadership, 219–220; Imperial Rule Assistance Association, 220–221; Tripartite Pact, 221; educational reform, 221–225; strengthened, 230

Shinto: Japanese nationalism, 9; mythology, 17; Fujiwara Seikwa and Hayashi Razan on, 51–52; Yamazaki Anzai founds new school of, 52–53; Kumazawa Banzan influenced by, 53; Kamo Mabuchi propagates principles of, 55–56; furthered by Hirata Atsutane, 65–66; state religion, 101–103; missionary program, 101–103; shrines graded, 102; hereditary priesthood abolished, 102; given higher status by Constitution, 115; emphasized in Imperial Rescript on Education, 115–116; *Ishin Gakkai*, 116–117; conflict between Shintoists and Christians, 119–120; said to be only Japanese religion, 133; special position in schools, 137; spiritual mobilization, 211–212; government support removed, 245

Shōmu, Emperor: supports Buddhism, 18; builds Tōdaiji, 18

Shotoku, Prince: compiles "Seventeen-Article Constitution," 12–13; supports Buddhism, 17

Sino-Japanese War: popular demands, 125–127; popular response, 127–130; economic growth, 144–145; political unity, 145

Soga family, supports Buddhism, 13

Sonnō (Revere the Emperor) movement: Yamazaki Anzai, 54; Mitsukuni, 55; background, 58–60; *samurai*-scholar demands, 63–65; Hirata Atsutane, 66; Meiji Restoration, 87–88; as a manifestation of nationalism, 90

Spaniards: arouse suspicions, 44; banned, 45; position of, in Philippines, 48

Stalin, Joseph: agrees to neutrality pact with Japan, 225; New Year's message, 263

Sugita Gempaku, on Russian demands, 64–65

Suiga Shinto, established by Yamazaki Anzai, 52–53

Sun Cult: as Japanese religion, 8; dominant cult, 10–16; focus of recorded traditions, 16–17; adjustment to Buddhism, 17; state religion, 101–103; dissociated from the state, 245

Sun Goddess: ancestor of emperors, 9; emphasized in *Kojiki*, 16; victory against the Mongols, 26–27; theory of Kumazawa Banzan, 53; *Dai Nihon Shi* rejects theory, 55; ridiculed by Ichikawa, 57

Sun Yat-sen: aided by Black Dragon Society, 159–160; trip to Japan, 160–161; encourages support for Southern regime, 161

Taft-Katsura understanding, on Japan's position in Korea, 152

Tairo Dōshi Kai (Anti-Russian Comrades Society), activities of, 141

Taisei Yokusan Kai (Imperial Rule Assistance Association): established, 206; instrument of ideological control, 220–221; clarification of *kokutai*, 221; strengthened, 230; mobilizes labor resources, 232

Takano Nagahide, seclusion policy of, 69

Takashima Shuhan, introduces foreign military methods, 70

Takasugi Shinsaku, seclusion policy of, 86

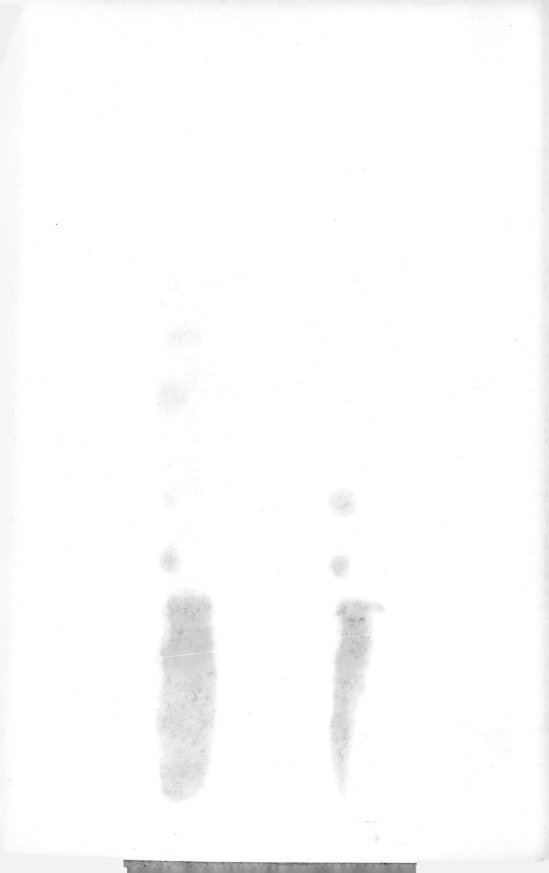

4/27/55

35801

DS
843
B76

BROWN, DELMER
NATIONALISM IN JAPAN.

DATE DUE

GAYLORD   PRINTED IN U.S.A.